The Cursillo Movement in America

THE CURSILLO MOVEMENT IN AMERICA

CATHOLICS, PROTESTANTS, AND FOURTH-DAY SPIRITUALITY

Kristy Nabhan-Warren

THE UNIVERSITY OF NORTH CAROLINA PRESS *Chapel Hill*

© 2013 THE UNIVERSITY OF NORTH CAROLINA PRESS

All rights reserved. Manufactured in the United States of America. Set in Utopia and Gotham by Integrated Book Technology. The paper in this book meets the guidelines for permanence and durability of the Committee on Production Guidelines for Book Longevity of the Council on Library Resources. The University of North Carolina Press has been a member of the Green Press Initiative since 2003.

Part of this book has been reprinted in revised form from "Blooming Where We're Planted: Mexican-Descent Catholics Living Out *Cursillo de Cristiandad*," *U.S. Catholic Historian*, "Remembering the Past, Engaging the Present: Essays in Honor of Moises Sandoval," 28, no. 4 (Fall 2010): 99–125.

Library of Congress Cataloging-in-Publication Data
Nabhan-Warren, Kristy.
The Cursillo movement in America : Catholics, Protestants, and Fourth-Day spirituality / Kristy Nabhan-Warren. — First edition
pages cm
Includes bibliographical references and index.
ISBN 978-1-4696-0715-3 (hardback) — ISBN 978-1-4696-0716-0 (pbk.)
1. Cursillo movement in the United States. 2. United States—Church history—20th century. I. Title.
BX2375.A3N33 2013
269'.6—dc23   2013008286

cloth   17 16 15 14 13   5 4 3 2 1
paper   17 16 15 14 13   5 4 3 2 1

To Steve, Cormac, Declan, and Josie
for your love, patience, and belief in me

Contents

PREFACE
New Beginnings, xi

INTRODUCTION
Finding Christ and Community in America, 1
The Significance of Catholic and Protestant Cursillos and the Fourth-Day Movement

CHAPTER ONE
Los Orígenes Mallorquines, 20
Eduardo Bonnín Aguiló and the Birth of the Cursillo de Cristiandad Movement

CHAPTER TWO
Coming to America, 56
The Early History of U.S. Cursillos de Cristiandad

CHAPTER THREE
A Focus on Christian Experience, 84
The Protestant Cursillos (Tres Dias, Walk to Emmaus, Via de Cristo) and the National Episcopal Cursillo

CHAPTER FOUR
Blooming Where We're Planted, 127
U.S. Catholics and Protestants Talk about Living Their Cursillo

CHAPTER FIVE
Teens Encounter Christ, 166
Pioneer in Young Adult Weekend Experiences

CHAPTER SIX
Feeding Bodies and Souls, 199
Kairos Prison Ministry International

CHAPTER SEVEN
Maverick yet Mainstream, 226
Christ Renews His Parish and Great Banquet

EPILOGUE
Cursillo Weekends, Fourth-Day Spirituality, and the Future, 245

APPENDIX ONE
Cursillo Chronology, 255

APPENDIX TWO
Glossary, 257

Notes, 259   Index, 303

Illustrations

Eduardo Bonnín with his mother and siblings, ca. 1918, 23

Eduardo Bonnín as a soldier, 25

Cursillistas at the first weekend Cursillo,
Cala Figuera, Mallorca, ca. 1944, 38

Eduardo Bonnín, 82

Robert Franks and Eduardo Bonnín, Palma de Mallorca, 1998, 89

Tracy Schmidlin and Jerry Lemcke,
Via de Cristo Ultreya, Orlando, Florida, 2010, 146

East Chicago cursillista Adelina Torres, 2008, 149

The TEC Hippy Jesus, 1968 TEC rally, Battle Creek, Michigan, 174

1968 TEC rally, Battle Creek, Michigan, 175

Dorothy Gereke and Father Matt Fedewa, 183

TEC boys' weekend, ca. 1966, 184

Hauling food and supplies for a KI weekend,
Rockville, Indiana, 2010, 200

PREFACE

New Beginnings

Heather Rankle and Judy Woolverton say they became good friends in Houston's Tres Dias community and turn to each other for support and guidance. Tres Dias weekends in Texas are "more elaborate" than elsewhere because "well, you know how everything is bigger in Texas!" exclaims Heather, an attractive, enthusiastic blonde in her forties with a ton of energy. Both women talk about their experiences as both pilgrims and team members. Christ's suffering and sacrifice are emphasized in their weekend courses, and when the pastor reads the story of Jesus' crucifixion, as a team member Judy has hit a pole with a hammer to make the sound effects of Jesus' hands and feet being nailed to the cross. "It really gets to people, you know, and we focus on all of the senses—sight, sound, taste, and hearing—in our weekends because we want people to get involved with their whole selves," Heather says. The Via de la Rosa, Jesus' final walk before his death, is reenacted during their Tres Dias weekend, and it really "hits home" with the women who "make" the course, according to Heather and Judy.

Heather says she was not brought up in the church and that her parents were just teenagers themselves when they raised her. The lack of God in her childhood home was a "generational curse," she believes. After she took a "wrong turn" in high school, her life began spiraling downward, out of control. By the time she turned eighteen, she had been pregnant twice, and before she turned twenty-one, she had overdosed on cocaine twice. The second overdose led Heather to a drug rehabilitation center, and while she says she "cleaned up [her] life" for a while after rehab, she still felt "empty" inside. And yet Heather did manage to graduate from high school, take some college courses, and get a good job. She says she knows that it was "God's handiwork" that she stayed alive and out of jail, because when she met the man she thought she would marry, her life began another downward spiral and she was again addicted to drugs and "unhappy times."

Heather's life took a turn for the better when she finally listened to a woman from her apartment complex, a hairdresser who was "always offering to do my hair for free as she knew this would be her chance to witness to me." One day, she responded to the knock on her door and welcomed her neighbor. "She didn't even have to say anything, I just cried and cried." That night, Heather accompanied her neighbor to church, where she was "saved." Heather interprets this day as "the first day of the rest of my life." That week she received salvation and was water baptized. She also received baptism of the Holy Spirit that week and has been "on fire for the Lord" ever since. As a new Christian, Heather turned to the Bible for guidance on how to live her life. She has studied Scripture ever since her conversion experience and cites Jeremiah 1:5, "Before I formed you in the womb I knew you; before you were born I set you apart." Heather says that God knew she would witness to others one day and that her once ungodly ways would turn to godly ones. As part of her recovery and her entrance into a spiritual life, Heather read the Bible and popular Christian devotionals such as *From Faith to Faith* by Kenneth and Gloria Copeland.[1] In those early days as a "new on-fire Christian," Heather was like a sponge trying to soak up everything she could. She had never felt so good in her life and wanted to do everything she could to keep it that way. She found herself wanting to learn more, and she would wake up in the morning two hours early to read, pray, and "just sit still and listen for His guidance." According to Heather, "the more I read and obeyed, the more things in my life started to improve. I quit all my bad habits, drugs, cussing, and the hardest of all—cigarettes. The Lord took all those desires away and replaced them with a desire to know Him and work for His kingdom to do His good will."

Heather moved back in with her parents, started going to an "awesome" church and began seeing an "awesome" Christian counselor. She says she never felt so much love and freedom in her entire life. It was during these first few months as a new Christian that Heather was invited by her aunt to go to a Walk to Emmaus retreat in Baton Rouge. Heather says that "for me if it was a place I could learn more about Jesus, I was all in. She did tell me they had a waiting list so she wasn't sure if I would get in this time. But it must have been my time to go because she called me a few weeks prior to the weekend and said she didn't know how but my name got to the top of the list. That was God at work."

Soon after her Emmaus experience, Heather found herself in her hairdresser's shop. Her life was now radically different from the day her hairdresser first witnessed to her. Heather was now a committed, practicing Christian, clean and sober, and in a relationship with a "really, really good man" named Richie. Her hairdresser again "put God into my life" by mentioning the local Christian movement Tres Dias. She shared the information with Richie. "God puts certain people in your life for a reason. We had been going out for a while and I thought that this might be 'the one,' you know?" Richie agreed to make his Tres Dias weekend before Heather made hers because "it is really important for the man to make his first because he is the head of the relationship, as it says in the Bible."

When we first met at the northern Illinois Tres Dias gathering, Heather beamed when she talked about then-boyfriend, now-husband Richie, who returned from his Tres Dias weekend "totally pumped, on fire for Jesus, in love with the Lord." Especially memorable was Richie's marriage proposal to her soon after his Tres Dias weekend. Heather made her Tres Dias weekend shortly after, and says it was the best experience of her life. "If God can love someone like me who has made many bad choices in my life and can make me new again, clean, then He can love anyone." Her Tres Dias weekend was "an amazing experience" during which she "felt Christ's love in ways I had never felt before."[2] Making her Tres Dias weekend showed Heather that she was worthy of Christ's love and that she had a lot to offer the world. After her weekend encounter was over, Heather wasted no time finding a reunion group that gathers every week for prayer and conversation over lunch. The group continually renews her and gives her the strength she needs.

Heather has served on every Tres Dias weekend since her own weekend experience and, along with Richie, sits on the local secretariat for South East Texas Tres Dias. They serve as the "preweekend couple" and in this capacity handle the registration for all the candidates for upcoming weekends. Heather has continued to flourish in the movement. In the summer of 2010, she was elected to sit on the board of International Tres Dias, and that October she was elected to the International Board as secretary of International Tres Dias. In a recent e-mail to me, Heather wrote:

> The Lord has changed my life in so many ways. The training of Tres Dias has helped me in all parts of my life. It has helped me to grow as a Christian so I can take what I have learned back to my church so I can show others through my actions the Love of our Lord and Savior. I dedicate my life to helping others to have another chance

of living a Godly life and to help Christians to grow in their walk with Christ. Today my husband and I serve in leadership roles at our church. We co-facilitate with another couple a Dave Ramsey Financial Peace class in our church that helps people get out of debt and grow their finances. When I look back at where I came from and where I am now all I can say is WOW THANK YOU JESUS!!!!

I first met Heather and her "sister in Christ" Judy at a northern Illinois Tres Dias gathering the spring of 2010. Heather's story of healing, renewal, and awakening is deeply personal to her, but it is also in many ways a universal story of how a three-day weekend in spirituality has impacted the lives of hundreds of thousands of Christian men and women in the United States. While the men and women who make a Tres Dias weekend may know some of the history of their movement, what they usually do not know is that it is part of a global movement in Christian spirituality that traces its origins to 1944 Mallorca, Spain. It was then and there that Eduardo Bonnín Aguilo crafted the Cursillo de Cristiandad, the three-day weekend in Christian spirituality for men that would eventually move from the island and would have a global impact on millions of Catholics and Protestants. This larger weekend Cursillo and "Fourth-Day" movement is the subject of my ethnographic and historical examination.

The research and writing of this book have been a truly pleasurable journey. I have so many people to thank—without their support for this book it would never have come to fruition. I must start with my family, for they have been with me every step of the way. I want to thank my husband, the historian Stephen Andrew Warren. Steve has supported my intellectual life and work since we met as undergraduates at Indiana University in 1990. He has provided a constant dose of love, support, and the best editorial advice since we first fell in love. It was you, Steve, who lifted my spirits when I doubted whether I could finish this book, given the pleasures but also demands of juggling family, work, and other life commitments. From driving me all over Mallorca in our rented Citroën Berlingo with the children for my interviews with cursillistas to taking the kids to the park to play when you knew I need some time to write, you have shown your love and support for my work. Even more, you have always encouraged my spiritual growth, and you calm me down when I get stressed out about all of the work that needs to get done at home and at work. Moreover, you have always been a fantastic editor and have provided incisive editorial remarks that have helped me strengthen my authorial voice and the manuscript as a whole. Thank you for all of this and more, Steve.

I thank our three wonderful children, Cormac, Declan, and Josie, who have traveled with me in the most literal sense on my ethnographic and historical journeying. You help keep me centered and you ground me with your wisdom. I love you so very much. You have asked me, "Mom, who are you going to talk to today?" and were just as excited as I was (or so it seemed!) to stay for a week in Cala Figuera, Mallorca, home of the first Cursillo de Cristiandad (1944). Visiting the chalet with you and your dad where the first weekend was held (and taking all of those photos!) was and remains a sweet memory for me—not to mention the ice cream bars and figs we enjoyed afterward. I look forward to accompanying each of you in your own spiritual and intellectual journeys as you grow and mature. You inspire me and bring me joy each and every day. *Me llenan de alegría cada día, niños.*

Right up there with the love and support of my family has been the unflagging willingness of Catholic and Protestant cursillistas across the United States, from California to Indiana to Florida, to help me understand the power of a religious movement that has touched the lives of millions of Christians around the world. Without the help of the cursillistas I have met, interviewed, and shared many a meal with, this book would be a bland historical overview of the Cursillo de Cristiandad movement. *A mis amigos cursillistas, especialmente en Mallorca*; San Diego, California; Houston, Texas; Phoenix, Arizona; Festus, Missouri; Des Moines, Iowa; the Quad-Cities, Rockford, and Peoria, Illinois; East Chicago, Rockford, and Indianapolis, Indiana; Miami and Boca Raton, Florida; and Poughkeepsie, New York—*gracias para todo*. I am eternally grateful to each of you for the time you took to share your testimonies with me and for helping me more fully understand the importance of this religious and social movement. I hope that this book captures a fraction of what you have shared with me and the richness and beauty of your experiences.

The seeds of curiosity that grew into this book were planted in me in the early 1990s when I was interviewing Mexican American devotees of *la Virgen* in South Phoenix, Arizona. The vast majority of my interlocutors had made a Cursillo and claimed it was one of the most significant experiences, if not the most important experience, of their entire lives. I vowed then that I would study this movement at a later date and honestly did not imagine that it would preoccupy me as much as it has. Thank you friends, for introducing me to a movement that has touched the lives of millions since 1944 and for providing me with yet another teachable moment. As with all of the cursillistas I have met since, you do your best to live your faith each day, and you inspire me with your centeredness, your strength, and your commitment to serving others.

Another *gracias muy grande* goes out to my San Diego *amigos, veteranos* of the U.S. Cursillo movement, among the first to make their Cursillo in the United States. You opened your hearts and homes to my family and me and convinced me of the importance of writing a history of the Cursillo de Cristiandad movement in the United States and of showing how U.S. Mexican-descent Catholics have been at the forefront of perhaps the most important Christian social movement in the late twentieth century. Thanks especially to Enrique Méndez, former director of the Office of Hispanic Ministries, San Diego, for all of his help in connecting me to the center of the movement in the greater San Diego area. Jesse and María Ramirez, Carmen Uriostegui, Enrique and Rosita Aldrete, Francisco and Sofía Pintado, and José and Juanita Herrera—your stories have greatly added to my understanding of the power and importance of the Cursillo *movimiento* and convinced me that this was a story that needed to be told. *Gracias por demostrar el poder del amor, la fe y el compromiso con la comunidad.*

I am also grateful to John Thompson of Kairos Prison Ministry International (KPMI) for allowing me to observe a Kairos Inside weekend. A special thanks goes out to JoEllen Rowe with the Indiana branch of KPMI. JoEllen and all of the Kairos Team that weekend welcomed me as an observer and made me feel at home during those three days. Thanks to Rita Steed of Rockville's facility for accommodating my nursing needs that weekend. Another thanks goes to Father Duane Jack of Colona, Illinois. Father Jack was an early supporter of this book and encouraged me to make my Cursillo weekend at the Believers Together Center in Moline, Illinois. My sponsor, Doris O'Keefe, has been a supportive and understanding friend, and I value her insights and wisdom. The team of women who organized and ran my Cursillo weekend, number 959, in March 2011 were supportive and understanding of my work. Thanks for everything, ladies!

My ethnographic journeys for this book began in the desert climes of Phoenix in the early 1990s and ended in 2011 on the beautiful island of Mallorca (also with desert topography). To my Mallorquín cursillista friends who spent so much time sharing their memories of Eduardo Bonnin Aguiló, initiator of the Cursillo de Cristiandad movement—especially

Miguel and María Sureda, Cristina González Duqué (and husband Juama and son Juama), Bartolomé Arrom, Catalina Granados Carreras, Vicente Patrol Gallefa, Jaime Galmés, Ramón Rosselló, Guillermo Estarellas, and Don Antonio Pérez Ramos—you have convinced me of the necessity of internationalizing the study of U.S. Catholicism and broadening out Catholic studies. Thank you for your testimonials and for clarifying the early history of the Cursillo movement as well as its present state in Mallorca. Miguel and Cristina went out of their way to organize the interviews, to invite me to a weekly ultreya, and to make sure that Steve, Cormac, Declan, and Josie were having fun when I was conducting fieldwork. The kids had a wonderful time at the beach and we all enjoyed what was our best meal—the paella was *simplemente incréible*—during our stay in Mallorca that afternoon.

I also want thank the leaders of the Catholic and Protestant Cursillos documented in this book. Victor Lugo of the National Secretariat of Catholic Cursillos; Tracey Schmidlin, then-president of the ELCA Via de Cristo; Steve Gielda, vice president of Via de Cristo; John Thompson, director of Kairos Prison Ministry International; Greg Engroff, director of Walk to Emmaus; John McKinney and Paul Weiss of Tres Dias; and Thom Neal, then-president of National Episcopal Cursillo (NEC), have given information on the history of their respective movements and have willingly shared their testimonies, which have all enriched this book. Sharing a meal with you in Orlando was a highlight of my research as you shared more than good food and wine with me—you shared your deep enthusiasm and commitment to the organizations that you head.

Ron Reiter, former director of Teens Encounter Christ (TEC), has been consistently helpful and forthcoming with information on the TEC movement in the United States. He even set up a weekend interview experience with the cofounders of TEC, Father Matt Fedewa and Dorothy Gerecke (formerly known as Sister Maria Concetta), and sent me home with a large box of original, previously untouched TEC documents. Ron's generosity as well as the generosity of the cursillistas I have met have been truly humbling. You have shared your personal narratives with me, your movement's history, even home-cooked meals. A special thanks here to Kay, Ron's wife, for a delicious five-course meal prepared and served in the Reiter home in Festus, Missouri. I must say that Ron has been one of the most enthusiastic supporters of this book and checks in frequently to inquire about its progress. For their part, Father Matt and Dorothy have also been generous supporters of this book. Dorothy calls me from her retirement home in Boca Raton to see if I have any more questions for her and to see when I am coming to visit her. I promise I will try soon, Dorothy! I am humbled by your sincerity and generosity of spirit and thank you for caring so much about this book.

I want to thank Augustana College, which supported me with research grants and a two-term sabbatical leave in 2010–11. The 2005 New Faculty Grant made my trip to San Diego possible and jump-started what became this book. A Faculty Research and Sabbatical Leave grant of 2009–10 helped me take several ethnographic research trips that were instrumental in the writing of this book. My journeys across the United States have been aided by the support I have received from Augustana. The college's Freistat Center for World Peace gave me the funding to travel to Mallorca for two weeks in June 2011 to conduct archival and ethnographic research important for the completion of this book. Former colleagues at Augustana College and new colleagues in the Department of Religious Studies at the University of Iowa have shared their enthusiasm for this project, and I thank them for the concern they have shown and the questions they have asked.

Colleagues around the country have offered encouragement and help along the way. Bob Orsi has been a stalwart mentor since he was my Ph.D. advisor at Indiana University. He has always believed in this Cursillo project and has offered up many words of encouragement over the years. Thank you, Bob, for serving as a role model for caring and engaged scholarship for many years. You have helped shape a generation of scholars and our work. John Corrigan and Judith Weisenfeld were amazing mentors in the Young Scholars in American Religion Program of which I was blessed to be a part in 2005–6. John, thank you for encouraging me to stick with this project and for believing in it when it was in its early inception. Judith, thank you for your mentorship through the years and for your ever-helpful advice on seeing the big picture in American religious historiography.

A special thanks to my 2005–6 Young Scholars in American Religion (YSAR) cohorts. The weekends we all spent together in Indianapolis are important moments in my professional life. I thank Courtney Bender, Sylvester Johnson, Tracy Neal Leavelle, Eve Sterne, and Kathy Cummings in particular for the intellectual proddings you have given me since our YSAR weekends, and Phil Goff, who has committed himself to the continuation of the YSAR program.

Tom Tweed has been a supporter of this project from the beginning as well, pointing to the significance of this book for the internationalization of U.S. Catholicism. Jim Fisher has also been an active supporter of my work to broaden Catholic studies. The Catholic studies seminar of which I was a part in 2007 was an important professional experience for me; thanks to Jim and to Maggie McGuinness for inviting me to be a part of this dynamic group working to reshape Catholic studies.

Tim Matovina of the Cushwa Center for American Catholicism at Notre Dame has been a big supporter of my work and has always understood the significance of the Cursillo movement for American Catholic history. Thank you, Tim, for offering me sage professional advice from the time I was a newly minted Ph.D. to the present. Your own work has continually inspired me, especially the care and concern you have given U.S. Latino Catholic history. Another strong supporter of my work has been R. Stephen Warner, who has offered support and sound critiques of my work for the past ten years. Thank you, Steve, for being an example of invested, engaged scholarship and a really good person to boot. Thanks to Steve and to Nancy Ammerman for inviting me to participate in the 2008 Louisville Institute Engaged Scholars in the Study of Religion, one of the many events that helped me realize the potential of this book.

The "Reimagining Religious History of the American West" conference at Arizona State University in fall 2006 offered an important venue for sharing my work-in-progress, and I thank the group's conveners, especially Tisa Wenger and Moses Moore, for organizing this event and supporting my work. Friends and colleagues Mary Thurlkill and Douglas Winiarski invited me to their campuses—the University of Mississippi (2007) and the University of Richmond (2008), respectively—to present working drafts of this project, and I have benefited from the responses I gained from them, their colleagues, and their students.

Thanks to Kathleen Sprows Cummings, friend and colleague for many years. Kathy has been an important sounding board not only for my intellectual work but in my quest to maintain a healthy balance of work and family. Thank you for being such a supportive friend, Kathy, and for inspiring me in your own carefully rendered, lovingly crafted, work. Thanks to other friends in the disciplines of anthropology, history, political science, religious studies, and sociology, including Jason Bivins, Cathy Brekus, Doug Burton-Christie, Amy DeRogatis, Margaret Farrar, Marie Griffith, Amy Koehlinger, Tracey Neal Leavelle, Kathryn Lofton,

Jason Mahn, Gerardo Marti, Charles Mathewes, Maggie McGuire, Quincy Newell, Sue Ridgely, Omid Safi, Jim Spickard, Ann Taves, Sarah Taylor, Tom Tweed, and Cyrus Ali Zargar, for offering their encouragement and support over the years.

My pastor, Katherine Mulhern, has been an important source of inspiration and wisdom in the later stages of writing and in life in general, and I thank her for that. Sister Marilyn Ring, O.B., has been a very special friend and spiritual mentor for the past eleven years, a stalwart woman of faith who always challenges me and those around her in profound ways. Thanks to friends Margaret Morse, Jane Simonsen, Katie Strzpak, Katie VanBlair, and Heidi White, who each in her own special way reached out to care for my family and me these past several years. I am blessed to have a close circle of friends. And my dear friend and neighbor Missy Bohonek, her husband Chad, and their children Luke, Carson, and Madeline have offered their love and support of my work and family since we moved across the street from them in 2005.

Jacqueline Bussie has been another important source of friendship and has consistently offered good advice and input. I greatly enjoyed organizing the Midwest American Academy of Religion (MAAR) conference with Jacquie in 2010 and 2011 and value her effervescence, wisdom, and strength. Working with Tom Pearson and Scott Paeth with the MAAR was a real privilege, and thanks to you both for all your support and wisdom.

I want to offer here a heartfelt thank you to our in-home daycare provider, Diann Gano, who for more than nine years helped care for Cormac, Declan, and Josie, providing them with a loving, nurturing environment. Maintaining a balance between work and family is not always easy, and we have been so fortunate to have had Diann's help in the raising of our children. A special thank you is in order for Kate Horberg for staying with us and helping out with the children for two months in summer 2011 so we could spend time writing our books. I wish you all the best in the Peace Corps and know you will continue to do amazing things in your life. You inspire Steve, our children, and me.

Another word of thanks needs to go out to my former Augustana students, especially those who were in the American Catholicisms course I taught there from 2002 to 2012. You have provided me with helpful feedback and have asked very good questions about my work. Your enthusiasm for it helped keep my spirits up, at times when I most needed the extra support, and I thank you for that. Particular thanks to my Augustana

College students Courtney (Anderson) Bruntz, Sarah DuRocher, Pat Fish, Kate Gibson, Maggie Hayes, Laurel Householter, Mohammed Hussein, Nick Kalina, Colleen Kilbride, Grace Kolaczek, Jaron Gaier, Constance Mithelman, Emily Petersen, Dorothy Williams, and Maureen Zach, all of whom have helped me in their own way to conceptualize this project and inspired me with their commitment to a life of learning and service to others. Thanks, too, to Mary Koski in Augustana's Deans Office, who provided me with a quiet office space where I could finish this book.

A big thank you to my stalwart University of North Carolina Press editor, Elaine Maisner, who saw the potential of this project when it was in its early stages. Elaine, you have been a wonderful editor, offering sharp and incisive criticism and pushing me to turn in what I hope is a great story of how a religious movement has been a catalyst for changed lives and communities in the United States and abroad. Thanks also to Alex Martin for his expert copyediting; to Paula Wald, associate managing editor, for helping to keep me on task; and to Caitlin Bell-Butterfield for her assistance these past several years. And, finally, a big thank you to Dino Battista, UNC Press's marketing director, who took an early interest in this project. As a cursillista, Dino understands the significance of this weekend course and movement for Christians around the world. I sincerely hope that my rendering of the history and experience of the Cursillo de Cristiandad and its various Protestant manifestations is an accurate portrayal of the essence and purpose of the movement and the beauty of the weekend for those who have experienced and continue to live it.

The Cursillo Movement in America

INTRODUCTION

Finding Christ and Community in America

The Significance of Catholic and Protestant Cursillos and the Fourth-Day Movement

The Cursillo Movement in America: Catholics, Protestants, and Fourth-Day Spirituality is an ethnographically oriented history of the weekend Christian Cursillo movement, the "short course in Christianity," among American Catholics and Protestants. What is today known interchangeably as the Cursillo (Cursillo de Cristiandad, or CdC) short course in Christianity or the Fourth-Day Christian movement began in 1944 on Mallorca, the largest of the Spanish Balearic Islands, as an effort at religious revitalization for Spanish Catholic men.[1] In 1957, thirteen years after their Mallorquín inception, Catholic Cursillos came to American Catholic culture by way of two Spanish Catholic air force pilots stationed in Waco, Texas. From the beginning, the weekend Cursillo movement was geared toward men, to provide them with a place to experience Christ and the Holy Spirit and a setting where their spirituality could grow. For men unaccustomed to showing their emotions, the weekend Cursillo offered the time and space to talk about their personal lives with other men in a safe space. For some, participating in the weekend events was a conduit toward a deeper spiritual life; for others it led to a revitalized participation in church. For most cursillistas—those in 1944 as well as today—making a Cursillo was and is about several things: discovering their potential as individuals, becoming connected to a faith community, and becoming more active members in their church.

The first Cursillo weekends were linked to the larger lay-initiated Catholic Action (CA) movement of the 1940s and 1950s that spanned Europe, Mexico, and the United States. Catholic Action predated the Vatican II Council by twenty years; its vision was to motivate laypeople to transform their society via their Catholic faith. Yet Eduardo Bonnín Aguiló, the primary initiator of what is now known as CdC, was critical of the top-down, hierarchically run Catholic Action. Bonnín and a small group of friends crafted a weekend experience that blended elements of the CA Cursillo and made it more lay-focused and less dependent on Church authorities. They called their weekend experiences "Cursillos for Pilgrim Leaders" and hoped that the three days would encourage men to *become* Church. The idea of "being Church" was that laymen would embody their Catholic religion and become more proactive in their faith lives. The goal was for Catholic men to claim and take ownership of their faith and to renew not only themselves but their Church and the surrounding Catholic culture. Bonnín and friends branched off of the more ecclesiastically focused and arguably fascistic Catholic Action, formed a weekend of spirituality, and encouraged cursillistas to live a deeper spiritual life. These weekend Cursillos sought to remake Spanish Catholicism. While masculinist-sounding language was used by Bonnín and the men involved in the early weekend Cursillos, these weekends were the inverse of mainstream Catholic Action Catholicism. The Catholicism of Catholic Action was a manly, embodied, pilgrimage-making Catholicism. Bonnín's Catholicism was something else—a deeply reflective, intellectual, and emotional experience and faith.[2]

Since the late 1950s, millions of American Catholics and Protestants and Christians around the world have participated in a seventy-two-hour Cursillo weekend course, or one of its many spinoffs. Catholic and Protestant graduates of the weekend Cursillo claim to be new individuals, refreshed and renewed. Cursillistas seek to demonstrate their new identities by living a life they believe Christ would want them to live. They share a desire to become part of a community of committed Christians who are, in their words, the "hands and feet of Christ." Catch phrases such as these reflect a common language that connects cursillistas around the world, whether they are Catholic or Protestant. Denominational and theological differences tend to be downplayed for an overarching, common identity as renewed Christians. Cursillistas' shared language emanates from a yearning for love, acceptance, and community.

Moreover, the linguistic markers of "De Colores!," "blooming where we are planted," and "reaching the faraway" point to cursillistas' dissatisfaction with institutional churches. While most cursillistas are churchgoers who deeply love their churches and their traditions, they have wanted more than the theology, rituals, and traditions contained inside their churches. They have wanted more from their churches, their pastors, and from each other. They have called for a new spirituality that speaks to their modern condition—a spirituality centered on a more mystical, loving Christ who cares less about denominations and more about Christian universalism. Since 1944 in Mallorca, cursillistas have sought to connect with the Holy Spirit. They say they feel the "fire" of the Spirit and have become reborn Christians who have examined their own lives and emerged as Christians ready to change their immediate environments. For their part, Protestant cursillistas have given the phrase "Bloom where you are planted" new layers of meaning as they spread their Cursillo movements globally.

A history of the larger Cursillo movement in the United States complicates the prevailing and pervasive Protestant narrative that implies and assumes that heart-filled, emotional religious praxis and discourse stems primarily from the Great Awakenings of the mid-eighteenth and nineteenth centuries. Much American religious historiography has reified the Awakenings to the point that contemporary phenomena continue to be viewed and interpreted through lenses now often two centuries old.[3] While much of today's Protestant religious enthusiasm and language of the heart can certainly be traced to the Awakenings, we have overlooked the profound intersection of more recent and relevant international and American Catholic and Protestant social movements. Since the 1950s, the ecumenical language of emotion and healing has increasingly stitched American Christians together.

Cursillistas, both Protestant and Catholic, share and promote a common discourse and a similar means of being in the world. My study of the Cursillo movement in the United States shows a new way of looking at denominationalism. The history of the Cursillo movement forces us to acknowledge that American Catholic and Protestant cursillistas emphasize their denominations much less than a Christian universalism of beliefs and experience. For most cursillistas, their denominations matter to them, but they are willing to transgress denominational boundaries for an experience with Christ, the Holy Spirit, and each other that universalizes Christianity and enables them to see Christ in each other.

What has kept the Cursillo movement alive is the dynamic combination and application of piety, study, and action, since 1944 the triple touchstone of the Cursillo movement. The individual's heart is the main focus—turning the pilgrim's heart to Jesus Christ to bring about a reawakening. I have been told by my interlocutors in Mallorca and all across the United States that during their Cursillo weekend, "Christ moved from my head to my heart." It is precisely this intense emotionality and focus on the heart in the Catholic Cursillo weekend that attracted Protestant Americans in the 1960s—*not* Catholic theology per se. The experience and renewal that the Cursillo weekend offered laymen and women in 1960s and 1970s America dovetailed with the larger church renewals and reforms that were taking place in every U.S. Christian denomination. The time was ripe for experimentation and reforms and reform-minded laity and clergy were drawn to the Cursillo weekend experience. Cursillistas' very language distinguished them from other Christians, as "De Colores!" emerged as a marker, a kind of lingua franca, of a new Christian identity. This new Christian was centered in the "heart" and linked Protestants and Catholics across the country in a chain of newly awakened, "on fire" Christians. "De Colores!" became a new linguistic for American cursillistas, whether they lived in California, Iowa, or Florida. Mallorquín cursillistas and cursillistas around the world greet each other with the saying and sign their correspondence with the words and an exclamation point. "De Colores!" has become a global password affording entry into a culture of renewed and committed Christians. For Bonnín and the architects of the Cursillo weekend, weekly meetings, reunions of cursillistas, were crucial to maintaining a renewed Christian life. The Cursillo weekend itself was designed to nurture a dialectical relationship between the individual, the larger community of Christians, and Christ, and the postweekend gatherings of cursillistas was intended to reinforce these ties. The reunion group remains central for twenty-first-century cursillistas as they work to maintain a spiritual life.

My study of Fourth-Day Christian movements in America is about how religion is made and experienced by people. The women, men, and young adults I have interviewed and encountered all talk about seeing the world in a different way after participating in their Cursillo weekend. Cursillistas, both Protestant and Catholic, say that they saw the world in "black and white" before their Cursillo, but that they now see and appreciate the world in its splendor and many colors. The rooster (with its multicolored plumage) and the rainbow are two symbols that these Fourth-Day movements use to advertise their new, postretreat perspective. The Mallorquín Catholic cursillistas' symbol is a tricolored origami bird, a creation of Eduardo Bonnín while he was at his group reunion meeting in a café. For Mallorquín cursillistas, Bonnín's bird reminds them of his playfulness and humor as well as the deeper meaning of making something beautiful (four-dimensional art) out of something ordinary (a paper sugar container).

Despite the historic and cultural importance of the Cursillo de Cristiandad movement and the variety of Christian movements it has inspired and nurtured, no one has written a comprehensive academic study of it. This is puzzling, since it is one of the most important American and global Christian lay movements since the 1950s.[4] An ethnohistory of the Fourth-Day ecumenical Christian movement shows us that mainline Catholicism and Protestantism have been shaped by laypersons and clergy who have worked together to transform their churches and surrounding communities. U.S. Cursillo communities have been enormously successful in helping the movement spread across the globe, as cursillistas have taken it upon themselves to be ambassadors of spirituality. In order to fully appreciate the ways U.S. Catholicism and Protestantism is situated within a network of international Catholicism, we must begin on the island of Mallorca, the birthplace of Cursillo and a place whose lay spiritual culture has had a profound impact on that of U.S. Christianity.

An ethnographic study of this movement shows that American Christians have been undergoing profound spiritual experiences from the late 1950s to the present, and that they are working to infuse their communities and churches with their newfound zeal. *The Cursillo Movement in America* captures what much recent historiography on American Christianity has missed—that mainline Catholics and Protestants, as cursillistas, are doing nothing short of reforming themselves as believers and as individuals.[5] Cursillistas share this newfound spirituality friends and family, an energy felt in churches, parishes, and dioceses across the United States.

I decided to write this book—in many ways it chose me—and have persevered because since the mid-1990s, I have spoken with and encountered men and women across the United States whose lives have been transformed by their weekend Cursillo retreat. Friends and neighbors have spoken positively of their high school experiences with Cursillos, and even the taxi driver, Craig, who drove me to the airport where I was on my way to a seminar to discuss my Cursillo project, talked at length about his Catholic Cursillo weekend. As we drove from my home in Rock Island, Illinois, Craig pointed down the street to where he had made his Cursillo fifteen years prior—at the site of the former Villa de Chantal convent and Catholic girls' boarding school. Craig, like the vast majority of cursillistas I have spoken with over the past six years, said his Cursillo weekend was an "awesome" experience that "changed [his] life forever."[6]

Tragically, the historic French Catholic Villa burned to the ground in 2005, soon after my family and I moved into our home three doors down from its splendid ten-acre lot. What I did not know then was that the Villa was the primary location for northwest Illinois Cursillos for over thirty years.[7] And to add yet another personal vignette to my attraction to the history of Cursillos, as I was researching the Lutheran Via de Cristo movement, one of the Protestant branches of the Catholic CdC, I discovered that the Nineteenth National Lutheran Secretariat (NLS) meeting of July 19–22, 1995, was held in Rock Island, at Augustana College, where I taught in the Religion Department from 2002 to 2012.

My interlocutors in the movement would make sense of these discoveries as "not coincidences but God incidences." My interlocutor John McKinney of Tres Dias, a nondenominational Fourth-Day movement, coined this phrase and believes, as do many of my interlocutors, that these events and discoveries have occurred because I have been "called" by the Holy Spirit to write this book. I can say with certainty that coming across the compelling historic and ethnographic details that I have been privileged to encounter cemented my dedication to writing this book. Whenever it seemed that I would never complete it, given the pleasures and demands of caring for my three children with my husband, Steve, of balancing family and work, I would speak with a cursillista or read a document and be reinspired.

Each time I look outside at my back garden I see the statue of Saint Juan Diego, given to me by Carmen Uriostegui, a San Diegan cursillista and one of the first people I interviewed for this book, and I am reminded of her powerful story of suffering and triumph. I was touched by the sincerity and love that my fellow Diocese of Peoria Women's Cursillo no. 959 participants showed me and each other in March 2011. I was deeply moved by the Kairos Prison Ministry volunteers who ran the weekend I observed at a medium-to-maximum-security prison in southern Indiana. My trip to Mallorca in June 2011 was another source of inspiration as I met Mallorquín cursillistas who shared their memories of Eduardo Bonnín Aguiló, and who eloquently spoke of the power and beauty of the movement. I have been deeply moved and inspired by the close to 250 cursillistas I have interviewed over the past seven years, and I have felt a duty to contextualize their stories with the larger history of Cursillos in North America and with American religious history more broadly. What they say matters on so many levels, and it is my job as an ethnographer to detail the larger cultural and historical significance of their individual stories.

Most of the men, women, and young adults I interviewed gave their enthusiastic permission to provide their full names in the book. For those cursillistas who asked that only their first names be given, I provide only their first names. And for those incarcerated women whom I interviewed and observed during the Kairos Inside weekend that is the focus of Chapter 6, I provide pseudonyms. Moreover, for reasons of confidentiality, I have altered some personal details in chapter 6 so as not to divulge the inmates' identities. I have also altered the names of the women I met on my Catholic cursillo weekend who either made the course as candidates or volunteered since I was participating as a cursillista and not as a scholar and my scholarly identity was unknown to everyone but the weekend leaders and the priest. I do refer to Father Duane Jack and my sponsor Doris O'Keefe by their given names since they knew about and encouraged my weekend experience and the research for this book.

A Cursillo is a seventy-two-hour-long "little course," a lay-sponsored, church-supported weekend retreat that addresses individual Christians as important, vital members of the larger church body. Groups of twenty to thirty "candidates" eat, sleep, pray, and worship together for three days, from Thursday to Sunday evening. The course, usually planned for months and carefully orchestrated, is run by a team of dedicated Cursillo leaders. Candidates have been carefully screened by veteran cursillistas. A candidate deemed ready to make a weekend Cursillo through the pre-Cursillo, a period of sponsorship. During this time before the actual course is held, which can last for months or weeks, each candidate meets with a veteran cursillista who helps to prepare him or her for the experience. Ideally, the sponsor continues to be a spiritual mentor long after the course is over, in a period known as the post-Cursillo. Following their Cursillo weekend, American Catholics and Protestants consider the Fourth Day to be the rest of their lives.

One dialectic that I explore in this book is the tension between popular and official piety, primarily seen in how members of the church hierarchy and laity interpret the weekend's meanings. While the weekend Cursillo was envisioned as a movement for laymen, its history and how that history should be interpreted have been marked by power struggles between clergy and laity that continue today. Bonnín was marginalized from the movement he initiated by bishops and priests who have wanted the weekend Cursillos to be more clerically driven and less ecumenical. It was my San Diego interlocutors in 2005 who first informed me about Eduardo Bonnín Aguiló and told me he was the "true founder" of Cursillos—not Bishop Juan Hervás, whom they insisted was an important supporter of the early Cursillo movement but one who "took over" the movement and "has gotten all the credit."

My San Diego friends were right—Bonnín was omitted from most Church-directed histories of Catholic Cursillos and even those of Protestant Cursillo offshoots. Hervás, not Bonnín, has been officially called the "founder" of the movement.[8] And U.S. clergy who acknowledge and even embrace Bonnín as the movement's founder today have their own agendas that can cause them to posit Bonnín and his three-day movement in the way they want to remember them. For example, the U.S. National Catholic Secretariat interprets Bonnín as antiecumenical in his concerns and outreach, yet there is evidence to show that Bonnín was ecumenically minded and not a Catholic triumphalist. Moreover, Bonnín never insisted that husbands make their weekend before their wives—this rule was a U.S. invention and is not observed in Mallorca. An ethnographically informed history helps us understand that just as the movement's history is contested, so too is Bonnín's legacy. I examine all of these tensions here and seek to unpack the cultural history of the weekend Cursillo as it arose in Mallorca and was transplanted in the United States.

Rooted in fascist Spain, Bonnín's "Cursillos of Conquest"—later named Cursillos de Cristiandad by Hervás—challenged the authoritarian Spanish Catholicism of the 1930s and 1940s in a quietly subversive way. Bonnín was no firebrand—he never explicitly challenged fascist Spain or its Church. Complex and at times paradoxical, he and the weekend he developed incorporated masculinist and fascistic-sounding language, in addition to the language of mysticism and lay empowerment. The deeply spiritual and intellectual Bonnín, a cradle Catholic born into privilege in island's capital, Palma de Mallorca, loved his country and his Church but sought to reform the way Catholicism was practiced. He initiated an alternative way of being Mallorquín and Spanish Catholic, wanting for Catholics to practice a faith that bound them in *amistad* (friendship) rather than separated them with mistrust and individualism. The three days were intended to bring people together and initiate a movement of love and renewed Christian spirituality that would have a pay-it-forward effect on individuals and society.

Since the first three-day Cursillo in 1944, Catholic clergy have given rollos ("short talks"), have administered the Eucharist, and have heard confessions. American Protestant clergy have been involved in the various Protestant Cursillos since the earliest ones were formed in the 1970s. Clergy's primary purpose is to serve and to support the laity on the weekend, and they are in turn served by laypersons, who cook and care for them. Veteran cursillistas volunteer to make meals, clean, and give talks. It is they who gather the palanca (literally "lever" in Spanish) letters, those personalized letters written by veteran cursillistas in a spirit of sacrifice and support for the candidates. Palanca letters are usually given to the candidates to read during the second day of the course and are cited as instrumental turning points by cursillistas in their weekend experience.

The three days of the Cursillo weekend consist of a series of fifteen rollos, five given by clergy and ten given by experienced cursillistas who have completed the movement's leadership training.[9] Spanish terminology has been kept intact by the mainstream Fourth-Day movements to maintain a sense of authenticity and connection to their origins. The Fourth-Day movements which include Catholic Cursillos (CdC), the nondenominational Kairos Prison Ministry International (KPMI), the Lutheran Via de Cristo, the nondenominational Tres Dias, the Methodist and ecumenical Walk to Emmaus, and the nonecumenical National Episcopal Cursillo (NEC) consider themselves to be "in covenant" with the original Mallorquín weekend Cursillo and follow as meticulously as possible the methods Bonnín set out of piety, study, and action. By calling themselves "in-covenant," these organizations indicate their genealogical authenticity as direct outgrowths of Eduardo Bonnín's weekend. By naming themselves as such, they self-consciously set themselves apart from more recent branches of Cursillo that they consider less authentic. The three days are carefully scripted and consciously return to Bonnín's directives. In all of the Fourth-Day movements, the rollos are followed by breakout discussion groups, and time for individual prayer and reflection is also built into the three-day schedule.

Another dialectic I explore in this book is how cursillistas balance their church involvement with their Cursillo-inspired new spirituality and their new place in the larger world. Adult Catholics who make a Cursillo and young adult Catholics who make the youth version of the Cursillo weekend, Teens Encounter Christ (TEC), hear talks on the sacraments. For them, the rosary and the Virgin Mary are important components to their weekend experience. Catholic cursillistas also place great emphasis on the Sacrament of the Eucharist, the centrality of Christ's body and blood via the doctrine of transubstantiation, which is key to their weekend events and defines them as Catholic. While the larger Cursillo movement downplays denominational differences in favor of universalism, Catholic Cursillos are the most denominationally oriented, and with a few exceptions, are in most U.S. dioceses not ecumenical. For all of cursillistas' discourse on universalism, denominational tensions remain, and Protestant cursillistas tend to be more comfortable with a universal notion of Christian spirituality. Like Protestants who make a Cursillo, Catholic cursillistas talk a lot about grace and about living out God's call to live grace-filled lives. But they also tend to hold on to what separates them from their Protestant peers—in some cases this comes across as Catholic triumphalism, but mostly it is a Catholic expression of spirituality and denominational difference. Catholic cursillistas find inspiration in the calls to evangelization by Popes Paul VI and John Paul II and feel a strong sense of responsibility as leaders and "prophetic instruments" of the Church.

Ethnography as an Essential Method

When we examine the history of the weekend Cursillo experience starting with the original 1944 weekend in Cala Figuera, Santanyí, Mallorca, and compare it to American Catholic and Protestant Cursillos, we find that the American Cursillo weekends have closely followed the method, purpose, and structure of the Mallorquín weekend. We find that Mallorquín Catholics, American Catholics, and American Protestants, from the 1960s to the present, have wanted essentially the same thing: a powerful encounter with Christ and the Holy Spirit, a renewed self, and a community of supportive, loving individuals with whom the individual has shared a profound experience. The far-flung U.S. Cursillo movement is a kind of grassroots Christianity that envisions laypersons as being church and transforming not only themselves but the world around them.

An ethnographic and historical examination of the U.S. Cursillo movement challenges much historiography of American Catholicism and mainline Protestantism by showing that since the late 1950s, Catholic and Protestant narratives have overlapped in significant ways. This book documents how, since the late 1950s, millions of ordinary, mainstream American Christians have wanted to—and have—experienced Christ, a renewed self, church, and community of fellow believers and worshippers. These men and women desire to live their renewed faith, and they set out to change the world, whether via social justice, evangelizing their newfound and refreshed faith, or continuing to work on and maintain their piety. What cursillistas share is a commitment to sharing their spiritual renewal with others.

As an ethnographer of American Catholicism and Protestantism, I document my interlocutor's stories by contextualizing them within American religious history more broadly. Moreover, I want to globalize the study of American religions, and in this book I show the profound impact of Mallorquín Spanish Catholic culture on post-1950s American Christian culture. If we are to understand the depths of American Christian experience and expression, we must seek out the origins of movements and must, if at all possible, travel to those places to conduct research.[10] My ethnographic research in Mallorca in the summer of 2011 greatly enriched this book by providing important historical contextualization for the Cursillo movement in the United States as well as globally. My conversations with Mallorquín cursillistas, most of whom were part of the early history, have convinced me that U.S. scholars of religion must broaden our geographic focus and look outside the United States to understand religion inside its borders.

A third dialectic I explore in this book is the relationship between international and U.S. forms of Christian expression. This book is about the importance of globalizing American religious history, and about how and why cursillistas' stories help us understand American Christian history and contemporary forms of Christian expression. The qualitative ethnography I have conducted since 2005 provides the data to challenge some assumptions long held in American religious historiography. Ethnography matters, not only because it enables scholars to connect with people but also because of what those connections afford us. The connections we form with our interlocutors allow us insights that cause us to ask questions that cannot be asked from a purely historical study. Ethnography as a method can reveal what really matters to contemporary Christians, but it can also provide necessary correctives to what has been considered the standard narrative—in this case—of the genealogy of a movement. As a methodology, ethnography shows us what other methodological approaches cannot.[11] If scholars of religion in America truly want to understand what is important to contemporary American Christians and to document what has been referred to as "lived religion" by an increasing number of scholars, then it is essential to study the Cursillo movement through ethnography.¹²

As a scholar of American Christianity I situate myself as much as possible in the lifeworlds of those I am studying. I have combed archives at universities and at the home offices of Cursillo and Fourth-Day movements. I have been given access to personal archives as well. Cursillistas have been generous in sharing photographs, memorabilia from their weekend Cursillos, and their reflections on their experience. Some have dug out old boxes that had remained tucked under beds, in drawers, and in closets, and have shared priceless materials that document their Cursillo experiences and post-Cursillo lives. I have been touched by the outpouring of support of these men and women, who have willingly shared so much.

Ethnography truly is a form of human relationship, and as a method it connects scholars and their interlocutors in ways that make our scholarship rich and multilayered. During my second visit to her home in San Diego, Rosita Aldrete asked how my son, then two years old, was doing, and when I showed her a photo of him she asked if she could have it to place on her *altarcito*. When I handed her the photo of Cormac, she kissed it and promptly placed it right next to the statue of the Santo Niño de Atocha. I was touched by her gesture of affection in including my child in her family and faith. While the archival work has been an important research site, it is the interviews and home-based archives that are the primary sources of information.

I first learned about the importance of the Cursillo weekend and movement from my South Phoenix interlocutors when I was interviewing them about their devotion to the Virgin Mary in the 1990s for my first book, *The Virgin of El Barrio*.¹³ These conversations convinced me that my next book should be should be on Cursillos. I was immediately intrigued by the rich and complex history of the Cursillo movement and just as surprised that no other scholar of U.S. religious history had written a book-length study of it. Between 2005 and 2011 I conducted one-on-one and group interviews with cursillistas, both by phone and in person. Over the past seven years I have also attended numerous group reunion meetings, secretariat meetings, and ultreyas (gatherings of group reunion meetings) across the United States, and even some in Mallorca. I have participated in a Kairos Prison Ministry Inside Weekend held at a women's correctional facility (spring 2010).¹⁴ I have also made my (Catholic) Cursillo weekend in March 2011 at Christ the King parish's Believers

Together Center in Moline, Illinois. Most recently, I traveled to Mallorca with my husband and three children to conduct interviews and archival research, my family and I sharing meals and beach time with our Mallorquín friends. In the chapters that follow, I will delve into the history of these Fourth-Day Christian movements and will showcase ethnographic data from my fieldwork, which adds an experiential texture to the history. Each chapter offers a combination of diachronic and synchronic analysis. Ethnography must be historically contextualized if it is to address the bigger picture.

Before I say more about the specific content of this book, I want to briefly outline the methodology and organization of the seven individual book chapters. Because I am trained in religious studies and in its multilayered methodological approaches, I am inclined toward an interdisciplinary approach to the study of religion. This book reflects that inclination. While my larger methodological approach is both ethnographic and historical, the way I have written the chapters is not uniform and is more of a blending of approaches. In some chapters, specifically chapters 1, 2, and 3, I draw on ethnography to enhance the historical narratives, making these chapters appear as ethnographically informed histories of the early Cursillo movement in Mallorca, the United States, and the in-covenant U.S. Protestant Fourth-Day movements.

Other chapters are more substantively ethnographic, drawing on history and theory to contextualize the ethnography-as-center. In what I will call a historically influenced ethnographic method in chapters 4, 5, and 7, my historic and contemporary interlocutors' narratives are the focus. These chapters tell the particular histories of U.S. Catholic and Protestant Cursillo movements from my interlocutors' perspectives and read more as "histories" than as "ethnographies," though the blending of methods is certainly present.

Chapter 6 reads differently from the other chapters. Based on my participation and observation during a women's Kairos Inside weekend, it is more deeply ethnographic in method and in content. In this chapter, history and theory enhance the ethnography and are acknowledged mostly by way of annotated endnotes, with my interlocutor's voices at the narrative center. My anthropologically and sociologically inclined readers might feel more at home in this chapter (and perhaps chapters 4, 5, and 7 as well), as the qualitative research that informs them—the interviews, the ethnographer's embodied research, and the observations gained during fieldwork—come through more explicitly than in the rest of the book. I hope that this religious-studies approach to the Fourth-Day movement is interesting and compelling to a wide variety of readers.

As a religious-studies scholar who has focused mostly on U.S. Catholicism in my research and writing, I have taken my cues from my interlocutors themselves. Believing (incorrectly) when I began that the Cursillo movement was primarily for Mexican American Catholics, I realized, the deeper I went into ethnography and historical research, that something bigger was going on, and that Catholics and Protestants alike were part of this Fourth-Day movement. The Cursillos have impacted the lives of hundreds of thousands of Catholics and Protestants in the United States and created a movement of Christian laypeople and clergy who want to reform the world in which they live. In working with laity and clergy involved in these various Cursillo weekend retreats and Fourth-Day movements, I have been given the opportunity to see the kind of commitment that these individuals have to becoming better people and better Christians.

An American Christian Story

I am a non-Catholic ethnographer of religion who, until recently, has worked mostly within U.S. Mexican-descent Catholic communities in the Southwest, West, and Midwest. In this book I raise some questions and concerns that have come up for me as an ethnographer who focuses on expressions of Christianity in the United States. I continue to work with Mexican-descent Catholics and have broadened my scope of inquiry to include white, non-Hispanic American Catholics and Protestants from a variety of traditions, and I am convinced that the subfield of Catholic studies and the larger field of religious studies can learn much from histories and ethnographies of Catholics as well as Protestants. I am also convinced that studies of U.S. Hispanics must be interwoven with the histories of U.S. Catholicism and U.S. Christianity more broadly. It is possible to reflect the uniqueness and richness of Hispanic lived religions in articles and books with an exclusive focus, but U.S. Hispanic religious histories must also be interwoven with others' histories in order to reflect common humanity and experience. U.S. Hispanic Catholic history is part of U.S. Catholic history, and both must be integrated into larger narratives of U.S. Christianity. In separating out U.S. Hispanic Catholic history from the larger narratives we risk exoticizing and romanticizing it, making it seem other and foreign to what U.S. Catholics have experienced.

Studying religion via ethnographic and historical methods gives us a fuller perspective on American Christian life and thought.

Main Arguments

My primary arguments throughout the book overlap and point to a new understanding of post-1950s American Christian history. This book is an ethnographic and historical examination of the Mallorquín and U.S. Cursillo movement and as such offers an entrée into a reexamination and new understanding of a sixty-year span of American Christian history. Fourth-Day movements can be seen as an important part of the small-group movement in America (studied by sociologists of religion such as Robert Wuthnow),[15] which emerged after World War II aims to reconnect Americans with the feeling and reality of meaningful community. What cursillistas have told me over the years supports Robert Putnam's assertion in *Bowling Alone* that post-1950s Americans tend to be disconnected from one another and have few meaningful social outlets. They would agree with his argument, in *Better Together* and *American Grace*, that people who are involved in their communities live fuller, richer lives.[16] They would second the thesis, offered in *Bowling Alone* and reinforced in *Better Together*, that religious communities have done a better job than secular social movements in addressing Americans' disconnect. It is during the Cursillo weekend and in the post-Cursillo phase that cursillistas find a sense of meaning and purpose in their lives. For many cursillistas, the weekend experience is just the beginning. These men and women continue to form and find community in the post-Cursillo—primarily in the form of the many reunion groups (ultreyas, etc.) that are part of living the Fourth Day. These reunion group meetings provide a spiritual and communal center for Christian cursillistas who want to continue to walk with Christ and to live Christ-filled lives.

Many cursillistas feel disconnected prior to experiencing the weekend retreat, but most end up finding a new meaning and a sense of purpose in their lives afterward. In postwar America, white, non-Hispanic families became more nuclear, as they moved from inner cities to suburbs and lost the connectedness to place and the extended kinship that their immigrant relatives had experienced in urban dwellings and ethnic barrios.[17] In the United States, men and women of Mexican-descent were living official as well as unofficial transnational existences and often felt out of place and even unwelcome in their new homes. For them, making a Cursillo weekend offered a welcome sense of place among men and women who had experienced a similar religious and personal awakening. While Putnam does acknowledge that "religious involvement is a crucial dimension of civic engagement," he bases his assessment of what he calls "religious involvement" almost exclusively on rates of church attendance.[18]

But church attendance is only part of the story, as "religious involvement" has meant a lot of different things to American Christians, and includes those events and gatherings that take place in spaces outside of churches. The rise of the Christian Cursillo movement in post–World War II America was part of a larger movement, the small-group movement, among American Christians. The small-group movement, as the sociologist of religion Robert Wuthnow has shown, arose in response to American Christians' desire for intimate communities of likeminded believers.[19] While Catholic Cursillo and Protestant Cursillo weekends take place in churches and retreat centers, Fourth-Day or post-Cursillo reunion groups—Cursillo small groups—meet in churches, bakeries, restaurants, and cursillistas' homes. In Mallorca, the United States, and wherever Cursillos are held internationally, group reunions function as small groups and give cursillistas a sense of purpose and community. Cursillistas' "religious involvement" is evidenced in a variety of ways and locales and is not exclusive to church buildings. While some small groups are linked to churches, even these meet outside of the church itself. The Fourth-Day Cursillo movement in America and elsewhere is fundamentally a popular Christian movement of men and women searching for spiritual intimacy, community, and connectedness.

This searching for meaning and connectedness is what captivated Eduardo Bonnín Aguiló, who wanted to provide the space and time for men to experience a radical transformation and more fully understand themselves, Christ, and each other. The Spanish Catholic men of the 1940s with whom he worked were not churchgoers. Most were soldiers and were citizens of a larger Mallorquín and Spanish culture of fascism and authoritarian Catholicism. While Bonnín Aguiló and his movement were not fascist per se, they could not escape the realities and rhetoric of their time, and a masculinist, disciplined language was incorporated into the weekend events of spirituality. Bonnín wanted to offer a place where men would be able to pour out their hearts to each other and to God, and to experience friendship and Christian brotherhood. In *Colaboración en la revista "Testimonio,"* he wrote, "The message of the short course, in synthesis, is only the proclamation of forgotten evidence. It is the best news: that God loves us, communicated by the best means which is friendship, led to what is most worthy of each individual, to the personal capacity of conviction, decision, and steadfastness."[20] Bonnín's weekend Cursillo offered an alternative to mainstream cultural Catholicism and aimed to "change the environment" of the authoritarian Church by easing mistrust and inculcating *amistad* and goodwill among Mallorquines. The focus of the original Cursillo in 1944 Mallorca was to help laymen find spiritual renewal, not to fill church pews. The weekend Cursillo movement has always been about helping individuals craft more spiritually meaningful lives.

Post-1950s U.S. cursillistas do tend to populate their respective churches, but heightened church involvement is a by-product, not the main goal, of the original movement. The cursillistas I have interviewed stress that they are part of a community and feel connected to Christ and to the men and women in their group reunion meeting. Through fellowship with other Christians who have made a retreat, these men and women say, they continue to grow as individuals in their faith. And like other Christians who experience change upon making a retreat, cursillistas want to make their faith work for others. Whether it be volunteering at a soup kitchen or helping undocumented workers adjust to the harsh realities of living without papers in America, cursillistas take what they have learned from their weekend experience and "bloom where they are planted" in the world.

This study of the U.S. Cursillo movement also challenges much of American religious historiography, which has tended to focus on movements in the East and in the West, with a nod to the South. For the most part, religion in the Midwest—Illinois, Iowa, Michigan, Missouri, and Ohio—has been overlooked. This study of Cursillos shows the region's centrality to the expression of American Christianity since the 1950s. A study of the Cursillo movement in the United States also shows the instrumentality of particular dioceses and the ecumenicism of American Catholic laity and some clergy in these places. In the Diocese of Peoria, Illinois, under the tutelage of Bishop Edward W. O'Rourke and Father Tom Henseler, ecumenicism among U.S. Catholics and Protestants was nurtured and encouraged. It was also in the Diocese of Peoria that Protestant Cursillos took shape and branched off. Nowhere else in the United States do we find the levels of cooperation and reciprocity between Roman Catholics and mainline Protestants that we do in the 1960s, 1970s, and 1980s Midwest. Protestant Cursillo movements and branches would simply not exist had it not been for ecumenically minded Catholics in the Diocese of Peoria. The history of the U.S. Cursillo movement and the importance of the Midwest to U.S. and global Cursillo history should prompt scholars of U.S. Catholicism and Protestantism to look more closely at regionalism as a way to understand how religious movements take root and spread.

This study of the Cursillo Fourth-Day movement also shows that Mexican-descent Catholics initiated a popular spiritual movement in American Christianity. My study of the Fourth-Day Christian encounter or retreat movement challenges our still mostly dichotomized view of American religious history, which continues to allot much time and space to Puritan Protestants and their descendants and much less to Spanish-speaking Catholics. While there have been some excellent revisionist works in recent years, most studies of American religious history still begin out East, with Anglo-American Christians, and not out West with Spanish-speaking Catholics.[21]

While the Cursillo was disdained by many Anglo-American Catholics in its early years because of its intense emotionality, by the late 1960s, more white, non-Hispanic American Christians were drawn in by the experience and saw the weekend as part of the exciting renewals of a Vatican II American Catholic Church and late-twentieth-century Protestantism. The late twentieth century was an exciting time for American Christianity, as Catholics and Protestants alike were experimenting with liturgical renewals and laity were seeing themselves *as* church. American Catholics and Protestants alike were searching for a religious experience that moved them and that put them in touch with Christ as much as they were looking for communities of loving Christians with whom they could nurture their faith. A history of the Cursillo movement, then, shows how Spanish-speaking Catholics, first in Mallorca and then in the United States, have deeply influenced white, non-Hispanic Catholics and in an even larger sense, impacted American Catholicism and Protestantism.

Finally, a close look at the Cursillo movement in the United States tells the story of twentieth- and twenty-first-century American Christians who for the most part were still faithful churchgoers but wanted more. They wanted a certain kind of experience that they were not getting in their churches, plainly put. They wanted their faith to "leap outside of the walls of the church," as one Catholic cursillista told me. Catholics and Protestants alike craved personal renewal and spiritual refreshment, as well as communities of believers who lived their faith in their everyday lives and not just in the pew on Sundays. They wanted to band together with other Christians who were unafraid to talk about their faith openly, the kind of folks who would pray together at a restaurant before eating. A history of the Cursillo movement and what cursillistas call the Fourth Day, from the first weekend in 1944 Mallorca to contemporary Catholic and Protestant manifestations, is a history of Christians seeking a deeper spirituality, a living Christ, and new, intentional communities.

CHAPTER ONE

Los Orígenes Mallorquines

Eduardo Bonnín Aguiló and the Birth of the
Cursillo de Cristiandad Movement

The Cursillos in Christianity Movement has a single purpose: that the Spirit of the Lord in Christ meets with the freedom of the human person and that this person, on discovering that they are loved by God, changes their horizon and perspective because they realize that God has them in mind.
—Eduardo Bonnín Aguiló, *My Spiritual Testament*

Eduardo's greatest gift was making people happy.
—María Sureda, Mallorca, June 2011

Sitting around the table in the office of Fundación Eduardo Bonnín Aguiló (FEBA) in Palma de Mallorca, a group of longtime colleagues and friends of Eduardo Bonnín talked at length about his profound faith, humility, and sense of humor. During the course of our conversations that afternoon in June, these Mallorquín Catholics wept as they shared their profound gratitude, and laughed when they recalled funny moments spent with a man they credit with changing their lives. They remember him as an intellectual, a man who "always had a book with him," and as someone who "never turned anyone away."

Some of his colleagues and friends say he was "like a priest because he was always praying with people who came to him for help." They say that "Eduardo," as they refer to him, a life-long bachelor and ascetically minded, had a deep and abiding passion for helping laity develop their spiritual lives. The slightly built, bespectacled Mallorquín, a cradle Catholic, was always "on the move," a man who "walked everywhere, and who would think deep thoughts as he walked." An intellectual and profoundly spiritual man, Bonnín initiated the three-day Cursillo weekend "Cursillos for Pilgrim Leaders" today known as the Cursillos de Cristiandad or simply "Cursillos," to bring a revitalized Catholic spirituality to the streets and the Church.

According to Bonnín's longtime friend and collaborator, Guillermo Estarellas de Nadal, "It is important to understand that Eduardo wanted the culture of the time to change. He wanted people to *want* to change the culture and he wanted people to be great friends." The culture he wanted to change was one marked by authoritarianism, fascist rhetoric and violence, and a deep sense of mistrust among Mallorquines. Bonnín, all of his close associates told me, encouraged *amistad* and wanted people to get along and accept their differences. He wanted to erase the sense of cultural anomie that so many Mallorquines experienced as a result of the Spanish Civil War by initiating a movement that emphasized new selves, new faith, and new communities.[1]

All of the Mallorquín cursillistas I spoke with emphasized Bonnín's sense of humor and zest for life. They spoke at length about his profound Catholic faith, which included his attending daily mass and praying the rosary regularly, but they say Bonnín never took himself too seriously. He was a practical joker, a man who loved making people laugh. "Always keeping busy," he made paper origami birds out of scraps of paper during Cursillo group reunion meetings, the first from a paper sugar container at a Palma café. For his ninetieth birthday celebration, cursillistas from around the world sent in their origami bird contributions, which were assembled by FEBA archivist Cristina González Duqué (the organization's only paid staff member) and volunteers and framed for Bonnín.

Moreover, his colleagues say, Bonnín was exceedingly humble and unassuming. In keeping with the man, FEBA, the nonprofit organization dedicated to maintaining his memory, is a modest storefront building situated in Palma's Calle de la Ferreria, in plain sight but easily missed, much as Bonnín has been overlooked as the initiator of what is today a global movement of Christian spirituality.

Bonnín, says his close friend Miguel Sureda, shunned the title "founder" of the movement. "He would say, 'El Fundador is the name of a brandy and I am *not* a brandy!'" While he was uncomfortable with the honorific designation, Eduardo Bonnín Aguiló (1917–2008) is indeed the founder of the Catholic Cursillo movement. Bonnín's Cursillo at its origins was a weekend experience for young Mallorquín men. The three days offered them the time and space to share their emotions, to talk about their personal lives and ambitions.[2] While they were indeed a part of the sociocultural milieu in which they arose, these "Cursillos for

Los Orígenes Mallorquines

Pilgrim Leaders" represent as much of an embrace of 1930s and 1940s Mallorquín island culture and its Catholicism as they do a rejection of repressive mainstream Spanish Catholic society. The society in which Bonnín's weekend arose was one marked by nationalism, fascism, Catholic authoritarianism, and intolerance toward dissenters. Bonnín was a complex man whose formation of the Cursillos blended his love of tradition and deference to the institutional Church with a profound challenge to these same structures and ideologies. It is to an examination of his life, Mallorquín sociocultural realities, and the origins of the now-global movement in Christian spirituality that we now turn.

The Education of Eduardo Bonnín

Eduardo Bonnín Aguiló was born May 4, 1917, in Palma de Mallorca, the island's capital, the second of ten children to Don Fernando Bonnín Piña and Doña Mercedes Aguiló Forteza. Amalia, the eldest child, was the only one who went on to marry and have children. Sister Luisa was the third born, followed by brother Jordi, who worked for the family's cereal and nut export business, where, according to FEBA archivist Cristina González Duqué, "he worked many hours and often with Eduardo."[3] Josefa, the fifth born, was followed by Fernando, who in his young adult years "spent a lot of time in mission work in Peru and who for a long time was a taxi driver in Palma, combining that work with his pastoral work."[4] María, the seventh child, was a Carmelite nun. The three youngest Bonnín Aguiló children, all women, are the only surviving siblings and share a modest home in Palma. Mercedes, like María, became a Carmelite nun, later leaving her order to become a social worker. The two youngest siblings, sisters Elvira and Pilar, also became social workers.

Eduardo was close to his parents and siblings and "always made a point in his life to be home for important feast days and celebrations."[5] He was brought up in a world of middle-class material privilege, devout Catholicism, and the opportunities that went along with his social status. Palma was urban and fast-paced, quite unlike the rural interior filled with groves of olive, fig, almond, and citrus trees. Eduardo grew up on an island that was and is breathtakingly beautiful. Palma is surrounded by the Mediterranean, and everywhere he looked, Eduardo had views of the sea and the bustling port. The west coast is rugged and hilly, long-known among hikers and pilgrims to the northern Santuari de Lluc for its challenging terrain, notably the famous Serra de Tramuntana, the mountain

Eduardo Bonnín (far right) with his mother and siblings, ca. 1918.
Courtesy of the Fundación Eduardo Bonnín Aguiló.

range that runs southwest to northeast.[6] The views out west are stunning, the beaches and *calas* (coves) are rocky, and the waters ultramarine blue. The central part of the island is flatter, replete with fragrant orchards, while the east coast has mixed geographies of sandy beaches and coves, deserts, fishing villages, and even today a slower pace of living.

According to González Duqué, the Bonnín Aguilós were neither poor nor rich but "normal," yet in the 1940s they were most certainly among the island's elite. The family was not ostentatious with its wealth. They blended in with Palma society and were known for their Catholic piety and outreach to the community. Catalina ("Cati") Granados, a longtime friend of the Bonnín Aguilós, says that she stopped by the family's store several times each week to buy milk and to chat with Doña Mercedes, who "was like a mother to all of us. I looked forward to going to the store and always enjoyed our conversations."[7]

Thanks to the success of the family's export company, Don Fernando and Doña Mercedes had the means to educate all of their ten children with private Catholic tutors, Augustinians. Like his siblings, Eduardo was exceedingly well-read and received a Catholic liberal arts education. His family's library was well-stocked with books, a luxury and indicator of

Los Orígenes Mallorquines

their social status. He and his siblings were encouraged to read widely and broadly, and this familial, social, and educational milieu predisposed them toward a well-rounded, liberal arts way of viewing the world. Eduardo came to believe that "at the center everybody is the same" and that intellectually and spiritually enlightened people could bring about reform in their communities—their workplaces, their Church, and their homes.[8]

The Bonnín Aguilós were immersed in a nationalist, authoritarian society, and my ethnographic research reveals a conservative Catholic family that nurtured devotional piety in its children as much as it encouraged them to read widely and to expose themselves to a broad range of ideas. As the son of upper-middle-class merchants, Eduardo soon learned that reading was his escape, that he could travel and experience the world through books. Yet his immediate reality was that he was raised in the closed cultural and religious world of Mallorquín Catholicism, a Church and faith that emphasized tradition, embodied piety, and sacrifice. The Bonnín Aguilós' Palma home was near the Plaça Santa Eulalia and its famous Cathedral of Santa Maria, "la Seu," the towering, gothic structure that overlooked the Mediterranean and dominated the city. As it does today, la Seu was a symbol of Catholic triumphalism over Islam and the "Moors," whose mosque was displaced by the cathedral when the latter was begun in 1229 and eventually completed in 1601.[9]

The cathedral, 121 meters long and 55 meters wide, with a nave 44 meters tall, is the most imposing of the many Catholic architectural sites that dot the island landscape. Mallorca is famous for its twelfth-century Lluc monastery, dedicated to the Virgin Mary and located in the island's northwest. Mallorquines then and today climb the rugged terrain of the Tramuntana to pay their respect to *la Virgen*.

Eduardo Bonnín loved the universal Church and had a deep devotion to the Virgin Mary. He began attending daily mass as a young child, drawn to a disciplined life that included prayer, fasting, and pilgrimage. The first Cursillo weekend he offered at age twenty-seven incorporated Catholic spirituality, Marian devotionalism, readings in psychology, and Catholic social teachings he encountered and nurtured in his young adult life. When he was seventeen, he attended La Salle College in Palma, located in the city center at 4b Avenida Sant Joan de la Salle, in the shadow of the massive Seu. He was influenced by the faculty's emphasis on training Christian teachers who would help spread peace and justice. At La Salle, he continued to read voraciously and fed his liberally minded

Eduardo Bonnín as a soldier. Courtesy of the Fundación Eduardo Bonnín Aguiló.

spiritual and intellectual disposition. After a year at La Salle, at age eighteen, Eduardo Bonnín joined other able bodied Spanish young men at the time and entered military service.

For the first time in his life, he confronted young men who were neither devout Catholics nor well educated. His nine-year military service was a pivotal juncture in his life, and his outlook was indelibly changed forever. He served for as long as he did out of a sense of duty and because he was drawn in by privates' oral histories. While in the barracks, he began to test the many theories he had gained through reading and contemplation, and he began earnestly working on making religion meaningful and relevant to the men around him. The "conflict" between his nurturing family environment and the "completely different" environment of the barracks led to his ethnographic, spiritual, and psychological efforts to make religion meaningful and freeing for men. He came to believe that the war and the Church's authoritarian stance led most youth to have "a wrong and fearful concept of religion" and that, for them, "religion was just a series of prohibitions placed upon them which hindered their lives and prevented them from using the freedom they could enjoy according to their own whim."[10]

During these nine years Bonnín spent all of his extra time in the barracks as an ethnographer, "trying to find out what people were like" and came to the conclusion that "at the very centre, everybody is the same."[11] He writes in *My Spiritual Testament* that "the underlying original seed of Cursillo grew out of the conflict that took place in me, when the education I had received from the family environment that I had always lived in collided with the environment at the barracks."[12] After his compatriots visited prostitutes in Palma's red-light district, he talked with them, asking if they "enjoyed themselves." Although they always replied "yes," the deeper they went in their conversation, each soldier would share his guilt, shame, and remorse.[13]

This life-changing experience of military service led to his epiphany that the environment is instrumental in shaping a man and his culture, and he decided that he wanted to help change the environments in which these men found themselves. His experience in Palma's barracks, combined with his readings and reflections, led him to introduce an alternative way of thinking about and experiencing religion. At the age of twenty-three, he read Pope Pius XII's 1940 papal letter on Catholic Action (the worldwide Catholic revitalization movement), a document that "had an unusual effect on me" and led him to examine "each of the constellations of individuals in the world, in my world and in the Church that I knew and frequented." He was excited by the pope's commitment to "good pastors" who would lead "lost sheep" into the "safety, life and joy in the return to the fold of Christ."[14]

While never referring to himself as a leader, Bonnín came to see himself as someone who could help bring lost sheep (in this case, soldiers) back to Christ, and he dedicated himself to this challenge. In 1943, he was swept into the Spanish Catholic Action (CA) Cursillos by his godfather, José Ferragut, the architect and president of Catholic Action for Youths in Mallorca. Bonnín was twenty-six at the time and attended the Cursillos for pilgrims at the Lluc monastery. He was involved in CA Cursillos as a rector, a teacher, in the prepilgrimage Cursillos. Recognized for his intelligence, wit, and ability to connect with people, he was asked to present his lecture "Estudio del ambiente" ("Study of the Environment") to young men training for the pilgrimage to Compostela.

Spanish Catholic Action and 1930s–1940s Mallorca

Bonnín, and the weekend-long Cursillo he would develop, was deeply influenced by Spanish Catholic Action in the late 1930s and early 1940s. This worldwide Catholic movement came into being after the publication of Leo XIII's 1891 encyclical *Rerum Novarum*, "On the Condition of Workers," which encouraged Catholics to initiate a "network of clerically led associations for social, benevolent, economic, and political purposes."[15] Pope Pius XI's 1931 encyclical *Quadrasegimo Anno* "Reconstruction of the Social Order" similarly "offered official social teachings about the application of faith to matters of social concern" and "advocated reform capitalist solutions to deepening social tensions and divisions in Europe."[16] Both encyclicals resonated deeply with Bonnín, who interpreted them as calling him and other Mallorquín men to action to change their environment.

The environment of 1930s and 1940s Spain was one of extreme tension and violence. Bonnín came of age during the ideological and bloody Spanish Civil War (1936–39). The war was, according to historian Stanley G. Payne, "the greatest and last struggle between traditional triumphalist Catholicism and liberal-proletariat secularism."[17] This internal conflict predated the Second World War and continued off the battlefield well into the 1960s early 1970s. Church officials supported the counterrevolutionary Nationalists in their efforts to defeat the revolutionary, anticlerical Republicans. In both word and action, they legitimated Nationalist soldiers' acts of violence and repression as necessary to conquer what they viewed as Republicans' godless secularism and communism and to create one Spain. In 1937, the Spanish bishops issued a collective letter that lent official support to the Nationalists' "civic military uprising" and violence, and effectively legitimated the execution of Basque priests as a necessary rooting out of Republican sympathizers.[18] In the letter, the bishops characterized the war as "an armed plebiscite . . . a struggle between irreconcilable ideologies" and "a conflict between Bolshevism and Christian civilization."[19]

For their part, Republicans valued regionalism, ethnic diversity, and secularism, and were disgusted by clerical privilege and centuries-old Catholic triumphalism. Operating under the ideology of fascism, the Spanish Catholic Church "provided the soul of Spanish authoritarian rightism" and successfully rallied a wide array of supporters, from agrarian farmers to mothers to discontented youth, who formed the Confederación Española de Derechas Autónomas (Spanish Confederation of the Autonomous Right, CEDA) in 1933 and viewed the war as a struggle between good and evil.[20] As revisionist historians of fascism concur, fascism was (as neofascism is today) a political ideology that encouraged an extreme form of "nation-statism," and its adherents, fascists, advocated for an "organic nation" and saw violence as necessary to solve conflicts.[21] As the historian of the Spanish Civil War Francisco J. Romero Salvadó writes, Nationalists and Republicans were both authoritarian and shared in the "fascisticization" of Spain during the 1930s.[22] Spanish fascism was "highly repressive," what the sociologist Michael Mann calls "a mixture of semi-reactionary and corporatist authoritarianism," one that enjoyed the full support of the Catholic Church in Spain.[23]

Moreover, the Catholic Church was complicit in acts of violence committed by the Nationalists, and it "blessed the orgy of blood, since in its eyes the nationalists were engaged in a holy Crusade against Godless heretics of the 'anti-Spain.'"[24] Members of the Church hierarchy "embarked upon the enforcement of Christian principles with a combination of zeal and compulsion reminiscent of the Middle Ages," and the Church rallied a wide social force in Spain, including farmers, merchants, traders, and middle-class men and women—all of whom were frightened by the "Red Spectre."[25] By 1938, when Franco had risen to power, Spain had become a "fusion of modernizing, totalitarian tendencies with medieval and religious-absolutist elements, a marriage that can be defined as National-Catholicism."[26] Adding to the Spanish bishops' compromise with a regime that engaged in violence was the "tragedy" that close to one-eighth of the clergy were killed by anticlerical Nationalists while the rest of the Spanish clergy failed to protest—what José M. Sánchez calls the "scandal of silence."[27] Mallorquines, like all Spaniards, continue to make sense of the violence and the collective silence.

In this larger political and social context of internal war, Spanish Catholic Action aligned itself almost seamlessly with 1930s and 1940s Spanish Falangism, the nationalist fascist ideology of José Antonio Primo de Rivera and General Francisco Franco. Spanish Falangism was distinctive from Italy's and Germany's fascism, the historian Gerald E. Poyo writes, because "where Fascism and Nazism undermined church authority and power, Falangism under Franco remained in alliance with the church and even evolved an ideology that emphasized many aspects of Catholic social thought."[28] Church authorities like the Jesuit José Joaquín Azpiazu "openly accepted dictatorship" as a way of "making the state assist the Church in achieving her most holy goal of the salvation of man to the greatest possible degree possible."[29]

It is difficult to disentangle fascism and Catholicism in late 1930s and 1940s Spain. Some leaders in the Falangist party, the Falange Española Tradicionalista (Traditionalist Spanish Falange, FET) and the affiliated

Juntas de Ofensiva Nacional-Sindicalista (Boards of the National-Syndicalist Offensive, JONS), such as Arias Salgado, of "uncertain Falangist" identity and part of the hardcore wing of Catholic Action, promoted what Payne has termed "Catholic Integrism," advocating for a right-wing Catholicism permeating all aspects of Spanish culture.[30] The ideology of Catholic integrism fused strong Catholic identity with authoritarianism and was the dominant worldview in pro-nationalist Spanish society from the 1930s to Franco's death in 1975.

Spanish CA sought to empower laymen but legitimated clerical control and authority, and supported falangist-styled nationalism. Throughout Spain, CA took on fascistic tendencies and was a charged blend of Church Catholicism, popular Catholicism, prowar language, and masculine Christianity. In mainland Spain and on the island of Mallorca, the movement was initiated by Church authorities to show support for General Franco's push to educate young men and women and to provide athletic outlets for them.[31] CA was divided into four branches, one for mature men, one for mature women, one for young men, and one for young women. Making Spanish men good soldiers for Christ and pilgrimage became the rallying cry for Church officials, CA leaders, and nationalist leaders alike.

Catholic Action spent much of its time and energy promoting the pilgrimage for men to Santiago de Compostela, a world-renown pilgrimage destination to pay honor to Saint James the Greater, one of the twelve apostles of Jesus. The magazine *Proa*, published by the Diocese of Mallorca, tirelessly promoted the pilgrimage, setting the goal of 100,000 pilgrims. The Cathedral of Compostela was established in the ninth century and is believed to house the remains of Saint James, the miracle-worker who inspired Spaniards during the Crusades against the "Moors." Compostela is symbolic of Catholic triumphalism over Islam, national Spanish Catholic identity, and ethnocentrically fueled anti-Moor or anti-Muslim sentiment. The pilgrimage to Compostela, called "The Way" by devotees, is an especially arduous journey over rugged mountainous terrain. For Mallorquín men the journey would be approximately 640 miles, or 1,030 kilometers. Pilgrims in 1948 took ferries from Mallorca to southeastern Spain and from there trekked to Santiago de Compostela, capital of Galicia. Because the Spanish Catholic Church has long encouraged embodied forms of devotion and sacrifice, this journey was considered the penultimate test of physical and spiritual endurance for Mallorquines.

Proa made the 1948 pilgrimage its rallying cry, summoning nationalist rhetoric, and setting a goal of 100,000 Spanish men. This *peregrinación* for young Catholic men to Santiago de Compostela in August 1948 was a direct outcome of the second Congreso de la Juventud Masculina de Acción Católica (National Congress of Young Men's Catholic Action) that had been held in 1932. Young men prepared for the national pilgrimage in the Juventud Española de Acción Católica (Spanish Youth Catholic Action, JEAC).[32] In August 1948, 70,000 young men from Spain and Latin America heeded CA and *Proa*'s call to make the "Great Pilgrimage."[33] These young men, called "Pilgrim Scouts," had been preparing for the arduous journey for years as part of their faith formation. CA Pilgrim Scouts were required to attend week-long Cursillos, short courses, that were run seminar-style. These Cursillos were authoritarian and rigidly structured. The *jefes de grupo* (captains) who were in charge of the Pilgrim Scouts were required to give the young men militant spiritual training.[34]

The pilgrimage to Santiago was part of a larger cultural world of pilgrimage in Mallorquín and Spanish society more broadly. In Mallorca, churches all over the island sponsored pilgrimages for youth, men, and women. The embodied devotion of pilgrimage was the quintessential Catholic way of proclaiming one's faith. Mallorquín pilgrimage honored Christ and his mother, the Blessed Virgin Mary. Pilgrimage to the northwest Lluc monastery to honor the "Queen of Spain" as well as to the southeast San Salvador shrine were important components of the island's Catholic pilgrimage network.[35]

Pilgrimages to Mallorquín Marian sites were mandatory in Catholic schools and were district-wide. During the 1947–48 school year, for example, the southeastern seaside districts of Manacor and Felanitx sent 800 students to the mountaintop *ermita* (hermitage sanctuary) of San Salvador. San Salvador has been an important pilgrimage site since the mid-fourteenth century, when the original hermitage was built 509 meters above sea level. In the 1930s and 1940s, children were part of the widespread culture of embodied Catholicism on the island, and as a rite of passage they walked the steep route, approximately ten kilometers from Manacor and six from Felanitx. Once they reached the top of the hill, the young pilgrims walked through the large gates, past the fourteen-meter cross and thirty-five-meter column on top of which perched a statue of Christ with an outstretched right arm. Devotion to the Virgin was evidenced inside the church itself in alabaster, as well as in the side gatehouse, where petitions and prayers to the Blessed Mother filled the space. Children's pilgrimage to San Salvador was part of the lifecycle of Catholic pilgrimages, culminating with "The Way" of Santiago de Compostela.

Proa authors tirelessly reported on the pilgrimage preparations taking place across the island and on the Spanish mainland, viewing the ritual action as an essential component in maintaining Spanish Catholicism and Spanish identity. Under a fascist-linked and authoritarian Spanish Catholic Church, pilgrimage took on masculinist and militaristic overtones. *Proa* made every effort to masculinize pilgrimage. Church officials were troubled by what they perceived as a feminized faith, and they decried churches as places where women and children gathered but where men were mostly absent. In fascist-controlled Spain, women were taught that family and children "were their only goal to achieve in life."[36] Yet work they did, and in addition to being wives and mothers, women who were part of the FET's Sección Femenina "continued to outperform other auxiliary services of the FET," which was "a remarkable achievement for a fascist movement ardently devoted to the principle of masculine superiority."[37] Women were continually told by Church and party leaders that, while their talents were recognized, their place was in the home, and that they "never discover anything." Female leaders in the FET internalized the misogyny of the time and externalized the rhetoric, asserting that they (women) "lack creative talent, reserved by God for virile intellects; we can do no more than interpret what men present to us."[38]

Proa's diocesan editors wrote editorial after editorial inciting young male Catholics to train themselves spiritually and physically for the long pilgrimage. In its numerous articles on pilgrimage, this officially sanctioned bulletin of the Diocese of Mallorca emphasized the important sacrifice that these young men would be making and that they were imitating Christ and being good, manly Christians. After the Civil War, poverty was widespread, and these young men traveled with few luxuries. Their methods of travel were "incómodos y rudimentarios," and they journeyed believing themselves to be walking as much for their country as they were for Christ.[39] The magazine promoted a masculine Catholic piety in a discursive language that dovetailed with the state's rhetoric. *Proa*'s emphasis on manly piety directly responded to what the Catholic Church and state perceived to be a feminized Church and culture. In the July 1938 issue of *Proa*, young men were told, next to a hand-drawn image of a sword, that they would "take back" Spain and re-Christianize not only their nation but the rest of the world, with the help of saints such as Saint James who were on their side.⁴⁰ These soldiers for Christ and Saint James would, as young Spanish men were told over and over again in *Proa* in the late 1930s, 1940s, 1950s, 1960s, and early 1970s, that they were not only capable of but *responsible* for remaking Spain into a Catholic Christian nation and that their efforts would remake the world order. Fascist Spanish authorities' agenda was legitimated and actively promoted in *Proa*, and young men were seen as vital members in the necessary fight for a hypermasculinized state. Soldiers attended these CA Cursillos and encouraged the young male pilgrims, whose Catholic Action speeches they applauded.⁴¹

In a marked shift from other Spanish Catholic pilgrimages, the one to Santiago distinguished itself in its embodied hypermasculinity and a championing of Christ and his male apostles, rather than the Virgin Mary. CA Cursillos had their roots in the wider culture of pilgrimage and discourse of masculine Catholicism. Although they maintained the larger Marian devotion in Spain, they redirected their focus to Jesus Christ and to masculinizing Spanish Christianity. A direct result of their campaign was that devotion to the Virgin Mary became less pronounced. Cultivating manly men for Christ is nothing new historically, and the masculinization of Spanish Catholicism in the 1930s and 1940s is analogous to the masculinization of American Protestant men during World War I. In Mallorca as in America, clergy called on men to publicly exhibit strength because they were understood as embodying "the spirit of Christ most perfectly" and as such were emboldened and empowered to fight their enemies.⁴² Church and state worked as one in the United States and in Spain to embolden men to reclaim society and religion. Fears of a feminized, weak society and religious institutions abounded in both places, and the prescribed inoculation against perceived weakness was a masculine, misogynist religious rhetoric and action.

In 1930s Spain, for example, the heightened discourse of mortification and sacrifice that we find in texts preceding and following the Great Pilgrimage to Compostela illustrates the Church's preoccupation with issues of gender and piety. Clergy were aghast at the dangerous gender imbalance they perceived in the pews.⁴³ A "feminized" Catholicism would mean a weak state. *Proa* editors incited their young male and adult male readers to apostolic action: "We must conquer the world! Christ is waiting for us. Our work carried out in unison must be strong, tireless, with the help of our Patron, Santiago . . . who is afraid?"⁴⁴

The Cursillos sponsored and inspired by Catholic Action in the 1930s and 1940s were militant and for men only. In part they reflected the fascist ideology that defined Spanish society and required a curious blend of deference and strength. Catholic Action encouraged acquiescence to authority figures, whether priests, generals, or Christ, and they supported the language and actions of the Nationalists. The earliest Church-sponsored Cursillos: Cursillos de Adelantados de Peregrinos (Cursillos for Advanced Pilgrims) and Cursillos de Jefes de Peregrinos (Cursillos for Pilgrim Leaders) reflected the larger Spanish religio-cultural milieu of nationalism and authoritarianism. Catholic Action's workshops to train pilgrim leaders, the earliest Cursillos on record, reflected masculinist nationalism and deference to authority and were part of the larger Spanish fascist ideology.

Catholic Action Pilgrim Scouts' weeklong Cursillos emphasized order and discipline, patriotism, and God's ultimate grace. The drama of sin, and the need for suffering and redemption, were emphasized in their courses and institutionalized in the Promoter's School. Held in the parish Center of Saint Eulalia, the pedagogy of these earlier Cursillos was lecture-driven. Each morning during the Cursillo a priest, who was the young men's spiritual director, would lead a meditation session and give a talk (a total of five during the week) on God's grace. He would administer the Eucharist each morning and was aided by laymen who also gave talks on prayer, study, and action throughout the week. The weeklong course was also joyful, and folk and religious songs were sung.

Graduates of the 1945 course received the "Promoter's Crucifix."[45] The Promoters' Crucifix initiated a history of cross-giving in Cursillos—both Catholic and Protestant—that continues today. The young men who completed the 1949 San Honoratio weekend received the first CdC cross.[46] Catholic and Protestant cursillistas around the world today receive a signature cross from their respective movements upon their graduation on the third night of the weekend.

The CA-organized Great Pilgrimage to Santiago de Compostela for young men in 1948 reflected the masculinist fascist thought of the time, and "The Way" of the pilgrimage symbolized a new era for Spanish Catholicism. According to Bonnín, his own Cursillos were "born in the womb" of the Diocesan Council of Catholic Action Youth and its focus on preparing youth for the Great Pilgrimage.[47] Six of his Cursillos de Adelantados de Peregrinos were held between 1941 and 1948, preparing young men for the pilgrimage. Young men were trained to be spiritual warriors for Christ and to be the public face of the Spanish Catholic Church, as well as of Spanish patriotism.

The January 1941 issue of *Proa* ended with a call to Mallorquín young men: "Youth of Palma: The 23rd, to Cursillo!" This battle cry was ensconced among the issue's reports of successful CA Cursillos in San Salvador (Felanitx) and the advertisement of the upcoming Palma Cursillo on January 23. The San Salvador Cursillo was characterized as having "pure, angelic apostles" and as communicating "their fire on the earth and making it burn, serving the evangelical judgment."[48] Bolstered by the masculinist rhetoric of fascism, Church authorities, CA, and *Proa* focused their energies on making Catholicism a robust, manly, and embodied faith.

Both Franco and the Spanish Catholic Church stood to benefit from a successful Great Pilgrimage. Within Spain's dictatorship, religion "became the main single ideological force invoked to legitimize the new regime, with official support for Church activities and the formation of numerous *juntas ciudadanas* citizen committees) to ensure the orthodoxy of social and cultural activities."[49] According the Catholic theologian Ivan Rohloff,

> The Catholic militancy that flourished under the fascist regime, gave a spirit of obedience to the pope and to the hierarchy as though to military officers. Welfare was easily sublimated and conquest of souls in Cursillo as in holy warfare led to triumph and victory."[50] The seven hundred Mallorquín youth left as "pilgrims" and returned as "apostles" and were charged by the diocesan spiritual director to take their own renewal and share it with the community and renew the Church. Seventy thousand men from Spain and Latin America had successfully made the pilgrimage, arriving in Santiago de Compostela "exhausted but full of hope, a hope nourished by the vibrant message of His Holiness Pius XII.[51]

Proa praised these pilgrims in its January 1949 issue, dedicating the majority of its text to the pilgrims' journey and its implications for the Church and Spain: "We cannot live off memories. Life is something more. We cannot stagnate thinking about the greatness of yesterday. One must project toward tomorrow the imprint and lesson of the days which, by the grace of God, we have had the fortune to live. . . . It is now time to act.

We must place our intelligence, heart, will, arms, and knees in our apostolic enterprise."[52] For CA leaders, the physical pilgrimage was essential for young Spanish men to revitalize themselves and their Church. The arduous pilgrimage would create stalwart soldiers for Christ. Yet CA's idea of conversion and evangelization could also conceal sinister intentions. Those who refused to convert were considered dissenters, and violent acts committed by Spanish authorities in the name of a reformed nation are well documented.

The Mallorquín cursillista Bernardo Vadell writes that after the Great Pilgrimage 1950s Spain continued to be characterized by a harsh dictatorship, a Catholic Church that went along with the fascist government, and a society in which citizens were constantly under surveillance. He writes of the "religiosidad impuesta," the religiosity imposed on people, and the "integrismo absoluta," the absolute integrism of the Church, its clergy, and fascism. Local priests had the authority to grant *certificados de buena conducta* (certificates of good behavior) to men who proved their loyalty to the Church and state. "During Lent," Vadell recalls, "star preachers would come from other provinces to threaten us with eternal flames, and, so that no one would lose the Word, they installed loudspeakers in the streets."[53] A conformist Catholic culture was guaranteed by the civil union between the Church and the fascist state.

At times, the Church did exert some degree of independence from the state. At the Seventh Diocesan Gathering in 1947 for example, clergy, not party leaders as was the ritual, made enthusiastic speeches to the youth assembled there. Prominent in assemblies before the Great Pilgrimage, military figures were notably absent from this one. As José Ángel Sáiz has written in *Génesis y teología del Cursillo de Cristiandad*, "In this one we detect a different, renewed, more jovial style, one that is basically more ecclesiastic and independent, without the presence of civil and military authorities."[54] Yet while Spanish officials relaxed their oversight at the 1947 gathering, authoritarianism manifested itself in visible ways across the island and mainland in the 1930s and 1940s.

Bonnín and a close group of friends who had been affiliated with Catholic Action built on the idea of pilgrimage that was central to Spanish Catholicism. They reimagined conversion, evangelization, and pilgrimage as an internal process, an intimate relationship between God and the individual. Bonnín's weekend-long "Cursillos for Pilgrim Leaders" branched off of the Catholic Action Cursillos for young men, yet they envisioned an alternative way of living out one's Catholic life. Bonnín's weekends blended official and popular forms of Catholic piety and praxis and embraced the intellect as well as the heart. In a larger cultural milieu that included fascist, militaristic, and Catholic integrist components, they offered a contrasting view, but quietly, so as not to draw too much attention.

Cala Figuera: The First Weekend Cursillos

The young Eduardo Bonnín was restless, increasingly dissatisfied with Catholic Action's lecture and seminar-style methods and its focus on physical pilgrimage. He knew from his conversations with other soldiers that they were disenchanted with the official Catholic Church. He wanted to provide a truly lay-run experience for young men that would make religion meaningful to them in ways it had never been before. After participating in CA's weeklong seminars, Bonnín came to fundamentally disagree with its methods. His longtime friend and colleague Guillermo Estarellas de Nadal remembers him as

> a very liberal Catholic who did not like Catholic Action's dependence on the clergy. He was critical of priests because he felt that they had too much of an influence on people. He wanted a break from the Church. He was an apostle who developed a method that was spiritual and where the Holy Spirit was present. He did want priests to be involved in the three-day Cursillos he developed, and they gave five of the rollos [short talks]. In Catholic Action you see, priests controlled Cursillos and dominated them. Eduardo didn't want any of that in his Cursillos.[55]

Bonnín's weekend-long Cursillos for Pilgrim Leaders emerged shortly after the end of the Spanish Civil War in a fascist political climate where authoritarianism and rigid ideological power was abetted by the Spanish Catholic Church.[56] While Bonnín had been involved for a time with Catholic Action, he left the movement to form his own version of Cursillos, one unmarked by fascist rhetoric and authoritarianism. In *My Spiritual Testament*, he goes so far as to deny involvement in Catholic Action, asserting that its approach was troubling to him and that he disagreed with its intentions and purposes.[57] The rollo he developed in 1943 for the weeklong Catholic Action Cursillos for young men, "Study of the Environment," derived its inspiration, as we have seen, from his military service and his desire to reach what he came to call "the faraway." Always a voracious reader, he began to read cutting-edge works in Christianity, philosophy, and psychology, declaring that his "usual urge to read focused now on the books whose authors at the time were at the crest of the wave of the Christian world: Hugo Rahner, Karl Rahner, Fr. Plus, the husband and wife Raïsa and Jacques Maritain, Karl Roggers, Maslow, Leon Bloy, Van de Meer of Malcheren, Rene Schwob, Gustavo Thibon, Erich Fromm, Jacques Leclerc, etc."[58]

Bonnín and a handful of leaders from Catholic Action's young men's branch went on to form the weekend Cursillos.[59] José Ferragut, the brothers Jaime and Bartolomé Riutort, Juan Mir, Andrés Rullán, and Guillermo Estarellas de Nadal had also seen how lay Catholic men were empowered by their Cursillos and pilgrimage and wanted to offer something that would help laymen thrive in their immediate environment and be like Christ; each man was "to fully immerse himself in the earthly city to which he belongs, and build it according to the will of God."[60] Bonnín, as all of his Mallorquín friends like Guillermo emphasize, wanted to offer a shorter course than the weeklong CA one, a more condensed version during which Catholic men would have the opportunity to experience the Holy Spirit away from the controlling Church. According to Guillermo, Bonnín "was brilliant, really. He developed a weekend that was also a fabulous psychological discovery, you see. The Cursillo weekend gets people talking, it gets them to share their thoughts and for men in the 1940s this was truly a radical thing."[61] Bonnín and his friends shifted the focus from the physical act of pilgrimage to a focus on preparing one's body, heart and mind for Christ. They began having conversations in the picturesque seaside village of Cala Figuera, Santanyí, Mallorca about forming a Cursillo movement that was influenced by but separate from Catholic Action.

These first non–Catholic Action Cursillos were held by Bonnín Aguiló and friends August 19–22, 1944, at Mar i Pins, a chalet in Cala Figuera that directly overlooked the cove. The location of this East Coast seaside village where Bonnín's Cursillo weekend was held is significant as it was far removed from Palma, Catholic Action's center and stronghold, as well as the fascist-controlled and authoritarian Church's center of power. Bonnín's Cursillo weekend was aided by the support of Catholic Action in the west coast town of Felanitx, "and especially its president, Francisco Androver, "who provided the candidates, a cook, and cart for transporting the food.[62] Recalling this first Cursillo, Bonnín writes: "Someone

Cursillistas at the first weekend Cursillo, Cala Figuera, Mallorca, ca. 1944.
Courtesy of the Fundación Eduardo Bonnín Aguiló.

brought a loaf, another brought a 'sobrasada' (sausage), rice, a chicken, etc. We settled ourselves on the floor as best we could, the leaders sleeping on the floor. There was no electricity in the house and we had to use a 'petromax' (a light used by fisherman to dazzle the fish)."[63]

This first weekend Cursillo established the blueprint for the thousands of Cursillo weekends that have occurred since 1944; candidates gathered together for an intimate weekend of rollos, food, fellowship, experiencing the love of Christ. One of these "little talks" was centered on the Virgin Mary, *la madre* of the Church. Bonnín's lifelong devotion to the Virgin, his time at the Lluc monastery where Marian piety to La Moreneta is encouraged and lived, and Mallorquín Catholic culture which is steeped in Marian piety, helped shape the weekends and their Marian-infused piety. Bonnín's weekend experience for men reenvisioned Catholicism and lay activism but also emphasized Catholic devotionalism and adoration of the Virgin, and her role as Mother of the Catholic Church.[64]

In his reflections on his participation in the 1944 Cala Figuera Cursillo, Salvador Escribiano Hernández writes that the "Grace of God and intercession of the Blessed Mary, which without doubt accompanied us at every moment and made it possible to crown this first stellar moment successfully."[65] Hernández, at age fourteen and one of fourteen participants ranging in ages 14–27, the camaraderie, fellowship, the joy, and the sense of humor and the magnetic personality of Bonnín, "from the first moment impacted us positively."[66] When Hernández wrote his testimony sixty years after his Cursillo, he emphasized that he had been in "group with every Thursday at six o'clock in the evening" since the 1944 weekend. In his recollections of his experiences at the first CdC, Hernández makes special mention of the simplicity of the environment—a water hose to quench thirst and to bathe, simple cots with army blankets, the good, simple Mallorquín-style food that he ate, and the care and concern given to the fourteen cursillistas: "Don Sebastián de San Gayá, our generous benefactor, who was in charge of supplying and transporting the food and supplies in his "carreto en molles,' his cart, hauled by a mule, without failing a single a day. And how could we ever forget 'Papa Consuelo' who was always punctual, opportune and of good will. He was in charge of preparing foods (stewed meat, vegetables, chips, fried eggs, also sobrasada), which we gladly went to gather at the kitchen."[67] Hernández ends his personal essay by thanking God for the "solid and fraternal friendship that has given back my life, confidence in mankind, and a desire to live."[68] While Escribano Hernández, like the thirteen other young men who attended the Cala Figuera weekend, had been on retreats before, but none, he stresses in his testimony, had the emotional, spiritual or communal impact as did this particular weekend. They were being asked to bring about a transformation to their immediate environments—to transform the culture of fear and violence through love and understanding.

According to Bonnín Aguiló, what made these Cursillos "completely different" from the Catholic Action Cursillos for Pilgrim Leaders was that in Mar i Pins, the weekend had a different structure, where ideas were emphasized more than doctrine, and where men gathered to "spread the ideals of Christ in a warm, sincere, friendly and festive atmosphere, sprinkling the rollos with anecdotes that we had carefully collected."[69] The three days kept some of the group dynamics of the CA Cursillos, which included poster sessions and small-group discussion, and added time for individual reflection, which its predecessor lacked. The real significance of the Cala Figuera Cursillo, according to Francisco Forteza, participant in Bonnín's movement, was "to remove Christianity from the road of bitterness and place it on the freeway of cheerfulness."[70] What Bonnín insisted upon was that a friendship with Jesus would remake the world. He wrote that "Jesus must be visible in our friendship with others.

It is this kind of friendship that has the creative power necessary to transform the world as Christian men and women acting as leaven in their environments."[71]

Life, Bonnín thought, was a pilgrimage, and he wanted to help young men prepare their hearts, souls, and minds for the long journey. Bonnín may have had issues with the Church hierarchy and its control over laity, but he was fundamentally a devoted Catholic who heeded Rome's call, instead of Spain's Falangist Church, for a more engaged and dynamic laity. Bonnín believed in men's potential and believed that laymen could revitalize the Church and their immediate surroundings. The Catholic weekend in spirituality that came to be called the Cursillos de Cristiandad were deeply influenced by Pope Pius X, whose aim was to "restore all things in Christ," as well as his successor, Pius XI, who in his push for his new evangelization, pointed out a difference between Christians in name only and practicing Christians; "It is not enough to be counted in the Church of Christ, it is necessary to be in spirit and in truth living members of the Church." Bonnín followed Pius XI in his aims to encourage a Christianity "in which all the members keep watch over themselves . . . can and should be an example and a guide for the profoundly sick world."[72]

Weekend Cursillos offered a remedy for intimate, spiritual experience for Catholic laymen. During the three-day-long course, men could cultivate a deeper piety and form a community of apostles who sought to ameliorate the mistrust and fear that characterized their society. Pius XII's call motivated Bonnín and his friends when they set out to draft their version of Cursillo, especially his entreaty to Catholics to "bring Christ into life again: to our daily life; our private and public life; and not rest while His doctrines and His law have not renewed and formed it completely" made an impression on Bonnín as he set out to revitalize his Church and to provide laymen with a greater role in their Church.[73] The goal of the Cursillos, according to Bonnín, was to "structure Christianity by means of practical Catholics who through their lives give a Christian impetus to a life which has ceased being Christian."[74] Bonnín, with his emphasis on apostolic action and a more involved and active laity, was part of the widespread pre–Vatican II discussions about theology of the laity, and Cursillo was part of "a larger lay movement and theology, which actually shifted (but was not first articulated) in Vatican II's theology of the laity.[75] Bonnín was aware of and was an avid reader of theologians such as Yves Congar, whose own writings on the need for authentic reform deeply influenced Pope John XXIII's reforms and the resulting Second Vatican Council.[76] Pope John's 1959 encyclical *Princeps Pastorum* addressed Catholic Action and the necessity of laymen transforming their immediate environments. In *Princeps*, Pope John exhorts lay Catholics to engage in apostolic work. He speaks at length on mission work and calls on Catholics to spread their faith through their actions: "We wish to renew urgently the exhortations and appeals of Our predecessor Pius XII: 'It is necessary that laymen give their generous, zealous, and active cooperation, joining the clergy in their apostolic work and swelling to large numbers the ranks of Catholic Action.'"[77]

Bonnín's Cursillo weekend and movement predated Pope Paul VI's 1964 *Lumen Gentium* by fourteen years with its emphasis on laity as church and part of the body of Christ. "I wish to place it on record . . . that the original idea was lay. I have always been surprised by the fact that all initiatives to ferment the Gospel in the hearts of people had always been the work of consecrated people, priests, monks, nuns, lay brothers, and so on."[78] Much of what Pope Paul writes about the role of laity in the Catholic Church in the 1960s was envisioned by Bonnín and some close friends—Estarellas de Nadal, Ferragut, Mir, the Riutorts, and Rullán—all of whom had all been involved in planning the Great Pilgrimage and were affiliated in some form with Spanish Catholic Action. They wanted something influenced by but ultimately separate from Catholic Action. They all believed that Spanish Catholic Action was excessively influenced by the Church hierarchy, which had removed the crucial component of "environment" from Cursillos. Bonnín and his friends emphasized that it was not enough to impact men individually through pilgrimage; the cursillistas must also be challenged to channel their newfound piety in their immediate, local environments in what was later called the "Fourth Day." Laymen were the key to the future of the Catholic Church, Bonnín and his friends believed, and the Cursillo weekend was designed to create Catholic soldiers for Christ in a way fundamentally distinct from CA's cultivation of Catholic Christian soldiers. Bonnín's cursillistas would be motivated not by fear but by the Holy Spirit, who inspired them to become apostles in their communities and reform Spanish Catholicism through a lay Catholic revitalization of faith and friendship.

Guillermo Estarellas de Nadal emphasized the radical nature of Bonnín's ideas to me during our interview at FEBA in June 2011: "You have to understand that Eduardo was very liberal, a very liberal Catholic. He had a deep respect for priests but was insistent that Cursillos were for the people and that the clergy would not take over." These non-CA affiliated Cursillos were meant to be "adapted to today's world." To look to the past or to hypothesize how individuals should live in the future would be "to cripple the Cursillos."[79] According to Bonnín, the nine major thrusts of the newly imagined Cursillos emphasized from the very first were (1) a "triumphant concept of Christianity"; (2) a "dynamic and militant Catholicism"; (3) a principle of "sincere, honest, and open-eyed dissatisfaction"; (4) a "profound and exact knowledge of modern men, of their problems and their anguish"; (5) a "profound conviction of the insufficiency or inflexibility of certain methods for the carrying through of the whole apostolic work"; (6) a "firm conviction that it is truly possible that anyone who is living on the fringe of religion, if he is hit with a fist full of Grace, would be able to surrender himself completely to Christ"; (7) the hope that after completing a Cursillo, "the same thing would happen as in Christ's time: The Samaritans and the Zaccheuses would be converted into the Lord's most dynamic apostles"; (8) a "relentless attempt to find a technique of concrete application, modeled on apostolic methods, which would take account of the personal problems and concrete needs of each individual, and solve these at their root"; and (9) the "conviction that the solution is simple and, because simple, universal. The effective catholicity of the faith must be lived in a Cursillo."[80]

Bonnín acknowledged that his weekend Cursillos were rooted in the weeklong Catholic Action courses for young men, but he stressed that the three-day Cursillos were something new and more timeless, since they equipped the individual Christian with the skills for living a successful, Christ-filled life.[81] The weekend-long Cursillos promoted community, individual Catholic Christian expression, lay empowerment, sanctifying grace, public confession, and popular language that resonated with Mallorquín men in the late 1940s, 1950s, and 1960s—as it has with Catholic and Protestant cursillistas since then precisely because the weekend and the movement it spawned championed a positive view of laity as being church. Bonnín's Cursillos were a call to Catholic action and trusted laymen to revitalize their church and society and to use a kind of Catholic imagination that they had not been given permission to use before.

Moreover, Bonnín's Cursillos offered young Mallorquín Catholic men a guide to live what contemporary American evangelical Christian pastor Rick Warren has termed a "purpose-driven life." For Bonnín and his associates, the purpose of a Catholic man's life was to become more spiritual and to know Christ on a deep level. Once this relationship was established, laymen were expected to be apostles by impacting their environment with their newfound spirituality. Indeed, the message preached by evangelical Christian pastors of the late twentieth and early twenty-first century—loving Christ, heeding his message, and as a result, living a good life—is a recent manifestation of living one's faith in the way that Bonnín envisioned in 1940s Mallorca.[82] Yet while Warren is seen as a sage by hundreds of thousands of contemporary American Christians, Bonnín was (and is) less known because the contentious climate of Spain in his day prevented him from marketing his kind of Christianity. He was a spiritual leader of the three-day Cursillo movement and an intellectual. As is evidenced in his books, diaries, and in the powerful memories of his friends, he wanted people to think deeply and act spiritually.

Bonnín believed in "apostles of the street" and felt that laymen could have greater impact on their environments than could clergy.[83] His lay movement was revolutionary for the time because it trusted men to be able to reform their Church and society. Bonnín wanted laymen to be spiritual soldiers for Christ and to bring about a peaceful era in Spain. He lamented the passivity that the Church cultivated in laymen and sought nothing short of a revolutionary grassroots Catholicism by laity and for laity.[84] The men who met and crafted the first Cursillo weekend felt called by the Holy Spirit and were reluctant to take credit for these courses because they saw themselves as mere instruments of the Holy Spirit. They believed that the real author of the weekend was God.

The second Cursillo weekend not affiliated with Catholic Action was held January 7–10, 1949, in San Honorato. During this second Cursillo the rollos that appear in the guidebooks today were developed. According to historian Julio A. Gonzalo González, "one of the motives for choosing San Honorato, many kilometres away from 'civilization,' was to ensure that the cursillistas were spared from being distracted from the real business of the Cursillo."[85] The geographic isolation also protected the cursillistas from the prying eyes of authorities. The Cursillos of 1944 and 1949 set the standard of fifteen rollos: five to be given by the spiritual advisor, a priest, and ten to be given by laymen. Father Juan Julió, an army priest, was chosen as the spiritual director of the 1944 and 1949 Cursillos because he had experience with the Catholic Action Cursillos and was well liked.[86] Bonnín writes that he wanted a more intensive experience because the weeklong Cursillos attracted a limited audience. He wanted to attract a greater diversity of cursillistas who would commit themselves to a three-day encounter with Christ.[87]

The Cala Figuera Cursillo was quietly radical. It offered a blend of the old and the new and sought to subvert the mainstream, fear-inducing Falangist Catholicism. Bonnín's Cursillos were a paradoxical and fascinating blend of masculine, warlike rhetoric, devotional Catholicism, and a life of the mind. Out of necessity, they had to incorporate some of the language of mainstream CA Cursillos. This way they could blend in more easily and operate off the FET's radar. The manly militancy of Catholic Action and Spanish nationalism, for example, made their way into the weekend's three days, but rather than preaching Catholic integrism, they offered the individual a spiritual experience in a closed, retreat-like setting unmediated by the state.

Bonnín's agenda was an evangelizing one and he encouraged graduates of the weekend Cursillo to "reach the faraway"—men who were far from God. His weekend Cursillos cultivated a male-centered grassroots piety that would work to end the widespread suspicion Mallorquines and Spaniards had of each other, and to encourage *amistad*. The Cursillo weekend experience Bonnín initiated in 1944 would become the catalyst for a worldwide Christian renewal movement, renamed in 1946 by Bishop Juan Hervás as the Cursillos de Cristiandad ("Cursillos in Christianity"), which in the United States would become perhaps the most significant movement of post-1950s Christian renewal.[88]

When I asked Mallorquín cursillista Miguel Sureda about the relationship of Bonnín's Cursillo movement to fascism, he replied, "We are still trying to understand that ourselves." Sureda acknowledged that while the movement itself was not fascist, it was influenced—it had to be—by its social environment. He talked to me about the sense of order and discipline that characterized the early Cursillo weekends, and that has carried over to today's movement. While Bonnín was part of the sociocultural milieu of Spanish fascism, neither he nor his movement was fascist, but his weekend Cursillos took on the rhetoric of fascism as a protective mechanism. Bonnín loathed the intense discipline and order imposed on the state and resented how the Catholic Church and Church movements like Catholic Action dictated belief and thought. He hated the idea of laymen as automatons, merely responding to the state's wishes. As much as he could rebel against the idea that laymen needed to be told what and how to believe, he did, and in doing so crafted a weekend during which laymen were introduced to a new way of being Catholic. Yet the weekend he designed had an ordered method and required discipline: everything participants did—listening to talks, reflecting on the messages, talking with one's tablemates—was on a planned time schedule. Paradoxically, "the Cursillo weekends' order led to freedom for laymen. In disciplining them, it gave them a means to exercise an influence on their own faith outside the bounds of clerical control."[89]

Bonnín's weekends incorporated militaristic, mystical, and practical language in the rollos and activities and emphasized laymen's spiritual empowerment through a relationship with Christ and the Holy Spirit. The Christ that men were introduced to during these weekends was manly and mystical. He was a man whom Bonnín imagined would walk the streets of Mallorca and one who was to be experienced in a profoundly personal and spiritual way.[90] Unlike the institutionalized Christ of 1930s and 1940s Spanish Catholicism, Bonnín's Cursillo Christ was to be encountered in an intimate setting, removed from "the world"—apart from the mediation of the fascist state—with a small group of laymen who for three days all sought a connection with the divine and desired to improve their lives. Bonnín conceptualized Christians as integral components of the Mystical Body of Christ and he saw the Cursillo's purpose as "vertebration," the linking together of Christian leaders in a dynamic Christian community.

Bonnín devised the concept of vertebration, the "orderly and systematic evaluation of the truths that are embraced, actually or potentially" in Cursillo.[91] These "truths" of a particular method, mentality, and purpose are experienced and lived in the course of a three-day weekend and, ideally, are lived during what Bonnín called the "Fourth Day." From the beginning, he intended for those who make the seventy-two-hour course to be mindful of their connection and commitment to Christ and to "bloom where they are planted."[92] Cursillistas are to share their newly recharged faith with others and to change the environment in which they live—whether it was fascist Spain or the contemporary American milieu.

After the 1948 Great Pilgrimage to Santiago de Compostela sponsored by Catholic Action, Bonnín and his friends officially branched off of CA to form their own movement. According to Bonnín, they called this Cursillo the "Cursillo for Pilgrim Leaders" so that the Church hierarchy would allow them to hold the retreat. For this reason, the date of the first three-day Cursillo has been recorded by most as 1949 and not 1944, the year Bonnín and his friends in fact organized the first Cursillo in Cala Figuera. Yet Bonnín emphasizes that the 1949 San Honorato Cursillos and those of Catholic Action were the same in name only as his Cursillos of Conquest were lay-run and had a new method and vision of outreach to laymen.

According to his longtime friend and colleague Bartolomé ("Tomeu") Arrom, "Eduardo always emphasized that you live Cursillo in your life. It is not a movement of the church; it a movement of the people to improve their faith and to improve the church as a result."[93]

Bonnín's early manuals written and coauthored in the 1950s and 1960s incorporate and reflect the militaristic language and comportment of the 1930s and 1940s. They incorporate the language of sacrifice, sacred metaphoric violence, and pain for a purpose, advocating "the stabbing technique" in the Cursillo weekends; "hurling the Truth (or truths) sharply so that it sticks: placing the cursillistas in the Truth and injecting the Truth into them."[94] Moreover, "the stabbing should be specific, sharp enough to stick. It must be the decisive arrow at the heart of the problem."[95] Moreover, the rollos given by laity and priests "should be a necessary consequence of militant Christianity, forming the plot and essence of the whole Cursillo."[96] A sense of urgency pervades these guides, a necessity to be like Christ and to affect the environment to bring others to Christ. This militancy with which cursillistas are to bring others to Christ is softened by the language of a mystical Christ. Bonnín was deeply influenced by his experiences in the military, and he took seriously Pope Pius XII's encouragement to conduct a "detailed study" of a situation before attempting to win men over to Christ.[97] From these sources Bonnín formulated the core of the weekend Cursillo, the "Study of the Environment." He committed himself to reaching those who are "farthest away" from the Gospel and believed that an understanding of these individuals' environments would enable the Cursillo weekend to propel them to embrace Christ and a Christ-like existence. Bonnín understood the cynicism that existed among young Catholic men who had grown up in a culture of fear and violence reinforced by the institutional Church. He believed that sin proliferated as a result of this collective cynicism and climate of mistrust. Bonnín wanted to save his Church from itself by bringing these men who had sinned back into the fold, and by igniting them to become part of a grassroots Catholicism that depended on their willingness to commit themselves to Christ.

For Ramón Rosselló Nadal, another longtime friend of Bonnín's and Guillermo's nephew, the weekend experience showed him that the teenagers he was hanging around were bad influences, and that other young men could show him a better alternative. Bonnín's use of the phrase "the far away" to refer to those who were furthest from God applied to him, says Rosselló Nadal. Bonnín had a powerful impact on his life and

Bonnín's influence and the weekend itself helped him "get the courage to change friends and get on the right track in life. No more loose women either." Rosselló Nadal emphasized Bonnín's impact on him and others: "What was so great about Eduardo was that he was always clear in what he wanted to say. His ideas were so original. He had the capacity to distill many ideas and to get his points across. He also had a great sense of humor. He always made people laugh and he always wanted people to enjoy themselves."[98]

Another distinguishing factor of Bonnín's "Cursillos for Pilgrim Scouts"–turned Cursillos de Cristiandad was that they emphasized not a historical Christ but a living Christ who can be loved, experienced, and taken into each cursillista's heart. Leaders in what came to be called the Cursillos de Cristiandad movement point out that the historical Christ is not sufficient because "he walked the earth two thousand years ago."[99] The mystical Christ, unlike the historical Christ, is thought to be timeless and because of this timelessness can have a greater impact on the Christian and his or her environment. According to Alphonsus Duran, CMF, Claretian Missionary, an early promoter of the Cursillos de Cristiandad movement, the mystical Christ, unlike the historical Christ, is in "the soul of each of the baptized, of Christians."[100] The Cursillos de Cristiandad focus on the mystical Christ and the deep connection each cursillista has with him. Getting cursillistas to see that Christ is inside of them is a major thrust of the course and is meant to empower each cursillista to be an apostle for the rest of his or her life. Bonnín emphasized this by asserting that "people gradually begin to discover themselves as free persons and as liberated by Christ, so that they can understand and value the dignity and greatness of being a baptized person."[101]

A group of Catholic Action Pilgrim Scouts realized this "dignity and greatness" and went on to write the ten rollos of Cursillos de Cristiandad, the short talks given by laymen during what developed into the three-day Cursillo. The first groups of men to make the Cursillos after the Great Pilgrimage were all soldiers and war veterans "accustomed to a life-style which was highly disciplined and structured."[102] Spanish Catholic Action's emphasis on "the lay apostolate as conquest of the world for Christ, and a willingness to accept the cost of discipleship," a militant Christianity that helped to give birth to what became the Cursillos de Cristiandad.[103] Acknowledging the influence of Catholic Action, Bonnín asserts that his Cursillos are separate from the earlier ones held for advanced pilgrims and pilgrim chiefs. He asserts that they were "something new

Los Orígenes Mallorquines

and distinct. They [were] the result 'of a tireless labor, miraculously fruitful! Toward the creation of a new kind of course.'"[104] But while the Cursillos were influenced by Catholic Action, they branched off in significant ways. In Catholic Action, lay Catholics followed the orders of the bishop. Pope Pius XI shaped the contours of Catholic Action as an organization of laypeople participating in the apostolate of the hierarchy. While laypeople within this movement certainly felt as though they played a role in reforming their church, their actions were governed by clergy and they were expected to follow the directives of their bishop. Bonnín's Cursillos, while they maintained strong connections to the Catholic Church and integrated clergy in the courses, were devised to be lay-run, and their explicit aim was to renew the faith of individual Catholics.[105]

The Spanish folk song "De Colores" that became the anthem of Bonnín's Cursillos was sung and performed for the first time at the third weekend Cursillo in San Honorario, according to Guillermo, who was present at the San Honorario Cursillo and who helped draft the rollos. "Eduardo wanted the young men to sing," says Guillermo, "and they chose the song 'De Colores.' They really enjoyed themselves, and after this Cursillo, the song became the trademark song for the weekend."[106] Bonnín's account of the event is slightly different, as he credits Guillermo Estarellas de Nadal, not the youth, with choosing the song: "We were looking for a song to sing, precisely something other than a pious song, so as to not frighten away the 'faraway' and with the song 'De Colores'— taken from folk music—the goal was squarely met. The 'De Colores' has in the course of time become the anthem and symbol for Cursillistas from around the world."[107] The young men, who were in groups of ten, wrote on the wall each night of the course, sharing their insights with everyone. The week culminated in each young man receiving a cross from the presiding priest, who would drape it around the graduate's neck.

"Cursillos Clandestinos": Bonnín's Ostracization and Clerical Takeover

Bonnín's Cursillos proved to be popular among Mallorquín male Catholics, and he hoped to expand the movement outside of Mallorca and to train Cursillo leaders to spread the weekend-long course. But Bonnín was viewed with suspicion by members of the Spanish Church hierarchy, and even those who were sympathetic to the movement marginalized Bonnín as the CdC founder.

In a move that points to the evolution of the Cursillos as a religious and social movement, a Diocesan Secretariat of Cursillos was established twenty years after the first Catholic Action Cursillo and ten years after the first Cursillo of Conquest weekend in Cala Figuera. The 1954 creation of the secretariat had the effect of officially separating Cursillos from Catholic Action. According to Rohloff, "The removal of Cursillo from Catholic Action was a traumatic experience for the latter since it deprived it of its energetic leaders and took away most of its life."[108] But for Bonnín and Mallorquín Catholic men committed to offering to laymen Cursillos not affiliated with Catholic Action, the split was liberating. According to longtime friend Guillermo Estarellas de Nadal, "You see, Eduardo believed that it was the Holy Spirit leading men to Christ, not necessarily priests and the Church. He believed in apostles of the streets, and his weekend encouraged them to take charge in that way and be apostles."[109]

Bonnín and the newly established separate Cursillo movement was supported by Juan Capó, the diocesan spiritual director of the Cursillos de Cristiandad, as well as Monsignor Juan Hervás, who, like Capó and Bonnín, saw in weekend Cursillos a way to enact Pius XII's call to laity. Paradoxical as this might initially appear, however, clerical support also hurt the CdC as Hervás in particular brought Cursillos more under clerical control, partially in response to attacks from those opposing them. Moreover, also partially in response to attacks on the new movement from the more conservative, pro-hierarchical ranks of Spanish clergy, Hervás named as the first president of the secretariat not Bonnín but a lesser-known, less controversial layman, Pedro Sala.[110] While he was openly a supporter of Cursillos for lay Catholics, Hervás himself was wary of the influence Bonnín had garnered and used his own power and authority to keep the popular layman from an official position. Many clergy, such as Bartolomé Torres, then rector of the seminary in Mallorca, were suspicious of the movement, which they saw as threatening episcopal authority and upsetting the power relations between clergy and laity. In response to Torres's criticism of the Cursillos, Hervás removed him from his seminarian post. In retaliation, Torres, through personal contacts including General Franco himself, had Hervás transferred to Ciudad Real.[111] Hervás was in a difficult position as he valued the lay focus of Bonnín's weekend but understood the threat that it to the hierarchically driven Church.

In the February 2009 newsletter of the Organismo Mundial de Cursillos de Cristiandad (World Organization of Cursillos in Christianity,

OMCC), President Juan Ruiz chronicled the early years of the CdC in Mallorca, writing that Hervás, "from the inception of his pastoral work was bound and very committed to Catholic Action" and had a "reputation for focusing on more traditional theological plans, with a great sense of authority and hierarchy."[112] On March 1, 1947, three years after the first non–Catholic Action Cursillo was held in Cala Figuera, Hervás arrived in Mallorca as bishop coadjutor with right of succession to the Archbishop of Mallorca, José Miralles. According to Ruiz, Hervás "was hailed upon his arrival in Mallorca, in a very special way by the youth of Catholic Action" and that the youth, "led by Eduardo Bonnín in front, as president of the Council, immediately shared with him 'what' they were doing over the past few years."[113] The excitement this caused led the bishop to offer these "bold" young people a weekly Mass, with a small gathering after the Eucharist. Hervás continued to support the Cursillos from his new position but advocated for a parish-based movement, not one based on the environment. He understood the parish more as an "apostolic community"—a community of apostles—than as the "locus of Christian fellowship" envisioned by Bonnín and the initiators of the movement.

For Bonnín and his supporters, the place for the most fully realized apostleship for laypeople was outside the walls of the Church, in the streets. Yet it was precisely Hervás's understanding of the layperson as "merely an extension of or a participant in the clerical priesthood" that won clerical support for the movement. Hervás was attempting to encourage the movement but understood its limitations during a particularly contentious political climate. If he had written about Cursillos in the manner of Bonnín, emphasizing the laity as their backbone, the Spanish hierarchy would never have officially approved the movement. And despite the tensions between them, Bonnín gives much credit to Hervás: "Without any doubt we owe it to him that the Cursillo Movement was accepted by the Church." Indeed it was Hervás's pastoral letter "The Cursillos in Christianity, an Instrument for Christian Renewal," Bonnín said, that "will always be the Magna Carta of the Cursillo Movement." Hervás was "the one who achieved the entry of the Cursillo Movement through the main door of the Church."[114] Hervás did much to legitimate and popularize the CdC and should be credited not only with providing the name that continues to define the movement but also with helping to legitimate the movement officially, which was crucial for the CdC's long-term success. In his widely read *Leader's Manual* and *Problems Concerning Cursillos in Christianity*, both published in the early 1960s,

Hervás addressed the need for a diocesan secretariat and for the Leader's School to be "in the hands of competent priests who represent it, and of laymen or lay organizations which it judges most appropriate for these functions."[115] The historical reality is that popular, lay movements like the CdC have required official support for their transmission and longevity.

In reading Hervás's published works, however, the degree to which Bonnín has been occluded from the official history is striking. It is no wonder that the origins and early years of what were then called the "Cursillos of Conquest" are mostly unknown today. Despite his championing of the movement, Hervás's words and actions were a double-edged sword: while the Cursillos de Cristiandad did win formal approval, the courses held after the letter was published were much more conservative than the earlier courses had been. The courses had lost some of their fire and the "domestication of the movement" had begun.[116] The courses, under Hervás, became less about influencing the individual's environment, less about "vertebration," and more about what the priest could teach the cursillista, closer to the Catholic Action version of the courses. The theology and structure of the courses became, under Hervás's tutelage, more clerically driven and top-down, an upright triangle rather than the inverted triangle of Bonnín's Cursillos. Under Hervás's direction, married men and women were encouraged to make the course and as a result, the culture of Cursillos shifted and fewer young, single men, former soldiers in the case of Mallorca, made the course. Hervás makes mention of the "experiments" in offering Cursillos for adolescents with "rather gratifying results," but he sends out a note of caution, asserting that "though the fruits may be bounteous, perseverance is much more problematic. The danger in the case of adolescents is that this instrument of Christian renewal may not have lasting effects and may become permanently 'ineffective.'"[117] As a result of the new emphasis on married, adult Catholics as ideal candidates for the weekend CdC, the movement lost much of the youthful enthusiasm of 1944 Cala Figuera and became more middle class-focused and conservative. The weekend experience became more about the priest influencing cursillistas and by extension, the parish. Those who did enroll in the weekend experience tended to be wealthier, more conservative members of the parish who were not interested so much in transforming the environment or being the vertebrae of Christ's community on Earth as in maintaining the status quo of power relations in their communities and parish. Moreover, the role of the Virgin Mary, central in Bonnín's weekend Cursillo, was deemphasized in

Hervás's weekend. He asserted that "devotion to the Blessed Virgin is not obligatory" and that this devotion "may be given greater or lesser importance in the Cursillo work, given the circumstances of time and place."[118]

This domestication of the Cursillos de Cristiandad was coupled with the open hostility to the movement by select, vocal clergy, including Hervás's replacement as bishop of Mallorca, Jesús Enciso Viana. Enciso made it a priority during his tenure as bishop to all but eliminate the Cursillos de Cristiandad, which he viewed as destroying Catholic Action for Young Men and causing serious divisions in the diocese.[119] The CdC were bearing "frutos malos" (bad fruit), wrote Enciso in his August 15, 1956, pastoral letter on Cursillo. His sixteen-page "Carta pastoral sobre los Cursillos de Cristiandad" was damning and was sent to all members of the Spanish hierarchy. In it, Enciso blasted what he considered theological transgressions committed by cursillistas, as well as what he considered the CdC's faulty theology. He dismissed the idea that laity could be theologically empowered during a CdC weekend, and he took special aim at the CdC's concept of sanctifying grace, grace available to everyone who seeks it. For Enciso, this idea of grace was a Protestant idea that was theologically dangerous and charged. He made it clear that Catholics must attend confession to receive this kind of grace and called the CdC's suggestion that laity could achieve it in a place other than the confessor's booth preposterous.[120] He further attacked the CdC's focus on laity, a more approachable Christ, and said that the CdC took Catholicism out of the Church. He was particularly perturbed by what he considered to be the presumptuousness of laypeople's leading other laypeople, and while he did not use the term *heretical*, he used strong condemnatory language. For all effects and purposes, Enciso's letter outlawed Bonnín's Cursillos of Conquest. Enciso ended his letter with the announcement that, effective immediately, the weekend Cursillos would be restructured with Catholic Action–affiliated priests leading the movement. Priests hand selected by Enciso himself would run the movement and no laypeople would be in charge on weekends. Moreover, laypeople unaffiliated with Catholic Action would have no role in Enciso's reconfigured movement.[121]

With the publication of Enciso's "Carta pastoral," Bonnín was forbidden to speak or write about the movement publicly. As a result, he took Cursillos underground and they became what Miguel Sureda, a close friend of Bonnín's and a leader in the Mallorquín Cursillo movement today, calls "Cursillos clandestinos." Over cups of *café con leche* at the

FEBA office, Sureda shared this piece of history that has gone undocumented: "What happened after Enciso's letter was that the movement became clandestine. Cursillistas would meet in the Plaza Major under the arcades and in cafes and they kept the movement going during this time."[122] Ramón Rosselló Nadal emphasizes that a hallmark of the "Cursillos clandestinos" were the 7:30 P.M. weekly ultreyas held in la Plaza: "We met in la Plaza and in each other's homes. We kept the movement going, against all odds. After the new bishop was installed in 1966, Eduardo was able to do ultreya in the open."[123] Their meetings in the plaza, in plain sight of "la Seu" and the bishop who outlawed their Cursillos, were a visible and symbolic protest against the hierarchy's ban.

Despite the forces of domestication and clerical control, Spanish men in the officially recognized, priest-led Hervásian Catholic Cursillo movement were often profoundly moved by their weekend experience and changed men by the end of the three days. Carlos Calatayud Maldonado, a lawyer and father of eight children, made the seventh Cursillo given in Ciudad Real on March 24–27, 1956. In his article "I Went to a Cursillo," Maldonado writes, "I went to the Cursillo just because people gave me no peace. At the club, at the town hall, at the County Council, on the telephone, in short in all places and on all occasions, those of my friends who had attended a Cursillo were continually bothering me, saying that I ought to experience it, that it was the most interesting thing I could do in my life."[124] Like many men who ended up making a Cursillo weekend, Maldonado bowed to social and peer pressure, and went to the three-day experience as an interested skeptic, not sure what would happen but intrigued by the transformations he saw in his friends. Maldonado went on to experience "a restlessness, a feeling of uneasiness" that led him to rethink what it meant to be a Christian man. He writes that for him and the men on his Cursillo weekend, "the language, unaffected, hard, manly, struck home. Our feet must be firmly planted on the unshakable rock of a supernatural inner life; we must conquer the world and offer it to the Father with our arms. It was impressive to hear a layman speak of these matters; especially for those who were not churchgoers and had an idea that all that was the business of the priests and women."[125]

Maldonado's testimony, first published in 1964, is among the earliest recorded testimonies of a Catholic Cursillo weekend and shows the emphasis of masculinization and the empowerment of laymen. In this precise, fifteen-page essay, he details the three-day events as well as his and his fellow candidates' reactions to the rollos as well as to the social encounters, some of which were new for Spanish men of the 1950s. Wealthy engineers from prominent Spanish families shared sleeping quarters with barbers, cooks, and gardeners. For Maldonado, seeing a table full of tobacco and caramels where wealthier men would pay extra for them and men who could not afford them could "take what they needed free of charge" brought home the social leveling that is part of the Cursillo method and mentality: all men are brothers in Christ.[126] Significantly, social leveling was emphasized by fascism and the Spanish authoritarian state, and we are able to detect an internalization of this ideology in the rhetorical devices of the Cursillo weekends, those sponsored by Bonnín as well as those more Church-oriented during the official ban.

This intentional breaking down of socioeconomic ranks impressed Maldonado, himself a man of means, who writes that the actions he observed and lived during his weekend were the grace of God; the "fact of serving is a small matter; what is important, is to be imbued with the spirit of brotherly service."[127] "For the first time in my life," he writes, "the grandeur of the Christian's vocation became clear to me." He discovered that "the highest destiny a man could dream of is to be like God, to be a participant in divine nature. I was dazzled and filled with enthusiasm."[128] After a weekend that he describes as life-changing, Maldonado went on to become active in the Ciudad Real Cursillo community.

Like Maldonado and countless others in the Mallorquín CdC movement, contemporary U.S. Hispanic Catholic cursillista Damien Rico says that "we need to help each other in our Christian journey, and there is no better place to do this than in your group reunion meetings."[129] What mattered to Maldonado then and Rico today is the combination of individual renewal and group support featured during the weekend and in the post-Cursillo, "Fourth-Day" period. The CdC's focus on individual spiritual renewal, a living Christ, and lay-initiated Catholicism set the stage for a mid-twentieth-century spiritual revitalization of Christianity that has spanned dozens of countries and impacted millions of Catholics and Protestants. The CdC became a global phenomenon in a relatively short amount of time, and the United States was one of the first places where it took root outside of Mallorca and mainland Spain.

The U.S. Cursillo movement's origins were close to the spirit and vision of Bonnín's lay-focused weekend: a grassroots Catholic movement that emphasized lay empowerment and laity as the backbone of the Church. In 1957, when Mallorquín laymen Bernardo Vadell and Augustín Palomino became corectors of the first CdC in the United States, Bonnín's vision of lay-focused Catholicism arrived in the United States. Over time, the U.S. movement became more institutionalized and hierarchical, much as its Mallorquín parent had under Hervás. As in Mallorca, when we examine the U.S. Cursillo movement we find that priests and bishops became increasingly instrumental. In short, the U.S. Cursillo movement in the 1960s, 1970s, and 1980s moved away from its lay origins and from Bonnín's intentions. But the original idea of grassroots Catholicism remained a strong undercurrent, and U.S. cursillistas took it upon themselves to maintain Bonnín's vision of lay empowerment and of channeling their newfound spirituality into their surrounding communities. In the next chapter, we explore the U.S. history of the Cursillos de Cristiandad.

CHAPTER TWO

Coming to America

The Early History of U.S. Cursillos de Cristiandad

For the first time in my life, the grandeur of the Christian's vocation became clear to me: a holy man, a participant in divine nature, a living temple of the Holy Spirit, a member of Christ, a friend of God, a brother of Jesus, and heir of heaven.
—M. Carlos Calatayud Maldonado, 1964

Every week from San Antonio, Texas, I sent letters to cursillistas in Palma to help them continue to live their new way of living. What was occurring there was a distillation, an obsession for the soul. I related my projects, my conversations with friends, commentaries and orations with much happiness, as if I were with them. I had not yet encountered in the United States the possibilities for such an apostolate.
—Bernardo Vadell, *Los orígenes mallorquines de los Cursillos de Cristiandad en EE. UU. (Texas, 1957–1959)* (2008)

Carlos Calatayud Maldonado made his Cursillo in Ciudad Real in 1956, at the cusp of the Cursillo weekends' worldwide expansion. Despite Bishop Jesús Enciso Viana's 1956 pastoral letter that sent Bonnín into exile and forced the three-day Cursillos and group reunions to operate clandestinely, what were now known as Cursillos de Cristiandad, the Hervás-renamed "Cursillos for Pilgrim Leaders," supported by both Hervás and Bonnín, began to spread around the globe. Mallorquín and other Spanish cursillistas who knew Bonnín and Hervás introduced the weekend course in spirituality abroad.[1] From 1956 until Enciso's death in 1964, one kind of Cursillo weekend was officially offered—the more ecclesial Hervás weekend. After Enciso's death, Hervás-influenced CdC weekends became even more prominent, and he was credited with being the founder of the weekend Cursillo.

When we examine the first Cursillos brought to the United States in 1957 and attempt to understand them in the context of their Mallorquín origins, it becomes evident that they came to America in the spirit of

Bonnín's lay Catholic weekend experience. The two cursillistas responsible for bringing the weekend Cursillo to the United States, Bernardo Vadell and Augustín Palomino, were close friends of Bonnín, whose lay-focused Catholic Cursillos had changed their lives and motivated them to what they believed was the apostolic action of spreading the Cursillos de Cristiandad to the United States. As Vadell indicates in the quotation at the beginning of this chapter, he was deeply invested in Mallorca's CdC movement, and during his stay in the United States, he kept in frequent contact with his Mallorquín cursillista friends. Vadell and Palomino worked closely with laymen and priests to spread Mallorca's Cursillo zeal in Texas. As Catholic Cursillos spread outside of Texas and across the United States, they became a blend of Bonnín's more lay-focused weekend experience and Hervás's more ecclesial weekend.

It was Mallorquín and mainland Spanish male cursillistas who made a distinctively Mallorquín Christian experience a global Christian movement. From Palma de Mallorca and Ciudad Real, these men first introduced Cursillos to Colombia (1953), Catalonia and Segovia (1954), and Rome (1955), then beyond Europe to the United States (1957), Mexico (1958), Brazil (1962), the Philippines (1962), and Argentina (1964)—countering the isolationism and parochialism that peaked, for Mallorquines, before the Spanish Civil War and World War II.[2] Through a weekend-long course in spirituality this branch of Spanish Catholicism migrated, morphed, and impacted Catholic and Protestant cultures around the world.

In this chapter, we will examine the early history of U.S. Catholic Cursillos, emphasizing its rapid spread and success, especially among Spanish-speaking Americans. In the United States, Cursillos were conducted exclusively in Spanish from 1957 to 1961. The world's first Cursillo in English was a men's weekend in San Angelo, Texas, November 9–12, 1961. Father Fidelis Albrecht, OFM, served as the spiritual director for the weekend which was held just over a month after San Angelo was granted diocesan status.

Starting in the 1970s, Protestants who had made a Catholic Cursillo weekend formed a variety of offshoots. Hispanics as well as white, non-Hispanic Catholic men and women all shaped the movement in the United States. Like the original Mallorquín weekend, the first U.S. Catholic Cursillos were offered only to men, but as the wives of cursillistas made their wishes known, the movement quickly became one for Catholic men and women. By 1960, three years after the CdC's introduction into the United States, separate weekends were offered for women and men. This practice continues today in the United States and in other countries.[3]

It is important to note that there was no "one" Cursillo de Cristiandad during the early years of expansion, and in many ways there is still a lack of cohesiveness today. Similarly, there are many competing and oftentimes conflicting versions of the history of the Catholic Cursillos de Cristiandad (CdC), making it a challenge to sort out the movement's origins and early years. Most official accounts of Cursillos call Bishop Juan Hervás the founder of the movement, and, until recently, few sources have included Eduardo Bonnín in the history of the movement, much less credit him with being the founder of weekend Cursillos. As we saw in chapter 1, an ethnographically informed history of the Cursillos' origins and early years makes it clear that Bonnín and a handful of friends—José Ferragut, the brothers Jaime and Bartolomé Riutort, Juan Mir, Andrés Rullán, and Guillermo Estarellas de Nadal—were the architects of the movement.[4] Other Mallorquines, including Bishop Hervás, Vadell, Francisco Forteza, and Juan Capó Bosch, authored and coauthored books that offered their views on the meaning, essence, and purpose of the weekend.[5] If Bonnín is viewed as the initiator and primary architect of the weekend, these men are considered by Mallorquín cursillistas to be among the CdC's founding fathers and early promoters of the movement.[6]

An attempt to write a linear history of the Cursillo movement is quickly complicated by two notable historical moments: (1) Hervás's reassignment to Ciudad Real in 1955 as a penalty for his promotion and support of weekend Cursillos and (2) the publication in 1956 of Bishop Enciso's anti-CdC "Carta pastoral sobre los Cursillos de Cristiandad." During their nine years underground, from the "Carta pastoral" to the appointment of Enciso's successor, Bishop Rafael Álvarez Lara, in 1965, Bonnín's Cursillos were restructured and reimagined. During this period, the Cursillo weekends that were officially held satisfied Enciso's requirement that Cursillos be clerically run and reflect the views of Catholic Action. In Palma de Mallorca and Ciudad Real, respectively, Capó and Hervás were the public voices of Cursillos from 1956 to 1965, and their weekends were more parish-based and clerically driven.[7] In these two men's defense, we must note that the greater clerical bent of the weekends during this time was made necessary by the hostile environment to the CdC, but one of the outcomes of the shift from a lay movement to a more clerically influenced one was that Bonnín was shut out from the official leadership and not mentioned as the movement's founder in published literature on the CdC.[8]

The effect of competing visions for the weekend was exacerbated by a lack of centralization. In some countries, such as Mexico and Colombia, Cursillo movements had national secretariats, but not all did. While the lack of centralization was a problem for leaders like Hervás and Capó who advocated for a more top-down, hierarchical Cursillo, it was not as problematic for Bonnín, whose Cursillos were structured from the ground up. For Mallorquín cursillista Guillermo Biblioni, a contemporary of Bonnín's who has written what insiders consider to be the definitive history of the Mallorquín Cursillos, Bonnín and his fellow laymen emphasized the grassroots nature of the movement: "They were the ones who conceived and developed with stubborn effort a new form of apostolate that gave life to the squalor of Catholic Action in which some of them were active. They were all laymen, friends who shared each other's experiences and projects and were concerned about friendship. MCC's [Movimiento Cursillos de Cristiandad] origins have two hallmarks: first it is a work in teams, as we just saw; second, the team is composed exclusively of laymen."[9] Bonnín's weekend Cursillo, as we have seen, encouraged laity to take charge of the weekend but to also work with clergy, and left room for creativity and adapting to the environment in which the Cursillo was held.[10]

An examination of their early history shows that the Cursillos that spread across the globe were not uniform and were informed by both Bonnín's lay vision for Christian men and Hervas's more clerically organized weekends. Bonnín, Hervás, and Capó all were prolific writers, but Bonnín's books and articles were not published by a national secretariat because he was a vocal critic of the direction the movement had taken since Enciso's pastoral letter.[11] Like their Catholic Action and Cursillos de Cristiandad predecessors, the men who introduced the CdC across several continents had experienced a personal renewal and commitment to Christ and saw their work as apostolic.

The U.S. origins of Cursillos—Catholic as well as the multiple Protestant versions—resemble those of other countries. As in Portugal, Austria, Germany, France, Spanish Guinea, and Mexico, Spanish soldiers (in this case, two young Air Force pilots) introduced the Cursillos de Cristiandad in the United States, with the support of local priests.[12] The men who introduced Cursillos in the United States saw themselves as soldiers for Christ, called to share their personal renewal in the communities in which they resided and to make Christianity more lay-focused and not run by corrupted Church authorities. These men had experienced personal renewal, an experience with Christ, and they emerged from their weekend Cursillo changed men. They vowed to be better individuals and more committed Christians, and they were "on fire" for Christ.

When we examine the early history of U.S. Catholic Cursillos, it is clear that, as in Mallorca, the emphasis was on spiritually empowering Catholic laymen and bringing them to a place where they could see themselves as "being church." The role of priests envisioned by Bonnín was to nurture laymen's spirituality, and the Franciscan Father Gabriel Fernández, the first spiritual advisor for U.S. Cursillo weekends, energetically took up this charge to encourage young men's spirituality and help them continue to live "in grace."[13]

Fernández, Vadell, and Palomino wanted to motivate young Catholic men to demonstrate their "apostolic action" by holding group reunions, ultreyas, and being trained each Saturday in the leaders' school. Because Fernández, Vadell, and Palomino were mentored by Bonnín and heavily involved in the Mallorquín Cursillo movement, the early U.S. Cursillos closely resembled the first CdC at Cala Figuera in 1944.[14] The focus of U.S. Cursillos was on laypersons' spiritual renewal and revitalization and on becoming apostles for Christ. U.S. Protestant versions of Catholic Cursillos, born in the 1960s and 1970s spirit of ecumenicism, retained the early Mallorquín emphasis on lay spiritual empowerment and renewal.

Spreading "His Kingdom" in the United States

The first CdC held in the United States, in Waco, Texas, in 1957 was close to Bonnín's original version and set the template for U.S. Cursillos. Father Fernández, who sponsored the first U.S. CdC in his Texas parish, knew Eduardo Bonnín and Juan Capó and was involved with the Palma de Mallorca Cursillo community.[15] For his part, Bernardo Vadell, one of the two laymen who contacted Fernández about bringing CdC to Texas, was Mallorquín and deeply involved in the CdC community there.[16]

The Mexican-descent male cursillistas with whom Vadell and Palomino worked in the late 1950s in Waco, Mission, and Laredo were, as Vadell describes in *Los orígines mallorquines de los Cursillos de Cristiandad en EE.UU. (Texas, 1957–1959)*, emotionally charged and moved by their experience. In Texas, the reception to the weekend was overwhelming, as Vadell recounts. As the rector of these first U.S. Cursillo weekends, he was humbled by the outpouring of the Holy Spirit he observed during the three days: "We encountered a group of young people, directed by a Franciscan, who had an intense spiritual life, who possessed a mentality and seemed to have a great spirit."[17]

The first U.S. Cursillo was held in Waco on May 27–30, 1957, at St. Francis of Assisi Catholic Church, in the Diocese of Austin. Fernández, St. Francis's priest and an early champion and promoter of Cursillos in the United States, was the weekend's spiritual director, and Bernardo Vadell served as rector. A Mallorquín from Palma, Fernández could trace his involvement with the Cursillos de Cristiandad back to one of the earliest Cursillos in Mallorca with Juan Capó and Eduardo Bonnín.[18] When recalling the events that led to the first U.S. CdC, Fernández writes that "we had to start something, there was nothing organized at that point and our beloved Catholic Action came to mind." He writes: "In less than a year we had 80 young men; not only did they live in grace already, they would encourage others to live that way, showing their apostolic action. These young men had weekly reunions, what we nowadays call Group Reunion and Ultreyas, School of Leaders also weekly."[19]

Bonnín's weekend Cursillo joined Spanish and American Catholicism in the United States. The military-friendly state of Texas was fertile ground for the weekend, which emphasized spiritual discipline and a sense of order as much as it honored individual freedom and dignity. The weekend, popular with soldiers in Mallorca and across Spain, was brought to the United States by way of two Spanish pilots, and it spread rapidly among male Air Force cadets. The history of the Cursillo movement is a history of poor men of Mexican descent who sought out a unique spiritual experience as much as it is a history of soldiers, cadets, and pilots whose lives were deeply impacted by the weekend experience of spirituality. The three days of Cursillo appealed both to men of Mexican and white, non-Hispanic origins, to day laborers, Air Force cadets, and U.S. Army soldiers. These men's histories as well as their futures would become intertwined with their involvement in the Cursillo movement. The weekend dynamics appealed to a cross-section of men because they spoke the language of healing and renewal and offered a disciplined masculine piety. Moreover, the Cursillo weekend, while legitimating manliness, also encouraged emotional outpourings in a nurturing and safe environment.

The story of how Cursillos came to the United States begins with a letter received in 1956 by Vadell, then a young pilot. He opened the official-looking envelope to find out that he had been selected to "assist in flight courses for approximately two years in the United States."[20] Vadell was in Madrid at the time, where he had been taking English-language classes. He was excited by the opportunity to improve his English in the United States, although he would miss Mallorca's sea. Vadell, along with Palomino, who also received a letter of invitation, were soon after stationed at San Antonio's Lackland Air Force Base. Lackland was roughly 180 miles from Waco, where the two would help sponsor the first U.S. Cursillo.

Vadell and Palomino's letters of invitation were part of U.S. president Dwight Eisenhower's anticommunist programs. Eisenhower, fully embracing the domino theory, feared communism's spread throughout the world.[21] This fear trumped his fear of fascism, and because fascist Spain had defeated the procommunist Republic, Spanish air force cadets were welcome at U.S. training sites to further not only their own training but to serve as anticommunist leaders.[22]

One year later, in April 1957, when Vadell and Palomino were at Lackland to help with the training school, Vadell wrote Father Fernández asking if he could help "spread His Kingdom" throughout the United States. In the letter, Vadell emphasized that Cursillo was transforming Spain and other countries, and that if it was God's plan, he believed they could transform the environment in the United States. "This masterpiece is transforming Spain and other nations from South America," he wrote. "I know that it is a strong undertaking, as the Cursillo is a very delicate matter; but if the Lord wills it, then it is possible, and I believe that we have to make everything in our hands to spread His Kingdom."[23] Vadell's enthusiasm and passion made him an effective ambassador for the Cursillo movement in the United States. In the influential *Structure of Ideas* (which he coauthored with Bonnín and Forteza), Vadell's masculinist and military language comes through. Cursillistas are to be determined men of action, part of a "squadron flight" to ensure that group reunions "bear more and better fruit."[24]

In *The Structure of Ideas*, Vadell, Bonnín, and Forteza argue that the Cursillos offer Christian men an opportunity to improve themselves, their brothers in Christ, and their communities. Using Spanish bullfighting terminology, they say the CdC weekend is a place where men should be "stabbed"; cursillistas must "aim high, implant truths in their aspirations, in their potentials . . . At any rate, the stabbing must penetrate them, pick at their conscience."[25] "The sharpness of the stabbing," Vadell, Bonnín, and Forteza write, "will always be determined by the hardness of the 'bull's' 'skin.' The essential thing is that it stick."[26] The "stabbing" is to be done when the time is right, when the Cursillo "is browning" and the candidates are open to receiving the truth.[27]

As we saw in chapter 1, while the Cursillo weekend was not fascist, it incorporated military language of discipline. The language of violence that characterized fascist, authoritarian Spain and its mainline Catholic culture in the 1930s, 1940s, and 1950s was reimagined in the weekend Cursillo. This reconfigured semantics of violence pointed to the necessity of apostolic action to reignite men's Catholic spirituality and re-Catholicize Spain for God and not for the nationalist, party-driven Church. The semantics of war, masculinity, and violence resonated deeply with men in the United States, who were immersed in a post–World War II culture and Cold War fears of communism and a godless world.

Vadell and Palomino believed that young male Catholics of Mexican descent in Texas were primed to receive Cursillo's "truths," and they were determined to establish the weekend in the United States. They believed that the Spanish, masculinist language would appeal to Mexican-descent Tejanos since they had long been victims of ethnocentric discrimination throughout the Southwest, and nowhere more than in Texas. According to historian Oscar J. Martínez, "Race relations deteriorated following Texas independence and the U.S.-Mexico War as a result of protracted confrontation."[28] He goes on to assert that "racism, segregation, and economic colonialism became the established pattern in Texas for the rest of the nineteenth century and for most of the twentieth. In New Mexico, Arizona and California the experience of Mexican Americans was similar but none of these states matched the deplorable record compiled in Texas."[29] Moreover, the poverty and racism experienced by Mexican-descent Catholic men and women in Texas in the 1950s were exacerbated by the ten-year Texas drought, the worst in the state's history.

For the sixteen young Mexican-descent men who made the first U.S. Cursillo weekend in Waco, and for those who followed soon after, the weekend was an alternative reality. During the three days, these young men experienced an environment free of the racism they experienced in everyday life.[30] Their identity as men and as Catholic Christians was affirmed and acknowledged, and they were given the task of revitalizing their communities and churches. The men who made the 1957 weekend in Waco were poor and marginalized, and lived in a city within a city, a barrio tucked away from the whiter, wealthier Waco. The weekend was held without any fanfare, quiet and hidden as the lives of these first U.S. cursillistas. The weekend was nonetheless successful, Vadell asserts in *Orígenes mallorquines*, because of the "indefatigable Father Fernández," who was there for the young men before, during, and after.[31]

Shortly after arriving at Lackland, Vadell and Palomino had heard about Fernández, a native of Palma de Mallorca, and his Catholic Action work with the young Mexican-descent men of his parish.[32] When he received the letter from Vadell, Fernández was thrilled at the opportunity to help initiate the CdC in the United States, likening the movement to a "fábrica de apóstoles [factory of apostles]," a weekend that would benefit individuals and the Church and churn out apostles for Jesus Christ.[33]

When he first arrived in Texas, Vadell lacked complete confidence in his ability to help spread Cursillos. In his account of the pioneer years of U.S. Cursillos, he writes about his passion and his self-doubt. He had heard about the famous radio priest Bishop Fulton Sheen, and hoped that this highly influential Catholic would help popularize Cursillos in the United States. After several unanswered letters to Sheen, Vadell gave up on getting his help. He realized that he would have to rely on his own ability to light the fire of the Holy Spirit in the United States, and he committed himself to doing as much as possible in his two short years in the United States. Vadell gained confidence when he observed the young men experiencing the power of the Holy Spirit. He came to see himself as a conduit for the Holy Spirit in Texas and realized that it was divine, not earthly help, that he needed most for the success of Cursillos.[34]

After completing the second Cursillo weekend in Waco, Vadell and Palomino were transferred to Mission, Texas, where they led a weekend in late 1957. Its impact increased by the fact that Mission was a small and close-knit town, so that news of the Cursillo spread rapidly. The parish priest, Father Daniel Ressetar, who was also an Air Force chaplain, worked diligently to publicize its success and, by the time Vadell wrote *Orígenes mallorquines*, was "already working on translating the course into English."[35]

From Mission, the two "traveling airmen" went to Brownsville in 1957 and then Laredo in 1958, where they organized further weekends. One year later, they were invited to introduce the movement in Corpus Christi, home of the Corpus Christi Naval Air Station.[36] Mexican-descent men in Corpus Christi, members of the Church-affiliated group Legionnaires of Mary, had heard about the Cursillo movement from two friends who had made their weekend in Laredo and returned to Corpus Christi "full of enthusiasm," dedicating themselves to introducing Cursillos there.[37] Vadell and Palomino worked closely with priests as well as with fellow laymen, like those in Corpus Christi, to further the movement. Their efforts helped establish what would become a nationwide pattern of lay and clerical cooperation.

Cursillo weekends proved to be tremendously popular in Texas: by 1959 eighteen men's weekends had been held in Waco alone.[38] Mexican-descent cursillistas spoke with friends about their experiences, creating a demand for the weekends among Catholic Tejanos.

Vadell writes candidly about the pioneer days of the Cursillos in Texas. Establishing the movement in Texas was enjoyable but also demanding and exhausting work. He writes about the letters of support that arrived from Mallorca, Ciudad Real, Madrid, and Reus, and how they kept him and Palomino spiritually fortified. He writes that they worked long hours studying the rollos, drinking Coca-Cola, and smoking cigarettes.[39]

The earliest U.S. Cursillos were all offered in cities that housed Air Force bases to which Vadell and Palomino were transferred several times during their two years in Texas.[40] For the first four years after Cursillos were introduced to the United States—that is, from 1957 to 1960—cursillistas were all Mexican-descent Catholic men. The first non-Spanish-speaking cursillistas were U.S. Air Force cadets who attended weekends in 1961 and 1962 in San Angelo, Laredo, and Dallas. The mobility of Air Force and other military personnel, typically transferred frequently during their careers, was a key factor in the geographic diffusion of the Cursillos.

Phoenix, home to a sizable community of Mexican-descent Catholics, became the U.S. center for the movement. The first national convention of spiritual directors of Cursillos was held in Phoenix in 1959, and one year later, the first issue of *Ultreya*, the official magazine of the U.S. Cursillo movement's National Secretariat, was published there. In a manner similar to how Mallorca's *Proa* magazine advertised Catholic Action's work, *Ultreya* promoted the Cursillos de Cristiandad. As a result, the CdC spread throughout the Southwest, across Arizona, California, and New Mexico.[41]

Paralleling their popularity among southwestern Mexican-descent Americans, Cursillos quickly became popular among New York Puerto

Ricans. Quoting the archdiocesan leader of Hispanic ministry Father Robert Stern, the theologian and historian Timothy Matovina writes that Cursillos were "immensely popular among Puerto Ricans and other Latinos" because they "provided a framework and community to the individual Hispanic immigrant otherwise submerged in New York's dominant non-Hispanic culture and in danger of losing his identity as Hispanic and Catholic."[42] For some Hispanics, like New York Puerto Ricans, making a Cursillo safeguarded ethnic and religious identities and empowered the men and women who became cursillistas. Making a Cursillo in their native language was just as important for first-generation cursillistas of Mexican descent. In 1960, Father Antonio Hernandez, Hector Torres, Juan Fonseca, Julio Sepulveda, and Severo Rivera traveled from Lorain to Waco to make a Cursillo weekend. Like other midwestern and East Coast Spanish-speaking Catholics, these Ohioans had learned about Cursillo weekends from other Catholics and from their parish bulletins and diocesan newspapers. The process of transplantation of Cursillos from Waco to Lorain was the template for the spread of Cursillos across the U.S. landscape. Priests, laymen, and laywomen made their Cursillo weekends in an established Cursillo community and returned to their communities on fire and motivated to spread the movement first in Spanish, then in English for their children, who preferred to worship in English.

Unlike Spanish-speaking Catholics in New York and Ohio, Mexican-descent cursillistas in Waco and other southwestern cities did not have to worry about losing their religio-ethnic identities: they were immersed in ethnoreligious communities. The Mexican-descent men who attended the first U.S. Cursillo in Waco lived in the exclusively Mexican Calle Dos barrio, attended St. Francis Catholic Church, and spoke Spanish almost exclusively. For them, the Cursillo weekend, offered in their native language, further legitimated their religious, linguistic, and ethnic identities and gave them an opportunity to improve their lives and their communities. All across the United States, Hispanic men and women of Puerto Rican, Cuban, and Mexican descent made their Cursillo weekend, from which they drew apostolic zeal and a strong sense of personal agency. These cursillistas came away from their weekend believing that they were the church; they were steeped in the Cursillo experience and semantics of religious, ethnic, and personal empowerment. They were motivated to put their renewed selves to the service of their immediate environments—their families, churches, and barrios.

In the late 1950s a "buzz" surrounded the Cursillo movement, and Spanish-speaking and English-speaking men and women alike were excited about their weekend experience and wanted to talk about it with neighbors, friends, and coworkers. Catholics who had not yet made their weekend received just enough information to convince them that they would have to experience the three days for themselves. And when Catholics were not talking, they were reading reports in their parish newsletters, bulletins, and in diocesan newsletters that promoted the weekend Cursillos.

The first English-language course was held November 9–12, 1961, in San Angelo, Texas. The city, just over 200 miles from Waco, was home to the San Angelo Air Corps Basic Flying School, which opened in 1941 and was renamed Goodfellow Air Force Field.[43] White, non-Hispanic Catholics in San Angelo who had read about the Spanish-language Cursillo weekends in their parish bulletins asked their priest, Father Fidelis, if they could experience one of the weekends for themselves. Other English-language courses quickly followed: in 1961 alone Cursillo weekends in English were offered in San Francisco; Gary, Indiana; Lansing, Michigan; and Gallup, New Mexico. By 1962, thirty English-speaking Cursillo weekends had been held.[44] The Cursillo Movement spread eastward, and in 1962 Cursillo weekends were held in Cincinnati; Brooklyn; Saginaw and Grand Rapids, Michigan; Miami; Chicago; Detroit; Newark; Baltimore; Kansas City; and Boston. And, significantly for the Protestant Cursillo movement, Catholic Cursillo came to the then-ecumenically oriented Diocese of Peoria, Illinois, in 1964.

Out west, Cursillo weekends were held in California (Monterey, San Diego, Sacramento, Los Angeles), Colorado (Pueblo), and Washington State (Yakima). By 1981, "almost all" of the 160 U.S. dioceses offered Cursillo weekends.[45] In 1965 the National Secretariat and the National Cursillo Office were established in Kansas City. The movement came to be joined to the National Conference of Catholic Bishops and is a member of the International Catholic Organizations of the Pontifical Council for the Laity in Rome.[46] In 1980 the movement established an international office, the Organismo Mundial de Cursillos de Cristiandad (World Organization of Cursillos in Christianity, OMCC), in Santo Domingo "to coordinate the three international "working groups" of Latin America, Europe, and the International English Language Group."[47] Today, there are close to 1 million Catholic cursillistas in the United States alone. The current U.S. National Secretariat is in Jarrell, Texas.[48]

U.S. Cursillos: Tensions between Popular and Official Catholicism

When we examine the U.S. history of Cursillos de Cristiandad, it becomes clear that in the early years of the American movement, there were two distinct Cursillo movements: one Spanish-speaking and the other English-speaking.[49] In the Spanish-speaking movement lay Catholics tend to have more control, and in the English-speaking Cursillo movement clergy have greater involvement. The Mexican-descent cursillistas I have interviewed who are part of the Spanish-speaking movement all emphasized their movement's ties the original Mallorquín Cursillos, and all of the first-generation Mexican-descent cursillistas I interviewed not only knew that Eduardo Bonnín was the movement's founder but had known him personally. Comparatively few white, non-Hispanic Catholic cursillistas I interviewed knew that Bonnín was the founder, and very few had met him. While some, like Ron and Marie Caronti of the Chicago English-speaking, movement knew that Bonnín was the founder, and say that their movement advertises that he is the founder of the Cursillos, the majority of white, non-Hispanic cursillistas I have interviewed believe that Hervás was the founder of the weekend Cursillos and (incorrectly) give 1949 as the year of the first Cursillo.

Some clergy active in the early U.S. CdC movement asserted (and seemed relieved) that "a significant factor that has been achieved in the USA regarding the Cursillo Movement is that it has been . . . de-Hispanicized."[50] In 1973, Bishop Joseph Green of Reno, Nevada, then episcopal advisor to the Cursillo Movement USA, reported that the vast majority of cursillistas were English-speaking, not Spanish-speaking, which points to an interesting tension in the movement that we will explore further in the next chapter. Some members of the Church hierarchy were eager for the movement to "adjust itself well to the American culture and mentality," and as Bishop Green noted, to lose its Hispanic cultural dimensions.[51] While some, like Green, were relieved that Cursillos, in his mind at least, were "de-Hispanicized," others had "grave reservations" about Cursillo for English speakers. These Catholics believed that Cursillos were "not the dynamic for American English-speaking apostles" because of their militancy and emotionalism but could work for Spanish-speaking Catholics who need "an emotional boot in the rear end to get them going."[52] While Bishop Green wanted to see the movement move away from its Spanish origins, one Catholic who identified himself as "Bill" argued that because of the movement's "fascistic implications," it should not take root among English speakers at all.

Moreover, not all U.S. Catholics appreciated the CdC's masculinist, militant rhetoric, its emphasis on creating soldiers for Christ in a country where Catholics were not known for having a public, evangelical kind of faith. Although by the late 1950s and early 1960s relations between Catholics and Protestants had come a long way since the mid-nineteenth-century era of migration and accompanying anti-Catholicism, these white, non-Hispanic Catholics knew that American Catholics had long been viewed with suspicion by their Protestant neighbors. They feared that an apostolic, publicly proclaimed Cursillo-style Catholicism would likely not diminish the lingering suspicions and would revive anti-Catholic rhetoric and actions.[53] However, history shows that rather than fearing the Cursillos, U.S. Protestants were drawn to the weekend and were helped by Catholics to establish their own versions of the three days. The Catholic Cursillo weekend offered what many U.S. Christians were wanting—the time and space to work on their personal spirituality and the encouragement to channel their personal faith into their surrounding communities. Moreover, cursillistas met frequently in small groups, group reunions, and this facet of the movement was immensely appealing to Protestant Christians.

The U.S. National Secretariat was formed in 1965 at the national Cursillo convention in Kansas City to oversee the movement and help direct its growth. In his 1973 report, Bishop Green of Reno wrote that while the movement was spreading rapidly across the United States, it was "not organized properly" and that because of this disorganization and "lack of understanding of the total Cursillo Method, when the initial enthusiasm wore off, movements began to flounder."[54] It is difficult to discern here what Green means by "properly" organized. Since he is referring explicitly here to the Cursillo method and the need for U.S. cursillistas to adhere to it, it seems that he wants the weekend-long course to be more clerically controlled, akin to what Bishop Hervás had desired. This kind of bureaucratic, more authoritarian secretariat was not in the spirit of Bonnín's idealized secretariat. Bonnín, Forteza, and Vadell, in *The Structure of Ideas*, asserted that the secretariat "must always be sufficiently flexible and Christian," that the secretariat was to discover the "leader group," and that it was a "summit group reunion, composed of spiritual directors and laymen—men and women—[that] takes the Cursillos as an authentic and apostolic plan."[55] Bonnín, Forteza, and Vadell envisioned and advocated for a movement with a leadership that served cursillistas and not the leaders' self-interest—they were against a secretariat serving as a "conning [surveillance] tower where the most expert people direct and command."[56]

Bonnín and his associates created and nurtured a movement that spread via transplantation by laypersons—cursillistas. When cursillistas, Catholics and Protestants alike, move to a new place, they take the weekend with them. While the larger Cursillo movement has been successful because of the efforts of laypeople and clergy to transplant the weekend and movement to the places where they geographically move, this fluidity also poses organizational challenges. The U.S. National Secretariat wants the various communities to operate in a largely uniform manner, but tensions arise between local Cursillo communities and the secretariat because the movement is fundamentally lay-run. Just how much freedom individual, diocese-affiliated Cursillo communities have and when they are technically under the jurisdiction of the National Secretariat is not always clear. In the 1970s by the National Secretariat, the episcopal advisor, and the executive director made a concerted effort to reorganize most of the U.S. Cursillo movements.[57] Promoting the Cursillo Leader's School was an important component of the effort to clarify organization and purpose so that the far-flung U.S. Cursillo communities had similar training and shared intentions.

Bonnín had helped develop the Leader's School—a weekend event during which Cursillo leaders were able to renew themselves and talk with other leaders in the movement. Bonnín certainly wanted a structure to help organize his movement, and his weekend Cursillo was—and is—as highly structured as it is a grassroots movement for laypersons to become leaders in their immediate communities. He wanted the movement to move organically, with cursillistas themselves, and to adapt to its environment. Leader's workshops and weekends were held to give the cursillistas "a much deeper knowledge and awareness of the true nature of the Cursillo Movement and a greater spirit of dedication to the use of the total method, especially the post-Cursillo phase of the Movement."[58] In the United States, despite the organizational problems the movement experienced in its nascent years, Bishop Green, like other clergy, had great hopes for the movement as cursillistas' "dedication and commitment" was viewed as "a source of inspiration to all who come in contact with them."[59] Like their priests and bishops, lay Catholics echoed Bishop

Green's sentiments when they expressed their hope that Cursillos would become the linchpin for church renewal, and they pointed to the weekend's focus on renewing one's relationship with Christ and a faith that reflects this "commitment to the Lord and our fellow man."[60]

Throughout the 1960s and early 1970s, white, non-Hispanic Catholics flocked to Cursillos. In some dioceses there were waiting lists; most parishes held between six and eight weekends a year for men and the same number for women, which was not enough to meet the demand. By 1970, the movement was functioning in 115 U.S. dioceses, and by 1972, in 120.[61] Reflecting the popularity of Cursillos in the Southwest, 69,122 Catholics attended Cursillos in San Antonio between 1962 and 1967.[62] In Chicago alone, by 1973 more than 2,200 men and women had made "the English Cursillos and an even greater number the Spanish ones." The movement came to Chicago in 1963 and became a popular method of renewal among clergy and laity alike. Cursillos were held at the Archdiocesan Cursillo Center then at 1300 South Wabash Street.[63] Ron and Marie Caronti, who have been involved with the Chicago English-speaking movement since the mid-1960s, say that Cursillos revitalized their archdiocese as well as individual laypersons, who were, according to Ron, "more involved in their parishes as a result of Vatican II. The movement's emphasis on piety, study, and action fit very well with what was coming out of Vatican II. The timing was perfect."[64] According to the Chicago diocese's associate director of Cursillos, Ed Salmon, "close to 400 men and women and 30 of our priests" were actively involved in organizing, staffing, and offering the Chicago English-speaking weekends.[65] Cursillos were so popular in the Chicago diocese that eight men's courses and eight women's courses were offered each year, in both the English-speaking and Spanish-speaking movements.[66]

The Cursillos de Cristiandad in the United States have always depended on the support of parish priests and the local bishop—even more than in Mallorca. As a historical rule of thumb, Catholic Cursillos have thrived especially in dioceses where the bishop is himself a cursillista. When we met in July 2005, San Diego auxiliary bishop Gilbert E. Chavez had been bishop for thirty-one years and a cursillista for thirty. From his perspective, the Cursillo movement was "the first innovative program for Hispanics. It called people to their faith and to be more participatory in the Church—especially men who would set up for festivals and such but who were not as involved in their faith and their Church as were the women."[67] Bishop Chavez, like Ron Caronti, observe that the spread of Cursillos in the United States came in the wake of the Vatican II Council and that the movement helped forge stronger relationships between priests and laypeople. Chavez thinks that "the majority of U.S. priests like Cursillos," but he adds that because there are so many demands placed on priests, even more since Vatican II, "they just can't get as involved as they would like, because of all of the demands placed on them already."[68]

Both the U.S. Cursillos and the CdC in Mallorca have experienced tensions between laity and the Church hierarchy. The Mallorquín cursillistas I have interviewed are well aware of the power dynamics in U.S. Cursillos. They emphasize the lay origins of the movement and Bonnín's desire to work with priests without clergy becoming overly influential in the weekend and the movement.[69] According to Miguel Sureda, a longtime friend of Eduardo and a leader in the island's CdC, a problem related to clergy's overinvolvement is the rule in most U.S. dioceses that wives should make their Cursillo weekend after their spouse. "I don't understand this rule," Sureda says. "Whoever the spiritual leader is in the family should make the Cursillo first. If it is the wife then she should be the one to make her Cursillo first."[70] Miguel and María Sureda and other Mallorquín cursillistas with whom I have spoken express some confusion as well as consternation about the more clerically oriented CdC weekends in the United States. They emphasize that Bonnín, and his friends who founded the movement, never wanted clergy to take over, and that this gender-based rule was created by national U.S. Catholic leadership of the CdC.[71] Moreover, in the United States, the National Secretariat has emphasized from the start that any Cursillo movement must have the sanction of the bishop of the diocese and that he "must be kept informed of the plans and functions of the movement."[72] The success of Cursillos in a particular diocese has always depended on the enthusiasm and support of the bishop as well as the parish priest. If Church authorities in a U.S. parish or diocese support the movement it takes hold, but if the support is lacking, the movement does not flourish.

To those most heavily involved in the United States, the most important component of a successful Cursillo movement is its Leader's School. Cursillo leaders guide the ultreya communities, which are essentially reunions of the various reunion groups in a diocese. Bonnín had envisioned the Leader's School as a place where leaders in the Cursillo community could be enlightened, encouraged, and where their ideas could be implemented. He cautioned against a Leader's School becoming "professorial," "boring," "a clique," or "a conning tower [dictatorial]." If the school becomes these things, Bonnín, Forteza, and Vadell cautioned, "it is no longer of value, even though it shines more than ever."[73]

The Rev. William ("Bill") Alcuin, OFM Cap., who was involved in the early U.S. Cursillo movement and wrote extensively on it, saw the leaders as the most important component in a successful Cursillo community. Alcuin pointed out that the leaders were handpicked by Catholic clergy and spent two hours a week studying the movement. He saw the leaders' school as fulfilling what Bishop Hervás had envisioned for the movement—weekly group reunions and regularly held ultreyas where the group reunions convene.[74] Alcuin interpreted the Cursillo movement as lay-inspired with clergy playing a more instrumental role. His diagram of the movement showed bishops and priests at the top of the movement, with laity under their bishop's and priest's directions. His vision of the Leader's School was the inverse of Bonnín's, who envisioned the two days as an opportunity for lay and clerical leaders to continue to grow spiritually and to continue to direct the movement together, as inspired Christians.

In Bonnín's Cursillo weekend, laymen were the ones who organized and ran the three days—not members of the clergy. Alcuin's interpretation of the movement reflects a post-Bonnín era where the U.S. movement came under greater clerical control. His naming Hervás as the founder of the movement also reflects the pervasive belief among clergy at the time. Alcuin saw his own role as helping to further priests' involvement in the larger Cursillo movement. Arguing that "most priests are afraid of spiritual direction," Alcuin in his correspondence with other clergy wrote of the importance of training priest leaders for the Cursillo movement.[75] He made no mention of the importance of laity in the movement's success; in Alcuin's assessment, the success depended wholly on supportive, knowledgeable clergy who were familiar with Hervás's writings.

Despite a tendency among U.S. clergy during this early period to favor clerical control, when Cursillos came to be offered in their dioceses in the late 1960s and early 1970s, many priests appreciated the enthusiasm and contributions that cursillistas brought to the parish and the diocese. These clergymen wrote approvingly, even glowingly, of cursillistas as among the most active and desirable parishioners. In some parishes, cursillistas revived struggling societies, reinvigorating them and making them "as good a group as any parish could hope to have."[76]

Yet while Church revitalization was a good thing, from Bonnín's perspective, it was not the primary purpose of the weekend. The main goal was to renew laity, who would go on to form intentional communities of "on-fire" Christians. Cursillistas would seek to transform their immediate environments and their societies. Enhanced church attendance and involvement were but welcome side effects of the Cursillo weekend and overall experience. For their part, U.S. priests appreciated the way that their cursillista parishioners were "awakened to the reality of Christian life by the Cursillo" and saw "that this whole Christianity bit is for real and that it's important."[77] They tended to focus on what the cursillista parishioner brought to the Church and cited increased involvement and commitment as welcome proof of the efficacy of the weekend. Some priests were dismayed by Cursillo's theology, which they viewed as "stone age," and by what they perceived as cursillistas' forming their own church within the parish, and even "badgering others" into making the course.[78] These fears and concerns centered on the degree of power laypersons had in the Cursillo movement. Written attacks on the weekend intended to discredit the movement as backward, nonintellectual, and even non-Catholic because Catholicism was known for its hierarchy, not its congregationalism where each community had a great degree of autonomy (even though the Cursillos answered to a national organization, the U.S. secretariat).

Thus, while many U.S. Catholic clergy appreciated the enthusiasm that cursillistas brought to their parishes, others were wary of this enthusiasm, which they saw as threatening their own position of theological authority in the parish. These anxieties hinged on post–Vatican II Catholicism's reconfigured power relationships between laity and clergy. Lay and clergy roles were being redefined and renegotiated during the 1960s and 1970s in the wake of the Vatican II Council (1962–65), during which time the Church underwent deep philosophical and theological discussions about its mission and purpose in the late twentieth century.[79] While most scholars today consider the council to have enacted only moderate reforms, it is undisputed that the Church changed and experienced Pope John XXIII's *aggiornamento*. Whether they liked it or not, priests in the United States and around the world had to contend with laity who were being asked, via encyclicals and pastoral letters, to become more engaged in the world around them and in their Church. For some clergy, the Catholic Cursillo movement was exciting and came at just the right time. For other clergy, cursillistas represented what was going awry with the Church—laity were trying to be priests and run their churches, overstepping their role in the Church.

But those priests and bishops who were supportive of Cursillos were vocal supporters and helped the movement gain respectability and momentum throughout the 1970s. In his personal correspondence, Father Timothy Joyce of Newton, New Jersey, wrote about his Cursillo experience: "The more I look back at those three days in Baltimore, the more I am moved by what took place.... It was a tremendous experience and three of the happiest days I have spent in my life. I only hope that they will have some lasting influence in making me a better Christian and a better priest."[80]

It was primarily pro-Vatican II priests such as Father Timothy who supported the Cursillo weekend in their dioceses and parishes and who were on the vanguard of an ecumenically inclined U.S. Catholicism. Yet Father Timothy's sentiments were not matched by those of the U.S. National Secretariat, whose leaders interpreted the movement as nonecumenical.

The U.S. National Secretariat's Position: Nonecumenicism

Catholic Cursillos inspired what has become a widespread, massive ecumenical movement of Fourth-Day movements and their offshoots, but some leaders in the American Catholic Cursillo movement were opposed to Protestants' adopting the word "Cursillo" because their courses were ecumenical or nondenominational. While lay Catholics and clergy welcomed Protestants into their courses and even helped them start their own Protestant Cursillos, such as the Upper Room Cursillos (now called Walk to Emmaus) and the Via de Cristo Cursillos (now affiliated with the secretariat of the Evangelical Lutheran Church in America), Gerald Hughes, a lay Catholic who was then the national coordinator of U.S. Cursillos, was not pleased. Despite substantial lay and clerical support for them, Hughes was opposed to ecumenical Cursillos. He argued that the Cursillo was a copyrighted and nonecumenical course and that Protestants could offer their own versions of it but could not call them Cursillos if their weekends were ecumenical. Yet ironically, when speaking at an Atlanta Catholic Cursillo gathering in 1974, Hughes warned cursillistas that Cursillos might be showing signs of becoming "ingrown, of being caught up in organizational activities and mechanics." The movement was designed to explore opportunities to "take the movement into the environments in which we live, work, and socialize."[81]

Under threats of legal action from Hughes, the founders of Protestant versions of Catholic Cursillos deleted the word "Cursillo" from their titles and manuals. Deleting "Cursillo" was painful for all of them, as they openly acknowledged the movement that began in Spain as their catalyst. For some, calling their courses "Cursillo" affirmed connections with global Christianity. Moreover, all of the founders of Catholic Cursillo branches had made their Cursillo weekend and called themselves cursillistas, "one who has made a Cursillo." Hughes's position is ironic from a historical perspective. As we have seen, the CdC's primary architect, Eduardo Bonnín, crafted the weekend as a venue for deeper spirituality, and part of his vision was to raise up laypersons to be Church. He wanted Catholic Christianity to be less about what the hierarchy wanted and more in line with living a life of Christ and bringing Christ to others. In analyzing Hughes's place in the CdC's history, we can see him as taking lay empowerment to an extreme, defying clergy's wishes for an ecumenical CdC, as well as out of step with the *aggiornamento* of post–Vatican II Catholic culture. In threatening to take legal action against Protestant spinoffs of the CdC, Hughes wanted U.S. Catholicism and by extension U.S. Cursillos to maintain a pre–Vatican II reality of triumphalism and nonecumenism.

Hughes addresses his concerns in the *Leader's Manual*, writing about some of the "problems" that non-Catholic participation in Cursillo weekends created—specifically intercommunion. He acknowledges that "the ecumenical policy of the Cursillo movement has been an evolving one over the years," and he specifically refers to the participation of non-Catholics in midwestern Cursillo weekends as problematic.[82] Hughes declares that "in keeping with Church discipline and good ecumenism," "there is to be no ecumenical activity *within* the Catholic Cursillo movement. Secretariats, leadership schools, Ultreyas, and weekends are to be strictly Catholic."[83]

The Mallorquín cursillistas I have spent time with all express confusion over this piece of U.S. Catholic Cursillo history. They all say that "Eduardo" would not have wanted this to happen because he was all about "bringing people together, not separating them."[84] Miguel Sureda says he is not sure what to make of what he calls the "franchising" of Cursillos in the United States. He thinks it is odd and does not completely understand why the word *Cursillo* has been copyrighted by Catholics in the United States. He emphasizes that those courses that are not three days and that do not follow the Cursillo handbook "are not Cursillos" and that coed weekends "are not Cursillos, they are something else," but he says that Bonnín would not have a problem with Protestant Christians calling their courses Cursillos if they adhered as closely as they could to his vision.

When we look to Bonnín's own writings, nowhere did he emphasize a desire to mark the weekend with Catholic triumphalism. The language of his weekend in spirituality was Christocentric but not exclusively Catholic. He wanted all Christians to be friends and to get along, and he emphasizes this ecumenism and *amistad* in his writings, published and unpublished. He created a weekend in spirituality that he hoped would connect men and women to the "living Christ of the Gospel" and show them God's grace.[85]

U.S. Protestants saw and heard about the transformations their friends and neighbors were experiencing and wanted that experience for themselves. In the 1960s and 1970s, a handful of parishes were supportive of Protestants making a Catholic Cursillo, yet because they feared reprisals from their bishops and the U.S. National Secretariat, their actions are off the record.[86] Only one U.S. diocese has publicly embraced an ecumenical stance—the Diocese of Peoria. This western Illinois diocese has been the U.S. center of ecumenical Cursillos since 1964, and under the direction of its spiritual director, Father Tom Henseler, a former chaplain in the U.S. Navy, midwestern Protestants have flocked to Peoria to take part in the Cursillo weekend.[87] Father Tom, as he is affectionately called by cursillistas, served as spiritual director for more than twenty years in the Peoria diocese and began the ecumenical Cursillo weekend in the Diocese of Springfield when he was transferred there in 1991.[88] One of the results of Father Tom's and Peoria lay Catholics' ecumenical outreach was the formation of Protestant Cursillo offshoots.

The National Cursillo Centers' stance was and still is that the non-Catholic branches and their offshoots are not true Cursillos because they are ecumenical and Catholic Cursillos were not and are not ecumenical because of the Sacrament of the Eucharist (Communion) and Reconciliation (Confession). If these branches of Catholic Cursillo became denominationally focused instead of ecumenical, according to Victor Lugo, the current executive director of Catholic Cursillos, "we wouldn't have a problem with them. You see, the word *Cursillo* was used by Methodists in their courses for Methodists and by Lutherans in their courses for Lutherans. This was fine, as long as the courses were designed only for members of those denominations. The problem was ecumenicism—Methodists started offering their courses to everyone, to all believers. This was a problem because the course was not designed to be ecumenical and it was being made into an ecumenical movement."[89]

The ecumenicism that Lugo is talking about here is Christian ecumenicism, and yet my ethnographic research, which includes conversations with Mallorquín cursillistas who knew Bonnín intimately, say something else, that the movement was designed for Christians to become closer to Christ and to reignite their immediate communities, and that Bonnín supported ecumenical weekends. The U.S. National Secretariat has a history of antiecumenism, and Lugo, who personally knew Bonnín and who has been involved with the CdC for over thirty-five years, is part of that larger history. While Mallorquín cursillistas remember Bonnín as an ecumenically oriented Christian, the U.S. National Secretariat has interpreted the founder of the CdC as having different orientations and motives.

Never in their history have the weekends been called "Cursillos de Católicismo." They have been interpreted as Christian. At times the three-day movement has assumed a more universal Christian identity and at others, a narrower denominationalism. The U.S. National Secretariat has interpreted the movement as having the latter history, while laypersons and some clergy, Catholic and Protestant alike, have leaned toward the ecumenical and universal understanding of the origins, intent, and purpose of the Cursillo weekend. Catholic and Protestant laypersons and clergy alike favor Bonnín's emphasis on the course's intent of encouraging *amistad*.

When Hughes ruled in 1981 that, according to the diocese's official rendering of the history, the Diocese of Peoria's Cursillo weekends "must cease being ecumenical or close down," Peoria's Bishop Edward O'Rourke, a supporter of the ecumenical Cursillo, "informed National Cursillo that Cursillo in the Diocese of Peoria would remain ecumenical. We are no longer connected with the national organization but still adhere to the Cursillo manual and structure."[90] The Cursillo movement in the Diocese of Peoria is especially significant to the spread of Protestant Cursillos in the United States as a variety of Protestants made their Cursillo in the diocese and worked closely with Peoria clergy and laypersons to establish their own denominational and nondenominational versions.

This part of U.S. Cursillo history shows lay ecumenicism operating at its fullest expression. Catholic cursillistas went out of their way to help staff the first Protestant versions of Catholic Cursillo weekends. We find an amazing level of cooperation and support that transcended denominations in the 1970s and 1980s, and the Diocese of Peoria was the center of this ecumenically oriented lay Catholicism. Bishop O'Rourke and Father Tom worked closely with Protestants to help form the Methodist Walk to Emmaus, the Lutheran Via de Cristo, and the nondenominational Tres Dias. If Hughes had taken a more ecumenical approach, the Fourth-Day Protestant Cursillo movement likely would not have mushroomed in the way it did in the late 1960s, 1970s, and 1980s.

The Midwest has been largely overlooked by scholars of American religious history, but a study of the Cursillo movement shows that this part of the United States was marked by ecumenism in the 1960s, 1970s, and 1980s. During these decades, midwestern Catholic laity and clergy alike worked with Protestants to spread the Cursillo weekend. The Diocese of Peoria was the hotbed of ecumenical outreach during the early years of the English-speaking Catholic Cursillo movement and the resulting Protestant Cursillo movements. A historical and ethnographic perspective shows us that while it is now one of the more antiecumenical and conservative dioceses in the United States, there was a time when the Diocese of Peoria embraced Vatican II reforms and was a leader in inter-Christian dialogue and experience.

Bishops and priests in this midwestern diocese embraced the reforms of Vatican II and the Church's call to ecumenical dialogue, especially with Protestant neighbors. As we have just seen, when the National Secretariat's Hughes demanded that the Peoria Cursillo community give up its ecumenical stance, Bishop O'Rourke opted to disassociate from the National Secretariat and operate as a separate entity. Peoria Catholic cursillistas believed that they were operating in the spirit of the founder, Eduardo Bonnín, as well as in the spirit of Vatican II, and that to become antiecumenical would betray both.

If the National Secretariat had taken a more ecumenical approach like the Diocese of Peoria, it might have achieved even greater successes in the United States and even globally, not only among Catholics but Protestants. The direction the U.S. movement has taken on a national level since Hughes's tenure is unfortunate from a historical perspective, as it was out of step with the spirit of Vatican II and represented a return to more triumphalist, pre–Vatican II Catholicism. Rather than embodying the *aggiornamento* of Vatican II and seeking inter-Christian dialogue and shared experiences with Protestants, the secretariat chose to embrace an exclusivist, nonecumenical stance, which its leaders believed was in the spirit of the founder of the weekend Cursillo, Eduardo Bonnín.[91]

Bringing Mallorquín Spirituality to America: Bonnín as Cursillo Ambassador to "Los Norteamericanos"

Peoria's Bishop O'Rourke is one of the many U.S. Church authorities who supported the Cursillo movement's emphasis on lay empowerment and saw it as an important movement of spirituality for laity and the Church. He followed in the footsteps of the Cursillos' primary architect, Eduardo Bonnín, who envisioned a weekend of renewal for laity and who launched a global movement of lay spirituality. Unlike O'Rourke and other U.S. priests, who were necessarily focused on the growth and maintenance of their parishes and dioceses, the lay Catholic Bonnín was able to assume a role as a globe-trotting, religious and cultural ambassador. He traveled extensively in the United States and was the primary global ambassador of the CdC from his first trip to the United States in 1961 to his final visit in 1998. Bonnín was a world traveler and spent much of his life on airplanes and in airports. For him, being the founder of a movement was not enough; he saw himself as an apostle and worked to see the CdC come to fruition globally. His friend and colleague Cristina González of the Fundación Eduardo Bonnín Aguiló (FEBA) says, "It was very important to Eduardo to visit the places where Cursillo was being lived and he was always traveling, always on airplanes because it was so important to him to see that people around the world kept experiencing Christ in Cursillo." During the course of an afternoon I spent at FEBA, González chronicled Bonnín's complex travel schedule. I had mentioned to her earlier that morning that I was interested in understanding Bonnín's impact on U.S. Catholic Cursillo culture in particular, and for several hours after my comment we sat together in the office while she went through his *diarios* (diaries), tracing his journeys in the United States and globally.[92] Bonnín wrote his journals in Catalan, and in tiny, precise script that was at times difficult for González to decipher. He wrote in a linear fashion, chronicling daily events, but in his small red *diarios* he also scribbled notes, names, and numbers in the margins of each page. González smiled and said that as FEBA's main archivist, she had gotten used to his writing style and the way he wrote his entries. She says that while she knew him personally it has been through her job—reading his writings, helping to translate them and make them available—that she has really gotten to know him: "He always began his diary entries by saying where he had attended mass that morning; he was a very devoted Catholic. And whenever he attended a Cursillo weekend, he would leave those three pages blank. It was the only time he did not write in his diaries." González's careful poring through the diaries shows that Bonnín traveled more to the United States than any other place in the world, a total of twenty-four times, more often even than Italy, his second-most visited country. When I asked about the travel logistics, González explained that Bonnín would visit various Cursillo communities and that they would pay for his plane tickets and would house him in their homes during his visit. Rarely, she emphasized, would Bonnín stay in a hotel. "He almost always stayed with a cursillista, and he really enjoyed that." When we compare the movement and transmission of the CdC in the United States to other weekend experiences whose histories are documented in this book, what binds them is that they are all supported by clergy but all are fundamentally lay-led. Laymen and women housed Bonnín during his travels, fed him, drove him to daily mass, and shared their spiritual experiences with him. As the founder of a movement in Christian spirituality who traveled extensively, Bonnín played an active role in maintaining its health and vitality.[93]

As I sat and listened to Cristina translate Bonnín's travels from his Mallorquín script into Spanish for my benefit, I was amazed by how much this man traveled—his schedule was grueling.[94] He visited countless Cursillo weekends, ultreyas, and OMCC gatherings—the man was a CdC ambassador like no other. He traveled to each community as an invited guest, at times speaking to Cursillo candidates during a weekend, at others, observing and offering his feedback. At times on his journey he assumed the identity of a tourist, but at other times he was on a pilgrimage to connect spiritually with other Christians, and to grow as a person of faith.

Bonnín was a much sought-after guest by U.S. cursillistas, in the Spanish-speaking as well as English-speaking movements. Cursillistas in the English-speaking "Ocean Bay," Massachusetts community, for example, invited him in November 1974 "to spend ten days with them as they celebrated the tenth anniversary of Cursillo in their area. Those who met him while he visited relate that 'He is a beautiful, simple, humble,

Eduardo Bonnín. Courtesy of the Fundación Eduardo Bonnín Aguiló.

Christ-like man. He is very monklike. He eats simply and he is like those in monasteries.'"[95] "Ocean Bay" was one of countless U.S. communities Bonnín visited as ambassador of the Cursillo method and movement. His U.S. travels, chronicled in relation to his interrelated global travels, include an August 1961 trip with stops in New York; Santa Fe and Albuquerque, New Mexico; Phoenix; San Antonio, Austin, and Ramos Rock, Texas (where he participated in the fiftieth U.S. Cursillo in the Diocese of Austin). From there he went to New Orleans and then Puerto Rico, where he helped to celebrate the fourth Cursillo in New Orleans and the fifth Cursillo in Puerto Rico, before finishing off in Miami. One year later in May, Bonnín traveled to New York, where he went to mass at St. Patrick's Cathedral. In his journal, he jotted that he saw the Empire State Building and was overwhelmed by its grandeur. From New York, Bonnín traveled to Guadalupe and Jalisco, Mexico, and in July of that year, he visited Kansas, and then San Francisco, where he took photos of the Golden Gate Bridge and commented on its impressiveness. Visits to Orlando and Venice, Florida, rounded out his summer travels.[96]

In 1971 Bonnín flew to Miami. Health problems kept him from returning to the United States until 1989, when he visited New York before continuing on to Madrid; Caracas; and Santiago, Chile.[97] In 1990 he went to Puerto Rico, and in the next year, to Los Angeles, Miami, Palm Beach, Tampa, Tokyo, Melbourne, Sydney, and Amsterdam. In 1992 he began his U.S. travels in Campeche, Mexico, and then went on a Pan-American tour during which he visited Guatemala; El Salvador; Miami; Toronto; Houston; Detroit; and Lindsay, Ontario.[98] In 1993, Bonnín visited Houston and while there went to the Johnson Space Center and wrote how excited he was to be there.

In 1994, he traveled to Tampico, Mexico; Houston; Toronto; and Los Angeles, where he visited Universal Studios and Disneyland. Showing me the photo of his visit there, González smiled and said, "Eduardo *amó* [loved] Disneyworld; he was like a little kid!"[99]

Bonnín's extensive travel schedule to the United States shows beyond a doubt that he was an active participant in the shaping and reinforcing of the U.S. Cursillo movement. He was the CdC's primary ambassador in the United States. Moreover, Bonnín saw his U.S. travels as an integral component in his efforts to ensure the CdC's global success. His trips to the United States were almost always linked to trips to other countries—he was a global ambassador and helped the movement he created spread far beyond the island of Mallorca.

When we look back to the introduction of the CdC to the United States and around the world we should remember that we are talking about the late 1950, not the twenty-first century. In Bonnín's time there was no computer, no YouTube, no cellphones or texting. The history of the CdC is a history of how a lay Christian movement was spread by word of mouth and by men and women who traveled to host weekends and to train others to do the same in their communities. It is a story about how an idea of revitalized Christianity caught on and, to use contemporary language, "went viral" before this was possible, linguistically or technologically. What is so stunning about this movement's history is that it is one of passion and commitment to an idea that Christian laymen and women can reignite their own faith and the faith of others.

A focus on renewed selves, spirituality, and commitment to their churches and communities is a crucial component of U.S. Catholic cursillistas' narratives and of U.S. Protestant cursillistas' stories as well. In chapter 3, we will encounter those adult-focused U.S. based Protestant Cursillo movements that trace their roots back to 1944 Mallorca and that acknowledge and advertise these origins. These Fourth-Day weekend encounters are based directly on Bonnín's methods and purpose, and their leaders are not only aware of their history, but are intentional in considering their movements "in covenant" with Bonnín's weekend. The resulting U.S. Fourth-Day movement showcases American Protestant Christian ingenuity and missionary drive, as these "Fourth-Dayer" cursillistas spread their Christian zeal in the United States and globally. Plainly put, U.S. Protestant cursillistas are the ones responsible for spreading the broad-based Fourth-Day movement throughout the world.

CHAPTER THREE

A Focus on Christian Experience

The Protestant Cursillos
(Tres Dias, Walk to Emmaus, Via de Cristo)
and the National Episcopal Cursillo

All of the Fourth-Day movements can trace their lineage back to Catholic Cursillos.
—Tracy Schmidlin, president, Via de Cristo, January 31, 2010

We say that the "Fourth Day is the rest of your life," and it is so true. The three days are important, but the weekend course is just the beginning. The Fourth Day is where the pilgrims' new life begins and where the work begins. It is all about the Fourth Day and living it the rest of your life.
—Greg Engroff, director, Walk to Emmaus, December 1, 2009

By the mid-1960s, mainline American Protestants like Bob and Rhoda Franks had heard enough about the Catholic Cursillo weekend to be convinced that they had to experience the three days for themselves. What they were hearing (and seeing) was exciting and intriguing; Catholic friends and relatives talked about changed lives, new relationships with Christ, improved marriages, and, generally speaking, new outlooks on life as a result of their weekend experience. American Catholic cursillistas spoke with enough conviction and passion that they inspired Protestants from a variety of traditions to seek out and make a Catholic Cursillo. In the 1960s and 1970s, Protestants like the Franks were able to make a Catholic Cursillo weekend in the Diocese of Peoria. It was a small group of Reformed, Lutheran, Methodist, Presbyterian, and Episcopalian laymen and women who, moved by their experiences during their Catholic Cursillo weekends, formed their own movements based directly on the Catholic Cursillo method.

The weekend Cursillos developed by Bonnín and his friends in the mid-1940s became standardized and institutionalized in print in the United States with the publication of Bishop Juan Hervás's *Leader's Manual*

(1967) and the U.S. National Cursillo Center's *Fundamental Ideas* (1974). Although there is disagreement today on the extent of standardization Bonnín and his friends intended, what is obvious from the ethnographic and historical records is that Bonnín wanted the weekend experience to become a movement. He dreamed big dreams and wanted the individual spirituality and group dynamics he witnessed in Cala Figuera to spread throughout Spain and the rest of the world. Bonnín believed that in order for the weekend Cursillos to become a successful movement, a specific method and purpose needed to be detailed. He envisioned the Cursillo as a three-phase process including the pre-Cursillo, the Cursillo, and the post-Cursillo. The pre-Cursillo is the process in which Cursillo leaders select promising men and, since 1952, women, to make the weekend course and prepare them as much as possible for the seventy-two-hour experience. The Cursillo itself is the highly structured weekend. Everything associated with the three days—everything—meals, talks, and sleeping arrangements—is planned down to the last detail. The post-Cursillo is called the "Fourth Day" and is said to be the rest of a cursillista's life. Cursillistas are to be apostles for Christ and to live a renewed life of faith and service in their "Fourth."

Months of planning go into the typical weekend, which is run by a team of dedicated Cursillo leaders. Candidates are invited by veteran cursillistas, those who have made the Cursillo themselves.[1] Once a candidate has been accepted for a three-day weekend, he or she goes through what is known as the pre-Cursillo, a period of sponsorship. According to official Cursillo literature, during this time, which can last for weeks or months, each candidate meets with a veteran cursillista who helps to prepare him or her for the experience. These official guidelines notwithstanding, however, most of the cursillistas I interviewed entered their Cursillo weekend with no preparation other than what they had heard anecdotally. The ethnographic research I conducted for this book shows that while some sponsors meet with candidates in the weeks and months before the actual weekend takes place, this does not always happen. Sponsors generally can be most helpful to their candidates during the post-Cursillo phase, guiding the new cursillista in living a Christian life in his or her Fourth Day. They help their candidates find a reunion group and meet with them when they need to talk. Cursillistas affirm the importance of reunion groups and ultreyas (called "secuelas" in Tres Dias), reunions of the reunion groups, in maintaining a healthy Christian life. Cursillistas look forward to their Fourth-Day activities and say that their meetings and activities nurture *amistad* and community as much as they support individual spiritual growth.

When we examine the history of the Fourth-Day Christian Cursillos in the United States, it becomes clear that the movement would not have come into being were it not for Vatican II (1962–65) and the climate of ecumenism and inter-Christian dialogue. For U.S. Catholics, the post–Vatican II climate was one of cooperation and the downplaying of differences in favor of what united Christians. For the first time in history, the Roman Catholic Church officially gave Catholics the permission and freedom to turn inward and to trust their consciences in matters of faith. U.S. Catholic laymen, women, and priests, caught up in this climate of Christian cooperation and reform, invited Protestants to make Catholic Cursillos; they sponsored Protestant men and women who made Catholic Cursillos and even helped them establish their own versions of the Cursillos. In contrast to Catholic Cursillos, which were only for men in the first eight years of the movement, the Protestant offshoots of Catholic Cursillos have always included men and women. The focus of this chapter is on four of the five "in-covenant" Protestant Fourth-Day Christian Movements, those three-day weekends, both denominationally and interdenominationally based, that follow the Catholic Cursillo guidelines and the spirit of Bonnín, emphasizing living a Christ-filled life in the Fourth Day.[2] When we closely examine the history of these movements and how they came to be formed, we see that they were shaped by Protestants and Catholics working together in the 1960s spirit of theological and liturgical ecumenicism. Simply put, if it had not been for ecumenically minded Catholics and motivated Protestants, the Fourth-Day movement would not exist.

The founding of these Fourth-Day movements begins in the 1960s and spans three decades, as Catholics and Protestants alike began to form courses and movements inspired by Catholic Cursillos. All of their founders had made a Catholic Cursillo and used the term *Cursillo* in the early versions of their spinoff courses. The history of the Catholic Cursillos and the Fourth-Day Christian movement was, from the beginning, a movement to empower laypeople, to enable them to "be free" and "live a new kind of life in Christ." This new life, the Fourth Day, entailed a commitment to bringing Christ into the world and sharing one's new perspectives with others in community.[3]

Throughout the 1960s, 1970s, and 1980s, American Catholics and Protestants were inspired by their churches' efforts to provide laypeople with a greater role and voice. What became a broad-based Christian Cursillo movement was in part a response to denominational concerns, mainline Protestant pastors' greater willingness to break down barriers of power and theological privilege in their churches, and laymen and women's hunger for more involvement in their churches and communities. The Fourth-Day movement was part of a new ecumenicism that swept across the United States and today continues the quest for personal and communal spirituality.

A case study of U.S. Protestant branches of Catholic Cursillo is enlightening on many levels, because it shows the possibilities of Christian ecumenism when Church authorities encourage laypeople's initiatives, as well as when the laity are proactive without requiring official sanction. The history of the U.S. Fourth-Day movement in spirituality is one in which laity and clergy work together to promote a method and experience of Christian spirituality. Yet this history also illustrates for us what happens when church authorities discourage or condemn ecumenical dialogue and outreach. In this scenario, movements become less ecumenical, turning more inward, and reach fewer people as a result. A history of Fourth-Day movements that base their method on Bonnín's triptych of piety, study, and action shows that the movements that reach the largest numbers of men and women are the ones that are the most ecumenically and interdenominationally oriented.

Tres Dias, a Fourth-Day movement rooted in the Reform Tradition but one that is interdenominational and evangelically leaning, continues to attract Christians from a wide variety of denominations and backgrounds. Via de Cristo and Walk to Emmaus, Lutheran- and Methodist-based, respectively, have maintained denominational roots but simultaneously emphasize their interdenominationalism. These three movements have also embraced intercommunion as an ultimate step toward Christian ecumenism. A fourth in-covenant movement, the National Episcopal Cursillo (NEC), remains nonecumenical and not interdenominational. The NEC has also been the slowest to grow nationally and internationally. While NEC leaders remain in conversation with leaders of the other in-covenant Fourth-Day movements, like the CdC, the NEC remains mostly its own entity, its nonecumenical stance precluding effective outreach to non-Episcopalians.

NEC members excepted, most Fourth-Day cursillistas have chosen since the 1960s to downplay denominational and theological differences in favor of commonalities and what links them. They are all believers in Christ; they believe that communion is necessary to feed their bodies and souls; and they seek out experiences such as intercommunion to put them in touch with the divine—even when these situations break with the church hierarchy's official position. The rise of evangelical Protestant Christianity and churches in the late twentieth century signaled the desire of hundreds of thousands of American Christians to emphasize experience over particular theologies. The theology that matters to contemporary U.S. Christians is shaped by the cursillistas themselves—a kind of experiential theology that trumps official church theology.

The first U.S. Protestant cursillistas in the late 1960s identified themselves denominationally but were part of the late-twentieth-century liturgical renewals and reforms that made it possible for them to focus on the possibility and reality of a universal Christian experience. Thus, the Roman Catholic Vatican II Council, the rise of Protestant evangelicalism, and the mainline Protestant denominational reforms came together in a dynamic way and opened the door for U.S. Christians to experiment. Nowhere in American religious history do we find as many Catholics and Protestants working together to promote an experience of Christian spirituality as we do in the Fourth-Day Christian Cursillo movement.

Encountering "Eduardo"

When the Franks traveled to Mallorca in April 1998 on an Elderhostel trip, the highlight of their journey was not one of the many enjoyable Elderhostel activities but a hastily arranged meeting with Eduardo Bonnín, a man Bob describes in his journal entry "A Visit with Eduardo Bonnin" as having a "kind and gentle voice and smile" that "added much to our welcome."[4]

When Bob recalls his and Rhoda's visit to Bonnín's apartment, he specifically mentions Bonnín's support for Protestant versions of CdC: "He showed us a newspaper from Peoria, Illinois, where he visited in April 1997 for a Walk to Emmaus anniversary."[5] During one of our conversations at a coffeehouse in Rock Island, Illinois, Bob recalled that "Eduardo," as he and Rhoda called him, was "very supportive" of the denominationally rooted, interdenominational Via de Cristo. Bonnín, recalls Bob, was "happy to hear" that Lutherans "had their own Cursillo" and "that other Christians could experience it."[6]

The Franks, lifelong Lutherans, agree with current U.S. Catholic Cursillo executive director Victor Lugo's insistence that Catholic Cursillos

Robert Franks and Eduardo Bonnín, Palma de Mallorca, 1998.
Courtesy of Robert Franks.

were and are attractive to Protestants precisely because of the *charisms* (gifts of grace) that individual Christians experience during the weekend retreat. As Lugo told me, "Protestants saw what Catholics were doing after making their Cursillos. They saw their awakenings. They saw that cursillistas were not just going to church and giving money in the basket; they saw that they were transformed. What happened was that the Cursillo methodology helped their faith communities encounter Christ. One of the major things with Cursillo is that the person learns that he is truly an image, a likeness of God. The person has the freedom to choose his faith."[7] It was precisely a profound encounter with God, spiritual renewal, and the promise of a new community that propelled U.S. Protestants not only to make a Catholic Cursillo but to develop offshoots of the three-day weekend.

Like the Franks and Lugo, all the leaders of the Fourth-Day movements agree that Protestant Christians are attracted to Catholic Cursillo weekends' emphasis on connecting with Christ, and they work hard to maintain their genealogical link, historical and spiritual, to Catholic Cursillos. The five major Catholic Cursillo-derived Fourth-Day movements that have sprung up in the United States before spreading internationally—Tres Dias, Via de Cristo, Walk to Emmaus, Kairos Prison Ministry International, and the National Episcopal Cursillo—are based

A Focus on Christian Experience   89

directly on the Cursillo purpose and threefold methodology of piety, study, and action; and their movements' manuals and handbooks were written with a deep knowledge of and admiration for Eduardo Bonnín's vision. The fifteen rollos are in the same spirit and purpose as the original Mallorquín Catholic Cursillo weekend, and veteran cursillistas in all the five offshoots adhere closely to the CdC's *Leader's Guide* and other literature.

Bonnín's vision and presence is very much alive today with the current leaders of the Fourth-Day movements, who talk about him in reverent tones and with sincere admiration. Each January, the leaders of the five in-covenant Cursillo Fourth-Day weekends meet for a weekend of good food, wine, and conversation and share their successes, challenges, and hopes with each other.[8] For Tracy Schmidlin, a third-generation German American Lutheran and president of Via de Cristo from 2009 to 2011, Bonnín has a special place in her heart as he ushered in a wave of revitalized Christian spirituality that continues today. At a 2010 Via de Cristo Ultreya, Schmidlin publicly praised Bonnín as "the founder of Catholic Cursillo who we all owe a debt of gratitude to. He helped to revive his church, and the course he developed has helped thousands of Christians experience Christ. We are part of that legacy."[9] Schmidlin's husband, Paul, a Lutheran pastor ordained in the American Lutheran Church and currently pastor of a Missouri Synod Lutheran Church in Berkey, Ohio, also admires Bonnín as a man who ushered in a new wave of Christian renewal. The Schmidlins honor Bonnín because he understood that Christians need to have an experience of the heart, an experience that fills them with emotion and puts them in touch with Christ.[10]

Greg Engroff, the international director of Walk to Emmaus, also acknowledges that the movement he oversees owes a debt of gratitude to Eduardo Bonnín and Catholic Cursillos, but he also expresses some frustration with Catholic Cursillos' nonecumenical stance. He believes that U.S. Catholic Cursillos' antiecumenical, anti-intercommunion position "has hurt it," preventing it from growing as demonstrably as have Walk to Emmaus and other more ecumenical movements. Engroff believes that anyone who desires to can walk with Christ and that the Christian ecumenical, interdenominational route that Walk to Emmaus has taken is the best path because it is reaching more Christians who desire an experience with Christ: "We're in arm with the Methodist Church. Upper

Room Ministries is ecumenical, and we're having a good ole time being ecumenical, and we're attracting thousands of people who want to take a walk to Christ."[11] Like the Schmidlins, Engroff is grateful to Bonnín for founding the Catholic Cursillo weekend, which he knows is the basis for his own movement, and he believes that the Catholic Cursillos' emphasis on transformation of self and environment has carried over into Walk to Emmaus, where Christians are transformed into the "hands and feet of Christ" in the world.

Unlike their leaders, most U.S. cursillistas (Catholic and Protestant) do not know about their movement's history, let alone its rootedness in Bonnín's weekend Cursillos. Even though the Fourth-Day movement's websites post a paragraph or two about the Cursillos' Spanish origins, the only lay cursillistas I have spoken with who were familiar with Bonnín's name were the Catholic cursillistas of Mexican descent I interviewed in Phoenix; San Diego; and East Chicago, Indiana. These men and women were proud of the weekend's Spanish roots. Some of them had even met Bonnín in person and enthusiastically spoke about him during our interview. Some of the Cursillo regions, like Region 7 San Diego, post an abbreviated history of the movement on their webpages, and sometimes they identify Bonnín as the Cursillos' founder. But for the most part, cursillistas display little awareness of the Cursillos' larger history. This is intriguing and even puzzling, given Bonnín's extensive travel the United States. By contrast, cursillistas in Western European countries such as Italy and Portugal are more familiar with the history of the Cursillos and recognize Bonnín as the movement's founder. It was Portuguese cursillistas who in the mid-1980s placed a plaque on the home in Cala Figuera, Mallorca, where the first Cursillo de Cristiandad was held in 1944. The plaque, in Portuguese ceramic tiles, reads, "The world's first Cursillo was celebrated here from August 20 to 23, 1944. Portuguese Cursillistas. De Colores."[12]

European cursillistas who today travel to Cala Figuera as pilgrims to visit the seaside home of the 1944 weekend Cursillo take photos, much to the puzzlement of the current owner, a German who, when he purchased the house in the mid-1980s, was unaware of its historical significance.[13] And although Mallorquín cursillistas are intimately aware of their founder and the movement's history, noncursillista Mallorquines are unaware of Bonnín's theological and historical significance.[14] It is striking that nowhere in contemporary Mallorca's voluminous print and web-based tourist literature does one find any mention of Bonnín or the now global movement he created.

When we turn our attention to the CdC's deep impact on the five major Protestant Fourth-Day Christian movements, we find the historical and intentional use of Catholic Cursillo design, intentions, and methods that exists alongside a lack of knowledge of its broader Spanish and Mallorquín history. When we closely examine four of the five in-covenant non-Catholic Cursillo movements in the United States—Tres Dias, Via de Cristo, Walk to Emmaus, and the National Episcopal Cursillo (NEC)—we find that their visions and intentions are remarkably similar. Leaders in all four movements cite Catholic Cursillo as their inspiration to provide an environment in which individuals can experience Christ, a renewed self, and a dynamic Christian community. Yet Protestant laypeople today are not always aware of their movement's connections to Catholic Cursillos, or of their interconnectedness with other Protestant Fourth-Day weekends. As we will see, the founders of all of the Protestant Fourth-Day movements were intimately aware of the Catholic Cursillo movement and its history, and they patterned their weekends after it.

Although denominationalism matters deeply to the Lutheran-based Via de Cristo and the Methodist-based Walk to Emmaus, they have chosen to operate interdenominationally, remaining open to all Christians to experience. The modus operandi of Tres Dias, which is inspired by the Reform Tradition and interdenominationalism, is openness to all Christians. The NEC is the only in-covenant Cursillo spinoff that is not ecumenical. Like the CdC, the NEC is open only to members of its faith tradition. And like the CdC, the NEC has clearly defined reasons for not being interdenominational, all the while maintaining friendly relations with the other in-covenant Fourth-Day movements. The NEC, like the CdC, maintains that the Cursillo weekend was not intended to be interdenominational—denominationalism trumps inter-Christian experience for these two movements. When we examine the histories of Tres Dias, Walk to Emmaus, Via de Cristo, and the NEC, we are able to understand that the commonalities outweigh the differences among these groups, and that they are all working, as my interlocutors have told me, toward the same goal, to have a renewed relationship with Christ and to share their apostolic action with the rest of the world. Taken together, the in-covenant Protestant Fourth-Day movements have experienced success in the United States as well as globally precisely because of their interfaith and evangelical Christian orientation.

Tres Dias: Interdenominational Success and Evangelical Outreach

Reformed Church deacon David McManigal "instigated" the Tres Dias ("three days") movement in 1971, after he made a Catholic Cursillo weekend in West Haverstraw, New York. McManigal was "unofficially" invited to participate in the weekend course by his good friend and fellow IBMer Ron Rupert, a Catholic cursillista. McManigal says he was the only Protestant at his weekend Cursillo, held at a Marian shrine, and emphasizes, "It took some getting used to. However, I still trusted Ron, so I was determined to go with the flow of events. The events of Thursday evening were strange to me, but so was my first day at boot camp when I joined the U.S. Navy, and that didn't turn out too badly."[15]

By Friday, McManigal "Began to get into the spirit of things," and by Saturday evening he was "completely sold!" He describes his weekend experience as "an indescribably marvelous spiritual journey."[16] McManigal emerged from his weekend experience renewed, refreshed, and committed to making the Catholic Cursillo weekend available to fellow Protestants. He recalls his eagerness after his weekend experience:

> My Cursillo weekend seemed to turn me into the Energizer bunny—an unstoppable bundle of frenetic energy! Of course, some people really would have preferred that I just go away, or at least shut up! A Cursillo cross—a beautiful silver-on-ebony crucifix—had been presented to me at the closing of my Cursillo weekend. I wore it on my chest almost everywhere, though I had to keep it under my shirt at work. I talked to anybody and everybody I could corner for any length of time about developing a Protestant Cursillo. I worked—at first unofficially but later as an official team member—on every men's Cursillo weekend for the next year. I attended meetings of the Cursillo Council, at first uninvited, but later as an invited, nonvoting member. I participated in a Cursillo de Cursillos, a Cursillo-like weekend designed to train Cursillo leaders. Once again I was the lonely Protestant.[17]

McManigal, unlike the midwestern Protestants who participated in the Peoria Diocese Cursillo weekends, made his Cursillo in a Diocese whose Cursillo movement was officially nonecumenical. Although ecumenically minded lay Catholics invited him and other area Protestants to experience a Cursillo weekend, he grew frustrated with their reluctance to help organize a Protestant movement, given external pressures: "I pleaded, begged, wheedled . . . in short, I made myself a terrible nuisance to all the Cursillo leaders! However, it wasn't just selfish reluctance to share that deterred those leaders from acting. The relatively new English language Cursillo organization was dependent upon the more established Spanish Cursillo Council for support—especially from the Catholic Archdiocese, which could have shut down the Cursillo movement with a single edict. After a year of total failure, I gave up. I shed a few tears, put away my Cursillo cross, and went to bed, totally beaten and broken in spirit."[18]

McManigal's frustrations point to overlapping tensions within the early Cursillo movement. While laypeople wanted to reach out to Protestants, apprehensions about the movement's hierarchy made them hesitant to do so. Moreover, at the time, the Spanish-language Cursillo movement was more established than the English-speaking one and viewed as the template for an authentic weekend Cursillo. Cursillistas in the fledgling English-speaking movement were unwilling to offend their predecessor by advertising Protestant participation. Yet what seemed to McManigal to be a total rejection turned into the inclusion he had hoped for: "the day after" he put away his Tres Dias cross, McManigal received a phone call from Catholic cursillista Helmut Maier, a member of the Cursillo Council, "who said that the Council had finally decided to take the risk in a limited way." The council allowed McManigal to contact members of the Cursillo community to solicit help, to use Cursillo materials, such as talk outlines and team handbooks, "so long as we did not use the Cursillo name or involve the Council directly in any way."[19]

With Maier's help and with a list of names of area cursillistas, McManigal contacted the small number of Protestants in the New York–New Jersey–Connecticut region who had unofficially, under the radar of the National Secretariat, made a Catholic Cursillo. McManigal asked for their help in establishing a Protestant version of the weekend. Weeks later, a small group met at Hopewell Reformed Church in Hopewell Junction, New York, where McManigal was a deacon and had the support of the church's pastor, the Rev. Ian Todd. The group unanimously voted to start a nondenominational Protestant version of Catholic Cursillo.[20] The first task was deciding on a name for their movement, and group initially chose "Taizé Weekend," after the popular ecumenical Christian renewal weekend in France. Yet Taizé told them they could not use the name, "someone . . . suggested that we call the weekend just what it is: 'three days.' Strongly in favor of honoring the Spanish origin of the Cursillo movement, I translated "three days" to Spanish: Tres Dias. That name was adopted by acclamation."[21]

The men who formed Tres Dias were mindful of maintaining continuity with what they understood to be a Spanish Catholic movement of spirituality. Deciding on a name for their movement was just the beginning of a year of hard work and dedication that went into initiating a nondenominational Christian weekend encounter. They faced financial challenges as well as difficulties in securing an affordable and sufficiently large space, finding men and women to staff the Tres Dias weekends, and deciding on a Tres Dias cross.[22] All of these issues and challenges were overcome, McManigal asserts, through the close working together of Catholics and Protestants, all of whom were dedicated to the creation of a Protestant version of the Catholic Cursillos. Catholic cursillistas from the three-state region, including George and Carol Burke, who owned the Christian bookstore that supplied the first batch of Tres Dias crosses (which became the movement's signature cross), supported the Protestant initiators of Tres Dias, including McManigal, Rev. Todd, Bob and Mary Essert, and Episcopal priest George Conger. Commenting on the first official Tres Dias weekend held at the Our Lady of Hope Seminary, the "Oblate House" training facility for priests of Oblates of Mary Immaculate in the village of Newark, New York, McManigal stresses that ecumenical cooperation trumped denominational fault lines: "On the weekend, I don't believe that most participants paid attention to who was Catholic and who was Protestant. It just didn't matter. However, I do recall one fellow from an evangelical church saying over breakfast, 'If Grandma could only see me now, sharing my faith with a bunch of *Catholics!*'"[23]

As McManigal's exuberance and recollection of events highlights, the post–Vatican II era of U.S. Christianity marked a significant shift from the participants' parents' and grandparents' generation in the value now seen in seeking out shared experiences across denominational lines. From this first Tres Dias weekend in the Mid-Hudson community in Newburgh/Poughkeepsie, New York, the movement quickly spread to Pittsburgh, then Fairfield County, Connecticut; Northern New Jersey; Long Island; Maine; Central Connecticut; New Hampshire; and South Hudson, New York.[24] The movement remains especially strong in the Northeast but is also vibrant in the Midwest, especially in Rockford, Illinois, home of the

Northern Illinois Tres Dias community (NITD), which recently hosted the International Secretariat Meeting. As Tres Dias gained momentum, it created its own national secretariat in 1979, when it also drafted a national constitution and a handbook, *Essentials*. *Essentials* maintains the continuity of the Catholic Cursillo weekend but identifies Tres Dias as an interdenominational Christian movement, open to all Christians.[25]

In 1980 Tres Dias took the final steps to becoming an official organization. On July 11, 1980, at Poughkeepsie, New York, Tres Dias's existing communities ratified and adopted the constitution and *Essentials*. Similar to the Catholic Cursillos' organizational structure, each Tres Dias community was chartered as a local secretariat. John McKinney was elected the first president. Like most of the early members, McKinney was an ex–Navy officer and brought his eye for organizational details to the fledgling movement. Later in the year, Tres Dias was incorporated as a not-for-profit corporation in the state of New York, and it was recognized by the Internal Revenue Service shortly thereafter.

An International Secretariat was formed in 1985, as Tres Dias spread to South Korea and Germany, thanks to the efforts of West Point and U.S. Naval Academy graduates. As the international communities burgeoned, Tres Dias charter member Peter Scharfenberg singlehandedly shipped Tres Dias manuals and other materials to communities all over the world for over twenty years.[26] Scharfenberg's labors underscore the great lengths laity would go to further their movement and show again that laity have been central to Fourth-Day movements' successes.

The Mallorquín Cursillo, U.S. Cursillo, and Tres Dias movements, all founded by men who served their countries and desired a more disciplined spiritual life, would continue to attract men and women from the armed services. The first international Tres Dias communities were established by men in the Navy who started communities where they were stationed, and we see this pattern of global outreach with all of the other Fourth-Day movements.[27] McKinney, a Navy officer for three and a half years, says that "for most of those years I was dealing with military attaches at the foreign embassies in Washington, DC . . . plus handling the formal visits of foreign heads of navies as well as the formal visit of the Minister of Defense of the Netherlands."[28] A graduate of Harvard University's MBA program, he describes himself as "an organizer who likes challenges." As the current executive director of Tres Dias, McKinney serves as a "clearinghouse of information" for the movement. He believes he provides an important sense of continuity, since he was one of the first members of Tres Dias as well as its first president. McKinney has a deep sense of how the movement began and of its need to maintain historic continuity. Today, McKinney serves an overseer role and visits new communities to give them support and direction, and he maintains the movement's website.[29]

McKinney says he "cannot emphasize enough" the ecumenicism that is "at the heart of" Tres Dias and its continued success: "I made the weekend number four, a year after it started. In those years Catholics were rectors in the early weekends. There was even a retired Catholic bishop there. I had met him when I served in the kitchen at a Catholic Cursillo. He gave me communion even though he wasn't supposed to. He had been in a Japanese prison camp and didn't listen to any hierarchy or authority. He had no problem with my taking communion."[30] Here McKinney testifies to the willingness of Catholic clergy and laity to overlook the National Secretariat's stance against ecumenicism and intercommunion in the interest of a truly ecumenical Christian movement. As with those of other Protestant Fourth-Day movements and their offshoots formed in the 1970s and 1980s, Tres Dias weekends were staffed by Catholic and Protestant clergy and laity. According to McKinney, the demand for Cursillos among Catholics in the Newburgh area was so great that not enough Cursillo weekends could be offered. Tres Dias appealed to Catholics because it had "the same essentials" as the Catholic Cursillo movement and because was interdenominational, offering a place where Protestants and Catholics could worship together. The formation of Tres Dias illustrates the desire on the part of many U.S. Catholics for a shared Christian experience.

Yet despite Catholic clergy and laity's desire to work closely with their Protestant brothers and sisters, Gerald Hughes, then the national coordinator of U.S. Cursillos, was anything but pleased with this ecumenicism, as we saw in chapter 2. One by one, he told the leaders of the various Protestant Cursillo movements to cease the ecumenicism. Says McKinney: "Gerry went on to tell me that I'd have to answer to God if I thought that the movement was ecumenical. I looked at him for a moment and said, 'You're absolutely right. I will.' He was doing what he thought was right, I suppose, but we felt that this needed to be ecumenical and that that is what the Lord would want."[31]

McKinney went on to tell me that he had met Eduardo Bonnín on two occasions: the first was in the mid-1990s, when Bonnín joined him and the leaders of the five major Fourth-Day movements at their annual meeting. At this meeting, according to McKinney, Bonnín "was very enthusiastic about Tres Dias. He was there in Jacksonville, Florida, for another meeting and came to ours. He was *very* supportive of Tres Dias being ecumenical and told me that he personally supported it."[32]

McKinney's understanding of Bonnín, like the Franks', differs radically from the U.S. National Catholic Secretariat's position, which describes CdC's founder and his resulting movement as exclusivist. Bonnín and his inheritors have faced a constant battle over his legacy and the meanings of the weekend Cursillo. As we saw in chapter 2, Spanish bishops, well before the formation of the U.S. National Secretariat, saw themselves as preservers of an exclusivist movement. Yet Catholic and Protestant laity and clergy alike have interpreted the 1944 Mallorquín weekend as a universal Christian weekend of spirituality, and they have persevered in their interpretation of what they believe to be Bonnín's true legacy by maintaining ecumenically oriented weekends.

Tres Dias has spread from its roots in the northeastern United States to more than eighty communities nationwide and abroad. According to McKinney, Tres Dias's interdenominational Christian identity gives the movement great flexibility. Free from having to answer to one church body, it can bring together laity and clergy from many denominational backgrounds. Tres Dias's interdenominational status may also cost it some participants, according to McKinney, since some people may be more "inclined to make the weekend that is part of their denomination. Catholics tend to make a Catholic Cursillo and so on."[33] Yet the movement's strengths seem to outweigh its disadvantages. In the Northeast, Catholics, Reformed Church members, Presbyterians, and even Pentecostals experience the weekend together. The U.S. Tres Dias movement has been successful in the South and is gaining momentum in the Midwest, both regions with large numbers of nondenominational evangelical Christians, who are attracted to the nondenominational weekends.

Married couples like Chad and Deb Smits of Rockford, Illinois, members of Rockford's largest Christian church, which is nondenominational and evangelical, say that what attracted them to Tres Dias was precisely that it was *not* affiliated with any denomination, sect, or creed and that it "was a place where people who love Christ can come together and praise His name."[34] With the trend in the United States toward blending traditions and downplaying denominational affiliation, Tres Dias is growing at a steady pace, especially in the South and Midwest. Christians like Chad and Deb work to "live their Fourth" by attending Tres Dias

International Secretariat meetings, attending group reunions, and going to the monthly secuelas, Tres Dias's term for the Cursillo ultreyas.

The founders and current leaders of Tres Dias lean toward Christian inclusivity, and Tres Dias's success is in large part because of its U.S. and global leaders' embrace of evangelical, nondenominational Christians like Chad and Deb. The Pew Forum's much touted 2008 *U.S. Religious Landscape Survey* reported that members of evangelical Christian Protestant churches account for 26.3 percent of the U.S. adult population, a figure the report predicted will continue to grow. With its evangelical-friendly, nondenominational Christian stance, Tres Dias seems poised for further growth.

Walk to Emmaus: Interdenominationally Methodist and Growing

Like Tres Dias, the Fourth-Day movement Walk to Emmaus, formed in the mid-1970 and affiliated with the Upper Room Ministries of the United Methodist Church (UMC), is ecumenically Christian and interdenominational.[35] Unlike Tres Dias, Walk to Emmaus maintains its denominational ties, but it is open to anyone who desires to make the weekend encounter and be a part of a movement where individuals "are the hands and feet of Christ." Like the creators of Tres Dias, the three founders of Walk to Emmaus— the Rev. Robert ("Bob") Wood, Danny Morris, and Maxie Dunham—are Protestant Christians who attended a Catholic Cursillo. Wood, Morris, and Dunham were motivated by their experiences with Catholic Cursillos and committed to the belief that all Christians could be renewed and inspired to revitalize their churches. Morris and his wife, Rosalie, Lutheran residents of Miami, had made a Lutheran Cursillo in Miami Springs, and Dunham and his wife, Jerry, both Methodists, made a Catholic Cursillo in the Peoria diocese. All three couples—the Woods, Morris, and Dunhams—experienced "spiritual growth" in their marriages, and when they later formed Walk to Emmaus, they funneled their experiences as couples into the movement's handbooks.

The origin story, or cosmogony, of Upper Room Cursillos–turned–Walk to Emmaus rests on the ecumenical spirit of 1970s Catholics and Protestants. Rev. Wood, who was in his late thirties when he moved from the New York United Methodist Conference to the Peoria, Illinois, Conference in 1973, says he was impressed as a young pastor by how active the 3,500-member Illinois conference was. Moreover, he noticed that "the people who were really involved in the life of the church, the most active members," were cursillistas. "I looked around the church and noticed that all of the people who were in leadership positions, whether it be religious education, evangelism, etc., were people who had gone through Cursillo. I was intrigued and wanted to find out for myself what this course was all about."[36] In addition to the energy of Methodist laymen and women, Wood was impressed by the then-bishop of Peoria, Edward O'Rourke, who had started Cursillos in prison. In the Peoria diocese at the time, Wood emphasizes, "Cursillo really was the springboard for all of the inner-city work that was being done."[37] Wood went on to make his Cursillo a year after his arrival to Peoria and says it was an important step in his Christian journey, propelling him to Christian action: "Cursillo was a renewing experience for me. I have been a Wesleyan all of my life. I have kept journals just as Wesley did. Cursillo has helped me put my faith into *action* and I have had a glorious ministry ever since."[38]

What also impressed Wood was the ecumenicism of the Peoria Cursillos. In his *Walk to Emmaus: The Early History*, he writes that the Peoria Catholic community was "deeply committed to Vatican II theology, which encouraged Catholics to Christianize their environments and become more accepting of other Christians."[39] During his own weekend experience, Wood observed men and women from a variety of Christian backgrounds who made the weekend and went on to renew their churches. While Wood's weekend was denominationally Catholic, he found the three days to be as ecumenical as a Christian gathering could be, with theological details downplayed in favor of what united the various Christian groups represented at the weekend retreat: "Cursillos in Peoria were ecumenical, catholic with a little 'c.' The priest at my Cursillo told me, 'I cannot invite you to take communion because you are not Catholic, but I cannot *deny* you communion.' So I took communion."[40]

I have interviewed dozens of Protestant men and women from the Midwest and Northeast who received communion from priests involved with the Cursillo they attended. The National Catholic Secretariat's official stance against intercommunion motivated Protestants like Wood to create Protestant spinoffs of the Catholic weekend. A lifelong member of the Reformed Church and a deacon, Wood quickly became active in the ecumenical Cursillo movement in the Peoria diocese; he served on teams and as an advisor to Protestant ministers who went through the weekend. He worked closely with Father Tom Henseler, a good friend and Catholic priest then working in the Peoria diocese. Father Henseler was the spiritual director of the Peoria diocese Cursillos when Wood made his Cursillo at Bradley University's Newman Center in 1973. The two later traveled to Hong Kong, where they helped establish a Cursillo community there. Wood was soon invited to Nashville to head what were then called Upper Room Cursillos. He moved there with his wife, Jan, and their family, wanting to help spread Cursillos among Protestants because he was "continually amazed by what I saw happen with people": "The benefits of the weekend experience are truly amazing—people's faith is recaptured. We find people go through the weekend and all of a sudden they get involved in their church again, they go from being nominal to active members. I've seen marriages renewed as a result of men and women making the course. The results of the weekend are wonderful."[41]

Wood was committed to furthering the Cursillo method and purpose because he saw for himself that it worked. Though he describes himself as a "lifelong Christian," he emerged from the seventy-two hours a changed man, ready to "tackle the world." In Nashville he found a "widespread hunger" for the Cursillo weekend among Protestant men and women.

> In Nashville we were developing a Protestant, ecumenical version of the Catholic Cursillo, and there was such a demand out there for the weekend experience. People would fly into Nashville, get trained, and fly home to start their own Cursillos. We trained Episcopalians who took Cursillo back to Mississippi, Texas, and Washington state, and we worked with Lutherans who took it home with them to Atlanta, Miami, and Virginia. What we found was a smattering of Protestants who had gone through the course and who needed help getting it started in their own communities.[42]

Rev. Wood provides a vivid description of the popularity of Cursillo weekends among American Protestants in the 1960s, 1970s and 1980s. Christians of all stripes were seeing their Catholic neighbors and friends make a weekend course and emerge new people with a new focus. They wanted this experience for themselves and they went to men like Wood in Nashville for training on how to spread the movement to their own communities and in their churches. I asked Wood how he went about forming Walk to Emmaus after Upper Room received word from Gerry Hughes that Upper Room Ministries could no longer use the name *Cursillo*: "We decided to keep as much of the weekend as we could. We asked, 'What is the kernel here? What is the guiding priority? We held onto the essence of the course—the theology of grace—which is the same for the Catholics. It doesn't matter if you are Episcopalian, Presbyterian, Catholic, or Methodist, you still believe in God's grace."[43]

With the emphasis on grace linking Walk to Emmaus to Catholic Cursillos and other Fourth-Day movements, Upper Room made some changes in terminology, including using the Greek word *agape* instead of *palanca*, which is Spanish for "lever" and is interpreted as "sacrifice" by cursillistas: "The Catholic Cursillo uses the word *palanca*, which means sacrifice. We chose the word *agape* because *palanca* is grace—Paul's grace. We decided to let agape, love, be the vehicle for grace. We took the course (Catholic Cursillo) little part by little part and tried to make our course as close as possible. We are close scripturally and our essence is the same, so we're *very* close to Cursillo."[44]

Wood and his Upper Room Ministries colleagues Dunham and Morris decided to develop Upper Room Ministries Walk to Emmaus, drawing on their experiences in the Catholic Cursillo movement and on Wood's observations of a Tres Dias weekend. As Wood emphasizes, Walk to Emmaus was the name chosen for the movement after they were informed by the National Secretariat of Catholic Cursillos that they could not use the word *Cursillo* in their weekends or in their literature. Wood named the movement Walk to Emmaus after reading Luke 24:13-32 and exclaiming: "What I have just read is exactly what happens on our weekends. We read scripture, break bread together, eyes are opened and hearts set on fire, and people's lives are changed so much that they can't wait to run back to their homes and tell how they have met Jesus in the breaking of the bread!"[45]

After renaming their movement, the Upper Room staff met to write the fifteen talks given by clergy and laity during the weekend. While the method and structure of the Catholic Cursillo weekend and its fifteen rollos remained the inspiration and basis for the structure of Walk to Emmaus, "we had to change all our manuals and terminology to appeal to Protestants."[46] The staff enlisted the help of theologians, psychologists, and church history scholars to ensure that "we provided the most theologically sound, spiritually uplifting, and emotionally supportive weekend possible."[47] Another aim was to base the talks in John Wesley's understanding of grace but retain universal appeal to all Christians.[48] The weekend talks were rooted in Scripture and the topics for the new weekend's talks were chosen, all of which discussed grace from multiple Methodist-inspired perspectives: prevenient grace, justifying grace, means of grace, obstacles to grace, and sanctifying grace.[49] Wood reports that "ninety-nine percent" of the established Upper Room Cursillo communities were pleased with the new course and that the talks reflected "a deeper Scriptural awareness" and a more ecumenical understanding of Christ. All but two of the then-seventy-two Upper Room Cursillo communities changed their name to Walk to Emmaus, and the two that refused eventually relented, given the legal arguments of the National Secretariat of Catholic Cursillos.[50]

Danny Morris, another of the three founders of Walk to Emmaus, draws a clear distinction between the National Catholic Secretariat and Peoria's Catholics. Like Woods and many other Protestant Fourth-Dayers, he had a run-in with Gerry Hughes. He claims that unlike the Peoria Catholic Cursillo community and Father Charles Giacosta, then the Nashville Catholic community's spiritual advisor, the National Secretariat was openly hostile to Protestants:

> The Peoria Cursillos were ecumenical, and this was a great problem for the Catholic Cursillo Center in Dallas. Upper Room Ministries has always been ecumenical and interracial, and this was a problem for the Catholics. I was on a trip with my family to New Mexico—part family trip, part helping to set up an Upper Room Cursillo there—and I stopped in Dallas to meet with Gerry Hughes, the director of the Catholic Cursillos. I talked with him about setting up Upper Room Cursillos and wanted to know if he could help us out. He told me to talk with Father Giacosta, who was then the spiritual director of the Catholic Cursillos in Nashville. I later realized that Gerry Hughes didn't understand or know anything about Upper Room Ministries when I spoke with him. When I returned to Nashville I met with Father Giacosta, who was two blocks from Upper Room Ministries, about setting up Upper Room Cursillos. He was very, very supportive and helped us get many Cursillos started. I called Gerry Hughes up on the phone to give him the good news of the Upper Room Cursillos, and he was livid. He was so angry and he chewed me out over the phone, saying that Father Gioacosta should have NEVER told us to do this. He was so angry and said that "this is the worst thing for Catholics!"[51]

While Wood is diplomatic in his depiction of Hughes, Morris depicts the National Cursillo Center as hostile to Methodists, adding that Hughes "threatened to sue Upper Room" if they did not change their movement's name and cease using the name *Cursillo* in their name and literature. Yet while the U.S. National Catholic Secretariat did not support ecumenical Cursillos, lay Catholic men, women, and certain diocesan priests worked closely with Protestants to get their own movements off the ground. Morris, like Wood, emphasizes the support and cooperation Upper Room received from Peoria- and Nashville-area Catholics and said, "We never would have succeeded as a movement if it were not for their help and assistance."[52]

The support of ecumenically minded lay Catholics and clergy has been instrumental in the formation of Protestant Cursillo weekends. As of 2011, there are 400 Walk to Emmaus ("Emmaus") communities worldwide, 302 of which are in United States. Ninety-three of the Emmaus communities are international. According to Greg Engroff, international director of Walk to Emmaus, African Emmaus communities are among the strongest: Mozambique, Ghana, and Zimbabwe. South Africa, or "Africa South," as Engroff likes to call the region, has a national board of directors and eighteen communities under the board. Emmaus is also strong in Australia, where there are twenty-five communities, as well as the United Kingdom, according to Engroff, where there are five communities.[53]

Engroff points out that Walk to Emmaus has been "very successful" in bringing people to Christ and having them become "the hands and feet of Christ." He believes that his movement has been successful largely because of its ecumenicism:

> We're still growing and others are not. Now, I don't want to brag or anything, and I need to be humble, but what we are doing works. I'm looking for people who want to be the hands and feet of God. I look for people who are dropping their nets and helping people. I look for people who sell their home and move to Africa, where they help AIDS victims. Now it doesn't have to be this radical, but I can't tell you how many stories I have heard from people who felt called by the Holy Spirit after the course was over, the Fourth Day, to make a major change in their lives.[54]

Engroff, like Wood, argues that Walk to Emmaus is "working" because men's and women's lives are transformed and they are empowered to "be the hands and feet of Christ." We are talking about a lot of hands and feet; Engroff reports that as of 2011, more than 1 million people have been through a Walk to Emmaus weekend.[55]

What Engroff does not mention is that Walk to Emmaus owes at least some of its success to the marketing prowess of Upper Room Ministries, an arm of the United Methodist Church (UMC). Even a brief glance at Upper Room's website will show the efforts the ministry has taken to advertise and sell Emmaus and related ministries. Of all of the Fourth-Day movements, Walk to Emmaus has the most sophisticated, professional website. There those interested can order a variety of books, magazines, zines, and other Christian merchandise. The selection is impressive, as is the website's efforts to reach as many demographics as possible. Like the other Fourth-Day movements and their offshoots, Walk to Emmaus sells its signature crosses, T-shirts, coffee mugs, buttons, and other Christian items. The movements are part of the larger history of American Christian retailing, what religious studies scholar Colleen McDannell calls "a striking example of how lay men and women successfully integrate religious concerns, popular culture, and profit making."[56]

While the Walk to Emmaus website offers information on where to find an Emmaus community and how to stay connected, the Emmaus movement continues to spread in the way the other Fourth-Day movements have spread: by word of mouth. In today's religious marketplace, "word of mouth" has taken on new meanings as movements' successes are enhanced by websites, the Internet, and Facebook, where cursillistas establish profiles and network with each other. The Internet and the web have enhanced the possibilities of movements' successes. Though the websites put a new spin on the weekend experiences and provide 24/7 information for all seekers, the manner in which the movements spread is still somewhat random. People hear about the courses from people they know, and they check out websites that give them more detailed information. More traditional "word of mouth" also remains an important marketing device for Cursillo weekends, with cursillistas telling friends, family, and neighbors about their weekend experiences and encouraging them to make a course.

According to Wood, the way Walk to Emmaus has spread has been and remains a random process, and he credits the Holy Spirit with leading people:

> It really happens almost by accident. Americans make the course and are renewed. Then when they visit another country they decide

to get a Walk to Emmaus community going. We've seen this happen time and time again, and people from other countries come to us and ask us to get the course started over there. The Hong Kong Walk to Emmaus community was started by Australians, Americans, and some folks from England. Then some Cantonese-speaking ministers asked us to get Walk to Emmaus started in Chinese churches. The Chinese president of the United Methodist Church went to Nashville and invited me and Tom Henseler to bring the course there. We went and helped them set up Walk to Emmaus in Cantonese! The Brazil Walk to Emmaus community got going after a Brazilian, who had made his course in Nashville, took it home. The African Walk to Emmaus community was started after a Nigerian student who made the course in Nashville went home and introduced it. This is the way the Gospel is meant to be spread and it is the Holy Spirit leading the way.[57]

Victor Pérez, international spiritual director of Walk to Emmaus, concurs with McKinney and Wood that the movement has spread because of the Holy Spirit working through people. The vivacious Pérez has a role akin to what Malcolm Gladwell called the "connector" in his popular book *The Tipping Point*.[58] Pérez says that the most exciting part of his job is "helping people to connect and to experience Christ's love. I love my job because I get to connect people. It is beautiful, just beautiful."[59] Pérez, a native Puerto Rican and "lifelong Methodist," made his Walk to Emmaus weekend in San Juan in 1997 because "I wanted to do the course in the language of my soul and with my people."[60] Pérez was appointed to his position, which is part of Upper Room Ministries, in 2004, and his job is to help start international communities as well as be a sounding board for questions and concerns that arise in the international community. When we spoke in 2010, Pérez was preparing to help a group of Christians in Sarawak, Malaysia, start a course. He had recently returned from Estonia, where he had helped Christians there start a course.

According to Pérez, international Walk to Emmaus communities are established because they are initiated by men and women who have traveled to the country or who have some kind of personal contact or connection to the place. This pattern is like that of Catholic cursillistas who have moved domestically as well as those who have been stationed abroad in the Navy or Army. Once a community is established internationally, Walk to Emmaus members there help spread the movement to nearby places, for example, Estonians introduced the weekend encounter to Russia, where there is today an active movement, according to Pérez. The Malaysian course he was preparing for when we spoke was organized and staffed in part by men and women from Singapore and Hong Kong. Returning to the important role technology and the web play in today's religious movements, Pérez mentioned that some communities have their weekly reunion groups online: "Some people hold reunion meetings each week via the Internet. They set up a chat group and are faithful to it. It really does work for them. They get together once a month in person or once every other month and have breakfast or lunch somewhere. These Internet reunion groups have been successful in Australia because people are very spread out there and have to be very intentional about getting together in person. Internet reunion groups can be done and there are many successful cases of this."[61]

While the Internet provides an important and even necessary medium for cursillistas to stay in touch, most reunion groups continue to meet in person, often for a meal. The majority of cursillistas I have encountered meet for breakfast, lunch, or dinner once a week, twice a week, or monthly. Pérez says that meeting over a meal ensures the success of the movement: "I've heard many stories of reunion groups that meet once a week for breakfast, early in the morning at 6 A.M. before work. Many of these groups meet at a Cracker Barrel, and the servers and managers get to know them. I have heard lots of stories of servers going up to the reunion group members and asking them to keep family members in their prayers. I have heard so many beautiful stories of this nature. The manager of the restaurant provides the space for these groups to meet and in turn receives a wonderful outreach. People realize that these groups are here for more than just breakfast. They are there for prayer and fellowship."[62] According to Pérez and others with whom I have spoken, Fourth-Day movements' reunion group meetings have become, advertently or inadvertently, a way of bringing others in to the movement.

Leaders in Tres Dias, Walk to Emmaus, and Via de Cristo confirm that their movements have spread in a similar way, by men and women who have been "moved by the Spirit" and who take the course to places they have visited, whether this is the local Cracker Barrel or a distant state or country. The most significant distances are not always geographic: sometimes the "faraway," as Bonnín referred to them, are removed from God spiritually but can be found at the local diner.

Wood, Pérez, and McKinney, and leaders in the other Protestant Fourth-Day movements, also highlight the ecumenical dialogue and the support that they give each other. Wood sent several letters to the National Lutheran Secretariat in the formative years of Via de Cristo, offering guidance and ecumenical outreach, and he worked with Tres Dias and Via de Cristo, as well as Peoria Catholics and Nashville Catholics as Walk to Emmaus was being established.[63] And, as Morris indicated above, Father Charles Giacosta and hundreds of other Nashville Catholics helped staff and run the first Walk to Emmaus weekends held there.[64] While the National Secretariat of Catholic Cursillos took issue with the ecumenical courses offered by Tres Dias, Walk to Emmaus, and Via de Cristo (formerly called Lutheran Cursillo), Catholic laity and priests worked hard to help their Protestant brothers and sisters launch their own weekends.

Via de Cristo: Lutheran and Ecumenical

Like its sister Fourth-Day organizations Tres Dias and Walk to Emmaus, the Lutheran Cursillo movement was inspired by and is deeply rooted in Catholic Cursillos. The Lutheran movement was affiliated with the National Lutheran Secretariat (NLS), formed in 1981. Thirty-two Lutheran men, women, and pastors gathered for the inaugural NLS meeting, and fourteen local Lutheran secretariats from across the United States were represented over the weekend. As we have seen with the other interdenominational movements, the majority of Lutheran Cursillos changed their official name from Lutheran Cursillos to Via de Cristo only after the leaders were specifically asked to do so by Gerry Hughes, then executive director of the Catholic Cursillos. According to the minutes of NLS of April 4–6, 1982, "Gerry Hughes, Exec. Director of the Roman Catholic National Cursillo Center in Dallas, Texas, presented us with an overview of their position on nondenominational versus denominational Cursillos and what is required to be authorized by them to use the name Cursillo."[65] The National Secretariat's position, as I have noted, was that movements could use the name *Cursillo* only if they were denominationally specific. The National Catholic Secretariat's reasoning has been that movements like Lutheran Cursillo and Walk to Emmaus could not maintain ecumenicism and stay true to the origins of the Cursillo de Cristiandad movement. Via de Cristo acknowledges the Catholic position in the notes from a gathering on February 4–6: "The Catholic Movement is requiring that all candidates be Catholic, and all team members and

Spiritual leaders also be Catholic. They are asking the Lutheran Movement to do the same [require all team members and spiritual leaders to be Lutheran] or change our name. Jerry [sic] [Hughes] supplied copies of the Episcopal Articles of Operation, stating we must have Articles of Operation that refer to the Lutheran Movement for the base doctrine."[66]

Via de Cristo's archived records from 1981–85 reveal men and women who were deeply committed to the purpose and methods of Catholic Cursillos de Cristiandad but wanted to maintain ecumenicism and to open the weekend experience to any Christian man or woman, not just Lutherans. Faced with Hughes's ultimatum, Lutheran secretariats had to decide either to remain ecumenical or enforce denominational exclusivity. The 1981–85 records show that while this was a liberating time for Lutherans who saw a split from Catholic Cursillos as healthy for the movement, some experienced a difficult split from their Lutheran brethren as they decided to go the Catholic route of denominational specificity. While the majority of the Lutheran secretariats voted to branch off of Catholic Cursillos and maintain ecumenicism, some groups, such as the North Carolina East group in 1981, decided to stay with Roman Catholic Cursillos and maintain a denominationally specific focus. The National Catholic Secretariat allowed these groups to continue using the title *Lutheran Cursillo*.

The Lutheran secretariats that voted to stay ecumenical adopted the following position statement at the February 1982 weekend gathering:

> Inasmuch as those convened together as the National Lutheran Cursillo Secretariat have determined the following to be our collective objectives:
>
> 1) Renewal should be consistent with Lutheran Theology and be "Lutheran based."
> 2) The Authentic Cursillo Method, as developed by Bishop Juan Hervas, should be maintained.
> 3) We wish to remain open to non-Lutheran participation.
> 4) We wish to provide a National organization to provide support and basic guidance.
> 5) We wish to develop and sustain a relationship to each of the Lutheran bodies.
>
> In that the General Secretariat of the Roman Catholics has determined that Authentic Cursillo requires that all team members and

all candidates be of the same denomination and in that one of the objectives of the Lutheran Community is to allow non-Lutheran participation: is therefore recommended by the National Lutheran Cursillo Secretariat that a change in name shall be adopted to allow our objectives to be accomplished.[67]

When we examine the minutes and notes from the Lutheran secretariats from 1981 to 1985, we find that Lutheran cursillistas entertained the ideas of merging with the interdenominational Methodist Walk to Emmaus Movement, merging with a then-existing Lutheran Kogudus movement, retaining the Cursillo name without licensing, or changing the name of the movement.[68] The name Via de Cristo was unanimously accepted as the name for the Lutheran movement at the February 6–8, 1986, NLS meeting at St. Michael's Lutheran Church in Ottawa Lake, Michigan. Via de Cristo was preferred over a long list of other proposed names, including Arnion ("lamb," in Greek), Christlich ("Christ-like," in German), Christlich leben ("Christian living"), Unterricht ("course" or "instruction"), De Colores, Open Door, Pilgrimage, Another Look, Sola Gratia ("grace alone," in Latin), and Christ Encounter.[69] Those involved with the newly named Via de Cristo believed that the movement's strength rested in its "ecumenical flavor" and that like their Catholic Cursillo parent, Via de Cristo and other "Cursillo-type weekends" were keys that, once turned by the Holy Spirit, "opened people's hearts."[70] An earlier vote to change "Fourth Day" to "Pilgrimage" was reversed, as the founders expressed a desire to keep the weekend encounter as close to the original Catholic Cursillo de Cristiandad as possible. As the historical records indicate, the founders and early leaders of Via de Cristo saw Hervás, not Bonnín, as the movement's founder, indicating the National Catholic Secretariat's influence. The current National Catholic Secretariat acknowledges Bonnín as the originator of the movement and Hervás as an important early supporter, and this interpretation has influenced current Via leaders, who all acknowledge Bonnín, not Hervás, to be the movement's founder.

Via de Cristo experienced impressive growth during its first ten years of existence. In the NLS March 1991 newsletter, President Wayne Ford expressed his enthusiasm: "We've come a long way, baby! We have grown from thirty delegates to fifty-six and from fourteen member secretariats to twenty-five. But more importantly, over 30,000 Christians throughout the United States have attended a Lutheran Via de Cristo/Cursillo."[71]

As in its sister movement Tres Dias, those involved in Via de Cristo today value their Catholic Cursillo roots and maintain that successful Fourth-Day movements model themselves on the seventy-two-hour experience that Eduardo Bonnín and his friends crafted in 1944. Today's leaders use words like *integrity* and *authenticity* to describe the importance of maintaining the link to Catholic Cursillos de Cristiandad as developed in Mallorca. As part of a history that links them to Bonnín's weekend Cursillo, an immigrant to the United States, Via de Cristo cursillistas carry "green cards" in their wallets and purses to show not just that they are dedicated to the piety, study, and action that are hallmarks of the Fourth-Day movements but also that they are mindful of their roots and that "we are all immigrants."[72] The Evangelical Lutheran Church of America, with which the National Lutheran Secretariat is affiliated, maintains a proimmigrant stance that includes outreach to Spanish-speaking migrants from Latin America.[73]

Although initiated by laypeople, Via de Cristo and other Fourth-Day movements adhere to their national organizations' rules and regulations. There is a hierarchy for each movement—for Via de Cristo it is the National Lutheran Secretariat—and while local communities and their members have certain freedoms when sponsoring courses, they have to follow a set of guidelines in order to maintain good relations with their national organization as well as other Fourth-Day movements. Communities that attempt to break from established Fourth-Day traditions are monitored, and if they continue to follow what the Fourth-Day movement leaders consider to be questionable, ahistoric practices, they are asked to disaffiliate and start their own movement. The Nebraska Via de Cristo community, for example, was "watched closely" in 1991 when it scheduled a two-day rather than a three-day weekend. Because they were not "keeping with the Method of the Movement," this community was asked to disassociate. Via de Cristo leaders, as with the other in-covenant Fourth-Day movements described in this chapter, consider the Mallorquín method laid out by Eduardo Bonnín and a small group of colleagues to be the standard by which they judge their movement's integrity. Cutting the weekend by one day, as the Nebraska community did, is seen as cutting out important talks and events that make an impact on the candidate. To the leaders in all of the Fourth-Day movements, the talks, poster sessions, small-group discussions, chapel events, and meals that take place during the seventy-two hours are considered crucial to maintaining the integrity and authenticity of the weekend.[74]

A Focus on Christian Experience

While the NLS, like the other organizations affiliated with the Fourth-Day movements, wants individual communities to express themselves during the courses in ways that reflect the surrounding culture and region, they do not tolerate deviation from what they all call "the essentials," which include the seventy-two-hour format, the fifteen rollos and topics, and the overarching principles of piety, study, and action—all of which were part of the original Cursillos de Cristiandad in Mallorca.[75] Tracy Schmidlin, president of Via de Cristo from 2009 to 2011, calls the many add-ons to a course "adiaphora," saying that the nonessentials such as elaborate skits, role-playing, and the abundance of gifts and food needs to be pared down to get back to "what is really important: study, piety, and action as outlined by Eduardo Bonnín."[76] As part of her role as Via de Cristo president, Schmidlin visited Via de Cristo communities across the United States and advised them on how to get back to the essentials and pare down their courses. She admits that this is difficult, as the cursillistas "love to make their courses elaborate. That's just what we do in America; we think that bigger is better."[77] Thom Neal, the 2009–10 National Episcopal Cursillo president, agrees with Schmidlin and asserts that there are "way too many add-ons in the courses. We need to examine this and make some changes, because it can be overwhelming for the candidates to have everything thrown at them."[78]

Fourth-Day movements' presidents monitor the adiaphora of weekend retreats and the overall health of their Fourth-Day communities. I was invited to attend a Via de Cristo ultreya, a reunion of reunion groups, in Orlando, Florida, in late January 2010. At that time, the Heart of Florida community was experiencing serious tensions, since the current president of its secretariat wanted to make substantive changes to the community's weekends, including shortening the weekend to two days (as the earlier Nebraska community had done). Moreover, the Heart of Florida community had failed to hold regular Via de Cristo weekends for two years and was on the National Lutheran Secretariat's "watch list." Schmidlin and Steve Gielda, Via de Cristo's vice president of outreach, spent the afternoon with approximately sixty men and women who were part of Heart of Florida to help them "get back on track." The president of the Heart of Florida community was notably absent. As one Heart of Florida Via de Cristo member told me, the president had "issues with the National Via de Cristo telling him how to run things."

All of the Heart of Florida men and women at this event expressed their hope that their community would rebound and regain the vibrancy of its early years, but as one woman told me, "it is ultimately up to the Holy Spirit. If this community is meant to continue and grow then it will." Her sentiments were echoed by the other cursillistas with whom I spoke; all of them emphasized that if "it is meant to happen it will because the Holy Spirit is behind it all. We are mere instruments." While the Fourth-Day leaders all say that the Holy Spirit guides their movements, they also believe that some human leadership is necessary as well to sustain the health of their movement. They do their best to help make their movements positive places for spiritual growth and Christian fellowship, and they work to keep their organization "authentic" and "in covenant." Via de Cristo's leaders believe that their movement has been successful in balancing the Holy Spirit's lead and humans' work. According to Gielda, as of the end of 2010, the number of individuals who have been through a Via de Cristo weekend numbers just over 100,000.[79] "Via," as members call it, is active in every U.S. state except Hawaii, Alaska, Idaho, and New Mexico. Internationally, Via is active in Finland, Latvia, Papua New Guinea, and Sweden.[80] It would seem that the movement's combination of denominational rootedness and openness to Christian ecumenicism is part of the reason for its success.

National Episcopal Cursillo: Nonecumenicism

Like its fellow Fourth-Day in-covenant movements, National Episcopal Cursillos (NEC) is rooted in Catholic Cursillos de Cristiandad. Also like the other Fourth-Day movements, the NEC is an apostolic movement that is reinvigorating churches, in this case those of the Episcopal Church. According to Sue Davis, the NEC's office administrator who has been a part of the movement since 1981, "one of the great strengths of the Cursillo movement is that it calls Christians to be what they are designed to be. The NEC, like the other movements, is working on building Christ-centered leaders."[81] Davis further emphasizes that "the bottom line is that the Cursillo movement is the best evangelizing tool the Episcopal Church has."[82]

Unlike its sister organizations Tres Dias, Walk to Emmaus, and Via de Cristo, however, the Episcopalian Fourth-Day movement has been able to retain the word *Cursillo* in its name and in its literature because it is not ecumenical. One has to be Episcopalian to make an NEC weekend. According to Thom Neal, "the other movements chose not to be constrained by the Roman Catholic licensing, but we have chosen to abide by the licensing and as such we are not ecumenical."[83] Like the National Catholic Secretariat, the NEC argues that "Cursillo was not intended to draw Christians from other denominations."[84] For the NEC, Cursillo is about "one thing: equipping Christians from specific denominations to serve Christ as His apostles in the world."[85] The NEC website nonetheless states goals remarkably similar to those of the other Fourth-Day movements: "The goal of Cursillo is to bring the world to Christ by empowering adult Christian leaders through the use of a specific method that is taught as part of a three-day weekend. The method, an evangelistic tool, enables and encourages Christians to live out their Baptismal covenant to serve Christ."[86]

Episcopal Cursillos have been around since 1970, when the first was held in the Diocese of Iowa, after the Episcopal diocesan bishop of Iowa sent leaders to Catholic Cursillo weekends for training.[87] In the NEC, an Episcopal team serves and leads Episcopal candidates. In 1972, the Diocese of West Texas became the second diocese to offer an Episcopal weekend. Iowa's diocese has always held separate men's and women's weekends, and West Texas has always held coed weekends. The Episcopal Cursillo movement spread from Iowa and West Texas, and those dioceses whose Cursillo weekends are rooted in Iowa offer separate men's and women's weekends, while those rooted in West Texas offer coed weekends.[88] This difference is significant, as my Mallorquín interlocutors emphasized that Bonnín was open to interdenominational Cursillos but not to coed Cursillos. Technically, coeducational Cursillo weekends (Via de Cristo offers coed weekends as well) are not in covenant with the CdC.

Like all of the Fourth-Day movements, the NEC adopted the symbols of crosses, caterpillars, cocoons, butterflies, rainbows, and roosters, which signaled new life and new ways of looking at the world. Episcopalian cursillistas were encouraged to join a reunion group, which in the early, formative years was called an "environmental group reunion."[89] Episcopalian cursillistas, like their counterparts in Tres Dias, Walk to Emmaus, Via de Cristo, and the Catholic Cursillos, were called on to "affect their environments," using Bonnín's term.

In 2009, the NEC changed its logo from a rainbow and a rooster to the Episcopalian crest with the motto "Growing Christ-Centered Leaders." According to Neal, the NEC adopted the new logo to "show that we are still a part of the Church" and because "the focus on the rooster and rainbow has become downright silly, and most Episcopalians cannot relate to these images."[90] Neal believes that the original meaning of the rooster and rainbow has been lost and that the song "De Colores" is done best in its original form or by an authentic mariachi band. He worries that the NEC will seem racist because "when you get a bunch of Anglo Episcopalians trying to sing 'De Colores' and dressing up like roosters and wearing rainbow gear, it takes away from the course and unintentionally makes fun of the foundations of the course."[91] Neal said that in his diocese, they have gone through "great pains" to deal with issues of race and that making "De Colores" into "a kind of 'Frito Bandito' kind of thing where Anglo Episcopalians are wearing sombreros and speaking with a bad Spanish accent[, which would be] ethnocentric, even racist, however unintentionally."[92] During our conversation he spoke about the separate Spanish-speaking and English-speaking NEC movements in Los Angeles. Neal said he has mixed feelings about the two separate movements because "we should really be part of one movement, but I do understand the need for Spanish-speaking men and women to have a place where they feel comfortable. My fear though is that we end up creating divisions instead of unity."[93]

Yet "including" Spanish-speaking Episcopalians in the English-speaking movement has not exactly been successful, either. In Neal's own diocese of Upper South Carolina, the 200-plus Spanish-speaking parishioners who attend St. Mary's Church in Columbia are being encouraged to make an NEC weekend in English because there is currently no Spanish-speaking course. Neal noted the delicate nature of accommodating Spanish-speaking Episcopalians and the dilemma of not wanting to create two churches and two movements but wanting to reach out to what Neal called the "hidden Hispanic community" of men, women, and children who are migrant farmworkers and speak Spanish exclusively.[94] Neal said that at a recent Episcopal Cursillo Leaders Workshop (ECLW) he attended, eight women leaders from the Dominican Republic attended who spoke only Spanish. These women had been on an NEC weekend and came to share their experiences as well as those of their community. To overcome the language barrier, interpreters at the women's tables translated everything the women said for the other leaders present. Neal said this "worked fairly well" but that it was not ideal, as the translations interrupted the flow of the meeting. He admitted he is unsure how to make the meetings run better. Neal's comments reflect the sentiments of the other Fourth-Day movement leaders, who all say they want to make their movements more diverse, but who do not want two separate movements (one in Spanish and one in English). The

Catholic Cursillo Spanish-language and English-language movements are mostly separate, and the Mexican-descent cursillistas I interviewed from the Spanish-speaking movement are fiercely proud of their culture and would not want to be part of the "blancos'" movement. While their children and grandchildren might join the English-speaking movement, these Latinos are satisfied with having their own movement within a larger U.S. and global movement.

All of the Fourth-Day movement leaders with whom I have spoken want their movements to be inclusive and are aware of cultural and linguistic needs that their movements need to address. They want to reach out to and accommodate Spanish-speaking men and women but are not eager to create separate, Spanish-speaking movements. Tres Dias, Walk to Emmaus, and Via de Cristo have translated their materials into Spanish, and in some places, Spanish-speaking weekends are held. And the NEC Committee announced at its February 2011 meeting that it was working on translating NEC Library materials into Spanish.[95]

In most places, the weekends are held in English. Whether their slogan is "Make a friend, be a friend, bring a friend to Christ," "Blooming where you are planted," or "Being the hands and feet of Christ," all of the movements focus on improving one's personal relationship with Christ. Drawing on Eduardo Bonnín's directives, all cursillistas work to share their newfound faith and zeal with others and work to "infect" or "impact" their environment. The conviction that having a newfound relationship with Christ is not enough, that one must share this newfound faith with others, is a thread that binds all of the movements together.

For Thom Neal, his Cursillo weekend was "enjoyable" but was not "the end-all-be-all for me, that is for sure."[96] Neal made his weekend after a good friend asked him to help out on a Kairos Prison Ministry International weekend. In order to do so, Neal first had to make a Fourth-Day weekend, so he signed up to make an Episcopal Cursillo in his diocese: "The way I was brought into the movement was definitely not the best way, as I made the course to help out my friend on his weekend. I think people should make the weekend for better reasons than I did. Now, I like to say that I am a 'recovering Southern Baptist.' I remember thinking during the weekend, 'I left the Baptist Church to *get away* from people like this!' I was proud to be a 'frozen chosen,' and the Cursillo weekend definitely challenged me in that area."[97]

It was not until one year later at a Cursillo Leader's School that Cursillo "ceased to be a warm and fuzzy weekend for me and became a method for living your faith." The workshop's emphasis was on pre-Cursillo and post-Cursillo: finding ideal Cursillo candidates and men and women to sponsor them, and helping cursillistas in their Fourth Day. NEC leaders who gathered at that workshop focused on the challenges facing the movement: not just finding people to make the weekend but finding the right people, men and women who could help revitalize the movement and ultimately the Episcopal Church. According to Neal, "We have a phenomenon of what I call 'sponsorship fairies': men and women who just want a warm body to sponsor and that is their focus. What we need are sponsors who see their role as mentoring their candidate and . . . focus[ing] on the Fourth Day. The weekend itself is important, but what I see happen in a lot of places is too much emphasis put into the weekend and not enough into what happens before the weekend and then after it is over."[98]

Cursillo has been an important component in the lives of Neal and his wife, Betsy. It has helped them become more active Christians and helped them revitalize their parish church, St. John's. Neal mentioned a recent service trip that St. John's youth made and said this kind of service work largely results from the influence cursillistas have made in the church. "Every part of the congregation has been invigorated by Cursillo, and we have moved from being a church of 'frozen chosens' to a church that wants to make a difference in the world."[99] The church's former pastor and his wife, both cursillistas, were instrumental in this "monumental shift," Neal said, noting that Episcopalians are "known for referring to history as an excuse not to make changes" and that it takes "a lot of work" to convince them otherwise, especially Episcopalians in the South. "Have you ever heard the joke, 'How many Episcopalians does it take to screw in the lightbulb?'" Neal asked. "The answer is 'none,' because someone will say, 'Well, my grandma put in that light bulb, and you can't change it!'"[100]

Indeed, the founding members of Tres Dias, who indicated their desire to move beyond their parents' and grandparents' nonecumenical faith, the NEC seems bent on maintaining the faith of its parents and grandparents, and this stance, coupled with its nonecumenical stance, has hurt it. The NEC has not seen the kind of national and international growth experienced by the ecumenical, more evangelical Fourth-Day movements Tres Dias, Walk to Emmaus, and to a lesser degree, Via de Cristo. The NEC's lack of growth parallels that experienced by the Episcopalian Church in America, as indicated in the *U.S. Religious Landscape Survey*. The 2008 study reported that 1 percent of the U.S. population declared membership in the Episcopal Church USA; another 0.3 percent claimed to be Anglicans, those who broke from the Episcopalians over gay marriage, and another 0.6 percent mainline Episcopal/Anglican not further specified.[101] Organizationally, the NEC looks a lot like Catholic Cursillos de Cristiandad in the sense that it is diocese- and not parish-based. The organization of the NEC is also like the Catholic Cursillos' in being overseen by lay Episcopalians and priests alike. The NEC consists of a General Counsel and a National Episcopal Cursillo Committee, the latter of which is comprised of one elected layman, one laywoman, and one clergy from each of the fifteen national districts. A variety of ex-officio members round off the NECC membership. NEC presidents serve a three-year term on the National Committee, the third year as president. In the history of the NEC, both laity and clergy have served as president. While Neal is a lay Episcopalian, his successor, Mother Pat Miller, is a priest in the Kansas City, Missouri, diocese. Like all members of the NEC National Committee, NEC presidents serve on subcommittees, and for the past three years, Neal has served on the committee that oversees membership and the "health of the movement." Neal said that in the past several years, "we have surveyed people half to death, but we have some important findings that are helping us as we strive to create a stronger movement." Saying that "Cursillo does seem to be in somewhat of a decline" among Episcopalians, Neal acknowledged that "we need to look at why we are doing it and how we are doing it." He argued that participants in the movement need to focus more on the pre- and post-Cursillo, not just on the weekend itself. Preparing men and women for the weekend experience is crucial for the health of the movement, and sponsors need to "step up" and work with their candidates before and after the weekend experience.

Ginny Schoneberg, NEC communications secretary from 1974 to 1990, refers to the phenomenon that Neal mentioned as the "disease we call 'Three-Day-It-Is,'" where cursillistas focus solely on the weekend and lose sight of the bigger picture: preparing for the weekend encounter and living the Fourth Day, also called the "post-Cursillo." Schoneberg writes about the dangers of thinking that the experience ends with the weekend itself. Laymen and women began thinking that they were better Christians than those who had not made their Cursillo. They used secret language and in short, turned other Episcopalians off to the experience and the movement: "Members of our parish and diocese began to think that we were a secret society or clique within the Church. We would not tell anyone anything about Cursillo, 'Come and See.' We talked in a foreign language—rollo, we greeted one another with 'De Colores' after a big embrace, talked of going to an Ultreya, and some of us were being called rectors, when we hadn't even attended seminary. Some became the Holy Joes and Joans of the parish. Was that what Christ had in mind when we were given the gift of Cursillo?"[102]

The cautionary tale that Schoneberg relates here is repeated by men and women in all the other Fourth-Day movements. The course experience itself is meant to be a first step toward a new life in Christ, and leaders of the Fourth-Day movements also emphasize to cursillistas that in order to "live the Fourth" they must join reunion groups and attend monthly ultreyas. The NEC and the other Fourth-Day movements stress that it is only by joining with other Christians in the small reunion groups that cursillistas will continue to grow and mature in their faith. As the NEC's "The Health and Well Being of the Movement" states, "An isolated Christian is a paralyzed Christian. Cursillo provides the means to break down the isolation so that in tandem with others, the purpose—not just of Cursillo but of the whole Church—can be realized."[103]

Yet while the NEC shares the other movements' concerns, its nonecumenical stance prevents it from reaching beyond Episcopalians—a problem for the movement, given the shrinking numbers of Episcopalians in the United States. As Sue Davis indicated, the NEC may be Episcopalians' single most important evangelizing tool.

In Neal's opinion, another area the movement needs to work on is reaching out to young adults and young married couples. Neal emphasized during our conversation that the NEC needs to reach out better to the younger generation "and make changes to reflect this generation's needs." When his then-nineteen-year-old daughter made her NEC weekend in October 2009, she "just could not relate to some of the seventies stuff" that was part of the weekend. "I grew up in a generation where you went to church, and church was at the center of everything. Young people like my daughter have many more demands and church is not the only thing they have in their lives. Young people use Facebook, Twitter, e-mail as forms of communication and we need to figure out how to reach them and deliver something they can relate to."[104]

Neal says his daughter is unusual in the sense that she chose to make an NEC weekend and neither Happening, the NEC weekend for teens and young adults, nor Vacari, the weekend for college students, interested her. At fifty, Neal says he is "in the younger set of folks" who attend the yearly NEC gatherings, where the average age is in the mid-to-late sixties. His observations are supported by the NEC-sponsored surveys, and the organization is responding by making greater efforts to recruit younger men and women to the movement, according to Neal. At nineteen, Neal's daughter was the youngest person on her weekend, while the average age of cursillistas in Neal's Upper South Carolina diocese is in the mid-thirties. This demographic reflects other Fourth-Day movements' constituencies as well; the average age of cursillistas is mid-thirties to early forties in Catholic Cursillos, Tres Dias, Walk to Emmaus, and Via de Cristo.

During our conversation, Neal also mentioned the NEC's goal of accommodating younger couples and families. While not all dioceses have coed weekends, Neal's diocese has always offered weekends where husbands and wives can make the course together. Yet coed weekends are not technically in covenant, as we have seen. Neal and his wife did not make their weekend at the same time, but he knows many couples who have done this and who insist it is the best way. Neal noted that the NEC has several options in terms of how the weekends are gendered: some dioceses like his offer coed weekends where men and women are together for the entire course but have same-gender sleeping quarters (even married couples are separated); some weekends are same-gender weekends (in some dioceses women's and men's weekends are held during the same weekends, but separately, so that male and female participants never meet); and some dioceses offer "conjoined weekends," where men and women attend the same weekend but have separate, same-gender tables and events. For his part, Neal does not think that same-gender weekends are essential for a successful course. It does seem curious that the NEC has accepted coed weekends, which are not in covenant, but still claims that they—and the Catholic Cursillos—are the most authentic because they interpret the CdC as denominationally exclusivist.

Unlike some men I have interviewed, who believe that separate gender courses are important, especially for men, to encourage them to open up and embrace the course, Neal said he had "no problem opening up during my weekend, even though there were women present." He said the other men on his weekend also opened up "and took away a lot from the weekend experience."[105] And in its efforts to address the survey findings, Neal's South Carolina diocese makes special efforts not only to recruit but to assist young families: "We encourage sponsors to talk with couples about babysitting their children for them while they are at the weekend course." Because it is difficult for young families to "get away" for a weekend, sponsors need to "step up their efforts" and offer to help care for the children of the candidate they have sponsored. According to Neal, sponsorship needs to be "comprehensive."

As with all the other Fourth-Day movements, the NEC has its own booklets, brochures, books, and even DVDs that detail the movement's essentials. The NEC's essentials come in the form of a bound "NEC Library," a three-ring binder filled with booklets titled "Introduction: What Is Cursillo?," "The Fourth Day," "Candidate Preparation," "The Three-Day Weekend," and "Administration."[106] Like the in-covenant Fourth-Day movements, the NEC encourages its graduates to evangelize, as summed up in its slogan, "Make a friend, be a friend, bring a friend to Christ."

Post-1960s American Christianity: Power to the People

Just as the 1962–65 Roman Catholic Vatican II Council gave laity expanded roles and opportunities in the life of their parishes and dioceses, 1960s Protestant church reforms gave rise to more empowered laymen and women.[107] As with Catholics who embraced Cursillos during and after Vatican II, Protestants craved more lay empowerment and greater working relationships with their pastors, and making a Cursillo was a way to enter into a new relationship with one's pastor. These relationships were more leveled, less hierarchical. Like U.S. Catholics, U.S. Protestants were increasingly using the language of spirituality and were looking to their clergy less for authoritative truth and more mentoring and guidance in their personal quest for truth and meaning.[108]

Members of the various Fourth-Day movements are today reaping the fruits of the reforms that took place in their various denominations in the 1960s, 1970s, and 1980s. All of the cursillistas I encountered in my research for this book, Catholic and Protestant alike, shared their enthusiasm for their churches and their subsequent involvement in the life of their churches and the Fourth-Day movement. Tanya Muzzarelli's Tres Dias weekend experience allowed her to appreciate her pastor more: "He is a great guy and is a lot of fun. When I ran a women's weekend, we had fun with it and dressed Dave up as a baby for one skit, to emphasize that we are to be like children in God's eyes. Pastor Dave is like one of us; he loves Christ and shares his love of the Lord with us."[109] Dave Smazik, the copastor of Tanya's church, Westminster Presbyterian Church in Rockford, Illinois, is deeply involved with Tres Dias as is Westminster's other pastor, William ("Bill") Ward. Pastor Dave came to Westminster in the mid-1990s with a plan to reinvigorate the laity. He had made his Tres Dias weekend and was "fired up," as he put it, to infuse Westminster with the Christian renewal and personal growth that he has experienced in his Fourth Day.[110]

Pastor Dave made his Tres Dias weekend in 1993 and afterward committed himself to bringing the weekend to his church. Since Dave's arrival the church has grown, and more than one hundred of the parishioners (approximately one-ninth of church members) have made their Tres Dias weekend in the past three years. According to Derek Schurman, a Westminster elder, nine of the sixteen church elders have made their Tres Dias weekend and they, along with Pastors Dave and Bill, are recruiting individuals for the course. The goal is that these men and women will make Westminster even more dynamic. Schurman proudly shared with me the church growth statistics that he pulled up for me on his laptop: membership has swelled to close to one thousand, and young families comprise a large percentage of church membership.[111] The case of Westminster Presbyterian church helps to illuminate the key role that pastors play in the success (or failure) of a church's Fourth-Day movement. While all Fourth-Day movements are lay-run, they depend on clergy to deliver five of the fifteen rollos and to administer the Sacrament of Holy Communion. For Catholic Cursillos, as we have seen, the centerpiece of the Eucharist in each of the three days makes it necessary for a priest to be present. He is also present for Reconciliation and is the only person who can fill this role in the weekend encounter. Tres Dias has taken root at Westminster Presbyterian because the laity are open to having an encounter with Christ and a new community but also because Pastors Dave and Bill have been enthusiastic champions of the movement and the weekend experience itself. Westminster Presbyterian is an excellent example of how the success of a Fourth-Day movement on the local level depends on a good working relationship between clergy and laity.

Jeff Johnson, the lay director for the Northern Illinois Tres Dias (NITD) community, emphasized how important pastors were to the movement. The laity, he said, needed to keep a pastor's participation from becoming stressful because "free weekends are hard to come by for pastors and being part of a Tres Dias weekend is a big commitment. It is up to us, the laypeople, to make sure that everything—I mean *everything*—is in place so that pastors can come and be a part of it."[112] John Connor, another member of the NITD, emphasized the intense planning and work that goes into each weekend: "I'm ex-military and I tell you I was blown away by the organization that went into my Tres Dias weekend. There is an astounding amount of moving people and things in an efficient way, and everything is taken care of down to the last detail. I have gained an even greater appreciation for all of the work that goes into a Tres Dias weekend since I have been on weekend teams and have been a *cha* in various capacities."[113]

Tres Dias weekend volunteers, called *chas*, as they are in the other Fourth-Day weekends, do all of the work for the weekend. They cook, serve, clean, organize, and attend to all of the details so that the weekend runs smoothly. These men and women do the work so that their pastors do not have to.

Tanya, who is Westminster Presbyterian's secretary as well as active member of Tres Dias, noted that the success of Tres Dias results from a combination of astute and active pastors, enthusiastic laity, and God's will: "Our pastors know what Tres Dias is bringing to the church community. We have better leadership at Westminster because of the Tres Dias members and the enthusiasm they bring. Our pastors target individuals for Tres Dias, but it is really God who does the targeting." For her own part, Tanya did not have a good Tres Dias experience. "It was terrible, I mean really awful. I had a roommate who just wouldn't stop crying and instead of tending to my own spiritual needs, which is what the weekend is all about, I focused on making the weekend a good experience for her and did not get that much out of it for myself." Despite this experience, Tanya became deeply involved in Tres Dias because of her motivation to serve and to "show my love of God with others." In her own estimation, Tanya has gained much from her involvement in the Tres Dias community; "I am surrounded by people who love God and who show their love of God each day."[114]

All of the cursillistas interviewed for this book, those in Fourth-Day movements as well as those in the offshoots of those movements, emphasized that while it is possible to feel close to Christ while in church, it was during the weekend that they truly experienced Christ and Christ's love. Sentiments ranged from "This is the closest you'll ever get to heaven" to "You'll never experience this kind of love anywhere else." Whether they were Tres Dias, Walk to Emmaus, Via de Cristo, or Episcopal Cursillo, these weekend encounters offered Christian men and women spaces where they could forge new relationships with clergy and with their religious traditions, which they in turn revitalized with their newfound energy.

The Protestant men and women I spoke with who are involved in Fourth-Day Protestant Christian movements are drawn to shared Christian experiences and want to talk about what connects Christians, not what divides them. They are fashioning a lay theology and point to a larger movement among Christians that has gone unnoticed by scholars of American religion. For their part, the Catholics I interviewed who support intercommunion and ecumenical Catholic Cursillos are aware of the hierarchy's stance, but they choose to downplay denominational and theological differences in favor of commonalities and experiences that link them. With the exception from the nonecumenical NEC, the vast majority of Fourth-Day Christian cursillistas seek ecumenical Christian opportunities and experiences that help put them in touch with the divine—even when those situations officially break from the hierarchy's position. They are called to live ecumenical, interfaith Christian lives.

Christianity on the Move

All Protestant Fourth-Day communities were founded by men and women who feel called to introduce the movements at home and abroad. It was a small group of men and women from Newburgh, New York, for example, who introduced Tres Dias to Atlanta, where it is, according to John McKinney, "one of the most active Tres Dias communities in the world." And it is men and women from the Atlanta community who have been especially active in spreading Tres Dias internationally. McKinney told of an Atlanta-based lawyer who felt called to give up his law practice, move to Russia, and start a Tres Dias community there. "He married a Russian woman and was the one who really got Tres Dias going there."[115] Sometimes "blooming where you are planted" can have international dimensions.

What McKinney points out here is fascinating on a larger scale, if we think about how movements start and how they spread. On the surface, the establishment of Tres Dias in South Korea and Germany may seem random, but we have seen that there is a reason behind the movement: laymen and women felt called by God to bring their respective movements to others.[116] As we saw in the first two chapters, the Cursillo movement has moved with cursillistas—from Mallorca to the United States and other countries. Religion moves, quite literally, with clergy and laity. Another way the Fourth-Day movement's growth can be interpreted is as ebbing and flowing with the participants' own movement. We are reminded of the religious historian Thomas Tweed's recent theory of religion as a series of confluences that ebb and flow.[117] The Cursillo movement moved when and how its members moved. Because it is a lay movement, Cursillo or Fourth-Day movements have expanded in precisely the places to which its members have traveled and moved.

It is important to emphasize that all of the men and women with whom I have spoken, those who started Fourth-Day weekends in particular places and those who are part of the movements, believe that the spread of their movement, whether it is Catholic, Lutheran, Methodist, or interdenominational like Tres Dias, is part of "God's plan, not man's plan," or as McKinney puts it, a "God incidence, not a coincidence." Catholic and Protestant cursillistas alike insist that the instigation and success of their movement is because of the Holy Spirit "shining its light down on us," as one women involved in Tres Dias told me at a recent gathering.

This language of the Holy Spirit reflects the rise of nondenominational Christian "megachurches" in the 1980s, 1990s, and even today, signaling the desire of millions of American Christians to emphasize experience over denominational identification. Theology matters to contemporary Christians, but it is a kind of theology that is shaped by the cursillistas themselves, what I see as a kind of experiential theology—a theology crafted out of lived experience rather than dogma and creeds that has appealed to mainline American Christians since the early 1960s.

Fourth-Dayers, cursillistas, the majority of whom attend denominationally affiliated churches, are the predecessors to megachurch Christians in the sense that their primary identities were as Christians who had had an experience with Christ. And as part of this new expression of Christianity—Christian first, denominational affiliation second—Protestant cursillistas seem to be more open to multiple expressions of faith and even to the blending of traditions. The Lutheran Kurt Horberg attends Catholic mass twice each week to "feed my soul." The beauty of the liturgy, the architectonics of the church, and the music all inspire him to be a better, more faithful Christian.[118] Current studies of American Christians that point to the blending of traditions show that Kurt is part of a larger trend and search for meaning. American Christians have gravitated toward the powerful experience with the divine made available to them during the Cursillo weekend. As we have seen in this chapter, the greater its openness to ecumenical Christian experience, the more successful a Fourth-Day movement has been. Given its history of ecumenical Christian dialogue and focus on what connects Christians, as well as its respect for evangelical Christianity, it would seem that Tres Dias is poised for continued growth across the United States.

Now that we have a sense of the history of the Catholic Cursillo and Protestant Fourth-Day movements, it is time to turn our attention to the inner workings of the weekends themselves—what happens on a typical Cursillo weekend and how cursillistas interpret the events. Chapter 4 focuses on the dynamics of the Cursillo weekend itself, and on what U.S. cursillistas say about their pre-Cursillo, weekend, and post-Cursillo or "Fourth-Day" lives. Catholic and Protestant cursillistas alike say that they are called to "bloom where they are planted," and that they work to "live the Fourth." As we will see, their use of this phrase is resonant with meaning.

CHAPTER FOUR

Blooming Where We're Planted

U.S. Catholics and Protestants Talk about Living Their Cursillo

I had forgotten God, all I cared about was money. I was having problems with my adolescent son at the time and other family problems. Like Saint Paul, I fell off my horse and was converted. My objective in making the Cursillo was to change my heart and mind and it happened. *Gracias a Dios por el Cursillo!*
—José Herrera, San Diego, July 26, 2005

If it weren't for my weekly group reunion meetings I would not be as centered as I am. I need those meetings to be the best Christian and person I can be, and it is my sisters in Christ who help me in my journey.
—Sue Davis, April 27, 2010

For the cursillistas interviewed for this book, making their Cursillo was about becoming a better person. They emerged from the intensive three days as renewed men, women, Catholics, Protestants, sons, daughters, mothers, fathers, husbands, and wives. For Catholic cursillistas like José Herrera, the weekend experience led them to nothing less than an epiphany. For the first time in their lives as brown-skinned Mexicans, they believed that their individual gifts were important to the future of their Church.[1] For those middle- and upper-middle-class white, non-Hispanic men and women like Sue Davis who made their weekend, the three days of their Cursillo affirmed their lay Catholic and Protestant identities. They returned to their homes and families rejuvenated, prepared to "be church." They were ready to take on increased responsibilities in the lives of their families, parishes, dioceses, and neighborhoods.

By examining Catholics' and Protestants' experiences and interpretations of their Cursillo weekends in this chapter, we are able to understand the power of the weekend, which transcends class, gender, and ethnic differences and offers a universal spiritual experience. When we pay close attention to cursillistas' stories of their weekend, we can begin to grasp why and how the Cursillo movement spread rapidly among U.S. Hispanic Catholics, as well as among white, non-Hispanic Catholics and Protestants, and why it continues to appeal to thousands of men and women each year.

The basic message is the same of all Cursillo weekends: God loves you, you are worthy of God's love, and God needs you to be a person of faith in the world and to reach others—called the "faraway" by Eduardo Bonnín Aguiló. All cursillistas are familiar with and invoke the mantra, "Make a friend, be a friend, bring a friend to Christ." They realize that they are vertebrae of a larger body, to invoke Bonnín's concept of Christian community, and that they are called to maintain the strength and integrity of that community through their leadership. While there are some denominationally oriented differences among the Fourth-Day weekends, these distinctions are muted in favor of what links them. For the men and women in Tres Dias, Walk to Emmaus, Via de Cristo, and Kairos Prison Ministry International, universality of experience trumps denominationalism. And many lay Catholics and Episcopalians, despite their movements' official antiecumenical stance, see themselves as part of a larger movement of shared experiences and experiential theology and do reach out in ecumenical ways to Methodists, Lutherans, and nondenominational Christians. All of the Fourth-Day movements point to Eduardo Bonnín's piety, study, and action—the three core principles of the weekend and in the Fourth Day. During the three days of the weekend itself, candidates have time and opportunity to work on their personal piety, and to learn about their faith from others. On the third day of the weekend, before they return to their families, candidates are urged to be strong and active apostles—they are told that to receive the full effect of the weekend they must "live the Fourth."

The inner workings of the Cursillo weekends offer what many contemporary American Christians have been searching for since the late 1950s: a renewed self, a meaningful Christian community and a connection with the divine. Contemporary weekend Cursillos, as counterpoints to Americans' increasingly hectic lifestyles and desire for meaningful community, offer the time and space for such intimate, spiritual experiences as well as important venues for "real time" community, in an age driven by a plethora of technologically mediated relationships. Cursillo weekend candidates are dropped off at the church or center where the weekend events will take place. Their sponsors help them carry in their luggage and pillows, give them a hug goodbye, and tell them they will see them Sunday evening. Candidates have been told by their sponsors to arrive at their weekend without a watch, cell phone, laptop computer, or other forms of technology and communication devices. In my own official letter of invitation to attend the Diocese of Peoria Northwest Area Women's Cursillo Weekend, March 17–20, 2011, I was told not to bring these devices because "Cursillo is time with the Lord, time to give our full attention to His message of grace and life."[2]

From the moment they check in to the church or center on Thursday night, weekend candidates are told that they are on "God's time" until the weekend is over at approximately 5:00 P.M. Sunday. They are told to not worry about what time or day it is since they will be taken care of for the next three days. While the weekend Cursillo movements eschew the word *retreat* for the three-day experience, believing the two to be qualitatively different, the setting for Cursillo weekends is that of a retreat. Candidates are cut off from the outside world, and for the next three days they eat meals together, sleep on cots in designated rooms, and sit at assigned tables in groups of six. The team leaders also share sleeping quarters and eat their meal with the candidates, bringing the total number of cursillistas—alums and candidates—to about fifty-five. The experience is like living in a sorority or fraternity house, with shared bathrooms, sleeping quarters, and dining facilities, complete with cooks and waiters, except that during the weekend the candidates do not leave the premises. For Catholic and Protestant cursillistas alike, the weekend is intense, exhausting, exhilarating, emotional, deeply cathartic, and challenging.

The cursillistas I interviewed for this book all talked about the importance to their spiritual growth of being "away from it all," in the words of one of my interlocutors. One of the cursillistas I spoke with at length is Sue Davis. Sue, now in her fifties, was raised in a conservative Jewish family in Southern California. Until her parents divorced when she was fifteen, Sue and her family worshipped together at San Fernando Valley's Conservative Temple. As someone who "has always felt God's presence in my life" and for whom "Judaism is definitely the foundation of my Christian faith today," Sue says she has "incredible memories" of her childhood, which included keeping partial kosher, the High Holidays, and reading Hebrew with her grandfather, who was "devoted to Scripture."[3] When Sue later met Jeff and when they began planning their wedding, it was important to Sue to worship with him in his tradition, which was Episcopalian. Sue chuckles when she thinks back because at this time, Jeff was "definitely not a practicing Christian." But Sue insisted that if they were going to be married at church then they must "follow through and attend church." Sue says she doesn't like the language of conversion, because "I didn't convert, I *transitioned* into a deeper relationship with God. I became aware of the Trinity and its part in my faith journey." In 1980, several years after their marriage and Sue's "transitioning" from Judaism to the Episcopal Church, she expressed a desire to make a Cursillo weekend. The U.S. Cursillo standard weekend practice was (and is today) that husbands were asked to make their weekend first and wives second, as men were considered to be the "head of the household" and were expected to be the spiritual head of their homes and families.[4] Somewhat reluctantly, but urged on by Sue and their priest, Jeff signed up for the weekend course. According to Sue, he was "completely transformed." She says that Jeff was "refreshed, excited, and eager for me to experience what he had. He was a different kind of Christian after his Cursillo, and seeing his response and change made me want to experience the weekend even more!"

Primed to "focus on my spiritual journey," Sue made her Cursillo several months later. During the weekend she realized that "God has a plan for each of us, and because of this 'aha' moment, my relationship with Christ just unfolded." Like the other Catholic and Fourth-Day movement cursillistas I have interviewed over a period of six years, Sue says that her weekend experience was "amazing and beautiful," a "first step" in her new walk with Christ. For Sue, as for the other cursillistas I have interviewed, the way the weekend was structured made them wonder what would happen next, and they eagerly awaited the next event. The rollos given by clergy and laity make an impact, and the table discussions and poster displays give participants the opportunity to reflect and share in an intimate setting. Breakout sessions, which always seem to be timed "just right," as one of my interlocutors put it, give participants the time and space to connect with each other—to share struggles they are having at home and at work, and to ask for prayers. Prayer is an important component of all Cursillo weekends, and participants have ample time to pray for their own families and for the families of their "brothers and sisters" on the weekend journey with them.

Deeply serious events, Cursillo weekends are also a time for enjoyment. Laity and clergy dress up in odd costumes, dance and sing songs, lightening the mood. During my Cursillo weekend, a group of alumna cursillistas dressed up like fully habited nuns and entertained the candidates with a song and dance routine. It was hilarious. The *pièce de résistance* was when Father Duane came out dressed as a biker with black leather jacket, tight pants, and a do-rag. For the team leaders who knew him well, the performance was so out of character for this gentle, soft-spoken priest that their laughter brought them to tears. The rest of the candidates laughed because the performance was so, well—unpriestly. The combination of rollos, group dynamics, time for personal reflection and meditation, and fun times have had a powerful impact on the hundreds of thousands of Christians who have experienced a weekend Cursillo since the late 1950s.

In living the Fourth Day, as a member of a reunion group, Sue says, her Christian journey is continually refreshed and renewed. For cursillistas, the Cursillo weekend catapults them into a deeper kind of faith—one that necessitates living their faith in ways they have not experienced before. After the "first step" of the weekend experience, Sue continues, cursillistas must join a reunion group (also called a group reunion) because "Christ doesn't ask us to do it alone. He wants us to gather with others and to hold each other accountable." A cursillista who does not involve him- or herself in a reunion group and who does not attend monthly ultreyas or secuelas is said to be missing the point of the weekend, which is to connect the individual to Christ and to connect Christ-filled individuals with each other to reach the "faraway."

While Sue's journey is unusual in that she "transitioned" from one tradition to another, what she says about her Cursillo experience and her Fourth Day is typical of cursillistas, whether Catholic or Protestant. Sue considered herself to be a Christian before she made her weekend course. And she discovered during the seventy-two-hour encounter a heightened level of self-awareness and a deeper, more intimate relationship with Jesus Christ. For Sue and the cursillistas I interviewed, two forms of awareness (self and Christ) were intertwined. Sue discovered that she was able to realize her full potential as a human by placing Christ at the center of her existence. She also realized that she needed others to help her in her walk, and for more than twenty years has attended a weekly reunion group meeting. For cursillistas, finding this small-group community is the third and vital component to this new life in Christ.

In this chapter, I will offer a firsthand phenomenological account and thick description of preweekend, weekend, and postweekend events from the perspectives of Cursillo participants. These men and women focus on the friendships they made, the emotional release they experienced, the sense of self they gained, and their encounters with the divine. I explore the richness of their descriptions and offer my own insights into the weekend, in part based on my own Cursillo weekend experiences.[5] In this chapter, I will do my best to honor the request of the men and women in the movements featured to not divulge too much, lest the "surprise" be ruined for future candidates. For my interlocutors in the Catholic Cursillo and Fourth-Day movements, "What happens on the weekend stays at the weekend." Yet Catholic and Protestant cursillistas alike did open up and share details of the experience, as well as their own interpretations, knowing that they were being interviewed for this book and giving me permission to share the details with my readers. They *wanted* to talk about what their weekend because for most, it remains a peak experience, a highlight of their lives. What cursillistas share when they talk about their weekends and their Fourth Day is the importance of having the time and space to experience God, Jesus, and their renewed selves. Their narratives show why the weekend continues to resonate with so many U.S. Christians today.

Weekend Preparations

Lay Christian men and women—everyday Christians—are the backbone of every weekend Cursillo and the larger movement, and they keep the movements going.[6] In each of the movements, whether it is Catholic Cursillo, National Episcopal Cursillo (NEC), Tres Dias, Walk to Emmaus, Via de Cristo, Kairos, Teens Encounter Christ (TEC), or one of the many Fourth-Day spinoffs, the lay director chooses team leaders who "make the weekend happen" organizationally. These leaders—women for women's weekends and men for men's weekends—put in dozens of hours preparing. The dates of the weekends are posted on websites and in parish and church bulletins at least six months in advance, and weekend candidates are solicited by cursillistas in person as well as on websites, where application forms are posted. All Cursillo movements have an application fee, today averaging around $100, to help defray the weekend expenses, which include water, electricity, and food costs.[7] Each movement is registered as a nonprofit organization and funded by donations. In the months leading up to the actual weekend, cursillistas' help is solicited. For women's and men's weekends, male and female cursillistas sign up to serve up palanca. Called agape in some of the Fourth-Day movements, palanca is broadly defined by cursillistas as a form of love offered through sacrifice.

Cursillo candidates offer palanca or agape by cooking meals, cleaning bathrooms, soliciting palanca letters, or praying—before the weekend begins and throughout the three days—in what is called the palanca or agape chapel. Before each weekend Cursillo, a designated lay coordinator sends out e-mails to cursillistas on the region's list, asking men and women to sign up to pray in the chapel. Veteran cursillistas are asked by weekend team leaders to serve as cooks, waiters, and waitresses. Cursillistas "offer up" their palanca for Cursillo weekend candidates in various ways. A veteran cursillista might clean the bathrooms, for instance, and make sure scented soap and other amenities are available. Palanca and agape are viewed as godly inspired, as ways of inviting in the Holy Spirit. The more palanca and agape, the better the weekend, it is believed.[8] By offering palanca and agape, cursillistas demonstrate their strength and integrity as the vertebrae, to invoke Bonnín's language, of Christian community.

What brings candidates to the weekend varies. Some men are invited by a priest or pastor, or have been told by a friend or relative that the weekend is worth their time. Some men are influenced by their wives, who want to make their weekend but must wait until their husbands have made theirs. Women whose husbands have made their Cursillo usually sign up to make theirs soon after, and single women who apply for a weekend Cursillo have been influenced by their mothers, aunts, sisters, and friends, as well as by priests and pastors.

Each candidate has a sponsor who meets with him or her in the weeks building up to the weekend, what is called the "pre-Cursillo" period. Sponsors can be clergy, family members, or friends. The sponsor is expected to meet with the candidate to go over what to bring to the weekend and what to expect. The initiative in starting the sponsor-candidate relationship can come from either person. I was atypical as a non-Catholic taking part in a Catholic Cursillo weekend. Moreover, my spouse, a non-Catholic, had not made a Cursillo weekend but did make a TEC weekend as part of his Catholic high school educational requirements, which seemed to please Father Duane Jack and Doris O'Keefe, my sponsor. So I required special permission to make my weekend—not because I was non-Catholic but because my husband had not made a Catholic Cursillo. Father Duane, the region's spiritual director since the 1970s, invited me to make my weekend and supported my research as well as my openness to having a spiritual experience. Doris, with whom I had had some great conversations, offered to be my sponsor. We met a couple of times before my weekend for coffee and to talk about what I should expect. The first time we met, she had some sponsor forms she needed to fill out and some questions to ask me. She emphasized that I should go in with an open mind and try not to anticipate the weekend events—which would be difficult given my six years of research into the movement.[9]

Making my Cursillo weekend in the spring of 2011 was the final component in the research for this book, which began in the summer of 2005.[10] The candidates I spoke with had experienced a range of pre-Cursillo activities. Some met with their sponsor weekly in the months before their weekend. Others met two or three times, and a handful reported meeting just once. The average was three to four pre-Cursillo meetings. While all of the female candidates I interviewed said they looked forward to the weekend, not all of the men I interviewed did, as some felt pressure from their spouses or friends to make the weekend. Male and female candidates alike reported being nervous about making the weekend, but they gave different reasons. The men were nervous about the unknown, since they were used to "being in control," as one of the men told me. The women tended to worry more about how their husbands and children would fare without them for three days. All of the candidates felt a heightened sense of excitement, a willingness to experience something new, and the desire to meet new people.

The Weekend Events

The weekend itself is highly structured, with three days' worth of carefully planned activities beginning at 7:00 A.M. and continuing until late in the evening. The schedule for all of the Fourth-Day weekends is essentially the same. All of the Fourth-Day movements have their own manuals, which, as we know from chapter 3, base the structure and content directly on the Catholic Cursillo movement's *Leader's Manual*. While the Protestant Fourth-Day movements have made adjustments, their structure and activities essentially follow the same script. Both Catholic and Protestant weekends are based on Bonnín's piety, study, and action, and the cursillistas who volunteer at the weekends are dedicated to helping their brothers and sisters in Christ have a fulfilling and spiritually rich experience.

The hope of weekend organizers is that each candidate will experience God's grace which will lead her or him to conversion. The conversion process is believed to begin in what is called the pre-Cursillo phase and continues during the three-day weekend and into the Fourth Day. At around 8:00 p.m. Thursday, candidates are presented with an opening talk that features two meditations.[11] According to the Catholic Cursillo *Leader's Manual*, the opening talk is designed to "arouse interest in the Cursillo," "to reduce as much as possible whatever psychological tensions the participants may be experiencing," "to awaken curiosity about the unknown that they are about to be living," and "to bring about a friendly collaboration in something that may be a turning point in their whole lives."[12] The "Know Thyself" meditation aims to "awaken consciences" by having the candidates think about their lives and circumstances. The "Merciful Father" meditation is "meant to illuminate with hope whatever anxieties may have been brought to the surface" in the first meditation. The focus shifts from the self to God and the promise of a new relationship with Him. The God that is portrayed during all Cursillo weekends is a loving God, one who is "already preparing a feast for our homecoming, ready to forgive and forget everything because we are His children," as we were told during my Cursillo weekend. We then were shown a PowerPoint slideshow with images of nature, children, and heaven. The tone for the weekend was set. The God of the Cursillo weekend is a God "rich in mercy," we were told, as is his son.

My Thursday night journal entry reads:

> After we were led into the large room we were told to talk with one other woman at our table and to learn her name, where she lives, family details, where she attends church, her occupation, and her hobbies and interests. I chatted with Julie, who attends a Catholic Church in a small town in western Illinois. Julie is married with one young daughter. She loves "outdoorsy things" and works as an interior designer. After ten minutes or so, we are asked to go to the front of the room and introduce our new friend to the audience. I was surprised how nervous I was. After the introductions were over, I considered the candidates—there were forty-two of us. The women were as young as their late twenties to as old as their mid-seventies. At age forty, I was one of the younger candidates and one of two non-Catholics. Most of the women on my weekend were from the Quad Cities area and from Geneseo, Illinois, a town about thirty

minutes away. After these introductions, we were assigned to a table, each designated with a female saint's name. I was assigned to the Saint Catherine of Siena table with six other women who will be my companions for the next three days. We were to eat our meals together, to make posters after the rollos, and to present our posters and summaries of the rollos to our fellow candidates and to the team leaders. Like the women at the other six round tables, we were to spend most of our time together this weekend. I'm looking forward to the weekend but really miss the kids and Steve.

FRIDAY

On the first full day, we were awoken very early by loud music being played from a speaker—I wasn't sure of the time, since there were no clocks or watches, but I have since learned from reading the *Leader's Manual* that it was around 7:00 A.M. We were told by a team leader to shower and to get ready to meet outside the cafeteria to pray before breakfast. Coffee and tea were available in the conference room for those who needed some caffeine before breakfast—our first meal together, featuring homemade breakfast casseroles, pancakes, and fruit salad. Afterward, we walked upstairs to the chapel, where Father Duane led a discussion and meditation on "The Three Glances." He focused on the three ways Jesus looks or glances at three individuals: the rich young man (enslaved by his possessions), Judas (enslaved by his ideologies), and Peter (enslaved by his belief that he needs no one but himself). As candidates we were invited "to define our attitudes towards Christ, who is looking at each of us," and to ask ourselves how God sees us. The self-reflexivity and inward-turning that began the previous night continued this morning as we were asked to meditate on our personal relationship with Christ.

After chapel, we went back downstairs for the first weekend rollo, the "Ideal" talk. Setting an ideal for ourselves is, according to the rollista, a "call to become fully human," and "the best way to meet God." We were asked to set a high ideal for ourselves so that we could be liberated from whatever enslaved us, whether this was lack of self-confidence, or fear of what others might think of us, or whatever prevented us from acting effectively. We were told that our focus "limits or extends the meaning of our life" and that in order to become fully human, we needed to not only choose a goal, but to "gain conviction for the goal, let it fulfill our aspirations, let it set the criteria for our actions, and that when we achieve the goal, it becomes a way of life and we set a pattern in motion."[13]

Like the "Ideal" rollo, all of the weekend talks are heavily anecdotal, and rollistas relate some of their own struggles and triumphs to the candidates in the room. The personal stories add an important layer to the rollos, as most of the details converge on the themes of marriage, motherhood, and balancing work, family, and faith. A common denominator of all of the rollos is a complete trust in God and Jesus. Rollistas try hard to connect their personal stories to the topic—whether it is the "Ideal," "Piety," or any of the fifteen weekend rollos—lest the talk seem solipsistic. The "Ideal" rollista wept as she recalled the especially trying moments in her life. She connected her personal struggles with the importance of creating ideals for her life so that she could endure the difficult times. She asked the candidates to write down their own ideals—what direction they saw their lives taking and what they thought about that direction. Was it their true ideal? Was God a part of that ideal? The weekend candidates were asked to reflect on these questions and to write down their answers. After writing in our journals, we were asked to discuss our thoughts with our tablemates.

The women at my table followed the rollistas' directions carefully. We thought, we wrote, and we discussed. Some of our discussion was lighthearted, but it took on a serious tone, too. One of our tablemates, who had serious physical impairment, talked about her husband's death and how she "took up the challenge" and learned how to drive after his death. She said she believed that God wanted her to set and to fulfill this goal—that his ideal for her was for her to be more independent. After we shared our thoughts and experiences with each other, we were given posterboard and markers by a team leader, who asked us to create a poster that reflected the essence of the rollo we had just heard. We received a large box of craft supplies—including glitter, stickers, ribbons, and glue—in case we felt extra crafty. A lot of giggling ensued as we attempted to make something that was both serious and creative. Judging by the whispers, giggles, and teamwork at the tables around us, the other weekend candidates were just as intent on fulfilling the task set before them. The atmosphere was one of friendly competition to make the best poster.

The deacon who presented the second weekend rollo, "Sanctifying Grace," built on the points laid out in the "Ideal" rollo by emphasizing that "an ideal life is a life of living in God's grace." According to the Cursillo *Leader's Manual*, this rollo one of the weekend's most important, because it lays "the groundwork for the living out of what is fundamental for being a Christian, by showing how grace opens us up to an encounter with God and one another in a new world of unsuspected realities, God alone being able to fill the emptiness of souls."[14] The deacon cited Scripture throughout his talk (2 Timothy 1:9, Acts 14:3, Wisdom 3:9, 1 Corinthians 1:4 and 15:10, Ephesians 2:8, John 2:43–50) to reinforce Jesus' gift of love, which is his grace. He was a gifted speaker, incorporating humor, events from his married life, and lessons learned to bring home the message that "sanctifying grace is a love relationship with God initiated by Him." Like all rollistas, the deacon worked hard to make the Bible relevant, referring to chapters and verses that have helped him personally and more deeply understand the meanings and importance of the rollo. While the weekend is not a Bible study per se, rollistas emphasize the importance of reading Scripture and making the Bible relevant in the candidates' daily lives. The third rollo was titled "Laywomen in Church," and the rollista focused on women's "special gifts and roles," citing Philippians 3:7-9 as her inspiration. She emphasized that "the ideal of grace is to be lived in community" and that "women are called to serve the mission of the Church, which is helping our neighbors, understanding evangelization, and being Church." Moreover, the place of women is "within the heart of the world; in a special way they are charged with temporal tasks." This third rollista also recited the Serenity Prayer during her talk, emphasizing that laywomen need to exercise humility in their lives.[15] Like with most of the rollistas, she invoked the gendered language of and women's "natural" gifts and abilities. Women can make the world a better place for people, she asserted, especially in the areas of education, right to life, and end of life issues. This would be the first of several rollos with a strong prolife message.

The fourth rollo given during my Cursillo weekend, "Actual Grace," was given by another deacon, who emphasized that grace is given by God and that it is "up to us" whether or not we accept it and God's call. "Actual grace," he asserted, "helped us come to Cursillo this weekend. We responded to this gift from God and said 'yes.'" The deacon emphasized that actual grace is "small moments, fleeting moments that we are given to either accept or reject God's grace." The opportunity to help someone at a grocery store could be an everyday moment of actual grace offered to us. The deacon stressed that "grace is given to us out of Christ's love for us, and it is damaging to our souls when we let actual grace skip away."

Accepting God's grace leads to piety, we were told by the fifth rollista in her "Piety" talk. "Our piety is our response to God's call," she said, and there is a distinction between ideal piety—"genuine and authentic piety"—and the "false piety of the Holy Hannahs, the Routine Rita's, and the Hypocrite Harriett's." Ideal piety can be nurtured by attending mass or worship, receiving Holy Communion, reading the Bible, and prayer. Piety, this rollista told us, is one of the three necessary components of a life of faith—the other two being study and action.

The rollos and the group dynamics that follow are a major focus of the three days. Candidates are asked to write in their journals, to talk with their tablemates, and to make posters after each of the rollos. At the end of the day, each table is called to come to the podium for a poster presentation and explanation of our artwork. The seven of us at the table of Saint Catherine of Siena weren't sure what time it was, but we knew we were exhausted from all of the careful listening, the intense discussions, and the tears shed as we talked about what the rollos meant to us. We all looked forward to supper and to some "down time," as one of my table sisters put it.

SATURDAY

In a Cursillo, the focus of Saturday is on the "Development of Christian Life." Our day's events began after breakfast, today a delicious buffet, with a meditation on the figure of Christ to help cursillistas start seeing Jesus as God "within reach."[16] The goal is for cursillistas to want to know Christ and His message, to appreciate everything that Christ has done for them, and to "want to follow Him as Master and as Friend, since he is still dynamically present among us."[17] The five rollos of the second day are "Study," "Sacraments," "Action," "Obstacles to Grace," and "Leaders." In the "Study" rollo, the sixth of the weekend, the rollista emphasized the importance of deepening our faith through studying the Bible, reading devotionals, and "carefully examining" our environments. Study, the "second pillar" in a life of faith, is "just as important as the heart," our rollista told us, "because we need a transformed mind as much as we need a transformed heart." The rollista recounted her busy travel schedule and her efforts to find new opportunities to grow in her faith through active study. Like the other rollistas, she used biblical Scripture to drive home the message of study, including Acts 17:11 ("Stay rooted in God's word. Read it and study it daily") and Jeremiah 15:16 ("Who will unlock His word for you? May God's word be the joy and happiness of your heart."). The rollista concluded her talk with recommended readings, all meant to help us study and to become stronger in our faith lives. She suggested the *Catholic Post, U.S. Catholic, Catholic Answers, Catholic Digest, Angels* on Earth, *Guideposts*, as well as more ecumenically oriented meditations like *Faith for a Lifetime, Our Daily Bread*, and Max Lucado's *Grace for the Moment*.

In the "Sacraments" rollo, Father Duane picked up on the theme of study, emphasizing that it is important to understand the meanings of the sacraments and not just "go through the motions." He explained that the sacraments are ways for each individual to be transformed into a sacrament, "into the sign and instrument of God for the building of the Church, the great sacrament of salvation."[18] In his presentation, conducted as a minilecture, Father Duane went through each of the Catholic Church's seven sacraments: Baptism, the Eucharist, Confirmation, Reconciliation, Anointing of the Sick, Matrimony, and Holy Orders, and emphasized that sacraments, for all Christians, are "celebrations of the Church gathered as his body" and "presume faith that Jesus is living among us today."[19]

My table's discussion centered on how we are to live the sacraments in our lives and what this means. "How do we say thank you to God?" one of my tablemates asked. "By living the sacraments and continuing to grow," responded another. Another tablemate, who has seen much suffering in her life, said that "suffering comes from sources other than God. God gives you what you can handle." Another woman at the table added, "We need to give honor and glory to God by and how we live." I wrote in my Saturday journal entry that "we all seemed to come to the conclusion that we suffer and we work through it—we have to—because we know that God and Mary lost their son. They suffered, too. We humanized God and Mary and that helped us see ourselves as living sacraments, as living, breathing bodies with minds able to honor God."

The objective of the "Action" rollo, the weekend's eighth, is to "live so that all who meet you meet Jesus," according to the rollista. Actively living one's faith, "demonstrating apostolic action" is "sharing your knowledge and love of Jesus, bringing people to Christ for the first time, and bringing others to a closer relationship with the Lord, people who have been members of the church for years," the rollista told us. She used the imagery of being invited to dine in "God's grace" at the "all you can eat buffet of peace, joy, blessings, confidence, assurance, hope, love, faith, and mercy." Like the third rollista, the eighth advocated involvement in the prolife movement as a way to actively live out a Christian faith.

The weekend's ninth rollo, "Obstacles to the Life of Grace," was given by a third deacon, who spoke of the constant presence of sin: "God has made us free, and we are capable of ruining His whole plan." Sin is "the biggest obstacle to a life of grace," the deacon informed us, and there are "many, many occasions for sin." The "remedies for sin" include the Sacrament of Reconciliation, sacrifice, prayer, and "contact with other vital Christians." He told us that "we cannot survive in this world without the support of a genuine Christian community."[20]

The rollista of the tenth talk, "Leaders," picked up on the deacon's emphasis on the importance of making the "choice" to remedy our sin. "Leaders," she told us, "influence the thinking and actions of others because they orient, guide, and direct." She urged us to use our talents, live out our responsibilities, and to engage in service to others. She cited Ephesians 4:1–6 as a guide for Christian leadership. Christians, the rollista told us, paraphrasing these verses, are called "to live in a manner worthy of the call we have received, with humility and gentleness, and in love." Christian women are to be "signposts who illustrate God, not us" in our actions.

After the day's rollos, personal reflections, and group discussions, after making and presenting our posters and enjoying a candlelight dinner, we were asked to form two lines and walk outside. Upon reaching the front doors of the adjacent church, we heard singing. When we entered, we saw about two hundred men and women, all holding candles and serenading us. There wasn't a dry eye among the candidates, including me. It had been a long two days, and I was processing all of the intense conversations we had had at my table. I also really missed my husband and children, unaccustomed to being away for this long with no contact, and I wondered how they were doing. The beautiful singing and glow of more than two hundred candles was emotionally overwhelming. Once I saw my sponsor, Doris O'Keefe, and her husband, Jerry, in the crowd, the tears flowed. The O'Keefes had supported me in my intellectual journey, and I knew how much they wanted me to have a spiritual encounter and meaningful weekend. I was deeply touched by their presence at this late hour. Looking around, I saw that most of the candidates were also overcome with emotion—tissues, sniffles, and shy smiles abounded.

SUNDAY

On the final day of a Cursillo weekend, the focus is on "Evangelization of Persons and of the World." Candidates are instructed how to live their lives most fruitfully as cursillistas. They are asked to meditate on Christ's message at the Last Supper, especially his instruction to "go out and bear fruit, fruit that will last" (John 15:16). Each cursillista is asked to "bloom where you are planted" and to bring Christ to the world.[21] In the "Environment" rollo, the eleventh of the weekend, candidates are asked to be the Christian leavening agents in their communities. The purpose of this rollo is "to help the cursillistas find their own ways and to strengthen them so that once they themselves have been converted, they can go about leavening their environments, as indicated in the Gospel parable."[22] The weekend candidates are urged to make choices that will positively impact their communities and to "seek out groups with caring people."

The "Environments" rollista on my weekend told us that she meets with a group of churchwomen every week to help keep her on track and to keep her in a good environment, and yet she also consciously seeks out women who might not themselves be in the best environment. She tries to "go slow" with these women by taking them to lunch or for coffee and to show them what being in a good environment can do for them. She emphasized that cursillistas need to go out of their way to show concern and support for those who are struggling, and she invoked the Fourth-Day slogan, "Make a friend, be a friend, bring a friend to Christ."

The twelfth weekend rollo, "Life in Grace," given by a deacon, underscored the "ongoing progression" of living a life in grace. We were told that living a life in grace is "a daily process by which we become more aware of God's gifts to us." Living a life of piety, study, and action "is living a life in grace." Prayer should be a central to our day because we need it to be "honest with God and to discern, listen, and wait patiently for Him to respond." Prayer builds strong individuals and communities, we were told.

The thirteenth rollo, "Christian Community in Action," built on this theme. The rollista emphasized living a Christian life to "leaven one's environment with the Gospel."[23] Cursillo candidates are called to be saints and to tend to Christ's vineyard. The rollista likened the parish to a village well, belonging to each member and nourishing everyone. She cited Matthew 18:20 to underscore the importance of Christian community and the possibilities of that community. In an analogy to the well, she referred us to our own recent experience: the "bonfire we saw last night in the chapel, where all of the cursillistas came together to show us their love and support."[24]

The fourteenth rollo, "Total Security," was given by the weekend team leader, and in her talk she told us that "the real question is—what will you do with your Cursillo?" She then reviewed the previous thirteen rollos, taking us on a journey from thinking about what our ideals are to considering how we see ourselves contributing to our communities. She told us that she has derived total security from her relationship with God and His son, Jesus, and that her reunion group reinforces this security in the love and support its members have shown her. She described how her reunion group cursillistas serenaded her husband into heaven when he was dying, and the comfort that brought her. She emphasized the centrality of being part of a reunion group, of attending a monthly ultreya, and of "putting yourself out there" as a cursillista.

The "Fourth-Day" rollo is the fifteenth and final talk of the weekend and builds on all the previous rollos by underscoring the vital importance of group reunions and ultreyas (reunions of various group reunion groups) for cursillistas in their new walk with Christ. This rollo emphasizes that the group reunion is based on friendship and that it needs to be kept small and in confidence, in a place where the "intimacy of friendship" can be nurtured and where it can grow.[25] All that is required of a group reunion is that it is kept small and that it is a place where members can share Christ and their ongoing formation as Christians.[26] All of the women on my weekend were told to be Christian soldiers, to "persevere in a life of grace, maintain contact with Christ and Christian brothers and sisters." "The Fourth Day," we were told, "starts tomorrow and continues for the rest of your life."

PALANCA AND THE FOURTH DAY

After the candidates had a late afternoon break and snack, we reentered the conference room to find that we had each been given a palanca bag. As a way of welcoming the candidates into the new community, each candidate receives a personalized palanca bag and a Cursillo cross. As we have seen, cursillistas believe that it is palanca or agape that makes the weekend run smoothly. The sacrifices cursillistas make before, during, and after the weekend are believed to maintain a successful movement. Some cursillistas pray rosaries for the candidates, while others offer their palanca by spending time away from their family to work at the Cursillo weekend. Called "chas" in Tres Dias and Via de Cristo, Cursillo weekend volunteers also prepare candidate's rooms, make sure there are extra towels in the bathrooms, and decorate the retreat center. On my weekend, a steady supply of pleasantly scented foaming hand soap was always available, as were bowls of candy.

While the soaps and candies are appreciated by the candidates, the palanca letters, or agape letters as they are called in some of the movements, are seen as the ultimate special touch to the weekend. Two cursillistas are usually in charge of the weekend palanca or agape and coordinate the letter writing and the filling of the gift bags offered to the candidates on the second or third day.[27] These coordinators solicit letters not just from family and local friends, but also from cursillistas in other locations. During my own Cursillo weekend palanca letters were read aloud by team leaders throughout the weekend. In U.S. Cursillos, these letters are usually given to the candidates to read during the second or third day of the course, but at my Cursillo each candidate was given hers to take home to read "in the privacy of your home where you can reflect on the words."[28] Pat wrote in her palanca letter, a copy of which was given to each of the forty-two women on my weekend, "My palanca for you was to give up my much loved morning coffee for Friday, Saturday, and Sunday. In place of this I spent one hour in prayer from 6:00–7:00 A.M. for you."[29] My palanca bag also included Hershey kisses attached to letters, rosaries, and bookmarks with inspirational messages. One of my palanca letters read:

> De Colores,
>
> Thank you for saying "yes" to Cursillo! Welcome to our family. My palanca for you has been to pray for you each morning and evening when I say my daily prayers. Whenever I wake up during the night I pray for you. I have prayed many rosaries for you as I travel to and from work.
>
> You are such a blessing—
> Happy 4th Day,
> Sheila

Palanca is continually invoked during the weekend as the glue that keeps the weekend running. Part of living the Fourth Day, cursillistas believe, is giving palanca, thus ensuring the continuation of Cursillo weekends.

The Fourth Day: De Colores! New Selves and Communities

During the Fourth Day or post-Cursillo stage, cursillistas aim to achieve the ultimate purpose of the Cursillo de Cristiandad movement, which is to "create core groups of Christians who leaven their environments with the Gospel."[30] The seventy-two-hour weekend encounter urges laymen and women to become Christians who will work to bring Christ to the world, specifically to their own environments (at work, in the home, in the neighborhood). This aim is remarkably similar for both Catholics and Protestants. The cursillistas I have met may have experienced significant challenges in their lives, but most emphasize the importance of having fun—what my Mallorquín cursillista friends call "tener mucho alegría." Cursillistas—Catholic and Protestant alike—enjoy life and say that they appreciate life more now than before they made their weekend. I have met some men in Orlando's Via de Cristo community, for example, whose reunion group meets weekly to eat, pray, and golf. Jerry Lemcke of the Heart of Florida Lutheran Via de Cristo community says that the camaraderie involves both prayers and the golf, bonding activities for the men of his group. "Hey, we get to pray together *and* we play golf, too—who can beat that?!" Across the United States and the world, cursillistas meet at each other's homes, in restaurants, in church halls, or on the golf course. Some, like a Moline, Illinois, women's reunion group, meet at Panera each week for coffee and dessert. A group of *sabatinas*, first-generation Mexican American women and men in East Chicago, Indiana, meet every Saturday at mass and then pray together afterward over coffee and *pan dulce.*

Wherever and whenever they meet, cursillistas come together as small accountability groups and recommit themselves to living their faith. For an hour or two they share food, friendship, and prayers, recognizing their strengths and weaknesses and helping each other on their Christian journey. In addition to meeting with their reunion group, Catholic and Protestant cursillistas strive to be active Christians in their communities. All of the cursillistas I have met and befriended in the course of my research—Hispanic and white, non-Hispanic; Catholic and Protestant alike—stress that the weekend course is "only the beginning," and that it is crucial to "live it" each day. Making the course but failing to become involved in a reunion group misses a main point of the weekend experience, they say, which is that Christians need each other to stay focused and on the right path.

After making their Cursillo, Catholic and Protestant cursillistas alike believe they are charged with an important task: the renewal of self, community, and church. While the weekend experience has universal appeal, individual cursillistas carry their own gendered, class, and ethnic situatedness and as such interpret their three days in complex ways.

Tracy Schmidlin and Jerry Lemcke, Via de Cristo Ultreya, Orlando, Florida, 2010. Photograph by Kristy Nabhan-Warren.

For first-generation Mexican-descent Catholics, the Cursillo weekend led them to the realization that they *are* the Church and that the Church is them. They felt empowered as individuals and saw themselves as a new *comunidad*. For these men and women, for so long been marginalized in society and in their Church, seeing themselves as important individuals and integral members of their Church was empowering indeed. According to San Diego *veterano* Jesse Ramírez, "The Cursillo is oriented towards the individual person. It helps a person seek a vocation and helps a person see where he or she is before God. You find out how well you know Christ; it is a Christ-centered movement and is an ongoing relationship and developmental process."[31]

Elva Hernández, a second-generation Mexican American cursillista in East Chicago said she is a more involved Catholic today, and that "before I made my Cursillo I was like a lot of Catholics, I was a pew Catholic and went on Sundays and then went home. I think that Our Lady wanted me to go make my Cursillo.... For my part, I feel more comfortable sharing my faith and challenging others to step up their faith life. I share my faith now—something I did not do before I made my Cursillo. We need to be good models for others but we also need to verbalize our faith."[32]

When we examine cursillistas' stories across generations, they point to the power of the experience and how individual selves are renewed. Cursillistas talk about the significance of the three-day weekend in terms of spiritual renewal, their deepened relationship with Christ, and their new understanding of themselves as part of a supportive community. Like José Herrera, whom I quoted at the beginning of this chapter, cursillistas emphasize that they are better people after making the weekend course. Their stories are often raw, full of emotion—many cry as they recall their experience—and they talk about the importance of emotion in the process of becoming a more real, more devoted Catholic Christian. Even cursillistas who made their course forty years ago recall it with an intensity and clarity that is astounding and deeply moving. Obviously, there is something about the dynamics of this course that propels the individual cursillista to embrace a deeper faith life. Although the course is well-rehearsed and planned, something profound happens there, and individuals take away life-transforming experiences.[33] Cursillistas stress that their faith is now more dynamic, palpable, and "real." While the majority of cursillistas considered themselves good Christians before their weekend, they emphasized that their faith was reinvigorated and that they are actively living that faith today.

The National Cursillo Center publications rarely delve into individual testimonies. The focus is on group dynamics and the results—how the movement creates strong group networks and how they ultimately benefit the Church. A close examination of the official literature reveals a preoccupation with community and subsuming the individual experience into the corporate Church. The National Cursillo Center has gone so far to dispute what it refers to as the "Three-Day Myth"—that the three-day experience is life-changing and altering. For the center's *The Purpose of the Movement*, "The 'Myth of the Three Days' goes something like this: Something sacred and wonderful happens in the three days of the Cursillo. Anyone who goes through it has been changed for life.'"[34] Yet when we turn to cursillistas' stories, they add complexity to the historiography and hagiography of the Cursillos de Cristiandad. Cursillistas point *precisely to* the weekend as a life-altering experience. Moreover, they realize that individual renewal translates into renewal of their church because *they are* the church. Even though the Cursillo Center's literature acknowledges the importance of the individual cursillista, it clearly conceives of the individual as part of a larger body of believers who will reinvigorate the Church. This was not Bonnín's main concern. As we have seen in chapters 2 and 3, his emphasis was on individual spiritual renewal.

As Louie González, a leader in the Diocese of Gary's Cursillo movement said, "It was at my Cursillo closing that I realized, 'This is church; church is the *people*. I looked around and saw the pure joy that people have—you can *see* it at the closing on Sunday."[35] As Louie points out, Cursillos have a corporate or communal aspect to them; cursillistas in both San Diego and East Chicago talked at length about the importance of their Cursillo community for them and said it has given them a sense of ownership of their Church.[36] The Mexican-descent and white, non-Hispanic cursillistas I interviewed all talked about the importance of making and sustaining their new selves and communities through regular group reunion gatherings.

Louie and his wife, Martha, made their Catholic Cursillo weekends because they were "so impressed" with friends who were "on fire" after making their Cursillos. Louie and Martha were also strongly encouraged by their parish priest.[37] The individual cursillista seeks a personal relationship with Jesus, but it is important to understand that in that quest and in the experience, cursillistas are intimately connected to other seekers like themselves who interweave personal and communal piety in the quest for empowerment and meaning.

Cursillistas I interviewed stressed the importance of the larger Cursillo community as a source of ongoing strength—and a constant reminder of the need to live a life informed by one's faith. As Damien Rico, a second-generation Mexican-descent cursillista put it, "What I've found is that I have a life that is closer to Christ now. . . . You become part of a community—something that is bigger than yourself. I remember that during mass one Sunday there was an anointing of the sick, and my friend was being prayed over by a cursillista who had been part of my group. After the service, he grabbed me and hugged me—there was this instant connection and memories came flooding back. De Colores, you know?!" As Damien points out, cursillistas believe that they *are* the church, and there is a deep connection between them—a special kind of bond.[38] "De Colores," interpreted by cursillistas as the course's embrace of many-colored peoples and cultures, is both a song and a greeting, which cursillistas usually exchange with a hug and a kiss. This

East Chicago cursillista Adelina Torres, 2008. Photograph by Kristy Nabhan-Warren.

camaraderie and love is further substantiated by Adelina Torres, a second-generation Mexican-descent cursillista in East Chicago: "Because of Cursillo, you build a lot of confidence with others, and you have this great relationship with Jesus. There is a camaraderie that you might have never had before. There is a love between cursillistas that is so strong—we're living the Gospel life. I wouldn't hesitate if one of my *compañeros* needed to talk. We are there for each other, and there is a special kind of security in our community."[39]

The cursillista's community is like family, and for those cursillistas like Mona Sandovál, who were hesitant to make their Cursillo, they discover that giving in to their emotions was essential to embracing this faith community:

> I never thought I had time to make Cursillo and I thought—I'm Catholic, I play Bingo! [Laughs] But when I decided to make my Cursillo I did it for myself—not for my family but for me. I was skeptical in the beginning—like Elva was saying, I was annoyed by some of the women in my group and I thought, 'Who does she think she is!' to myself, I admit! [Laughs] Before I made my Cursillo I thought that I knew how to pray—I had memorized the prayers, and I said them. But I really learned how to pray at Cursillo—I had to learn

how to pray right. A woman at Cursillo taught me how to pray. At our chapel visit, we all held hands and prayed—it was awesome! It was then that everything just poured out of me; I was bawling, my chest hurt. The Cursillo was very emotional for me. The eight of us who made the course together are tight like family. Even though we aren't able to get together as often as we might like, when we do see each other there is an instant connection. We know we're here for each other.[40]

Mona brings out several layers of experience: making the Cursillo was an intensely emotional experience in a safe and loving environment. All of the cursillistas I interviewed emphasized that becoming better people necessitated exposing themselves emotionally, spiritually, and intellectually in the presence of other cursillistas. Cursillistas today tend to embrace the language of emotions that made Cursillos seem problematic to white, non-Hispanic Catholics in the 1960s and 1970s. Mexican American cursillistas go so far to claim that Hispanics are "more emotional" than whites, so Cursillos "make sense" for them. This claiming of language inverts the emotionalist rhetoric that was used as an ethnocentric weapon against first-generation Hispanics and turns it into a desirable quality. As Catalina González, a first-generation East Chicago cursillista, put it, "The Spanish-language Cursillos are the *best* because we're Mexicans and we're *loco* for our religion!"[41] Moreover, all of the Mexican-descent and Puerto Rican Catholics I interviewed were proud that Spanish terminology such as *Cursillo*, *rollo*, and *palanca* had gone mainstream in the course.

The majority of cursillistas said they were healed as a result of the weekend. Rosita Aldrete, in a voice barely audible, spoke about why she made her Cursillo more than years ago. Looking down and twisting her wedding ring around her finger, Rosita talked about her daughter, who was killed in a car accident when she was in her twenties. "When she died, I lost it, I mean, I *really* lost it," Rosita said. "I lost my faith in God, the Church—everything. God led me to Cursillo so that I could get through the terrible pain and so that the hole that was left in my heart could heal. After my daughter died I wanted to die, too. I was a dead woman when I made Cursillo, and it made me alive again. I owe my life to Cursillo."[42] The Cursillo healed Rosita and restored her faith, not only in God and the Catholic Church, but in her fellow man. Today, she is active in the Spanish-speaking Cursillo movement and has been a key organizer of

Cursillos in greater San Diego. Rosita and her husband, Enrique, devote many hours to the movement and to creating an environment where fellow *mexicanos* can find themselves and Jesus, and so that they can experience healing they cannot find elsewhere. After her Cursillo experience, Rosita found the will to live and hope that continues to sustain her. As Mary Farrell Bednarowski writes, individually and communally, to be healed is to have hope, "that state wherein we know that some kind of response or change or reconciliation or transformation is possible."[43]

The hope that Rosita found is contextualized in a new *comunidad* and *familia* of cursillistas. In making her Cursillo, Rosita was personally renewed—she came to know herself in an intimate way. What Pierre Bourdieu calls "the micropractices of everyday life" embed Rosita in "interconnected . . . webs of significance" that govern "experiential engagements with the world."[44] Even though Rosita's experiences were deeply contextualized within the *comunidad* and *familia* of the Cursillo weekend, her experience was fundamentally her own. Community reinforced her self and her interpretations, yet she could still identify a renewed sense of self and purpose. While testimonials have similar structures and themes, they bear the individual stamp of each cursillista who, although she internalizes the social language of Cursillo, makes it his or her own. Rosita's self was enhanced through the structure of the three-day experience. We can thus see a deep interplay of the dialectic of self and community in Cursillo testimonials like Rosita's. The self is healed, renewed, and indelibly linked to a new kind of community.

Even though not all cursillistas agree that individual healing is or *should* be the main motive for making the Cursillo, it is an important part of the experience for many. As Louie put it, "The main reason someone should make their Cursillo is to have a walk with Christ, and if you have a walk with Christ your questions will be addressed—maybe not all during the Cursillo weekend, but it is a start."[45] Louie's note of caution seconds the deemphasis in Cursillo movement literature on individual healing and renewal and the greater emphasis on corporate, group dynamics and a renewed Catholic Church. Catalina González said that when cursillistas talk about healing, they are really talking about how they have learned to deal with life's blows: "Your problems don't go away, but you do handle them better."[46] Even those cursillistas who emphasized the healing that took place for them during the weekend acknowledge that the Cursillo was not a "quick fix" and that they must work hard to maintain the spiritual momentum initiated during the weekend.

Cursillistas' weekend and Fourth-Day narratives consistently point to emotionality—their outpouring of emotions—how they wept, broke down, and felt emotionally "spent" from the weekend experience, as the ultimate legitimation of the course. Cursillistas' interpretations of their experience hearken back to nineteenth-century American Protestant philosophical and theological traditions, linking this movement and the narratives of its members with larger American religious history. As John Corrigan has written about antebellum Protestant revivals, "emotionality was a claim for and a demonstration of the legitimacy of the subjective self, of the capacity of the self to freely choose."[47] For the antebellum American Protestant and the cursillista, the emotional testimonies offer the ultimate proof that their experience was real, life-changing, and sacred. And situating themselves in a larger emotional discourse—one that centers on healing, personal renewal, and a reborn faith—empowers and legitimates them as individuals.

In her testimony, Carmen Uriostegui, an eighty-six-year-old *mexicana* living in Oceanside, California, emphasized a legitimated self.

> I did not want to make a Cursillo—I resisted it, I did! I saw the changes in my husband, who had made his, I mean, his face was long and calm; he was a different man! I was frustrated with him—he was like, too good to be true! Me, I loved money too much. I worked in a factory and as a waitress—I loved the feel of money in my apron—in fact, I can still feel it now. How I loved to feel the bulge of money in my pockets! God really worked on me—it took two years—I made my Cursillo two years after my husband made his. Now, I don't want to say that my life has been easy since making the Cursillo; in fact it has been very, very hard, and I don't understand everything that has happened in my life. I have had two hip replacements and shoulder surgery. I have lost my husband and my children. I have gone through many, many tragedies. But it is God and the Cursillo that have enabled me to cope with everything, even though I don't understand why it has all happened. I *need* Cursillo, it is my life. Everyone is changed after making the Cursillo—everyone. Everything is different. And we see Christ in every one of us.[48]

Carmen spoke to me at length about her difficult life, which has included rape in addition to her sons' and husband's premature deaths. When she says Cursillo is her life, she means it—her identity is so deeply entwined with her Catholic faith, her community of cursillistas, and a Jesus she came to know in the course that without it, her self would be empty. Carmen stressed her need for a community that she help her continue to cope with life's difficulties. When Carmen says that she "puts Jesus in the driver's seat" and trusts that he will take care of her, she points to a language of love, "spiritualized in a way that rendered it extraordinary and private, a core reality of the self."[49]

Cursillistas of all ethnicities and denominations want to "bloom where they are planted." They want to share their newfound sense of self and God with others, and they hope to make a positive impact on their larger community and church. Experiencing the Cursillo and living out the Fourth Day gives these men and women a sense of religious, cultural, or gendered pride that they had not experienced before.

Unbound Men

In an essay published eight years after his Cursillo experience in 1956, Carlos Calatayud Maldonado, the Mallorquín cursillista we briefly encountered in chapters 1 and 2, focuses on the spiritual awakening he experienced and how the language of the weekend course, "unaffected, hard, manly, struck home."[50] The weekend-long course in Christianity that he experienced and that flourished in Ciudad Real became a global movement between 1955 and 1965. When Maldonado made his Cursillo, the weekend Cursillos were still an all-male movement. The first women's weekend was held in Bogotá in 1953, and from the mid-1960s on, separate men's and women's weekends became standard practice in Cursillo communities around the world. Women came to have an important role in the movement, leading women's weekends and having an important say in the direction of the movement. In the United States and worldwide, female cursillistas now occupy leadership roles in the movement.

Today's Catholic Cursillo movement offers separate women's and men's weekends, and cursillistas come together for the monthly coed ultreyas. Early correspondence and contemporary ethnography shows us, however, that until the early 1960s CdC was considered a movement exclusively for Catholic laymen.[51] As we saw in chapter 1, the movement was founded to reignite Mallorquín men's faith and to revitalize their Church and communities. Literature written by CdC's founding fathers used highly gendered, male-focused language. Men were charged with becoming soldiers of global Catholic spiritual revitalization, in line with the Vatican's calls for spiritual reawakening. The weekend in Catholic spirituality was meant to reignite men's faith and inspire them to transform their fascist Church and wider Spanish society. At the same time that the weekend courses encouraged masculine discourse and spirituality, they also nurtured submission to Christ and the language of healing and emotion. From the start, the spiritual yin and yang of the Cursillo weekends was a dynamic blending of idealized masculinity and femininity. Bonnín's intention was to create manly, strong, but also emotionally connected, soft patriarchal Christian soldiers for Christ—men who would be better husbands, fathers, and Christians.

Guillermo Biblioni, the most respected and trusted scholar of CdC history among Mallorquín cursillistas, writes that if it had not been for Bonnín's statement that "there are no male or female souls, only souls," the CdC would have remained an exclusive all-male movement.[52] Biblioni writes that high-profile cursillistas such as Juan Capó were against inclusivity and wanted Cursillos to be for men only: "Against those who wanted to open up the Cursillos, Don Juan Capó and his group used flimsy arguments based in machismo."[53]

While Bonnín initiated a movement initially focused on revitalizing Mallorquín men's spirituality, the consensus today among cursillistas who knew him intimately is that Bonnín supported and encouraged women's weekends. The Mallorquín female cursillistas I have met and interviewed all emphasized that Bonnín wanted all Christians to be spiritually empowered and insisted that he was most definitely not "machista." These women felt supported and say they were treated as equals in the movement, and they add that Bonnín always rose to defend their interests when some in the movement questioned women's involvement.[54]

While it is experienced by both sexes, the emotional release that leads to healing and wholeness for cursillistas is especially important for men. The Cursillo and Fourth-Day weekends give men a much needed emotional outlet. For some, the weekend offers them a chance to expand their definition of what it means to be a man. For others, the weekend reaffirms patriarchal marriages with the husband as head of the home and spiritual guardian. As we have seen, the practice of U.S. Catholic Cursillos differs from those on the island of Mallorca, where the movement began. U.S. parishes, whether predominantly Spanish-speaking or largely white, non-Hispanic, continue to encourage husbands to make the course before their wives, considering husbands to be the spiritual heads of their families. In the U.S. movement, wives who wish to go first must receive special permission from a priest. One of my San Diego interlocutors, Carmen, explained this rule by saying that "if the wife makes hers before his, then this can cause real problems in the marriage because the man needs to feel that he is the leader."[55] Carmen's sentiments were echoed by white, non-Hispanic female cursillistas such as Doris O'Keefe, who said the husband should have the experience first so he can "feel that he is doing something in the religious sense before his wife, and then he can encourage and support her when she makes her weekend."[56] Bishop Gilbert Chavez of San Diego argues that it is important for men, especially Hispanic men, to make their Cursillo first, to help maintain familial and communal structures. Moreover, Bishop Chavez views the Cursillo movement as offering an essential alternative to mainstream American life: "The Cursillo movement is an alternative to the American materialist view of life, which isolates individuals and can become antifamily and [anti]community. What Cursillo does is affirm family, faith, and community."[57]

Given these explanations and legitimations of the status quo gender-based rules of patriarchy, I was surprised when my San Diego interlocutors invited me to make my Cursillo in the Spanish-speaking movement. After all, they knew that I was not Catholic and that I was married to someone who had not made his Cursillo. In a fascinating exchange—I distinctly recall it and wrote about it in my field notes—my female cursillista friends assured me during one of our sessions, "Don't worry, *hija*, if you would like to make Cursillo for your book research you can. *We* are giving you permission." A few days later, I received a phone call from one of the women, who told me she had arranged for me to meet with the bishop the very next day. Apparently, the ladies had reconsidered and decided that it would be a good idea for me to meet with Bishop Chavez to obtain his official permission to make my Cursillo.[58] What impressed me at this ethnographic moment, and still does, is the confidence that these first-generation Mexican-descent women displayed. My interview with Bishop Chavez (which they were able to set up in a stunningly short amount of time) reaffirmed for me the importance of lay women to the Cursillo movement. While Bishop Chavez and others in the U.S. Cursillo movement might bemoan the difficulty of attracting men to the movement and that maintaining men's involvement is a top priority, their respect for the female cursillistas in their communities comes through.[59]

For their part, Hispanic and white, non-Hispanic men I have interviewed focus on how the course enables them to transcend gendered shackles and become better men. As the anthropologist Elizabeth Brusco suggested for the Columbian context in her study of how evangelical religion has reformed men's machismo there, the U.S. Catholic Cursillos reform and domesticate the patriarchal leanings of U.S. Christian men. All of the male cursillistas, Catholic and Protestant, whom I interviewed discussed this.[60] To borrow the language of sociologist W. Bradford Wilcox, who writes about American Christian evangelicals and their experiences with faith and gender, these male cursillistas are encouraged to be "soft patriarchs"—men who are at the head of their homes but who exhibit a softer, gentler, and more emotional side.[61] Women who make the course are empowered to take up and own leadership roles, but these roles are seen as complementary to their roles as wives and mothers. What impressed me when I conducted fieldwork in San Diego was that the majority of the leaders in San Diego's Cursillo movement were *mexicanas* who were supported by their husbands. Cursillistas emphasize that the Cursillo enables them to become better men and women so that they can become better husbands, wives, church leaders, and members of their communities.

The cursillistas I interviewed thus stressed the importance of healing, renewal and emotional release in the course. They spoke at length about how they needed to be "broken down" in order to find and embrace a faith that was more real to them. Men who made their Cursillos were impressed with the changes they saw in their fathers, brothers, uncles, and male friends. They found the Cursillo a safe space for emotional release. John Blackwell affirms this need for a safe and nurturing place for men's emotions. "For the men who participate in the Walk to Emmaus," he notes, "the ritual also has certain latent functions. The ritual stimulates emotional feelings in the male pilgrims and functions as a sociocultural forum for the transformation of feelings . . . into emotions. The devotees are able, often for the first time in their lives, to express emotions freely. . . . expressions of emotion are stimulated, rationalized, and celebrated ritually."[62]

The men I interviewed, of whatever ethnicity or denomination, confirm Blackwell's observation that emotion is encouraged and celebrated during the Cursillo weekend. Men who make a Cursillo are immersed in what they consider to be a "safe space" in which they can weep and "let go" emotionally. The careful orchestration of the weekends is intended to help men and women let go and find Christ. According to Louie, a second-generation Mexican American from East Chicago who has sponsored many cursillistas and who has served as a Cursillo leader on many occasions, "Guys realize that the Cursillo is real and authentic. It is very liberating for them and they feel all the walls go down in ways that they haven't before. The floodgates just open up—everything that you've been carrying in your heart comes out. You discover that you can be a new person."[63] At first, men try to cover up their emotions, which is funny and predictable, said Louie: "Men don't usually open up until Saturday—it takes longer for them than women to open up. It's funny—it happens every time—when the men are given their palancas to read, they all go up to their individual rooms to read them, and they cry when they're up there. But they're not willing to admit that they were crying—they all come down with red eyes and pretend that they have allergies or something. They've splashed water on their eyes, trying to cover up the redness, and they do everything that they can to pretend that they weren't crying."[64]

According to Chris Sandoval, a second-generation Mexican American, "The machismo thing was working in me. When workers at the Cursillo offered to take my bags for me, my reaction was, 'I can carry my own bags!' The machismo thing had to go—and it did at Cursillo."[65] Several men interviewed confirmed Louie's observation that it was when they read the letters of support, the palanca letters from family members and other cursillistas that they broke down, "When you see a grown man put his guard down," said Chris, "you realize you can, too. The palancas were great—when I read mine I went to my room and cried."[66] Louie noted that "as team members we know that the barriers for men will be let down when they read their palancas."[67] In other words, emotional release is one of the intended results of the weekend because it is seen as necessary for a deepening spirituality. Male cursillistas say that they see the emotional release as a stepping stone to deeper relationships with others. As Miguel Arredondo put it, "Men are finally able to open up at the Cursillo, and this helps them with the rest of their lives. You can now open up to people, and that's what they were looking for."[68]

Rob Litavich, a deacon in the Roman Catholic Diocese of Gary, Indiana, entered his weekend "with the attitude of just get it over with," but he soon felt challenged by the other men on his weekend to open up and trust them emotionally. "The guys on my weekend really shared themselves and it drew me in, in a way I hadn't been drawn in before to talking with other men about my life and my relationship with the Lord."[69] It was the emotional encounter with other men and with God that impacted Rob, who describes himself as a "typical white guy," the most during his weekend.

Like Deacon Rob, San Diegan cursillista Jesse Ramírez emphasizes the importance of the Cursillo weekend in giving men the permission to exhibit emotions and their "softer" side. The Cursillo, according to Jesse, is also good for women because they can be in leadership roles in the Catholic Church and develop their leadership qualities. "I have seen great examples of women being empowered through the Cursillos. And men's eyes are opened to women's strength in the Cursillos." Jesse continues, saying, "We're Hispanic and we have machismo. Cursillos help to free men from useless traditions like machismo. You know that machismo is not just a Hispanic problem, all cultures have it. It's like baloney, no matter how you slice it is still baloney."[70]

Yet most of the Mexican-descent men I interviewed argued that although male chauvinism can be found in men everywhere, no matter what their ethnicity, *machismo* is culturally specific and pervasive. According to first-, second-, and third-generation Mexican American male cursillistas, because of intense expectations of men to be "men" in their culture, it is especially difficult for Hispanic men to "show their emotions."[71] Jesse talked about the importance of having separate spaces for women and men so that each can focus on personal improvement and not worry about what is expected of them by others. "Men and women have separate Cursillos but this is good, because in Cursillo the individual focuses on him or herself." He went on to discuss the importance for women, especially within Mexican American culture, of having their own space free from men and men's attempts to assert power over them. Jesse and his wife, María, both emphasized the intense change in Hispanic men during the course and underscored the loosening of gendered expectations. According to María, "A lot of men change as a result of making the Cursillo. Men cook at the Cursillos, clean. They are servers and are doing some things that they have never done before." Jesse added that the men are "unbound; and their wives, from their perspective, don't want to put up with machismo anymore."[72]

My interviews and conversations with U.S. Mexican-descent as well as white, non-Hispanic Catholic and Protestant cursillistas confirm that even though machismo may be a kind of culturally informed patriarchy for Spanish-speaking men, a deeply ingrained and culturally legitimated patriarchy binds all men who have made a weekend Cursillo. Father

Duane Jack, who made his Cursillo in Peoria in 1971, says that for him, a highlight of being involved in the movement is "seeing how other men have fallen in love with God—this is deeply influential to me and other men." On the weekend both women and men "bare their souls," but what makes the weekend especially significant for men, according to Father Duane, is that for most of them, this emotional outpouring is their first experience sharing emotions with other men on this level. During the Cursillo weekend, men "talk about their successes, their failures, and expose themselves in an intense way." This experience is "incredibly liberating" for them.[73]

The seventy-two-hour Cursillo weekend experience helps male candidates become "unbound men," to use Jessie's language. For Ron, a second-generation Italian American Catholic who has lived in Chicago his entire life, the emotion and spontaneity he experienced during his Cursillo weekend in 1965 was "so new to me and was new for the Catholic Church, which was just beginning to experience Vatican II changes." The "praying, sharing, and crying" among men was deeply moving to Ron, a cradle Catholic who in his Italian American Chicago world had rarely witnessed men showing outward emotion in an affirming environment. "I experienced men cry and I was moved to tears myself," he said.[74]

Learning how to open up to each other was also key to the Cursillo weekends of the white, non-Hispanic Catholic and Protestant men I met at a Tres Dias International Secretariat gathering in Rockford, Illinois, in March 2010. All of these men spoke of the freedom they experienced opening up to other men—as John Connor put it, "sharing my life story and my desire to become a better man." For close to two hours, I sat and listened to stories about how their Tres Dias Cursillo weekend gave them the courage to be "servant leaders," more loving husbands, and "real men." The dozen men who sat down to join the discussion at various intervals emphasized how humbling the weekend experience was and how they learned that Christ was the example of how to lead their lives. As John emphasized, "I learned that pride has to go. This was hard for me as I am an ex-military man! I learned how to be humble and that Christ needed to be my guide." Alternately described as "gentle leading" and being "smacked in the head," the weekend showed them how to be better Christian men.[75] "Many of us have that head knowledge but not heart knowledge," John said. "What Tres Dias does is opens up that eighteen inches not yet explored between your head and your heart."[76] All of the men I spoke with in Rockford emphasized that although both men and women experience Christ and new selves and community during the Cursillo, for men the weekend "packs an extra punch" because men are more resistant to religion and to intimate communities. Moreover, many men of the war generation, especially those who were military men themselves, are, as Tres Dias member Tom Miller emphasized, "just blown away by the weekend because they feel loved for the first time. They realize that 'Christ did it for me,' and this is mind-boggling for them—to experience this kind of love."[77] John described the weekend experience as "being hazed by the Spirit."

In contrast to their enthusiastic retelling of the weekend experience and their "Fourth Day," most of the men I spoke with confessed that they had not wanted to attend the weekend retreat and that they only went after being cajoled by their wives or friends. Most of the men said that they were "nervous" about what the weekend would entail and that they made up "all kinds of excuses" as to why they couldn't go. "I only went because my wife had packed my bags for me!" said John Connor, who went to his Tres Dias weekend "about as dubious as you could be." Similarly, Wayne went to his Tres Dias weekend "in the last hour—I mean, the *last hour*. I barely threw enough things in a bag for the weekend."[78] Catholic male cursillistas' retelling of their weekend experiences dovetails the stories Protestant male cursillistas tell. Most said they "dreaded going" to the weekend because they didn't know what to expect. Some felt it would be a "waste of precious weekend time." What connects the narratives of all of the men I have encountered is that even if they dreaded the weekend, what they experienced made them want to become better individuals, husbands, fathers, and Christians. They formed real and lasting friendships with other men and reinforced the weekend bonding experience with regular group reunions that continue to reinforce their new selves and the new relationships they formed through the weekend encounter.

Yet another group of men experience liberation from deeply ingrained gendered roles during a seventy-two-hour weekend retreat. As we will see in more detail in chapter 6, male offenders incarcerated in medium-to-maximum security prisons around the United States can apply to make a Kairos Inside Weekend, a retreat modeled after Catholic Cursillos. These men, according to Michael, a Kairos volunteer in southern Indiana, experience "radical transformations like you wouldn't believe." The male offenders, according to Michael, experience intense emotional release and "cry like babies."[79] Not used to an environment where they feel safe sharing themselves, these men tend to "open up" even more than female offenders, according to Michael and JoEllen, director of Kairos Inside weekends for women in the state of Indiana. Both Michael and JoEllen mentioned that male Kairos graduates from a Southern Indiana correctional facility make quilts for families of fallen soldiers. As JoEllen said, "Imagine this—a group of men convicted for serious crimes getting together to make the most beautiful quilts you have ever seen for families who have lost a son or daughter to combat."[80] Making a Kairos Inside weekend helps these men create new meanings of manhood, beauty, and expressions of love. Quilting becomes an expression of compassion as these men seek to connect to humanity outside the prison walls.

Cursillistas from all the various movements seek to improve themselves and to connect with Christ, and they understand making a Cursillo as just the beginning. As cursillistas in the United States as in Mallorca continually emphasized, the weekend is the first step in a lifelong journey. During the Fourth Day, largely through its group reunions, John Bruckman, a white, non-Hispanic Catholic, told me, "the individual person and the community he or she becomes a part of are one."[81]

When we go one step further and contextualize these Christians' stories with those of other Americans, we can see that cursillistas have not been alone in their quest for meaning. Their narratives of healing and spiritual wellness dovetailed the rise of small groups and the concomitant discourse of healing and wellness that begin to emerge in the 1950s. As the sociologist of religion Robert Wuthnow has noted, since the 1950s, "growing numbers of Americans spend weekends at retreat centers that give them a holy place in which to focus on spirituality."[82] And in their quest for new selves, new relationships with the divine, and new communities, American men and women began to incorporate a therapeutic language of wellness and healing.

U.S. Fourth-Day movements have been influenced by the therapeutic language of recovery programs. The largest of these recovery movements is Alcoholics Anonymous (AA), which was established twenty-two years prior to the first American Cursillo, in 1935, as a "fellowship of men and women who share their experience, strength and hope with each other so that they may solve their common problem and help others to recover from alcoholism."[83] For those in AA and in its many spinoffs, recovery is a life-long process. Regular attendance at meetings is crucial for those in recovery, and being held accountable in front of one's peers and before God is central to the movement's philosophy.

During the 1960s, 1970s, and 1980s, cursillistas, Catholic and Protestant alike, gave their discourse of recovery and health a decidedly Christian spin, distinctive from "12-Step culture's non-creedal spiritualism."[84] Sociologist Trysh Travis notes that when twelve-step programs like AA are considered, "recovery aligns somewhat awkwardly with the history of religious life as traditionally defined."[85] For cursillistas, their narratives of healing and renewal combine elements of twelve-step programs with decidedly Christocentric themes of sin, suffering, and salvation. During my Cursillo weekend, the deacon who presented the rollo "Obstacles to the Life of Grace," spoke about his recovery from alcoholism and how his involvement in AA led him to Cursillo. In his rollo, the deacon spoke at length about how sin is a major obstacle to an individual's grace and described the "remedies for sin," which include sacrifice, prayer, and working with a spiritual director. Lastly, he emphasized the need for Christian community because "we need others to keep us on track and in a life of grace."

The deacon's narrative illuminates the widespread language of renewal, recovery, and redemption that began to overlay the American religious landscape in the 1950s. Through Jesus Christ and the Holy Spirit, cursillistas discovered a new kind of awareness and new ways of being and seeing that would help them become whole. To use the language of twelve-step programs, the weekend is a way for candidates to take their "personal inventories." Cursillistas take stock of their past and present lives and reflect on how their lives can improve, with the focus on a new relationship with a loving God and His son, Jesus Christ. Like their counterparts in recovery programs, cursillistas rely on the small-group experience and its offerings of intimacy, safe space, and warmth. They gather for companionship and support, and, like members of AA and any number of its spinoffs, cursillistas challenge each other to continue to live a balanced life. Cursillistas push each other to grow spiritually and try hard not to take their new selves or relationships for granted.

Community: "My Group Reunion Meeting Is a Highlight of My Week"

Once their weekend experience is over, these newly inspired laymen and women form small groups, called group reunions (or reunion groups), which meet weekly or biweekly. While some find meaning in nonreligious clubs, groups, and civic organizations, others are drawn to religious and spiritual groups. The popularity of group reunion meetings and the key role that they play in cursillistas' living their Fourth Day is part of what Wuthnow and other sociologists of U.S. religions see as post-1950s Americans' new "quest for community."[86] Since the late 1950s at least, American men and women have searched for small groups that can satisfy their longing for friendship and spiritual growth. Like other Americans, cursillistas say they craved a meaningful community and true friends with whom they can share their spiritual journey. Group reunion meetings function as spiritual and communal touchstones for millions of cursillistas in the United States and around the world.

For Bob Franks, Friday breakfasts with his Via de Cristo reunion group help keep him spiritually centered. Bob has been meeting with his reunion group since 1989, and their breakfasts are "a highlight of my week and I always look forward to them." A retired college physics professor, Bob said that he was not the typical candidate in that he entered the Cursillo weekend skeptical and wanting to analyze everything. But at one point during the weekend, his faith moved from his head and reached his heart. While Bob's wife, Rhoda, said her weekend Cursillo is a highlight of her life and brought her to a new place with her faith, she has not had the same experience of a successful, regularly meeting reunion group. While she has maintained her involvement in reunion group meetings, hers have broken up due to some members' moving and other members domineering and pushing fellow members away. Like her husband, Rhoda stays active in Via de Cristo and attends the monthly ultreyas to stay connected and to continue to live "a life with Christ."[87]

Dialectics of Self and Community: "My Group Reunion Is Where I Am Held Accountable"

For many cursillistas I have interviewed, the devil has been all too real and has taken over their lives. In their single "Monkey Gone to Heaven," the 1980s alternative rock band the Pixies sing: "If Man is five. . . . if the Devil is six. . . . then God is seven."[88] Cursillistas conquer the devil during their weekend experience, and their reunion groups help them continue to keep their minds and hearts focused on God. For cursillistas, God (number seven in the Pixies' song) trumps themselves (number five) and the devil (number six). Moreover, cursillistas believe that it takes other devoted active Christians to help keep them accountable.

The rise of Cursillos among Catholics and Protestants also paralleled and drew on the recovery movement that has been part of American cultural discourse since the 1960s. Tanya, head secretary for Westminster Presbyterian Church in Rockford, Illinois, says that her weekly Tuesday night group reunion meetings are essential to her continual "walk with Christ" because the group "gives me and others accountability. We all need it, and it makes a huge difference to have people you trust tell you what you need to be doing better and what you are doing well. . . . The intimacy that you find in your group reunion is like nothing I have ever experienced. There is an element of love, trust, and support that you just can't get anywhere else."[89] Tanya went on to illustrate the deep bonds of love and friendship that form among reunion group members: "After my mother-in-law's son was diagnosed with cancer she just didn't have the energy or the heart to decorate her home for Christmas. Her reunion group met at her home and spent the afternoon decorating her house for Christmas. They set up the tree and everything!" In Tanya's estimation, reunion group members are like "stepping stones; each person is like a stone helping us in our walk to heaven."[90]

Tanya's emphasis on the importance of reunion groups for cursillistas in their Fourth-Day journey was echoed by all of the cursillistas I have interviewed. Steve Gielda, vice president of outreach for Via de Cristo and member of a Virginia reunion group, gave a Fourth-Day talk on this topic at an Orlando Via de Cristo ultreya. In it he underscored the importance of reunion groups and how members become like family, "even closer than family in many cases," for cursillistas. Steve says he was able to fully appreciate the significance of reunion groups when he attended his mother's recent funeral. Distraught over her unexpected death (the result of a car accident caused by a driver who fell asleep at the wheel), he was "moved to tears of joy" when, during the visitation, women who were members of his mother's three reunion groups entered the chapel singing. The women had come from three different cities where his mother had lived. "Their presence was powerful, and they witnessed a profound love and connection with my mother that made everyone in the room feel the love and bonds of friendship and commitment that existed. It was an incredibly moving testament of friendship, love, and devotion." In that moment Steve "really understood the power of love, friendship, and how we help each other in our walk with Christ."[91]

In our interview, Rita Gustafson, a member of Northern Illinois region Via de Cristo, also spoke at length about how her reunion group members "have really helped sustain me in times of trial and need." Rita offered a couple of examples to illustrate the important role reunion groups play in the lives of Fourth-Day movement members, citing her "transracial" adoption of two children and her father-in-law's hospitalization and death as moments when her reunion group members rallied behind her, going "above and beyond what even family members did" to show their love and support for Rita and her family.[92] Her reunion group members would bring over food for Rita and her husband, daughter, and two sons after she had spent the day at work, at the boys' soccer practice, and at the hospital with her dying father-in-law. Her reunion group members fully embraced her adopted children. "It was my reunion group members who made me feel that the only color that matters is the color of Christ's blood, and I felt fully supported by them as Jon and I went through the adoption process."[93]

While the majority of cursillistas I have interviewed, like Rita, have gone on to become involved in their Fourth-Day movement, I have met some who came away with mixed feelings about their weekend and are not maintaining any involvement. For these men and women, the weekend's rules and structure were overwhelming and prevented them from enjoying the three days. For Linda, the three days were "not so good" because she felt "confined and like I was being told what to do the whole time." While most of the men and women I interviewed said they were liberated and empowered by the weekend events, and they are the focus of this book, it is important to note that not all cursillistas come away with positive associations.[94]

In the next chapter I will discuss a movement for Catholic young adults, founded by two individuals motivated by their Catholic Cursillo weekends. As part of "living their Fourth," Father Matt Fedewa and Dorothy Gereke, aka Sister Mary Concetta, formed the Cursillo offshoot for young adults Teens Encounter Christ (TEC) in 1965. In creating TEC, Father Matt and Sister Mary Concetta initiated a weekend experience that took American Catholic teenagers seriously as young adults and counted them as important members of society and the Church.

CHAPTER FIVE

Teens Encounter Christ

Pioneer in Young Adult Weekend Experiences

I'm getting old and my back is starting to bend, but I decided a long time ago that I'd rather wear out than rust out.
—Dorothy Gereke, aka Sister Mary Concetta, RSM, aka "Mama TEC," cofounder of Teens Encounter Christ, May 25, 2010

TEC came about after a group of Cursillo men came to me and said they wanted a retreat for their sons that was based on Cursillo. You see, the old style of retreats for youth just wasn't working, and we needed something new and dynamic for the Catholic youth of the 1960s that was more than priests just lecturing to the youth.
—Father Matt Fedewa, cofounder of Teens Encounter Christ, June 18, 2010

Unless a grain of wheat falls into the ground and dies, it remains only a single grain; but if it does die, it produces a rich harvest.
—John 12:24

Meeting Dorothy and Father Matt

It is a humid and warm summer day in Festus, Missouri, when I finally meet Dorothy Gereke, one of the cofounders of Teens Encounter Christ (TEC), in person, after many long distance phone conversations. Ever the gracious hostess, she insists "Never mind, let's talk now!" when I unintentionally wake her from a late-afternoon nap at the Drury Inn, where we were staying. Dorothy, formerly known as Sister Mary Concetta of the Detroit-based Sisters of Mercy (1957–68), is now in her late eighties. Today, Dorothy is "a little bit slower than I used to be," largely because of circulation problems in her legs, which require her to wear support hose so that she can walk. Dorothy dislikes the hose, which take a long time to put on and are tight, but she sighs and says that it is necessary to wear them so that she can walk and "to do the work that I do for the Lord." Dorothy's spirit and determination make her appear younger than her age, and her easy laugh, sparkling eyes, and warm demeanor make it easy to see why she is affectionately called "Mama TEC" by her admirers in the movement. While our phone conversations that led up to our Missouri meeting had convinced me that Dorothy was indeed a spirited and spunky Catholic woman, spending time with her in person is another thing. This former nun is blessed with a keen intelligence and wit, and has more energy than most twenty-year-olds I know. A cradle Catholic, she has maintained a rigorous prayer life for over seven decades. Dorothy continues to attend daily mass and maintains a busy travel schedule, flying around the country to give talks at Catholic organizations such as the National Federation of Catholic Youth Ministry (NFCYM) and to attend TEC weekends as an honorary guest as part of her "ministry of presence." Our Missouri meeting marks the start of her five-week tour of the Midwest and West. Dorothy is eager to meet Catholic youth, the adults who mentor them and share in their journey, and to see her friends and family in Iowa. She chuckles and smiles when I express my surprise at her hectic schedule, given her advanced age, saying: "A friend of mine just the other day looked at my schedule and said, 'Wow! I'm tired just looking at it! Looks like you are, too!'"

For much of her adult life, Dorothy has channeled her deep Catholic faith and considerable organizational skills as a former hospital administrator, and has worked alongside TEC cofounder, friend, and collaborator Father Matt Fedewa, a now-retired diocesan priest and educator in the Diocese of Lansing, Michigan, to usher in one of the most significant and long-standing religious movements for Christian youth in the last century. TEC, cofounded by Father Matt and Sister Concetta in Battle Creek, Michigan, in 1965, was at its inception an intentional departure from other Catholic youth retreats. From the start, TEC took its participants, teenagers and young adults aged seventeen to twenty-four, seriously as individuals and as members of a cultural group with its own concerns and needs.

Most other youth-oriented retreats of the time which "talked down to youth," according to Father Matt and Dorothy. In this way, the early TECs were analogous to the first Mallorquín CdCs, which branched off of the hierarchically run retreats held by Catholic Action for young Catholic men.[1] Moreover, TEC was founded as a "multigenerational movement," according to Ronald ("Ron") Reiter, TEC's executive director from 2005 to 2012. This, too, is analogous to CdC's early years, when the weekend was geared toward young Catholics. Ron, Father Matt, and

Dorothy all emphasize the combination of adults and young adults working together as a key component of TEC's identity and a primary reason for its longevity.

TEC was the first Catholic branch of CdC to be founded in the United States amid the Second Vatican Council and the "winds of change," as Father Matt likes to say, that swept through the American Catholic Church as well as broader American society.[2] Part of the new American Catholicism of the 1960s, TEC experimented with new ways of teaching Catholicism and offered young adult Catholics new venues for their faith expressions. Progressive and traditional at the same time, TEC embraced both change and long-standing Catholic theological tradition. At TEC's core is an insistence on traditional Catholic teachings surrounding the Paschal Mystery of Christ—the theological triptych of Christ's Crucifixion, Death, and Resurrection.

As many scholars have pointed out, what it meant to "be" Catholic after Vatican II became more complicated and contested—distressful, even, to some U.S. Catholics.[3] But Vatican II gave Catholic reformers like Father Matt and Sister Concetta, and the young people with whom they worked, permission to explore their Catholic identity in new and exciting ways—all the while staying true to Roman Catholic tradition. To Father Matt and Sister Concetta, Vatican II was a time of opportunity that gave them the permission they needed, as a man and a woman who had taken vows of obedience, to usher in a spiritual renewal movement for young adult Catholics.

The Snow-Shoveling Photo and TEC's Beginnings

While the weekend itself focuses on Christ's love for the young adults in attendance, the history of TEC is about reciprocity and cooperation between priests, nuns, and laypeople who want these young Catholics to experience Christ's love. Father Matt and Sister Concetta were inspired by their own experiences with retreats, Catholic Cursillo weekends, post-Vatican II Catholicism, the burgeoning field of adolescent psychology, and their own observations and participation with Catholic young people.[4] They point to one weekend youth retreat in particular as a turning point for TEC and in their lives. Father Matt, who was in demand as a leader of youth retreats in the early 1960s, says that he was asked by the parents of teenagers to offer a Cursillo for their teens. These parents had been "profoundly moved" by their own Catholic Cursillo weekend and wanted a similar experience for their sons. According to Ron Reiter, "How it all started was that the Battle Creek Cursillo community wanted to share their experiences with their sons and daughters but didn't want them to have to wait until they were in their thirties to take a Cursillo. They asked Father Matt if they could have something for their children and it was Father Matt, who was experienced in holding retreats for youth, who designed the first TEC. Soon after, Father Jim [Brown] entered the picture and told Father Matt, 'You have a tiger by its tail here.'"[5]

In 1963, convinced that the time was right for a new kind of weekend experience for his high school youth, Father Matt took twenty-seven young men from the Diocese of Lansing to the University of Notre Dame in South Bend, Indiana, for a "Cursillo-type retreat." He says that they "had a great experience and came away refreshed, renewed, and ready to be of service in the world."[6] Father Matt says he aimed to offer a meaningful, contemplative rite of passage for the young men, something that was "good and positive and not moralistic and negative because that is precisely what a lot of them had been getting in their schools and churches."[7] At this point in our conversation Father Matt paused and said, "What became known as TEC is more than just emotion. It taps into initiation rites and the creation of a culture in which young men receive an identity which sacramentally they've been given but that they'd been taught. TEC gives young men a chance to become what they already are."[8] Like his Mallorquín predecessor Eduardo Bonnín, Father Matt, in his pre-TEC retreats, aimed to reignite young Catholic men's faith and to give them time to reflect on who they were as individuals.

In a retelling of a story that has assumed mythical, even sacred, dimensions for members of the TEC community, the day after the retreat, when the young men would normally have attended school, a winter storm hit the area and the young men went out and shoveled snow for the elderly all over South Bend. The Associated Press (AP) picked up the story because, according to Father Matt, "a bunch of young men willingly serving others was really newsworthy at the time, you see, because so many people in the 1960s had a negative impression of youth as lazy and self-centered. Well, these young men sure proved them wrong!"[9]

After the photo appeared in newspapers across the United States, Father Matt says he received "hundreds" of phone calls and letters from priests and parents who wanted to sponsor a similar retreat for the youth of their parishes. Father Matt remembers answering that if they were serious about starting a program in their parish or diocese, they would have to come and observe a weekend. Until the Notre Dame weekend, Father Matt and Dorothy had been leading weekends for young men and women, respectively. The Notre Dame weekend was the catalyst that brought them together to combine and formalize what they were doing independently. Father Matt smiles and shakes his head a bit when he thinks about the rapid expansion of TEC in the 1960s and 1970s: "The whole evolution of TEC is crazy, really. I never intended to start a movement. I just wanted to make a better retreat for my high school kids!"[10]

Dorothy and Father Matt realized that they would have to write a manual and sat down to do it while both were deeply committed to their own vocations. At the time Father Matt was a parish priest, a high school teacher, and was working on his master's degree from Loyola University's Institute of Pastoral Studies, a Vatican II–inspired and funded program to provide additional training to priests and sisters: "Basically, I would be at Loyola all week and would come home every weekend to say mass. I would stay at the Lodge [the retreat center owned by the Sisters of Mercy that was adjacent to Lila Post Hospital]. Then in July of 1965 I went to Dorothy and told her that we should create a new and dynamic retreat for youth, based on our experiences. I said to her, 'What would you say if we had 1,200 seniors go through the Lodge this year?' It was a busy, exhausting time but exhilarating, too!"[11]

Sister Concetta's response to Father Matt was an "automatic yes. . . . I'll get permission from the Sisters and you get permission from the diocese."[12] This sister and priest had gotten to know each other well as Father Matt was confessor to the Lila Post Hospital, which was run by the Detroit Sisters of Mercy and of which Sister Concetta was chief administrator. They found themselves talking a lot about young adult spirituality and what the Vatican II church could do to encourage their spirituality. They had both participated in the Catholic youth weekend experience Seeking Each Other and Receiving Christ's Hand (SEARCH) as well as the Better World Movement (BWM) and shared a deep commitment to Vatican II–inspired renewals.[13] Sister Concetta says she "had the full support" of the Sisters of Mercy "without whom TEC would not have been possible, for they helped make the weekends happen."[14] Fellow sisters helped to staff the early TEC weekends and the order made sure that TEC was first in line for reserving the Lodge for its weekends, given the many requests for weekend retreats during this time.[15]

The first two pre-TECs were for young men and were held at the University of Notre Dame. The AP story called the weekend retreat a Cursillo and put Father Matt in a position of authority in Catholic circles, catapulting him to fame among reform-minded U.S. Catholics. Father Matt chuckles when he thinks back to the Notre Dame experience, the media's coverage of it, and Catholics' response. He told me that the article "got it wrong—we weren't Cursillo but something else for youth. The Notre Dame weekend was like a Cursillo for young men, but it was then unnamed and was pre-TEC."[16]

Father Matt and Dorothy point out that when they were thinking about a name they were certain of one thing they would not call it: a weekend retreat. "We knew this would scare youth away because of all of the negative associations with the word *retreat*!" Dorothy says.[17] Father Matt acknowledges that times have changed and that youth today have positive connotations with the word *retreat*, but it was not this way in the 1960s.

The practical effects of the AP photo on their lives were astonishing to Father Matt and Sister Concetta. The two found that they worked well together, their many talents combined: as a high school educator, Father Matt had years of experience working with Catholic young men and knew "what worked with them and what did not." His studies at Loyola were grounding him in Vatican II–inspired catechetics and exciting him "to enact some of these new ideas" in his high school courses.[18] He would drive up to Battle Creek from Chicago each weekend to serve as the spiritual director of the early TECs held at the Lodge, and it was during a break from classes and ministry in July 1965 that he began drafting the TEC manual with Sister Concetta's input.

For her part, Sister Concetta brought her expansive hospital administrative skills to the weekend and, with an eye for detail, wrote the first lay director's manual.[19] The first TEC manual was written by Father Matt and Sister Concetta at the TEC Lodge on 65 Emmett Street in Battle Creek on the Feast of the Assumption 1965. The manual was presented by the Diocese of Lansing and the Sisters of Mercy, who deemed the manual "for private use only." The July 21, 1965, version of the proposal called the weekend retreat "Exercises in Christian Living for Youth," borrowing the name from retreats Sister Concetta had been involved in that were similarly community-oriented. But Father Matt and Sister Concetta wanted their weekend to have its own name, something that would speak directly to the central place of the experience of the Paschal Mystery. The next month, they took another priest's suggestion and renamed it Teens Encounter Christ.

Current TEC executive director Ron Reiter says that soon after the development of the manual, adults were sent to Battle Creek for training: "TECs soon spread like wildfire and had a life of their own—they were unguided in the beginning. National gatherings were held, and people came from all over to attend. The first one was held in 1970, and 1,500 people gathered for the convention."[20]

The Reverend William J. Fitzgerald, director of religious education for the Diocese of Lansing and affectionately called "Fitz" by Dorothy (who knew him when she was known as Sister Concetta), wrote the introduction to the first manual, in which he emphasized the "search for identity" as a "major preoccupation" of all adolescents. In TEC, he wrote, "the student is able to live what he learns. He is freed from the sometimes frustrating experience that comes from the limitations that time and place impose upon the classroom living situation. He is enabled to involve himself in the Mystery of Salvation as he lives a weekend with Christ in a Christian community."[21]

In their own introduction to the manual, the Sisters of Mercy emphasized the "real need youth has for help and support in the most important endeavor of finding self, finding God, and finding neighbors." The order expressed its desire to "assist in developing a continuing program that will give as many of our young people as possible the opportunity for a real personal encounter with Christ."[22] In the first TEC manual, speakers are explicitly told to avoid "talking about teenage morals, or sin, or indulge in any of the many forms of negativism with which our students have been too long confronted in the name of Christianity."[23] Rev. Fitzgerald and the Sisters of Mercy saw in TEC the possibility of reaching 1960s Catholic teens with a weekend encounter tailored to their generation. There were few rules and regulations in the early TEC weekends; "just don't hurt the property or anyone else," according to Dorothy. "We even allowed smoking during the weekend—can you believe that!" exclaims Father Matt. Sure enough, the "Announcements and Ground Rules" section of the manual states that "smoking will be permitted in the conference room, lounges on second and third floors, as well as the dining room."[24] And reminiscent of the early Mallorquín Catholic Cursillos de Cristiandad, at the early TEC retreats, change was made available for the participants to purchase cokes, cigarettes, and candy.[25] A social leveling was at work in both CdC and this Catholic spirituality movement for youth it inspired.

Casual clothing was also encouraged, except for designated liturgy and chapel times. The young women, or "girls," however, were asked to wear dresses or skirts. The Sisters of Mercy wrote in the manual that "the reason we request the girls not to wear slacks, etc., is that we are trying to inspire them to bring out all of their womanly virtues."[26] The weekend encounter for teens was in some ways a pioneering youth retreat in its tone and focus, but there were still limits on how far the founders would go. Gendered identities were upheld; in asking the "girls" to wear dresses or skirts, a specific kind of Catholic womanhood was promoted and maintained. As primary sources and secondary sources have informed us, U.S. Catholics still wanted their "girls" to look pretty and feminine, and to fulfill their godly duties of becoming wives and mothers.[27]

While TEC weekend dress codes for young men and women indicated a desire to maintain decorum and "tradition," women religious were experiencing their own changing dress codes in the wake of the Vatican II Council. For many U.S. orders of women religious, sisters' changing habits reflected Catholics' attitudes toward Catholic women.[28] Dorothy remembers wearing the full habit in TEC's inaugural year and in 1966 the modified habit, which was "freeing to her and many, many sisters." The Catholic manhood and womanhood maintained and promoted during the early TEC retreats reaffirmed what it had meant to be a good Catholic "boy" or "girl" but began leaving some room for negotiation. For women religious the visible signs of change were in the modified habit as well as in more public and vocal roles. Vatican II afforded young laywomen new opportunities to become leaders among Catholic youth through Vatican II initiatives such as youth apostolates.

While participants may have been conservatively dressed, the TEC weekends were new and experimental—even radical—for American Catholics at the time. These young adults and their adult mentors were pioneers in a new American Catholicism that built on the "old" Catholic faith and made it "new" and relevant for these young adults. The thirty-five Michigan State University Catholic students who participated in apostolic formation weekends at the TEC Lodge in Battle Creek were trained to be campus leaders on the Lay Apostolate, specifically the new roles for laity decreed by Vatican II.[29]

When the movement was three years old, at the time of the 1968 TEC rally in Battle Creek, a total of 249 TEC weekends had been held, with a total of 10,109 candidates and 5,057 volunteers.[30] Part Woodstock, part Catholic liturgy, the early TEC rallies came in the wake of the larger Vatican II reforms and were part of an exciting time of experimentation in

The TEC Hippy Jesus, 1968 TEC rally, Battle Creek, Michigan. Courtesy of TEC Conference.

ways of worship. At the early TEC events such as this rally, young Catholics smoked, played guitars, and sang folk and civil rights songs such as "We Shall Overcome"—all alongside supportive, habited nuns and priests.[31] While their "oppression" was a far cry from that of blacks in the Jim Crow South, these mostly white, non-Hispanic Catholic youth saw themselves as overcoming oppression from the institutionalized Church as well as from larger society. The songs of protest and empowerment appealed to them because for the first time in many of their young lives they were taking ownership of their faith and were agents rather than recipients of theology.

The rally was a big hit and the fieldhouse was packed with excited youth at 6:00 P.M. for the Folksong Concert. The TEC rally's symbol was a long-haired Jesus strumming the guitar in flowing robes and wearing a crown of thorns. Here was a hip and "new" but "old" Jesus—one who died for these youths' sins but also a younger man they could pray and sing to.[32]

In the three years building up to the 1968 rally, Father Matt and Sister Concetta put in "hundreds of hours" to ensure TEC's success. Indeed, the records from the TEC weekends held in the Diocese of Lansing list Father

1968 TEC rally, Battle Creek, Michigan. Courtesy of TEC Conference.

Matthew Fedewa and Sister Mary Concetta as director and codirector, respectively, for almost every TEC from 1965 to 1969. For her part, Sister Concetta spent her weekends overseeing TEC and put in long days Tuesday through Friday playing catch-up because of the days she had been absent for the hospital: "At this time I was so busy, I had a $3 million fund drive for the hospital that I was overseeing and all of these other responsibilities. Priests were wanting to hold Cursillos at the Lodge, and parents were wanting their teens to be in the retreat that Father Matt had held at Notre Dame. A sister friend of mine from Ann Arbor invited me there to hold retreats from Monday to Wednesday and Wednesday to Friday, and a priest from the student center went to Ann Arbor to help put in these courses. It was a busy, busy time!"[33]

She says that Father Matt was the "roots" of TEC and she was its "wings." They were a team, and each brought specific skills and gifts to the early TEC weekends:

We decided to have different teams each weekend. Father Matt is the theologian—much more than me. I was the catalyst, the coordinator, the supervisor. He'd get a team together and I'd say, "Well, who's going to be over at the Lodge that weekend?" Two of our sisters volunteered to be there, and then there was me. Father Matt brought the first team, and a priest from Flint [Michigan] would be there. They'd go home, and a month later we had a team of adults and students who had made the course, and all of these people would help it run.[34]

She describes the early days of the movement as exhilarating and exhausting.

We scheduled twenty-seven weekends that year, starting October 9, 1965. I was at each weekend, and the other two sisters really helped out. But sometimes one was sick or the other was working, so I always had to be there. I was so convinced that this was the Holy Spirit and the Lord's work that I gave my *everything* to TEC. So from Friday evening to Monday I was busy with TEC and from Tuesday A.M. to Friday evening I was doing hospital administration work. I was fortunate to have a very capable hospital administrative assistant, but I still had to work sixteen- to eighteen-hour days at the hospital to catch up.[35]

Dorothy recalls that in those early years of TEC, she and Father Matt fielded dozens of phone calls from priests and laity across the United States. All of the callers had questions about the weekend experience and wanted a TEC manual. When I asked her how she responded, she replied, "We told them that TEC isn't a cookbook. You have to come and observe how it is done . . . not just read about it."[36] Dorothy and Father Matt made it a point to welcome anyone interested in sponsoring a TEC to one of the many TEC weekends they hosted at the Lodge. Dorothy resigned from her full-time administrative position at the hospital to focus exclusively on TEC. She had been working two full-time jobs and it was exhausting her. In a Christmas letter to the then-Sister Mary Concetta, Father Matt writes that her resignation from the hospital to devote herself full time to religious education "was a fantastically generous move. I imagine there are times of regret especially when the adolescent is so much adolescent and so little adult."[37]

On a larger scale, the working partnership and friendship between Father Matt and Dorothy dovetails the history of women religious and priests, the sometimes lifelong friendships and the mutual admiration that accompanies those friendships.[38] The history of TEC elucidates the working relationships between women religious, in this case the Detroit Sisters of Mercy, diocesan priests, bishops, and archbishops, all of whom were committed to creating meaningful retreats for Catholic youth.

"There Is No Such Thing as a Coincidence"

In the course of conducting the research for this book I was told again and again that "there is no such thing as a coincidence." When I first spoke with Ron Reiter, then the executive director of TEC and told him a little bit about the scope of this book, he interjected, "You know, I just came back from a trip to Boston where we just had a TEC workshop. On the way home on the plane I thought about how great it would be if we could get the founders' memoirs in a book form and here you are calling me. I kid you not, I wrote this down! You called me for a reason, that's for sure."[39]

Ron's interpretation of my phone call and the meanings embedded in it is seconded by the leaders and members of all of the other organizations chronicled in this book. The people I have talked to, from all of the various Fourth-Day movements, believe that things happen for a reason, that God has a master plan, and we just don't know it. Moreover, they believe, we have to be open to God's leading us in new directions. My involvement and presence as a scholar was interpreted as a "sign from God" for them to "keep doing what we are doing," as many in the Fourth-Day movements have told me. The men and women who have been through one of the Cursillo-based Christian retreats covered in this book believe that God played a hand in their making their weekend retreat and coming away as refreshed and reborn Christians. Whether one understands these events as caused by God's will, the alignment of the stars, or just plain ole good luck, the same hermeneutics of events can be applied to the 1965 founding of TEC in Battle Creek.

Father Matt and Sister Concetta first met in the early 1960s when he was assigned to St. Phillip parish in Battle Creek and was confessor to the former Lila Post Montgomery Hospital, run by the Detroit Sisters of Mercy. As a diocesan priest, Father Matt's duties included visiting hospital patients and tending to the Sisters' confessional needs. At this time he also developed an interest in youth ministry, seeing a need for a more dynamic kind of outreach to young adults. In the 1950s and early 1960s, according to Father Matt, youth ministry was "the parish mission approach and was top-down in its style of teaching. Basically, the priests talked and the youth listened." After a "disastrous" retreat where "I basically did exactly what I hated, talking down to the young men for three days," Father Matt says he told God during the drive home, "See, I told you that I wasn't cut out for this kind of thing! Youth ministry is not my vocation!"[40] But God, says Father Matt, had a plan for him.

Father Matt also was inspired by Vatican II. "I remember it well," he says. "It was on the feast day of Saint Paul when I heard that the pope had called an ecumenical council. I about fell out of my chair from the excitement it stirred in me!"[41] Motivated by the ecumenical council, by what he calls its accompanying experimental climate of the 1960s, and by a mutual desire to make religion "fun" and meaningful for Catholic youth, Father Matt entered into an enormously productive and significant phase of his life. For her part, Sister Concetta was also motivated by Vatican II–related reforms and wanted to make the faith and tradition that were so dear to her more relevant for the young Catholic women she encountered. Like Father Matt, Sister Concetta devoted much of her waking hours to crafting a weekend encounter for young Catholic adults that would not only inspire them during the weekend but empower them for the rest of their lives. As Catholics, Father Matt and Sister Concetta were deeply committed to fostering a living experience with the Paschal Mystery of Christ ("Die, Rise, Go Forth"), which has become the hallmark of the movement. The challenge was to relate the Paschal Mystery in a way that would resonate with young adults. They wanted Catholic young adults to "move beyond the faith and reason they'd been schooled in and to venture into religion of the heart."[42] They designed TEC to be the "smells and bells—the experiential part—of Catholicism because Catholicism is based on liturgy, and we wanted something that was different from the priest preaching at them."[43]

It was precisely the weekend's focus on the Paschal Mystery that attracted a young priest named Roger Schwietz. Father Roger, or as he is known today, Archbishop Schwietz of Anchorage, Alaska, first became involved with TEC in the summer of 1975. At the time he was assigned to St. Thomas parish in International Falls, Minnesota. The parish held its first TEC and a group of TEC veterans from the St. Louis area went to International Falls to put on the course. In recalling the weekend events, the archbishop notes the joining of the Paschal Mystery with spiritual renewal:

> It was a moving experience, one I haven't forgotten. It was all about the Paschal Mystery of Jesus—dying and rising. This made a lot of sense to me, but it was even more than this—it was about a spiritual renewal. TEC gave people a sense of what Christian life was all about. I thought then and still do that TEC is a gift in which people are invited into the Paschal Mystery as well as a personal relationship with Jesus. Moreover, one can develop this personal relationship with Jesus in community. The course is very intentional in hitting on this.[44]

For his part, Father Matt wanted to make the Paschal Mystery exciting and meaningful to young Catholics. He wanted Christ to be more "real" to them and to be someone young adult Catholics could turn to. After experiencing "one boring retreat for youth after another," and even presiding over one of those "awful boring retreats" himself, Father Matt knew that there had to be a better way to bring "the mystery of Christ and His message of love and hope" to the 1960s generation.[45] Little did he know that someone else was thinking the same thing and starting to sponsor retreats for Catholic young women, someone who happened to be in the Michigan diocese to which he was assigned.

For Father Matt in particular, the "foundations of the faith," which are rooted in the Paschal Mystery of Christ, along with the new methods of holding retreats and the new adolescent psychology that were in circulation, all came together in a perfect storm of theology and science. As a Catholic high school teacher, he was up to date on new teaching philosophies that emphasized greater democracy in the classroom. Father Matt emphasizes that TEC was both old and new Catholicism: both rooted in Christ's life journey and embracing the new catechetical and liturgical movements.

Father Matt and Dorothy are the first to say that they did not do all of the work and that they received support and encouragement from many women and men, significantly the Sisters of Mercy and Father Alfonse Nebreda, then the bishop of Lansing. The Reverend Fitzgerald, director of religious education for the Diocese of Lansing, was another important early and enthusiastic supporter, well aware of the challenges of young adulthood and of the lack of meaningful outreach programs for religious youth at the time. In his introduction to the first TEC manual, Fitzgerald writes that the search for identity is a particular concern for Christian youth, whose search involves not only self-identification but Christ-identification. He described Teens Encounter Christ as a major contribution to the solution of that problem and the answering of that question.[46]

When Father Matt approached her about offering the youth retreats, Sister Concetta, in addition to her work as administrator of Lila Post Hospital, was also offering weekend retreats for female Catholic high school seniors at the Lodge. The Lodge had originally been the site of a three-year nursing program for the Sisters of Mercy, but when the nursing program was terminated in 1956, the Sisters were "challenged with finding the most effective use for the former student residence." The Sisters found that while the building did not adapt well to patient or hospital use, "it seem[ed] particularly well suited for various apostolic projects in this age of renewal."[47] The Lodge became the site for the early TEC weekends, the place where men and women religious and laity from the Diocese of Lansing came together to bring a new experience of Catholicism to young adults.

Dorothy describes the Lodge as a gift from God that was used for many good purposes in its time:

> The Lodge was just beautiful. There were forty-eight private rooms, a large auditorium, a large living room, just a lovely space. I feel that all of our resources are gifts from God and that we need to use and to share these gifts. I started working with diocesan social services, and I made room for unwed mothers. I counseled them, worked with them until they had their babies and either kept them or put them up for adoption with Catholic Charities. I did this for about two and a half years or so. I told my Sisters that I wanted them to enjoy the Lodge and wanted them to come for longer than the summer. The Sisters liked it so much that they requested to come more frequently and for longer. The Sisters of Mercy, who taught high school in Detroit [their provincial house was in Detroit], wanted to bring high school girls there for six-to-eight-day retreats.[48]

In addition to housing nursing students and unwed mothers and being a place for rest and relaxation for priests and sisters, the Lodge also was the site dozens of Catholic Cursillo weekends before becoming the first

TEC center. Cursillo came to the Lansing diocese in 1961, and for the first year the weekends were held in Spanish. Two years later, the weekend experience was offered in English. Father Matt and Sister Concetta, who had heard "many great things" about the Cursillo weekend and experience from friends, were among the first to make their Cursillos in Michigan, Father Matt in late summer 1963 and Sister Concetta several months later. Sister Concetta in particular had been drawn to retreats and had participated in several. Before her Cursillo weekend, she had experienced SEARCH, the California-based Catholic youth movement popular in the 1960s and 1970s. She was also involved in the Better World Movement (BWM), founded by a Jesuit in Rome who wanted to see laity and priests working together for their Church and faith. The BWM retreats, which lasted six days, were created in the spirit of Vatican II in that they emphasized laity and men and women religious worshipping together and learning from each other.

Dorothy says she was drawn to Vatican II–era retreats because of the possibilities they opened up for Catholics and their Church. Her experiences with BWM, Cursillo, an Exercise in Christian Living weekend, and a SEARCH weekend were life-changing and led to her commitment to youth.[49] Her Cursillo in particular, she says, was "very moving": "Cursillo really blew my mind. After my Cursillo I wanted to put on Cursillos for adults—I had never worked with young people at that time. But when I started to hear from parents that they wanted TEC for their sons and daughters, I held TECs alternate weekends as Cursillos at the Lodge. I remember the New Year's Eve TECs—parents would come from their happy hour at their parties and would have 'Holy Hour'—it was really moving. Cursillo made quite an impact on me, and TEC was very much influenced by Cursillo. Father Matt and I were very moved to take our Cursillo experiences and start a similar movement for youth." As Father Matt put it to me during one of our conversations, "There was nothing wrong with youth, and there was nothing wrong with the Gospel. . . . it was how we were doing it. The Cursillo table experience and the spontaneous sacrament, the Cursillo dynamic really inspired me when we were thinking about how to offer a new kind of retreat for Catholic youth."[50]

Archbishop Schwietz says that Father Matt's incorporation of group dynamics into TEC was "ingenious" and that it resonated with youth who he believes are subject to a cult of individuality that is ultimately damaging to them.

We as Americans value our autonomy, our individuality. There is a lot of individualism, but a hunger for community we don't always recognize. For young people they discover an intentional community outside their family. Young people are so subject to our culture—we are asked to keep our faith private, and I believe it is harmful to our faith and our youth and culture to do this. It's quite a discovery for young people to discover young people who desire to know Christ—it's a kind of "wow" moment. So it's the public recognition of faith in their community and the community that comes out of TEC that are vital components to its success.[51]

At the time they developed TEC into a spiritual renewal weekend for Catholic youth, Father Matt and Sister Concetta were aiming for the "wow" moment that Archbishop Schwietz describes. They wanted to offer a safe and nurturing environment, with adult guidance and supervision, for young Catholics to experience Christ's love and to come into their own as people of faith. They saw their role as that of Christian stewards who would encourage the faith development of the young people in their care.

The "Roots" and the "Wings": The Making of TEC

When we first met in June 2010, Dorothy was just starting her five-week travel schedule, which included consultant work for TEC and her "ministry of presence." Father Matt, in his mid-seventies when we met, was the intellectual force behind TEC's early years and remains a valued consultant for the movement. Teasing Dorothy at our June gathering, he told her that she does all of the running around for the two of them and that he is perfectly content to "be a homebody," which includes taking his morning walks (while praying the rosary on his fingers) and reading. After spending time with Father Matt, Dorothy, and Ron Reiter, the executive director of TEC who brought us all together, it was clear to me that the two are good friends and care deeply about each other.[52]

As they joked over drinks, Dorothy over a margarita and Father Matt over iced tea, at Drury Inn's happy hour, the two conveyed a shared faith that has made their friendship endure over the years. As old friends do, Father Matt and Dorothy finished sentences for each other and anticipated the direction of the conversation, peppering it with shared memories. Seeing the way in which Father Matt and Dorothy related to each

Dorothy Gereke and Father Matt Fedewa. Courtesy of TEC Conference.

other made it easy to understand how and why TEC was so successful in the late 1960s and 1970s. "I'll bet we kept the round table manufacturers in business for a while!," joked Father Matt and the former Sister Concetta, now known as Dorothy Gereke. One of the first things Father Matt said they did was to get rid of conference tables and bring in round tables where groups of six people, five young adults and their adult mentor, could sit together during the weekend encounter. The round tables used by TEC paralleled the Vatican II style of parishes built in the round and indicated a new outlook on the individual and the need for community.

Because they wanted to offer a new kind of retreat for Catholic youth, like SEARCH, that addressed young people's particular concerns and needs, they encouraged a more relaxed and open, intimate and interactive style of conversation. "We tapped into the inculturation which was an integral part of Vatican II—bringing the faith to the people in their style and language," said Father Matt. "We brought Catholicism to Catholic youth in a language and in a format they could relate to, and we took them seriously as young adults." Dorothy added, "Yes, we offered them

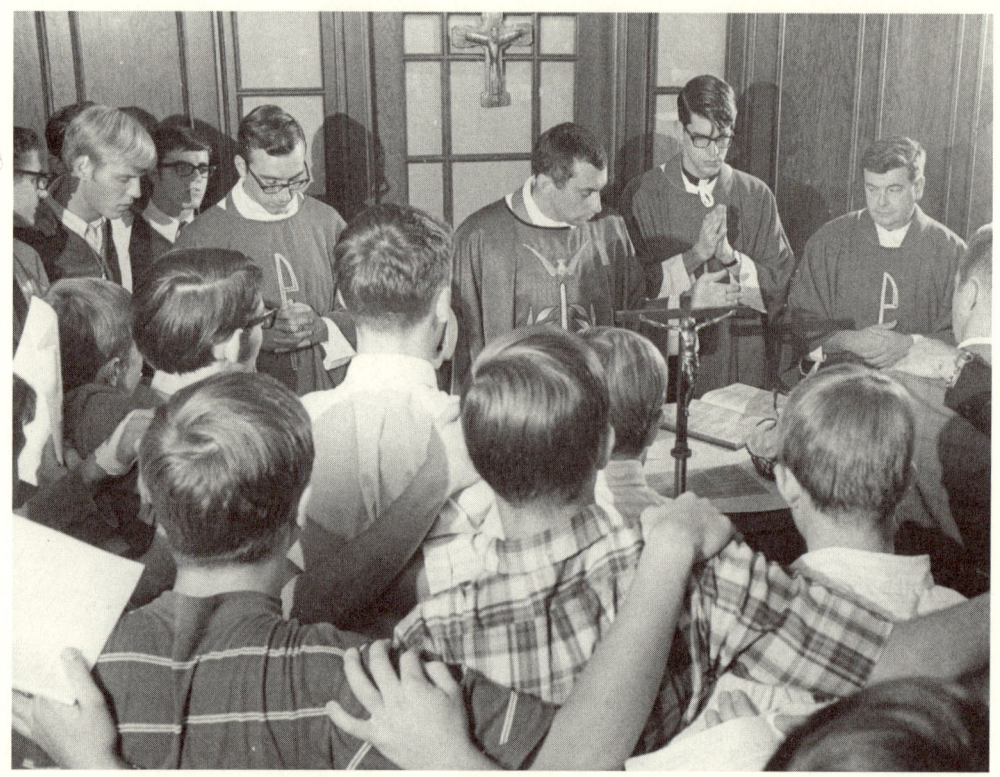
TEC boys' weekend, ca. 1966. Courtesy of TEC Conference.

solid Catholic faith in an environment where they were taken seriously as young people. We catered to them so much. . . . We wanted them to be as comfortable as they could be and if they smoked, well, then they could smoke!"

For all of their accommodations and relaxed demeanor, however, obstacles stood in their way. As Father Matt observed in the Christmas letter to Sister Concetta already quoted, "The students who drink, etc., give evidence that we are not just 'saving the saved.'"[53] One time, a group of boys overturned a trash can full of water on her as a prank: "It took a while for my habit to dry!" she recalled with a laugh. Dorothy credits her ability to work with such rambunctious young men to her growing up with four brothers, which accustomed her "to boys and their intense physicality.[54]

Father Matt and Sister Concetta were among those Vatican II–era Catholics who were eager to enact the reforms of their time. According to Father Matt, hearing the mass and blessing of the Sacrament in the vernacular, in English, was a "very moving" experience for the teens, who had felt distant from the Sacrament as it was "given to them in a language that was foreign to them." "As a result of Vatican II, young people could relate to their Church and faith in ways that they hadn't been able to before the Council," he said. Dorothy also wanted to reach out to youth in new ways: "We found that if we treated them well and didn't go down to their level, even the ones who were misbehaving, they saw that we respected them. That was a big thing for them because most adults did not show respect for teens. A major goal of ours was for these teens to be their own person and not a follower [sic]. We wanted them to find out who they were all about."[55]

As Father Matt and Dorothy reminisced at Drury's Inn on particularly meaningful experiences with TEC, Father Matt recalled an early boys' TEC weekend and what he called the "masturbation conversation." The topic came up during one of the weekend's open discussions, and the young men openly wrestled with the temptations, pleasures, and guilt they experienced while masturbating. Dorothy, who was present during this particular TEC weekend, said that she "just sat there and tried not to move because I did not want to distract them in any way. I don't think I moved for about twenty minutes!"[56] Creating an atmosphere of respect, support, and love was a major goal of the movement's cofounders and they worked hard to be empathetic listeners during the weekends they oversaw.

In their desire to show their concern and respect for American Catholic teenagers, Father Matt and Dorothy created a weekend experience geared toward the teenagers' particular needs and concerns. As a diocesan priest, Father Matt was part of the catechetical renewal taking place in the American Catholic Church. Predating the Vatican II Council by several years, the Office of Education in the Diocese of Lansing in 1957 undertook a new teaching curriculum that dovetailed with the larger, nationally based Confraternity of Christian Doctrine (CCD) teacher-training program reforms.[57] Inspired by his coursework at Loyola's Institute of Pastoral Studies, Father Matt was committed to figuring out a newer format of learning and experience for young Catholic adults. He credits the institute's Father Alfonse Nebreda, SJ, with providing the inspiration for what came to be called TEC. According to Father Matt, TEC benefitted from the resources provided by the Department of Religious Education, housed within the Lansing Diocesan Office of Education.[58] From the start, TEC was a diocesan-supported project.

The years 1965–69 were a whirlwind of activity for Father Matt and Sister Concetta, who oversaw hundreds of TEC weekends at the Lodge. As Father Matt wrote in 1967, "The doors of TEC Lodge, 65 Emmett Street, Battle Creek, Michigan, first opened on October 9, 1965. Some forty-five senior boys from ten different Catholic high school CCD programs participated. Their enthusiasm and conviction is the likely human explanation for the steady flow of candidates ever since. By Christmas, 1966, some forty-one TEC weekends had been conducted in the Diocese of Lansing, with a total of some 2,080 high school seniors participating."[59] In these formative years for TEC, each of the two founders had a specific role and relished it. As Dorothy puts it, Father Matt was the "roots"—the educator-theologian visionary—of TEC and she was the "wings," helping the movement flourish by facilitating the weekends' practical details. She recalls one day in particular,

> Father Matt came to my office with Father Alfonse Nebreda, head of catechetical at the time, and said to me, "If the Paschal Mystery is the central core of our faith"—death-resurrection-ascension—then we add group dynamics. We talked for a long time and decided that six tables with six people at each table was ideal because if you get too many more than this, there is no discussion. We set thirty-six as the ideal number.... I shared the experiences that I had with youth and retreats with the diocese and Father Matt shared his as well. Father Matt was wondering what to call [the weekend], and one of the priests present that day, Father Eugene Sears, said, "It's TEC: Teens Encounter Christ." So that's what we called it![60]

From 1965 to 1969, the four years Dorothy was involved in TEC as Sister Concetta, the Lodge was filled to capacity each weekend. Groups of teens had to "crowd into the chapel," and beds and mattresses were placed in each of the forty-eight rooms. The Sisters of Mercy were essential to the implementation and success of TEC, Dorothy says, because "it was they who provided us with the means for an effective, life-changing experience for youth.... I cannot thank them or stress their importance enough."[61] Writing in the first TEC manual of 1966, the Sisters of Mercy wrote that "the apostolate to youth remained our focal area of concentration in the use of the Lodge. So in the fall of 1964 we were asked to schedule closed retreats for high school seniors, and now it seems providential that a communitarian type of retreat was planned. As one retreat after another was scheduled during that year, the plan and format was modified so that it gradually began to be developed toward its present form of what we now entitle 'Teens Encounter Christ.'"[62]

The Philosophy, Nuts, and Bolts of a Typical TEC Weekend

TEC's motto, the verse from the Book of John quoted at the beginning of this chapter, has informed the weekend encounter since its 1965 inception. The goal is for young adults who participate in the encounter to "die" unto themselves on the first day, "rise" and become new individuals who have Christ on the second, and "go forth" on the third, committing themselves to bringing Christ to others as evangelizers. While the language of "Fourth Day" and "De Colores" is not used self-consciously by graduates of TEC, the "going forth" is what Catholic and Protestant cursillistas call "living the Fourth [Day]." TEC weekends held prior to the official publication of the first TEC manual in 1967 were called "Exercises in Christian Living" by Father Matt and Sister Concetta, but they knew that they needed a name for their weekend encounter for youth that packed a greater punch and that attracted Catholic youths' interest, especially given the negative connotations that surrounded youth retreats of the time. The Saturday through Monday encounter was intended to foster a greater sense of self as well as community, and to set the stage for individual and communal metanoia—a spiritual awakening and a powerful experience with Christ. Writing in 1967, Father Matt described the three days as being akin to Lent (Saturday), Easter (Sunday), and Pentecost (Monday).[63] From the start, writes Father Matt, the encounter was intended to share the "'good news,' the core of the Christian message, the mystery of Christ—the plan of the Father to call us in Christ by the power of the Holy Spirit to a life of personal intimacy with Him in the community of the Church."[64]

The Catholic youth who go through the weekend TEC are plugged into the Christological triptych and live out the experience for themselves. The pedagogy of the three days is to show the youth the Pascal Mystery and to involve them in it, and the adult mentors and TEC alumni who volunteer during the three days focus on ways to increase individual Catholic piety, strengthen the relationship with Christ, and offer a community in which this is possible. Adoration of the Eucharist is a central component of the three days, and events such as the agape meal served to the participants emphasizes sacrifice and love in the name of Christ. The course is unapologetically Catholic, and while non-Catholics are allowed to make the course, they are not permitted to take part in the distinctively Catholic Eucharist. Love and redemption have been hallmarks of TEC from the encounter's origins. TEC was imagined as part of a Church-based "total religion program," catechism and evangelization geared toward young adults with a new twist—offering a new rite of initiation that emphasized experience and the heart. According to Father Matt, the "TEC experience" was never intended to replace or supplant existing religious programs, but the hope was that it would "complete them."[65]

Father Matt and others involved in the religious education of youth incorporated the theologian Marcel Van Caster's experiential catechetics, which conceptualized the "triple task" of the catechist: to help inform youth, to form them, and to initiate them into a new life of Christ.[66] Once initiated, TEC alumni can go forth and evangelize. While the process itself was not entirely new, the dynamics accompanying each "task" during the TEC weekend was new, informed by the Vatican II reforms that gave Catholics, laity and women and men religious alike, new freedoms and possibilities by way of expressing and living their faith. And, as we have seen, TEC was deeply influenced by the Catholic Cursillo method. As cursillistas, Father Matt and Sister Concetta worked hard to integrate the group dynamics they experienced on their Cursillo weekends, along with the CdC's emphasis on lay empowerment via an encounter with Christ and the Holy Spirit. The question that TEC asks its youth participants, according to Father Matt when we met in 2010, is not "What am I going to do?" but "Who am I going to be?" The three-day course provides a setting in which young adults can look within themselves and ask how they want to live their lives, thus initiating lives of introspection. The encounter's events range from the deeply serious, such as meditating on Christ's crucifixion, to joy, as is displayed in Sunday evening's "hootenanny." The "hoot," as it tends to be called today, is a large and boisterous gathering of TEC candidates as well as TEC alumni, who "make evident the living church as a community of joy in Christ."[67] The TEC alumni I interviewed, even the two who were critical of the weekend, all spoke positively of the hoot and said it was a "big shot in the arm, a real boost of energy to see so many people this happy about their faith," according to Josh Lyphout, a TEC alumnus.[68]

Reminiscing on his involvement with TEC in the late 1960s and early 1970s, Archbishop Schwietz emphasizes the importance of good adult leadership and the possibilities of the weekend:

> For me, it is important to have a good process of discernment. The leaders are properly trained in the fundamentals of the faith, and they must have respect for young people and their freedom. On a personal level, I have found this respect to be a very important component in the success of TEC. When I was in International Falls, Minnesota, which is way up north on the border with Canada, there was a lot of historic tension between youth in International Falls and Fort Francis, Ontario. . . . There was this long history of violence and animosity between the two towns, and much of it centered on the rival hockey teams. As a result of this long-standing misunderstanding there were a lot of tensions between the youth of the two towns, a lot of prejudices. Well, the first TEC held in September 1975 in International Falls, Minnesota, really brought the youth together from these two towns. There was a melting of the barriers and the TEC group experience led to a real healing of community.[69]

What TEC Alumni Say Today

The TEC alumni I have spoken with all appreciated the love and concern that the adult peers showed them during the weekend. While some said the weekend ranks as one of "the best of my life so far," others were more measured in their comments and in their reflections on the experience.[70] Josh, for example, said that while he "got a lot out of the weekend, I mean, I was definitely more into my faith in the months after the weekend, and I was nicer to people," the intimate moments of the weekend made him a little uncomfortable as a young man.

> There is quite a bit of emotional stuff going on. The letters are very emotional, lots of men crying, and hugging. Many guys at my TEC just broke down. There is a lot of hugging at TEC, and I'm not really a huggy kind of guy. At the hoots, for example, people line the hallways in what is called an *abrazo* line, a "hug line." Imagine it: There were forty guys in my TEC, and there are two people per guy, so that makes eighty people hugging plus family members and friends who are there. There were probably around 200 people at the hoot—a whole lot of hugging. What I remember from my hoot was this sweaty bald guy who hugged everyone—not my kind of thing, you know?![71]

Even more than Josh, who made his TEC as part of a high school requirement, Kate, a college senior when we met, emphasized that TEC did not "click" for her when she made the course several years ago. She felt claustrophobic amid the windows and doors covered with paper and did not like feeling "penned in." "I wanted out of there. I really didn't enjoy myself at all mainly because I felt a lot of pressure from my mom to experience TEC." Kate says that she is open to retreats and wants to enjoy them. She contrasts her TEC experience with Catholic youth-focused retreats in Steubenville, Ohio, that she "really, *really* enjoyed." Kate says that part of her problem with TEC is that she does not like being served by others. "It seemed strange to me that my bed was made for me, my meals cooked for me. . . . pretty much everything was done for me that weekend. It wasn't the real world." Kate says that she wears the TEC hoodie that her mother bought her "only when my other shirts are dirty."[72] Kate admitted to me that she probably didn't get a lot out of the weekend because she "went in with a pretty bad attitude. I was trying to make my mom happy and probably didn't go for the right reasons."[73]

In contrast to Kate's mostly negative assessment of the weekend, Tim Murga, a recent college graduate, says his TEC weekend was a highlight of his high school career and motivated him to increase his prayer life. He says he took from his weekend a commitment to sharing his renewed Catholic faith and spirituality with his peers. Today Tim, who is preparing to start graduate school, regularly attends TEC hoots and serves on weekends.[74] Chris Scott, an opera singer and a doctoral student in music, seconds Tim's assessment of TEC, saying that it was "a real highlight of not only my high school career but my life so far." Chris has been too busy with school, teaching, and performing to participate in TEC hoots and weekends as does Tim, but says he hopes to make his Cursillo at some point, since his uncle, who is heavily involved in Cursillo, keeps saying he will love it.[75] Like Tim and Chris, Chad Bohonek, who made his TEC right before he attended college as part of his high school requirement, says his TEC weekend was "truly awesome" and that it introduced him to the Holy Spirit and "living a spirit-filled life."[76]

The TEC experience of Amanda Plesch, a college sophomore, also was positive.[77] "The course was really emotional and I'm not really an emotional kind of person. I still got a lot out of the course, though. I was touched but I didn't cry a lot. . . . I'm just not like that. Basically, TEC was a really good life experience for me. It was life-changing in the sense that I was able to make some really good friends through it. TEC has changed the way I look at things. I can get closer to people now because I have opened up—TEC helped me be able to do that."[78]

As she reflected on the future of TEC, Amanda said that she thinks that her generation may "fade away from it because we get involved in other things. Religion is hard to stick with for my generation. It is harder to maintain because we are into so many different things." But Amanda went on to add that she thinks the movement will be around for a while because "there is always a full group of girls or boys taking the course. TEC is a secret, and kids want to go experience what their friends have talked about. They are curious."[79] Since making her TEC weekend, Amanda has been on one "wheat" team, a group of TEC alumnae who return to work for a weekend course. Members of a TEC wheat team are "behind the scenes, cooking, cleaning, writing letters for the candidates. I was on one wheat team and really enjoyed it." Being part of this team involves performing short skits for TEC candidates. Amanda has good memories of performing a dance with other wheat team members to Matthew West's "More." "We wore gloves and used black lights. It was so awesome! We were told that it was the best TEC skit ever done!" Songs by contemporary Christian artists such as West, Jeremy Camp, Nicole C. Mullen, MercyMe, Casting Crowns, David Crowder B., and Jars of Clay pervaded Amanda's TEC weekend, adding a hip element to the three days. Being on a wheat team involves lots of work and planning. "If you are on a wheat team you meet every Wednesday to plan. We say, 'wheat, wheat, and more wheat!' Wheat is basically service to others, and when you are on a wheat team you are serving others for three days straight." While Amanda greatly enjoyed her wheat team experience, she says it is hard to participate in more weekends right now because she is away at college and cannot return home on a regular basis. Amanda's assessment of the three days is as follows:

> The first day, Saturday, was Die Day. It is pretty intense. The focus is on Jesus' death on the Cross and his sacrifice, and there is the Stations of the Cross. Candidates reflect on where they are in life, who they are and who they want to be. It is kind of dark, somber, and the food is not so great. You get a sandwich or something like that. Friday is a serious atmosphere for sure. Now Sunday, Rise Day, is much happier. When you wake up there are banners everywhere, and I mean, *everywhere*. It is colorful and happy. I loved it! The food is great; I loved the cheesy potatoes! On Sunday you get to eat

"fancy food," and the boys serve the girls. Sunday is also the hoot, which is so cool! It is a secret and is held Sunday night. People from way back go to the hoot. TEC graduates find out about the hoot from an e-mail telling them when it will be. That is how my mom found out, and she was there for mine—it was a total surprise! The candidates are completely surprised because we thought that we were just going to the gym to chill out after our fancy dinner that night where we dressed up and ate the fancy food dinner. When I saw my mom there I did cry, and I am not the crying type, as I have said. People sang "This Little Light of Mine" and held candles. It was beautiful, really. The wheat team performs skits and there is a lot of singing. There is an *abrazo* line where everyone gives the candidates a hug—it was a really long line. You hug every single person there. I absolutely loved it! Monday, the third day, is Go Forth Day, the day you are supposed to get excited about going into the world and telling people about your experience and Christ's love for us. You get a TEC cross and a Bible, and you go to school on Tuesday. Everyone is excited to wear their TEC gear. The TEC weekend is really exhausting; you are so tired to go to school on Tuesday but you *want* to go, too. You wear your gear: your TEC cross, your hoodie. It is kind of cool. I loved wearing my cross and hoodie and felt really special that day.[80]

Amanda has good memories of her recent TEC weekend and says that she enjoyed the conversations she had with her tablemates and the leader at their table, which they named "Five Fine Females Finding Faith." She says it was a bit strange to not have her cell phone handy but that she understands why phones cannot be used during the weekend. Leaders of her weekend, in keeping with TEC practice, stayed in contact with parents by e-mail. For Amanda, a highlight of the weekend was receiving the pile of "wheat" letters that people had written to her. She shared her letters with me, stuffed into two manila folders. Like the palanca letters of the cursillistas I have spoken with, these letters were deeply moving to the weekend participants, who were touched by the love and support they received from people who had been through the weekend, some of whom they knew, but many of whom they had never met. "The fact that all of these people took time to write letters to each girl on the TEC weekend really kind of blew my mind," says Amanda. Inspirational messages she received included: "If God can use an ordinary stick to part an entire sea, and ordinary spit and mud to make a blind man see, then He certainly can use ordinary you and me to accomplish extraordinary things!"; 'Nothing is real until it is experienced"; "Service isn't an option, it's a family obligation"; "God has a plan for you!"; and "God loves you and so do I!" An underlying theme of all of the letters is that Christ has unconditional love Christ has for the TEC candidates, that He is within each of them, and that each was being called by Christ to be "the best version" of her- or himself. TEC candidates also write letters to themselves, and Amanda showed me hers, which emphasizes self-affirmation and the desire to grow spiritually with others' help. "I was on a happy high when I wrote this letter to myself," she says, adding that whenever she needs a little lift she goes back and reads this letter and the others.[81]

The motivational slogans in Amanda's TEC "wheat letters," or very close approximations of them, are used in all of the Fourth-Day movements, as we have seen, as well as their spinoffs. God's unconditional love, the importance of experiencing one's faith during the weekend, the importance of being part of a small Christian community, and the call to be an active Christian are messages that pervade each of the Fourth-Day movements' weekend retreats. All but one of the TEC graduates I interviewed regard the weekend as a time during which they could experience God's gifts of graces—whether it be through making a new friend, discovering who they were as individuals, or recognizing Christ's importance for their lives.

"A Gift from God"

Dorothy Gereke says that she has been the recipient of "many, many gifts" from God during her lifetime. She remembers receiving a phone call one afternoon in February 1985 from Father Matt about a TEC reunion in Omaha, Nebraska, that was being initiated by a Father Jim Brown, then the in-residence priest at Creighton University's Boys Town. She had then been away from TEC for more than sixteen years and was caring for her husband, Paul, to whom she had been married since 1972, and who was dying from Alzheimer's. "At the time I was angry at God for my husband's illness. I loved my husband so much. I had absolutely no idea that TEC had become a big movement because after I left my religious order, I had 'died to TEC.'"[82]

The phone call was "a gift from God," she says, prompting her to become reacquainted with the movement she had cofounded. It was good for her to travel and to have a break from caring for Paul full-time and to reconnect with Father Matt and young Catholics. True to her strong work ethic and unflagging energy, Dorothy never left Paul's side until she was convinced by a niece to become reinvolved with TEC. The Omaha TEC conference "reenergized my soul," she says, and she uses TEC language of the Paschal Mystery of "rising" again to describe her reintroduction to TEC.[83] By 1970, both Father Matt and Dorothy had left TEC to engage in other vocational calls. For his part, Father Matt had "given up youth ministry altogether" and was focusing himself "100 percent" in inner-city ministry in Flint, Michigan. He worked at a Catholic school for African American youth "in a time when there were no choice programs made available to them as there are now."[84]

Sister Mary Concetta left her order in 1969, assumed her birth name Dorothy Neibauer, and married Paul Gereke in 1973. At the time of Father Jim's phone call, neither Father Matt nor Dorothy "had any idea whatsoever that TEC had become a movement"; at the Omaha conference, Dorothy was "simply amazed" by the testimonies of the men and women who came up to her and told her how much TEC had meant to them and their families. TEC graduates greeted her as "Mama TEC" and she was hugged by extended families of TEC alumni who shared their testimonies with her and thanked her for her "gift" of TEC to them. Dorothy left the gathering humbled and recommitted herself to the movement she cofounded. Since Paul passed away in the late 1980s, Dorothy has more than 700,000 miles in the United States and Canada traveling for TEC and the Sisters of Mercy, with some international trips to Ireland for good measure. "It is such an inspiration to me to come see young people just come alive during the weekend. I talk with parents and family members during hoots and hear from them how important TEC has been in their lives and in their family's life. It is great to show them that religion is FUN. I say 'Lord, you are so good to allow me to see the harvest and to share in it.' This is such a grace, a blessing to me."[85]

Mary O'Brien, who is involved with the TEC movement in Des Moines, says that Dorothy has quite an effect on young Catholics: "When the youth meet her they are so attentive. I have watched this many times. It is like a grandma-grandchild relationship, and they respect her so much."[86]

While Father Matt is content, as he says, to read and write, as the movement's "wings," Dorothy can't sit still. Father Matt's and Dorothy's efforts were recently honored when the two of them received the 2010

NFCYM Lifetime Achievement Award for their founding of TEC and their continued involvement with the movement.[87]

Conclusion: TEC's Relevance to Catholic Youth Today

Since the late 1960s, American Catholic and Protestant teenagers and young adults have been experiencing three-day weekend retreats modeled after Catholic Cursillos. Chrysalis is Methodist in origin and ecumenical; Kairos is a parish-based Catholic spinoff of TEC; and Awakening is the National Episcopal Cursillo for young adults. In the 1960s and 1970s, the young people who went through a TEC weekend were part of an intensive parish system that funneled high school students through the weekend course. Today Catholic high schools around the country similarly require a TEC or Kairos weekend as part of the students' junior year. Based on the research I have conducted, American Christian young adults are signing up to take these courses for a variety of reasons—some simply as a requirement for graduation and some (in places where it is not a requirement for graduation) because they know someone who has made a weekend and who recommends it.

While some of these youth were seekers before they made the course, others did not know what to expect and were swept up in the course. Wes Six, a Protestant eighteen-year-old college student at a midwestern liberal arts college, made a Kairos that was offered by his Catholic high school not because it was required but because he was curious: "I learned so much about myself and my relationship to God. I was shown things about myself, and I became a better person. My faith now is definitely stronger."[88] Justine Nguyen, who also made a Kairos course in high school, says the weekend focuses on "teenage angst and pressure," and she appreciates its being geared toward the needs and concerns of youth.[89]

While the young adults who make a weekend retreat see no conflict of interest in the variety of weekend retreats offered, Father Matt sees things differently. He views Kairos's success as directly related to TEC's demise in certain dioceses, noting that in his own Diocese of Lansing, the birthplace of TEC, there are no longer any TEC weekends offered—only Kairos. But Father Matt adds that while TEC's decline in some parts of the country distresses him, "maybe TEC needs to die, and some other encounter in spirituality will rise up in its place." While Father Matt has invested himself in TEC's success among youth, he says that the main point is that young Catholic adults are being moved by the spirit, and if Kairos is the weekend retreat that does it, then he needs to accept that as "movements come and go, what matters is that our young people are touched by God."[90]

As of 2011, more than 300,000 young adults have made a U.S. TEC weekend since the first weekend was held in 1965. According to former TEC executive director Ron Reiter, "the largest TEC Community, the Central Minnesota TEC, lays claim to touching over 30,000 youth, young adults, and adults during their history of over thirty years."[91] There are currently fifty-two TEC centers in twenty-four U.S. states and in forty-five dioceses.[92] During the late stages of his tenure as executive director, Reiter and the national officers were "in communication with" several communities to reopen their TEC centers and were also working with three communities to open new TEC centers by summer 2012.[93] Reiter's successor, Billy O'Regan, was responsible for establishing TEC of Central Texas in Austin as part of this larger TEC effort. There are six international TEC centers: in the Bahamas (Nassau), Canada (Thunder Bay, Ontario), Bolivia (La Paz and Riberalta), the Czech Republic (Uhonice), and Lithuania (Kaunas).

TEC remains strong in dioceses where it has a long history and where it is supported, as with the Diocese of Peoria and in St. Paul, Minnesota, where it is linked with National Evangelization Teams (NET).[94] In other places, such as the Diocese of Lansing, other youth retreats, like the parish-based Kairos, have proven to be more popular. Catholic young people today are part of a larger movement among Christian youth seeking to recapture a sense of tradition while combining it with new forms of praise and worship. To maintain a theological as well as cultural relevance, TEC, like other youth-oriented movements, must be willing to adapt in order to reach young adult Catholics.

TEC's focus on the Paschal Mystery of Christ can be seen as rooted in Catholic tradition, which it presents in a way young people can understand. Many young Catholics today yearn for tradition as well as a religion that speaks to their concerns, and if TEC continues to tap into youths' spiritual needs and concerns, it will be around for another fifty years. As it was in the 1960s, today's TEC depends on men and women religious, laymen, and laywomen working together to nurture and encourage a love of Catholic tradition as well as new forms of spirituality among young adult Catholics. Ron Reiter believes TEC will continue into the future because, unlike other forms of religious education, "TEC invites one to encounter Christ; it is a heart knowledge and not just a head knowledge. Much of what the youth have learned up to that point is head knowledge, which is important, but the heart knowledge they experience during the weekend helps them truly understand Christ. A response to an encounter like TEC may be immediate or it may take years. One thing is for certain: you will never forget the experience."[95]

Ron also notes that since 1997, TEC has become more centralized and organized, and he sees this evolution as key to TEC's longevity. During the years 1998–2006 workshops were held to oversee the formation of ministry teams and to check in with what was happening at the TEC centers scattered across the United States.[96]

The challenge for this Cursillo spinoff movement, as with all of the Fourth-Day movements examined in this book, has been how to combine newer forms of outreach and tap into the contemporary language of spirituality while maintaining a foothold in tradition. TEC was formed in the midst of the Vatican II Council, which aimed to offer an old faith with a greater openness to Catholic manifestations. During our interview in June 2011, Father Matt noted that "at one time TEC was the only show in town—we had no rivals in terms of successful youth weekends. Today each parish has a youth minister, and it is their job to work with youth, but youth ministers have really killed TEC in many ways because their focus is on their parish and TEC is diocesan-based."[97] For youth ministers today, parish-based events take precedence over diocesan ones, and the rise of Kairos and other parish-based youth oriented weekends makes sense in this context.[98] Father Matt, Dorothy, and Ron say they think TEC needs to make adaptations, and that the movement's dependence on priests has been a challenge, given the shortage and "overextension" of priests in the United States. All three would like to see the movement continue in a way that is rooted in its past, but they are pragmatic and understand that "new blood" needs to be brought into TEC in order to reinvigorate it.[99] The God of TEC is not the Moralistic Therapeutic Deity that the sociologist of religion Christian Smith argues typifies young adult Christianity today.[100] Although the God of TEC participants and alumni is all-knowing and loving, the three-day weekend has a theological core and familiarizes the young adults with Scripture and theological concepts on which they can base their renewed faith.

What distinguished TEC from pre–Vatican II Catholic youth retreats is that it reimagined youth retreats—calling them "weekends" and "encounters"—and offered a very different kind of setting from pre-1960s Catholic retreats, one in which adults and youth worked together.[101] While it is not technically one of the "in-covenant" Fourth-Day movements, TEC is a direct offshoot of Catholic Cursillo and incorporates Bonnín's theological triptych of study, piety, and action.

The next chapter turns to Kairos Prison Ministry International, a fifth in-covenant Fourth-Day movement in that it adheres closely to the method, purpose, and action of the original 1944 weekend Cursillo and uses the Cursillo method to reach out to incarcerated men and women. While it is an in-covenant Fourth-Day Christian movement with roots in the Cursillos de Cristiandad, Kairos is distinctive in that it focuses exclusively on bringing the Fourth-Day apostolic action and charism to inmates and their families.[102] In the next chapter, we examine ethnographically a Kairos Inside weekend.

CHAPTER SIX

Feeding Bodies and Souls

Kairos Prison Ministry International

I was in prison and you visited me.
—Matthew 25:36

What brought me to Kairos was that I wanted to change and have God in my life.
—Female offender, Rockville Correctional Facility, May 2010

I came for the food, but got *real food* instead.
—Female offender and Kairos "Angel," Rockville Correctional Facility, May 2010

I am here because I know that God is gonna rock this place this weekend!
—Kairos Prison Ministry volunteer, May 2010

We meet on a warm Thursday afternoon in May 2010 at a church in southern Indiana, just a few miles from Rockville Correctional Facility, the women's medium-security prison where the weekend events will take place. Approximately 1,300 female inmates are housed there. As the time neared for us to drive to the prison, the forty-six women present take a moment to hold hands and pray aloud for a weekend where Christ will "touch the hearts" of the female offenders we will be meeting. Hours upon hours of work have gone into the seventy-two-hour event for which these women have been preparing. Four women and their spouses have done most of the cooking and baking, and all of the forty-two weekend volunteers have written "agape letters"—letters of love, support, and encouragement—for the incarcerated participants. The cooks, wearing aprons, lift heavy crates of food and load them into two silver-colored trailers attached to pickup trucks. The trailers are quickly filled with containers of notebooks, pencils, posters, beverages, and food, including 20,000 chocolate chip cookies, bagged by the half dozen and stored in large plastic bins.

Hauling food and supplies for a KI weekend, Rockville, Indiana, 2010. Photograph by Kristy Nabhan-Warren.

When our caravan arrives, we walk into the huge gray building chatting nervously, holding the only items we are allowed to bring in with us: our driver's licenses and lip balm (no lipstick allowed).[1]

We survey each other's outfits and our own, as we have been told not to wear khakis, jeans, sneakers, or the colors maroon, khaki, or dark green—the colors the offenders wear. We are not allowed to wear any clothes with labels or anything too flashy that the offenders might "covet."

We are instructed to line up by alphabetical order in the facility lobby and wait our turn to sign in. There we show our identification, sign our names on the sheet provided, and one by one walk through a metal detector and are frisked by a female prison guard. We are then taken into the facility in small groups by the prison warden, Rita Steed, who is also the Kairos Inside (KI) liaison for this facility. We walk outside, past a group of offenders playing softball, toward the Kairos trailer, which has been searched and cleared for entrance by the facility's security guards. We then start unloading the food and items for the weekend, carrying boxes of carrots and loading bins of cookies onto dollies. Once inside the recreation building where the weekend will be held, food is unpacked in the gymnasium, which will serve as the retreat's cafeteria. Several Kairos volunteers busy themselves organizing bowls of raw vegetables, ranch dressing, tortilla chips, nacho cheese dip, salsa, and cheese cubes. On one long table we arrange pitchers of lemonade and water and carafes of coffee, caffeinated and decaffeinated; on eight round tables we set small Styrofoam bowls of vegetables, chips, salsa, and nacho cheese dip.

Once all the tables are set up and the name cards are in place, each Kairos volunteer receives a name badge with her name and a multicolored yarn string to drape around her neck. We also each get a name badge with the name of one of the offenders, the one we will "host." Then we wait, some of us fidgeting, all smiling, for the guard to bring in the forty-two incarcerated women who will be participating in the weekend course.

As each woman enters the room, her name is called aloud and one of us walks over to her, smiling, holding the name badge. My "guest" is Donna, an African American in her mid-fifties. I approach her, shake her hand, and, after she voices her consent, hang the badge around her neck.[2]

The women working this weekend are from southern Indiana towns and cities and from a variety of denominations, including Methodist, Catholic, Baptist, Presbyterian, and Disciples of Christ. Several attend southern Indiana nondenominational Christian churches. All but one of the white female volunteers are from middle- to upper-middle-class southern Indiana families.[3] Sister Demetrius, the only nonwhite Kairos volunteer this weekend, is an African American sister of the international African Missionary Order. Like her "sisters in Christ" who have gathered this weekend, Sister Demetrius says she is motivated by her desire to bring hope and love to incarcerated women and to share her faith in Christ. Denominational differences are set aside for the seventy-two-hour retreat in the interest of this greater goal.

Kairos Prison Ministry International (KPMI), founded in Florida in 1976 by Catholic cursillista and attorney Tom Johnson, is currently active in thirty-three U.S. states, as well as in Australia, Canada, Costa Rica, and South Africa. According to John Thompson, Kairos's executive director from July 2001 to April 2012, in August 2011 when we spoke, 250,000 incarcerated men and women had been through a KI weekend in 350 KPMI communities.[4] As of December 2012, there were 400 active KPMI communities in 32 U.S. states and 50 international communities in 9 other countries. Each year, 25,000 inmates and family members in the United States and abroad experience a KI or Kairos Outside (KO) weekend.[5] The KI weekends, retreats held inside medium- to maximum-security prisons, last from Thursday to Sunday evening (seventy-two hours) and are based on the Catholic Cursillo de Cristiandad method that originated in Mallorca in 1944 and came to the United States in 1957, seventy-two hours of "piety, study, and action" in the form of talks, breakout discussions, and prayer. The focus of the Kairos Inside weekend course is "bringing the love and forgiveness of Jesus Christ into prison"; the intent is to "change inmate attitudes," renewing their hope and sense of self-worth.

On the surface, with our manicures, abundant snacks, name badges, and general cheeriness, we Kairos volunteers could be mistaken for a gathering of church ladies or of the women's branch of the evangelical organization Aglow International.[6] Our weekend even bears resemblance to historically white sorority formal rush, as Kairos volunteers pair with women seeking admission into an exclusive club. My own experience with formal rush, as a Kappa Delta at Indiana University in the early 1990s, had many similarities with the Kairos weekend. The gendered power dynamics of rush—with seekers desiring to join an establishment and members of the establishment doing their part to evangelize the seekers—are present during a Kairos women's weekend.[7] The weekend "guests" were selected by Rita Steed, the facility's community services director, and twice as many volunteered as could be accommodated. But of course there are very real qualitative differences, as our participants are a literally captive audience with far fewer choices than those enjoyed by women at sorority rushes, church-based events, or Aglow gatherings.[8]

I was able to speak with twenty of the Kairos participants during the weekend. I learned that the Kairos weekend represents different things to different women. For some, the weekend offers a break from the everyday grind of inmate life and provides contact with the outside world, which most of them experience only during infrequent family visits. Some signed up for the course because they were curious, having heard good things about it from their "bunkies" or others in prison who had been through a previous Kairos Inside weekend. Other women admitted they signed up because they had heard how good the food was. One inmate I spoke with over snacks said she had "been around so many bad influences in my life that I thought for a change I could see what it is like being around some ladies who are different from all that." One thing is certain about the weekend: for seventy-two hours, the inmates are in close contact with a group of women who shower them with messages of hope and encouragement and offer them a reality different from the very difficult one they have known.

Most of the Kairos volunteers at this weekend are middle- to upper-middle-class, white, non-Hispanic women. These women are an impressive group and have excelled in their various professions. Sharon, the weekend's "leader," is a savvy businesswoman; Loretta, the "observing director," manages a major retail clothing chain; and Susan, the "inside coordinator," runs a family business with her husband, who is himself heavily involved in men's Kairos Inside weekends. Almost all of the forty-six women work full-time jobs. They say they volunteer their time (including several weekends training for this event) and money to Kairos because they feel called to share Christ's love with people, especially those who are forgotten by larger society. Mary, a pretty and petite blonde grandmother who is the weekend's "agape coordinator," says she has been involved with this ministry ever since she watched the television show *20/20* and learned about a notorious prisoner's enthusiastic conversion to Christ as a result of participating in a Kairos weekend. She was "truly touched" by this man's story and felt a strong urge to experience the power of "Christ's forgiveness and healing" herself. Mary has worked four Kairos weekends in Indiana and in North Carolina, where she used to live, and plans to "be an instrument for Christ" for as long as she was able.

Like their male counterparts in men's Kairos Inside weekends, the volunteers who work the women's weekends bring their (mostly) upper-middle-class, white, Christian sensibilities and theology to a group of black, white, and Hispanic women who are often from poor backgrounds and broken families. Here they overlap with the women's section of Aglow International, which has a prison outreach ministry that hopes to "teach the women how to receive the healing that God promises by releasing their pain, grief, unforgiveness or other emotional barriers."[9] Kairos volunteers want to be "instruments of the Holy Spirit" for the incarcerated "guests" and help them attain forgiveness, inner peace, and a life of faith. While Kairos volunteers say they are "blessed" by working with the female offenders who participate in a Kairos weekend, their main objective, as with members of the other Fourth-Day movements, is to "make a friend, be a friend, bring a friend to Christ." Kairos volunteers hope to share their love of Christ with prisoners and to help them forgive themselves and become grace-filled, renewed women seeking to make a positive impact on society, whether inside or outside the prison walls.[10] The faith-filled volunteers are full of excitement and anticipation as they hope and pray that their weekend guests will walk away healed, refreshed, renewed, and "blessed" by God's grace.

Like those of its sister Fourth-Day Cursillo movements, a Kairos Inside weekend weaves together various strands of post-1950s American culture, including the popularity of recovery and self-help movements and small groups, as well as the interrelated, pervasive longing for community. Kairos volunteers aim to bring their Christian convictions to prison inmates and to help them begin the process of transformation—breaking down the psychological walls they have built around themselves inside the very real prison walls. The Kairos "sisters" who converged here from dozens of small Indiana towns think of each other as kin and form intentional communities that provide familial love and support.

"The Prison Story"

What distinguishes Kairos Inside from the other in-covenant Fourth-Day movements is that it targets a very specific group of individuals, incarcerated women and men in state and federal medium- to maximum-security prisons. While all Fourth-Day Christian movements claim a historic and theological connection to Eduardo Bonnín, Kairos Prison Ministry also believes that its focus on inmates gives it a particular connection to Bonnín. In a 1995 newsletter, KPMI published "The Prison Story," which recounts a 1949 visit by Bonnín and a friend to two Mallorquín prisoners scheduled for execution the next day. According to the story, Bonnín and his friend asked the two men to pray for the success of the Cursillo movement, as they were "the only people we have met who know when they will meet the Lord face-to-face. We want you to say something to Him.... we feel it is so urgent. We have this wonderful project, from which we expect great fruits, but we have failed miserably so far to get it going. We want *you* to ask the Lord to help us."[11]

In "The Prison Story," Bonnín told the two young men that God loves them, that Christ is compassionate and forgives them. He then gave one of the prisoners his crucifix after the prisoner asked to hold it. Bonnín and his unnamed friend told the men about the "Good Thief" who had "stolen heaven." According to "The Prison Story," when the two prisoners were executed at the garroting post the next day, the prisoner kneeled and held Bonnín's crucifix, right up until the moment when the hood was placed over his head and the chain was pulled.[12]

The story's author tells it as a kind of cosmogonic myth—an origin story—of Cursillos and their slow beginnings. The author also reports that Bonnín first spoke of the prisoners, of his request and his belief that the prisoners did indeed ask God to bless the young movement, at a 1992 National Cursillo Encounter in Detroit.[13] There Bonnín "revealed that Cursillo was given its crucial push in its birth experience by two prison inmates." He also related the movement's early struggles and said that when the prison chaplain called to ask him to speak with the two condemned prisoners, Bonnín believed this was the opportunity the movement needed to grow. He showed his deep appreciation for the prisoners' "favor" by wearing his crucifix, which had been held by one of the executed men.

While this origins story was mentioned to me by a handful of Mallorquín and U.S. Catholic cursillistas, they were not sure what to make of it or how it was directly relevant for their movement's history. Their interpretation of the story was that the executed prisoner had indeed taken Bonnín's plea for a successful movement directly to God. It was John Thompson who talked about it the most, as Bonnín's stance toward the prisoners has had a profound effect on him personally and on KPMI's mission.[14] Thompson and his organization believe that it is a Christian's duty to reach out to prisoners as fellow human beings, and as children of God. Bonnín insisted on reaching the "faraway," and in this case two prisoners condemned to death in late 1940s Spain.

Food, Love, and Fellowship

Food, food, and more food. If you have ever been on a Fourth-Day Cursillo weekend in the United States, you know what I mean. As with all Cursillo weekend volunteers, the Kairos ladies shower their agape on the weekend guests in the form of food, and I can attest that these southern Indiana ladies and their spouses *can indeed cook*. This "Support Team" spends the weekend at a church near the prison cooking all of the food for the retreat, hauling it over periodically in the two silver trailers. Lasagna, fried chicken, meatloaf, mashed potatoes, salads, and brownie–ice cream sundaes with all the toppings are just part of the fare. We are even served bread pudding with lemon sauce. Food is a constant on these weekends and every single Catholic and Protestant cursillista I have interviewed over the years has mentioned the high quality of the meals on their weekend as well as how deeply impressed they were by the degree to which they were served. A hallmark of a Walk to Emmaus, Tres Dias, or Via de Cristo weekend is the candlelight dinner served Saturday night, and Fourth-Day movement spinoffs like Great Banquet include feasts as a crucial part of their identity and theology. Christian hospitality and the sacramentalism of serving food, abundant during any Christian Cursillo weekend, is especially pronounced on a Kairos Inside weekend, as the volunteers want to take extra special care of their guests, who have not always been treated very well by their families and by society at large.[15] Kairos Inside volunteers dedicate themselves to catering to the weekend participants' needs and take on the role of servant.

Cindy, an attractive and athletic fifty-something Kairos volunteer, says she loves working in the kitchen because it gives her the opportunity to see "Christ in action." She is always excited to see "the expressions on the ladies' faces when they walk into the room and see all of this wonderful food that has been prepared for them."[16]

Kairos Inside volunteers and their theology of compassion and outreach are part of a larger historical trajectory of American Christians' demonstration of love through feeding people's bodies and souls. This outreach is supported by denominations that provide funding and church kitchens where cooking and feeding can take place, but at its core, the history of American Christian food theology and praxis has been driven by laity. Everyday Catholic and Protestant men and women have given their time and labor to the goal of feeding hungry people in critical numbers since nineteenth-century waves of Eastern and Western European immigration. U.S. churches across the country have made feeding a priority since the turn of the twentieth century and continue to operate food banks, soup kitchens, and luncheons for the hungry. The theology of food that informs this Christian praxis stems from, in part, an interpretation of the Gospels as calling Christians to demonstrate love, charity, and hospitality.

In addition to being physically nourished, the weekend guests read literature and hear talks meant to help them forgive themselves and learn to love themselves as individuals. The volunteers build in time for the inmates to read and to reflect on what they have read, and table discussions follow each talk given by a Kairos volunteer. Each participant is given a copy of the "Freedom Guide," and chaplains are available throughout the weekend for private sessions. The guide, a green pocket-sized prayer book, holds up Jesus not just as an inspiring teacher and leader who can show them the way to freedom but also as a best friend who has suffered like them. The opening prayer of the guide, "Christ the Prisoner," emphasizes that Christ was a prisoner who was tortured, condemned to death, and publicly executed. As the sociologist Megan Sweeney has written, in her moving study of the importance of reading for female inmates, "encountering a character who inspires them, serves as a model to emulate, or demonstrates a capacity for change can seem vitally important to women who feel an urgent desire to change but a deep uncertainty about their ability to do so."[17] For the Kairos weekend guests, Jesus is someone they are encouraged to relate to and to turn to as they work to become healed and renewed individuals.

For many of the forty-two inmates on this weekend, family visits are infrequent and stressful events—reminders of what they have left behind. Most of the Kairos weekend participants are mothers whose crimes have separated them from their families. Many have young children who are being raised by family members or friends. The Kairos volunteers work hard to relate to the inmates by admitting publicly in the weekend talks that they are not perfect women either. One of the weekend presenters goes so far to say that she had done some "really bad things and unlike yourselves, I just wasn't caught." Oftentimes, says JoEllen Rowe, coordinator of the Indiana Kairos Inside women's weekends, "the ladies in here think that those of us on the outside have perfect lives and that we haven't experienced difficult times or even trauma. It is important that we connect with them to show them that they are not alone and that we, too, have suffered in our lives."[18] While rollistas in all of the Fourth-Day movements use anecdotes to connect with candidates, in KI the anecdotes do more than "break the ice"; they are a concerted effort to show the female offenders in the room that these mostly white, upper-middle-class women have had their own struggles, hurts, and sorrows. As I listen to the talks this weekend and observe the various group dynamics, I am struck by the extent to which the KI presenters emphasized sin, suffering, and salvation. While this theological trio is in play in the other Fourth-Day movement weekends, it is much more central in the Kairos Inside talks and makes healing and renewal even more central to the movement's mission.

Like the women and men who staff soup kitchens and food banks across the United States and places like God's Love We Deliver in Chicago, which cooks and serves food to people living with HIV, Kairos volunteers focus on feeding the bodies and souls of men and women who have experienced social dislocation and anomie.[19] When I ask the volunteers why they have chosen to be involved with Kairos, all of them say that they are individually blessed and that they want to share their "blessings" with women who have not had the kind of life they have been fortunate to have had. Kairos Inside volunteers aim to show the "hospitality of God" seen throughout the New Testament Gospels.[20] Volunteers enter the prison and share the primary goal of "building Christian community within the institution."[21] They feed their guests throughout the weekend, shower them with agape, and encourage them to form new families within the prison walls. The hope of all of the weekend volunteers is that the guests will form relationships with Jesus Christ and will leave the weekend events with individual and collective commitments to lead more Christ-centered lives. The weekend guests are assigned to tables of seven, and each table is considered a family and is given the name of a female biblical character. The table or family names during the Kairos weekend I observe include Elizabeth, Esther, Sarah, Ruth, Martha, Mary, and Priscilla. The weekend guests are encouraged to think of themselves as part of new families. The phrase "the family of" is used throughout the weekend in contrast to other Cursillo weekends, which refer to their "tables."

This language of family is intentional during a Kairos Inside weekend because for many participants "their experience with 'family' is a dark wound that must be addressed in the healing process."[22] The Kairos volunteers work hard to give the concept and kinship of family new, positive connotations for the female guests. Kairos volunteers call themselves "sisters in Christ" and make it abundantly clear during the three days that they want these female guests to join their family and that they are, moreover, worthy of being part of this family. The weekend team members are told to remember that "the purpose of Kairos is to build Christian community within the institution, and it begins with the family."[23]

Kairos volunteers' sense of responsibility is motivated by social as well as theological justice—they want to empower the women to break the cycle of self-hatred, anger, and violence. The language of "making better choices" made popular in the late twentieth century by Christian evangelicals is used throughout the weekend events, and the offenders are introduced to the "lifestyle choice" of being a Christian. They are repeatedly told, through the talks and in the many group activities, that this choice, unlike the ones they are making or have made, is one that will free them from the shackles of their own personal imprisonment and allow them to be "free" in prison, even if they are serving life sentences. The focus of the weekend is freedom not from the literal prison bars, chains, and fences that surround the inmates but from spiritual and emotional prisons. The Kairos volunteers fervently pray that the female offenders—their weekend guests—will make the lifestyle choice of becoming good Christian women.

As on the other Fourth-Day weekends, while the Inside Team on our KI weekend consists of a group of women, the Support Team consists of men and women. The Support Team cooks, transports the food from an off-site kitchen to the prison, and cleans up the dining areas after the inmates and volunteers have eaten. A crucial part of their mission is to demonstrate their agape for the women behind prison walls by feeding them. Calorie-dense, rich foods are served alongside fresh produce, and the inmates are encouraged to eat as much as they desire during mealtime. I have been told by cursillistas in all of the movements documented in this book that they were overwhelmed and "humbled" by the delicious food served to them during their weekend.[24]

A typical Kairos weekend with its excesses of food would seem a festival of gluttony to the mostly white, non-Hispanic Christians who are the focus of U.S. religious historian Marie Griffith's *Born Again Bodies*.[25] Kairos's theology of food, with its central emphasis on consumption, also seems unlikely to win the endorsement of Gwen Shamblin, founder of the highly successful Christian Weigh-Down diet. The seventy-two-hour KI retreat features abundant meals more akin to Father Divine's famous banquets and slogan "Good Health, Good Will, and Good Appetite!" than to mainline white, non-Hispanic Christianity.[26] Father Divine's food theology of love and abundance, as Griffith describes it, can be applied to Kairos's food theology: "Food was depicted as the concrete symbol of heavenly love, a love poured out upon all who were willing to partake of it; and the purpose of dining at this holy table was to tangibly unite body and soul."[27] The food served throughout a Kairos weekend is a testimony of the volunteers' love, concern, and Christian piety. For the volunteers, feeding inmates is agape in action, Christian praxis at its most tangible.

On our weekend in southern Illinois, exclamations of "this is so much food!" and "I can't believe how *good* this food is" are commonplace. One of the participants at my table Friday evening is excited to get fresh veggies, which she says she "can't stop eating!" She especially appreciates the baby carrots, cherry tomatoes, and ranch dressing, food she says she hasn't eaten in the ten years she's been in prison. Yet there is a downside to the abundance: several of the participants run to the bathroom during the course of the weekend, having literally eaten themselves sick. While the intention is to show love to the inmates, the rich and plentiful food caused these women diarrhea and bloatedness. They are not served fresh produce at the prison, and their bodies are no longer able to digest so much fiber.

The "guests" nevertheless continue to eat the food because of the taste and quality. And, as the weekend progresses, comments are made about weight gained and lost, with metaphorical overtones. As one participant says to me over cookies and coffee, "I have gained about ten pounds but have also lost a huge weight I have been carrying with me." She is referring to the guilt and self-hatred she has been carrying with her for the past twelve years. When we speak Saturday afternoon, she says she has "let go of" bad feelings that have "been weighing me down big time." The discourse of weight at this Kairos Inside weekend parallels American Christians' contested relationship with food and their bodies, highlighting the desire to be both "full with Christ" and "lighter." These female inmates want to lose weight or at least not gain weight, but they also want to eat what they consider godly, "blessed" food prepared for them by the Kairos volunteers. Although the bounty makes some of them ill, the perceived holiness of Kairos food, in the end, trumps its nonsacred effects. Inmates choose to focus on what they believe to be "holy food" that will help to sacralize and purify their bodies, and the binging and purging that sometimes accompanies the abundant food is considered a sacrifice for the greater good of becoming redeemed women. While home-cooked food is a feature of all of the Fourth-Day movements, it takes on special significance inside the prison walls, where the inmates are fed food that many of us "on the outside" would consider inedible. Prisoners I spoke with said they spent most of their money at the prison commissary, where they could purchase peanut butter, bread, and cheese crackers. During a Kairos weekend, everyday food takes on sacred characteristics as does the overall space of the rooms where the events are held. Actual food as well as metaphors of food are centerpieces of the Kairos weekend. Thursday night's opening talk for women includes the following passage:

> A Kairos weekend is sort of like baking a cake. There is a recipe for the weekend, this manual, which details what we will be doing over these three days. The recipe won't do you any good if you are eating

a cake right now. First, we have to gather the ingredients and measure them out. But if we tried to judge the flavor of our cake just by tasting a little of the flour or a little of the salt, we would be making a bad mistake. We must mix the ingredients and put them in the mix before we know how good the cake tastes. Even then we must add topping if we want the very best. Kairos is like that. The first day we are mostly gathering and sifting ingredients. Don't judge the cake on that day, and please don't stop there even though the mix doesn't look especially wonderful. Stay with it and things will get better, and Sunday will be a "topping" that produces the best experience you have ever had.[28]

Kairos weekends, as we see in this excerpt, are intensely gendered, and the language conveys heterosexual, middle-class, white, non-Hispanic norms for these mostly black incarcerated women: baking, cooking, and marriage. I find myself wondering in private that weekend just how many white, non-Hispanic women today bake cakes from scratch. The image of a home-baked cake not made from a box (just add water, oil and an egg) seems outdated, upholding romanticized, middle-class white ideals of womanhood. As dated as it is, however, the metaphor is intentional: the weekend encourages idealized Christian womanhood. Part of this ideal emphasizes the domestication and domesticity of women and their families, which is ironic since most of the Kairos Inside volunteers, on this particular weekend at least, are working women.

A new kind of womanhood is offered to these inmates: a forgiven, renewed woman who is submissive to God the Father and who is cherished in his eyes. These women have all been failed by their men, and Jesus is one man, Kairos volunteers repeatedly tell them, who will never let them down and who will "always be there" for them. The Christian womanhood offered to the Kairos participants this weekend is complicated, as it blends messages of submission to a Christian God and his son with messages of forgiveness and empowerment. The KI men's weekends are similarly engendered, using sports metaphors as liberally as women's weekends invoke baking. The men's weekend likens the three days to trying out for a football team, with the requisite "running laps" and "doing calisthenics." An underlying theme of Kairos Inside weekends is making good Christian women and men in very specific images. On the women's weekend the ideal is that of the woman who looks to God for guidance in all things.

Kairos Inside Angels: Serving Up Love

Unlike the other Fourth-Day weekends, a KI weekend is not staffed by graduates. On a women's weekend such as the one I observe in southern Indiana, the weekend is staffed by cursillistas from Fourth-Day movements as well as a variety of spinoffs such as Great Banquet and Christ Renews His Parish.[29] Until recently, inmates who have made a KI weekend have not been able to volunteer, but the weekend I observe is one of a handful of KI pilot programs being tested in KPMI communities across the country in the spring of 2010.[30] One of the proposed additions to the weekend is the addition of the "Kairos Angels," graduates of the KI weekend who remain residents in the facility. These Angels are chosen by the prison warden for their leadership skills, mentoring abilities, and for the positive changes they have exhibited since their KI weekend experience. Four Angels share their time and talents during the KI weekend I observe. Two serve on the music ministry team, and the other two help out in the kitchen and as waitresses. I speak with all four women at length during the weekend, and they are happy to share their thoughts on the experience and on their postweekend lives. Their KI experience helped them realize, as one of the Angels says, "that I am worth something." Self-hatred, longing for their families, and an intense guilt for the crimes they have committed link these women. All four Angels feel as though KI gives them a second chance to live a better life and to be "a better example for my kids." All four of the Angels talk about the importance of serving as "positive examples" for the other inmates, especially for the new intakes.

One of the weekend Angels, whom I will call Julie, tells me excitedly that her job this weekend is to be a "waitress for God." She sees her role as "serving up this good and godly food" made by the Kairos Team. Another weekend Angel, Shana, talks excitedly about how much she loves to sing and that being part of the weekend's music ministry "just means so much to me, you know, because I want to use my voice as a witness to God and his glory." Shana has mentored many young women since her KI weekend, and is seen as an elder in the facility. She admits that she has "messed up real bad in my life, and I just want to show that we can change and we can be instruments of peace and love instead of violence and anger." I sit at the same table as Julie and Shana all weekend and am able to see how much participating in a weekend as a volunteer means to them. They both say that they are honored to be chosen and take the role seriously.

Tiana, another weekend Angel, talks with me about the years of intense physical and emotional abuse that she endured—a pain and suffering that would be incomprehensible to most. She says she experienced healing and a "letting go of my anger, hatred, and violent ways" during her Kairos weekend. She felt "clean and fresh, not like trash" for the first time in her life, and emerged from her weekend committed to "doing right by God." Messages of "God loves you," "You are worthy," and "You are beautiful" resonated with Tiana during her own Kairos weekend, and she is "so happy," she says, to be invited to return to help out. When we talk over dinner, she speaks lightheartedly of her love of peanut butter mixed with cereal. ("You've just got to try it, for *real*, girl," she tells me. I tell her I will try it. And I can say now that, yes, it *is* good.) She also tells me about her job in prison. When our conversation turns more serious, Tiana says Kairos "changed my life in a really, really deep kind of way," and she emphasizes her hope that the retreat will have a similar effect on the participants this weekend. She says that she will "probably be in this place for a long time" and that she tries to make the most of her prison time by focusing on how she can help other women. Like Julie and Shana, Tiana says she would like to return to the "outside" one day, but she isn't sure when or how, so in the meantime, she tries to make life better for herself and others where she is.

The pilot Angel program is KPMI's attempt to integrate weekend graduates into its mission of reaching out to incarcerated women and men. Kairos's leaders understand that while the volunteers are effective, KI graduates bring knowledge, skills, and experience that most KI weekend volunteers lack. The team leaders I speak with during our weekend are all positive about what they are observing, and all of them say they hope that the Angels program will become a permanent part of the weekend because Angels can not only help during the weekend but also serve as mentors in the post-Cursillo, postweekend phase.

Cookie Love

The centerpiece of the message of love and support that runs throughout the weekend is Kairos chocolate chip cookies baked by dozens of volunteers. Kairos is known for its "cookie ministry." Each participant receives gift bags of the cookies throughout the weekend—and as welcome and farewell gifts. On Friday afternoon, Kairos volunteers stand outside the recreation facility where the weekend events are held and hand out bags of cookies to the newly incarcerated offenders, known in this facility as the "intakes," as they exit the cafeteria and head back to their dorms. The ceremony is unique to this Kairos group and facility. By the end of the day, every one of the facility's 1,300 prisoners will have received one dozen cookies as will have the staff members. As we hand out the cookies, we receive responses that range from shy murmurings of thanks to "God bless you" to confusion and even tears. The intakes, in their bright yellow and orange jumpsuits, stand out from the other offenders, who wear khaki, maroon, and forest green. These women, according to JoEllen Rowe, coordinator of Indiana KI women's weekends, are dazed and overwhelmed by their first week in prison: "Here they are newly incarcerated, and then they see a group of women handing out cookies. It must be a strange and wonderful experience all at once for them."[31]

The cookies are part of Kairos's message of agape, "God's unconditional love toward us," which informs the actions of the weekend volunteers. The cookies that we distribute over the four days were baked ahead of time, as a form of Christian service, by dozens of women, men, and children who attend various southern Indiana churches. The cookie bakers are given the official Kairos recipe and told to bake and handle the cookies with love and "in prayer." These "blessed" cookies, as they were called by volunteers, are distributed throughout the weekend by the Kairos volunteers as part of agape. The inmates who attend the weekend are asked not only to accept the "love offerings" and "agape gifts" given to them but to give the cookies to fellow inmates with love. The KI weekend is "bathed in agape—the unconditional love of Christ, delivered by the people of Christ."[32] The Kairos volunteers work in the spirit of the God's Love We Deliver volunteers Bender investigates, preparing and delivering food to nourish bodies and souls.[33] The significant difference is that the Kairos ladies have come here to share what they consider to be the redemptive power of Christ with women who have been largely been forgotten by the world outside the prison gates and barbed wire fences. To KI volunteers, the inmates are the "faraway"—those far removed from Christ—that Bonnín wanted cursillistas to reach.

For the volunteers, the cookies also symbolize forgiveness. Later that weekend, the participants take part in a healing ceremony and afterward receive a bag of cookies to present to another inmate they need to forgive. Susan, one of the weekend leaders, instructs the women "go ahead, do it while you're hot!," referring to their newly self-forgiven state. When the guests are told this, gasps are heard throughout the room. The next morning, several of the guests share with me their "forgiveness cookie" stories. Julie tells me about giving her bag of cookies to a bunkie who had "really, you know, made me angry. I needed to let go of the anger I had for her and yeah, she was surprised I gave her those cookies." Another KI guest tells how a tablemate gave her bag of cookies to her to give to another inmate (who is not part of the Kairos Weekend). A year earlier, the recipient of the forgiveness cookies had shot and killed the cousin of the cookies' original sender. The main topic of conversation over coffee this morning is this exchange and what it means. The guests express amazement and admiration that the giver of the cookies did this. When I ask the giver about it, she says, "I kind of surprised myself that I wanted to give her those cookies. Yeah, still kind of shocked I did it." While this weekend guests were prompted by the Kairos Inside leaders to give away cookies, the way this woman responded was spontaneous, and Kairos leaders understand her gesture as motivated by God. After hearing her story, Kairos volunteers smile, saying, "God is great" and "The Holy Spirit is powerful indeed." The weekend volunteers strive to make room in the course's planned format for such spontaneity on the part of the weekend guests. Kairos weekend leaders are mindful that the three days must adhere to guidelines set by the national organization, yet do not want the weekend to feel scripted. They try to downplay the tension between structure and inspiration by citing the "Holy Spirit," or "Jesus" at work. They understand the weekend to ultimately be on "God's time." Yet not all spontaneity during the weekend is welcomed by Kairos Inside volunteers. The manual warns, for example, against boisterous, call and response–type singing, which clashes with the ideal of white, middle-class normative Christian womanhood offered to the weekend guests.

Making "Holy Ground" and "Living Sanctuaries"

All Fourth-Day weekends are highly organized, scripted, and intentional. Each KI weekend has designated leaders who hold several Saturday's worth of training for the volunteers. Every KI weekend has a coordinator, who will be the next KI weekend leader; a leadership crew, which consists of an advising leader (a former KI leader who serves as a consultant all weekend), a leader, an observing leader, and a state observer. There is also a music leader and team, servers (a head servant and head servant assistants), a table leader and table assistant for each of the seven tables, and seven clergywomen, one for each table. Each KI volunteer is assigned a specific job, and she comes to the weekend having prepared through study and prayer. She has been part of an intensive, deliberate "team formation," which in southern Indiana includes between twenty-six and thirty-four hours of preparation before the KI weekend. She has studied the KI manual with her sister volunteers, and she has spent many hours praying for a successful weekend experience for the offenders.

In Kairos, as in all Fourth-Day Cursillo movements, individual "thumbprints" and experimentation during the weekend is discouraged, since this is seen as taking away from time-tested and proven weekend events. As in the KPMI program manual puts it, "Every element of the Weekend program is to be done, and done in its proper sequence. Don't rearrange elements to suit your personal opinion about what works better. The Wisdom of Kairos has established the program as the best method."[34] The lay and clergy talks that are given throughout the weekend—between thirteen and fifteen—are written out for the speaker, and she or he is asked to add only a few minutes of personal experiences or reflections that relate to the topic. Detailed outlines for the weekend talks, specific Bible verses, and questions for the offenders to consider are provided in the program manual. Chapel is an important part of the weekend experience, and at least twice each day, all of the weekend participants go to the chapel, held in the craft room at the facility the weekend I attend.

The Kairos volunteers emphasize the holiness of the chapel space and time and tell the participants they are standing on "holy ground." The prison's craft room and the entire recreation building become the site of personal and spiritual transformation. The weekend guests are told that they can make into "God's House." They are told that if they declare the space to be sacred and it will be so.[35]

The Sunday cross ceremony symbolizes the love that Jesus—the fellow prisoner and sufferer, the ideal man and spouse—has for each of the guests. As each woman receives a cross around her neck, she is told by the clergywomen conducting the ceremony that "Christ is counting on you." Some of the prisoners are weeping, some smiling, some making fist pumps in the air. Several of the women break into spontaneous song. We have been singing songs from the Kairos songbook, but these quickly give way to black spirituals. "I've Been Changed" and "Precious Blood" are sung by old and young guests alike, with a power that gives me goose bumps. Unlike other unplanned elements of the weekend, this one keeps on going, perhaps because the other KI volunteers have left the room to give the guests time for reflection and worship.[36]

While these women respectfully sing Kairos approved songs that have become favorites over the course of the weekend, like Randy Rothwell's 2010 hit "Sanctuary,"[37] at this moment they claim their own voice. The Kairos weekend events have shown them that they can refashion prison space into sacred space, and in the presentation of the crosses ritual, these forty-two women make the chapel their own. They sing of being healed, reborn, and renewed. For me this is the most moving part of the weekend.

Shortly after the crosses ritual, the guests are led back to the recreation complex for the closing ceremony. One hundred or so Kairos volunteers sit in rows of chairs and greet the inmates as they move to the front of the room. Sharon, the weekend's director, asks them to address three questions: What condition did you come to Kairos in? What did you find here? What are you taking away? One by one the guests walk to the microphone and speak. They talk about having "a new direction in my life," "finally [being] able to forgive myself for all the things I have done," "now know[ing] the meaning of family," losing "all that weight inside of me," and finding Christ. Several of the prisoners talk about the crimes they committed in front of their children and say they have forgiven themselves and are motivated to go home to be better examples to their families. One guest in particular focuses on her self-hatred and says she now knows that she is "lovable and worthy of God's love." The many prayers are intended to help female prisoners believe they can make prison space into sacred space. Moreover, the women are encouraged to reconsider their bodies as sacred sites—bodies that have been abused, neglected, and shamed. They are told to imagine their bodies as vessels for Christ's love and forgiveness, a kind of love that purifies and redeems.

In short, the Kairos participants are told that if they can forgive themselves, they can start the process of sanctification and freedom from what has been weighing them down and leading them to make "bad choices." While KI volunteers say that they realize that their weekend guests cannot change circumstances outside of their control, they emphasize personal responsibility for their own actions. The guests are asked to forgive not only themselves but also those who have hurt them.

The rice paper ritual is an important ceremony of forgiveness and renewal during the weekend, and one that builds on the weekend messages of suffering, healing, and redemption. For this ritual, the guests and volunteers are each given a slip of rice paper as they exit the chapel and return to the main room, where their tables were located. When they return, they see that the volunteers have moved the tables out of the room and rearranged all of the chairs into a large circle. At the front of the room are long rectangular tables covered in tablecloths. On each table are several water bowls. The participants are asked to write the names of people they need to forgive on their slips and then find a seat and sit quietly until they feel it is time to walk up to one of the tables and place their piece of paper in a water bowl. After each woman places her slip of paper in the water, a volunteer seated behind the table hands her a popsicle stick and she stirs it, under the volunteer's gaze, as it dissolves. This is an intensely emotional exercise for many—guests and volunteers alike—and many women weep as they walk to the bowl and drop their rice paper in the water and watch it dissolve.

Rituals and dynamics that emphasize forgiveness and freedom are important components of the KI weekend. The "Freedom Guide" given to each participant at the beginning of the weekend tells them that Christ died "to set us free" and that "part of being 'free' is to go the Father, through Christ, under the guidance of the Holy Spirit, as we bring our brothers and sisters along with us."[38] While some of the offenders in the room will never leave prison, they are given the message that even though they are in prison, perhaps even for life, prayer and a relationship with Jesus Christ will set them free. While its theology is radically different from the famous prison ministry of the Nation of Islam (NOI), Kairos Prison Ministry International shares the NOI's emphasis on reaching out to a forgotten group, sharing the good news of a savior figure, and helping inmates find "freedom."[39] With freedom comes the ability to make better choices, to love oneself, and to forgive others. The thirteen talks given at this KI weekend—"Three Encounters with Christ"; "Choices"; "You Are Not Alone"; "Friendship with God"; "I Will Never Forget You"; "Acceptance of Self"; "The Church"; "Opening the Door"; "Discovery through Study"; "Christian Action"; "The Wall"; "Obstacles to Grace"; and "Means of Grace: Walking Your Talk"—carry the message that the offenders are loved by God and that they have the ability to make changes in their lives to initiate spiritual health and happiness.[40]

Yet mixed in with messages of empowerment and turning to an all-powerful God are messages of submitting to men, specifically to husbands. One of the speakers, for example, emphasizes the importance of "following your husband's lead" in her talk, saying "that is how God wants it." This instruction seems out of place in a weekend that teaches self-empowerment, self-improvement, and making better choices. The

Kairos Inside weekend guests have had tenuous histories with the men, relationships often characterized by abuse, and emphasizing that "the husband is called by God to lead" seems dangerous and risks alienating the women in the room who are seeking healing and renewal. For the most part, the volunteers work hard to transcend their socioeconomic and racial privilege and relate to the guests, but differences remain and cannot be overlooked or glossed over. They also emerge in the imagery used in the course, such as the cake-baking metaphor examined earlier. Relational challenges remain, for all of the good intentions. When the guests stray from the songs in the program and into more energetic hymns, the KI volunteers on our weekend go along, but they also do their best to steer the singing and praising back to calmer, more manual-worthy expressions.

As I have noted, the talks in KPMI and other Fourth-Day movements are highly scripted. Each KPMI talk follows a prayer taken from the green Freedom Guide and runs approximately twenty minutes. The talk is broken into sections, which KI volunteer reads verbatim from the KPMI program manual, inserting a personal story where indicated. A poster, flip chart, or chalkboard may be used to illustrate some of the major points, but any visuals are to be kept simple, so as to not distract from the content of the talk itself. The volunteers' preparation prior to the weekend includes giving their talks and receiving critical feedback from their KI sisters. By the time she gives her talk, it should be polished yet retain intimate qualities. The talk is to draw in the listener—the female offender—by asking her to relate to the KI volunteer and to reflect on her own life and how she can live better. As one of the KI speakers finishes her Saturday talk, JoEllen beams with satisfaction. "She worked really hard on that," JoEllen says. "It has really improved from her practice talks."

Indeed, the KI volunteers who give their talks are polished as well as impassioned. Their personal stories are well-timed and placed, and, as the program manual instructs, they are brief, so that the speakers do not spend too much time focusing on themselves. Some speakers are overcome by tears during their talks as they recall troubled childhoods, abusive relationships, and broken marriages, but they are careful to loop their stories back to the talk's title topic.

A common thread of all of the talks is affirmation: Even though we sin and fall, God loves us, we are God's worthy, beautiful child, and we are worthwhile as individuals. For the female offenders, such messages of self-worth have been rare in their lives. These are women who have been abused in every way imaginable and in ways that the KI volunteers, even the ones who have themselves been abused, cannot imagine. One was locked in a closet for hours each day as punishment for not brushing her hair the "right way"; many were sexually abused by members of their nuclear families from an early age.

Affirmation for the offenders abounds when they share their "family posters" with everyone in the room. Table by table, each lady goes up the podium to discuss the poster she has made. After she has explained her artwork, her tablemates choose another woman from the table to walk around the room holding the poster aloft for all to see. The KI volunteers rave over the posters, exclaiming how "wonderful," "colorful," "creative," and "awesome" they are. JoEllen is a champion of affirmation, giving each poster individual attention and congratulating each artist who walks by. Sitting next to JoEllen, I am very moved by the outpouring of support and affection that the KI volunteers give these women and by the proud expressions of the women as they hold up their posters. I am also reminded of a critique of Fourth-Day weekends I have heard from people inside and outside of the movements: namely, that the message that "God loves you" is too simplistic. My experience with a KI weekend has led me to believe the contrary, that messages of love and acceptance are never simplistic and that the rise of small groups, which stress accountability and affirmation, attests to the power of "simple" affirmations. Moreover, men and women in medium- to maximum-security prisons need to hear these positive affirmations more than anyone. During our weekend, this need is movingly articulated on three occasions: after the women receive the agape letters, during Saturday's "open mic," and during Sunday's closing.

"Agape, Agape, and More Agape"

A highlight of the weekend is the agape letters, letters of love and support written for the KI participants. The KI volunteers arrive at the facility bleary-eyed and weary Saturday morning, having spent much of the night writing individualized letters for each of the forty-two KI participants. Sonia, a KI volunteer, tells me that she writes part of the letters in advance but completes them on Friday night after she has "gotten to know each of the ladies a little better. I want each letter to be personal and not generic." The letters are written on brightly colored notepaper and sealed in colorful envelopes. Each KI participant receives her own agape letter bag filled with forty-two letters—one from each of the KI volunteers—late afternoon Saturday. As the participants begin reading their letters, all of the KI volunteers exit the room for the cafeteria, where they sit and sing from the Kairos songbook. As one of the KI volunteers tells me, "We are singing for them; we are showing them that they are loved and that we care about them."

The KI volunteers sing for close to twenty minutes. A mother and daughter who have played the guitar and sung first soprano all weekend lead us, and two Kairos music Angels sing along and tell us which page is next. When we reenter the recreation room where the KI participants are sitting, the majority are crying and wiping their eyes with the Kleenexes provided at their tables. Applause breaks out as the KI volunteers walk in and sit down. It lasts for several minutes, despite the weekend leader's insistence that "we are not to be thanked; it is the Holy Spirit who should be thanked." One of the weekend participants stands up, overcome with emotion, and exclaims, "I know I can speak for all of my sisters here that we are so very touched by what y'all just did for us. To be able to read letters that haven't been looked at by the warden and letters written just for *us*, well, I can't tell you how much that means to us." Another inmate says, "You ladies, who don't even know us that well, took the time to tell us that someone *does* care!"

Eduardo Bonnín, the founder of the weekend Cursillos on which Kairos is based, was critical of what he called the various "oddities" of Cursillo weekends. In particular, he worried that the letters distracted the recipients from the *clausura*, the closing.[41] Yet in my experience, for women who have suffered as much as these women have and who are seeking a radical healing and renewal, the letters can provide them with a sense of love that they have lacked.[42] The weekend Angels all tell me that their letters were a highlight of their weekend and that they keep the letters and read them over when they are especially down or angry to remind themselves that someone cares about them. Some say that they never receive mail and that they will "cherish" and "take care of" these letters.

While a KI volunteer would say that all of the actions and prayers that go into hosting a KI weekend is a form of agape, some moments stand out as especially significant. After the volunteers make their way into the recreation room Saturday morning, they go to the designated "agape room." There Mary and Helena have been working hard on all of the weekend agape, including hanging posters made for this KI weekend by inmates of other facilities, assembling slips of paper that indicate prayers for the KI inmates into a prayer chain, and posting supportive messages sent from other domestic and international KI ministries. Mary, the head agape KI volunteer for the weekend, says she loves being assigned to agape because she sees how much joy it brings to the offenders. She has participated in four other KI weekends and has been heavily involved in southern Indiana's Walk to Emmaus community. She says she feels "always so blessed" to be able to share her Christian faith and love with others and see how "Christ's love just touches the hearts of these women here. It is just beautiful." After Sunday's closing, Mary and Helena, her assistant, are also responsible for burning all of the agape, as is Kairos Prison Ministry practice, to protect the privacy of the inmate participants. While Mary says she is a little sad to see all of the beautiful and inspired art go up in flames, she is happy and secure in the knowledge that God is smiling down on the event with pleasure as "all of the agape messages reach Him in heaven."

The open mic is a prelude to Sunday's closing. About twenty participants take the mic and give testimonies of how the weekend has affected them individually and as a group. All of them speak of the feelings of self-worth they have gained. One enthusiastically proclaims, "I know now that I made a bad choice that got me in this place, but I am really letting go of the hatred that I have felt for myself. I know that I am loved, I am worthy, and that we ARE the church!" Most of the women who take the mic say that their feelings of self-worth have radically improved.

The voluntary testimonies at Sunday night's closing ceremony are powerful and voice the affirmation that the participants feel from the weekend, as well as how they are moving beyond the past and looking toward the future. These are women who entered the weekend feeling resentful and angry and full of self-hatred, self-pity, or both. What the weekend has done for them, they say, is move them from self-hatred to forgiving themselves for the crimes they committed. As one participant says, "I came here after selling and doing drugs, even in front of my children! I know I made some terrible choices in my life and am committed to being be a better mother who will not surround her children with the kind of things I used to. I have forgiven myself and look forward to a better life." Another talks about her struggle to leave her abusive husband: "This is my fourth time in here, I am ashamed to say. Each time I got out I went back to him, thinking I could change him. I now know that I need to focus on changing myself now, and that he will never change. For the first time in my life I feel like I am worth more than a piece of dirt." Another young participant tells us of her journey to heal from grief: "I came here shortly after my baby died of SIDS. I went crazy after she died and turned my back on God. I can't say that I am anger-free, but I am working on it now and feel a whole lot better than when I came here Friday night." Some of the speakers say they are focused on finding a "new family" that will make their prison stays more bearable. Others speak of letting go of the guilt and remorse that consumed and crippled them, vowing to "do good" in prison and on the outside, should they leave the penitentiary.

"I May Still Be in Prison but Now I Am Free"

By Sunday night, the proclamation "We ARE the church" is heard repeatedly in the rooms where the weekend events are being held. The weekend guests have been working on forgiving themselves, have been praying for healing, and are privately as well as publicly vowing to change. For the past seventy-two hours they have remade the recreation room, craft room, and gym into sacred spaces—places of prayer, fellowship, and places where they eat and talk about issues important to them. At the Sunday night closing, Rita Steed, the facility's community services coordinator, tells them that the "hard work starts now." After the weekend is over, she tells them, they must go back to their dorms with their bunkies and all of the problems that were there before the weekend. The challenge to the forty-two women now, she tells them, is staying true to what they have learned at Kairos and maintaining community. "As you know," she tells them, "in prison you can't trust anyone, and you will be stabbed in the back.... The challenge to you is how you will respond. Hopefully you have experienced a change this weekend and will handle things differently. I challenge you to 'be the church' and to make good things happen here. You are all spiritual warriors now—you are armed with God. You don't need real 'arms,' just God. God is your weapon and is your ultimate defense." Rita continues by urging the women to attend the Saturday group reunion meetings that are held in the craft room every Saturday. She talks about living the Fourth Day and how maintaining the spiritual high they have now will be crucial if they are to endure prison and stay focused and spiritually centered. "You have been freed from the bondage of rage and imprisonment and you are now 'free.' I challenge you to keep it up." Rita's message is met with a resounding clapping and cheers from the forty-two women who have just made the weekend course. Several of the women chant "We ARE the church," and the fifty or so cursillistas who came for the closing ceremony clap along with the recent graduates. Women and men from the Indianapolis area Christ Renews His Parish (CRHP) are in the audience, along with men and women involved in Kairos Prison Ministry, Catholic Cursillos, Walk to Emmaus, and Via de Cristo. These men and women are all part of the larger Fourth-Day movement and have come to show their support for the inmate graduates.

The hope of Kairos Prison Ministry International and its volunteers is that the inmates who graduate from the weekend experience will "affect their environments" and "bloom where they are planted"—whether in prison or at home upon release. Kairos Inside volunteers bring their middle-class, mostly white, non-Hispanic religious and cultural sensibilities to the weekend events and aim to transform individuals and prison culture. They are intentional in staying close to the original CdC method of piety, study, and action, and through the CdC methodology they have adopted, they hope to bring healing and hope to the incarcerated women (and men) they serve for three days.

Post-KI Weekend

Another distinguishing factor of the KI weekend, when we compare it with the other Fourth-Day weekends and movements, is that the graduates are not able to join a reunion group of their choice—their choice is limited to the one Saturday reunion group that is led by a KI volunteer who regularly visits. Rita, the warden, says this group is small but fairly consistent. She also mentions that some of the weekend graduates meet with other religious groups that sponsor weekend events. The weekend team leaders I spoke with all said that they would like to see the guests go on to live better lives within the prison, but they recognize that it is more difficult to avoid bad influences "on the inside" than it is "on the outside." For her part, JoEllen says that she hopes the guests can go on to give each other the support and love they experienced here during the weekend, and that they can help each other live better lives on the inside than they had before the three days. While sponsors in all of the Fourth-Day movements are encouraged to maintain a relationship with their candidates well after the weekend is over, KPMI's regulations prohibit weekend sponsors from contacting their candidates once the course is over. KPMI focuses on helping the incarcerated to become Christ-filled leaders in their communities, and the organization fears that inmates will become too attached to and dependent on their sponsors if they maintain contact.

Anecdotal evidence provided to me suggested that when KI volunteers had maintained contact with their candidates through letters, this regular communication was not helpful for the inmates. The KPMI manual thus states, "It is critical that Kairos volunteers realize that the important relationships that need to be formed are between the Kairos Residents, and not between the Residents and the volunteers. Activities that make the Residents more dependent upon volunteers are counterproductive to the purpose of KPMI."[43] KI volunteers are also forbidden to visit the prison where they served as a volunteer, but they can volunteer at the Saturday reunion groups or Kairos Monthly Reunion gatherings at a different prison. While the other Fourth-Day movements seem to encourage and nurture attachments to other Christians, especially those who can help individuals in their walk with Christ, KPMI discourages and in some cases forbids contact between volunteers and graduates. The volunteers with whom I spoke said that they know this policy seems "a little harsh," but that it is a necessary measure for the organization to take so that inmates do not become too dependent on sponsors and volunteers. The tough-love approach stands in marked contrast with the weekend events, which, we have seen, seek to bridge differences between volunteers and guests and emphasize a shared emotional and spiritual experience.

While this chapter, like chapter 4, has focused on in covenant Fourth-Day Cursillo movements, the next chapter, chapter 7, examines two movements that have branched further outward from the original 1944 weekend Cursillo. Like Teens Encounter Christ (TEC), which we examined in chapter 5, the two movements examined in chapter 7 are Cursillo spinoffs. Yet unlike the Fourth-Day movements and TEC, these offshoots are self-consciously offshoots and see the changes they have made as improvements. The Catholic Christ Renews His Parish and the Protestant Great Banquet were formed to reach Christians unable or unwilling to make a mainline Catholic or Protestant Christian Cursillo. Their founders are self-conscious in their efforts to maintain continuity with the original Cursillo, but they insist that their movements are qualitatively different and are improved versions of the Fourth-Day weekends. Their movements' similarities to Fourth-Day movements nonetheless outweigh their differences and point to a shared desire by U.S. Catholics and Protestants for renewed selves and communities.

CHAPTER SEVEN

Maverick yet Mainstream

Christ Renews His Parish and Great Banquet

Cursillo was the catalyst for CRHP. People couldn't get into a Cursillo so we developed something in-house for them.
—Bob Edwards, president, Christ Renews His Parish, December 14, 2009

It was when I started to become a second-class citizen in the Kingdom of Heaven that I decided to go my separate way. It always happens; the Holy Spirit will have a movement in the church and then people come in and institutionalize it.
—Jack Pitzer, executive director, Lampstand Ministries

You can drink coffee from all different kinds of cups, from old Styrofoam ones to beautiful ceramic cups, but what matters is what is *in* the cup. It doesn't matter what weekend encounter it is, what matters is that Jesus is in the cup.
—Pastor John Herfurth, Trinity Lutheran Church, Indianapolis

While the mainline Fourth-Day movements we have encountered so far can trace their roots directly to the Mallorquín weekend Catholic Cursillos, still other movements and encounters have branched off of them. While technically not part of the Fourth-Day movement proper, the offshoots of Fourth-Day movements share in the major aims and goals of the Cursillo weekend encounters that inspired them. The proliferation of Fourth-Day movements and their offshoots indicates the depth of desire by contemporary American Christian men and women to encounter Christ, experience healing and renewal, and become part of a new community. These offshoots also signal something else that is peculiarly American—the pluralism of Christianity. In part because of the disestablishment clause, American religious history—in this case Christian—is replete with instances of sectarian movements. It would be historically inaccurate to say that America has a "Christian history." Instead, the history of Christianity in the United States is about multiple Christianities,

Christian *histories*. The absence of a legalized, nationally mandated religious tradition has allowed for the kind of experimentation and flowering of traditions that we find in U.S. religious history. What has always fascinated me about American religious history has been the inventiveness, moxie, and general chutzpah that men and women have shown. If Americans, especially Christians, do not like a tradition they try to reform it, and if their efforts fail then they break off and form their own movement. These breakaway movements are usually informed, at least in part, by the traditions from which they stem, and this historical link is part of the new movement's history, too, whether or not it is publicly acknowledged.[1]

Those Christian retreats and encounters that branched off from Catholic and Protestant Cursillos were both inspired and repelled by their parent movements. Their aim has been to improve upon the Cursillos to create a better encounter for the individuals involved and to facilitate the continuity of renewal. Some of the founders branched off because of dissatisfaction with their Fourth-Day encounter; others were told that they could not make certain modifications and still call themselves a mainline Fourth-Day movement. While some kept the seventy-two-hour weekend others shortened it, modifying the three days in ways that are not deemed in covenant by Fourth-Day movement leaders. Yet despite the disagreements and differences that prompted their formation, when we examine the nonmainstream "Fourth-Day-esque" encounters, these branches of the branches, we see that they aim for the same thing as do their mainstream Fourth-Day counterparts: to put men and women in touch with the Holy Spirit and Christ. They offer a lay-focused weekend and method to cultivate a renewed Christianity. Fourth-Day movements and all of their offshoots, in covenant or not, aim to create a revitalized lay apostolate. The men and women who go on these retreats want to experience community, healing, and wholeness, and many take their weekend messages and experiences and try to make the world a better place, which for them means to live their faith in their daily lives.

In this chapter I will focus on two of the more successful of these Fourth-Day movement offshoots, in terms of geographic spread and numbers of men and women who have made one of their retreats: Christ Renews His Parish (CRHP), the Catholic encounter that branched off of the Catholic Cursillos in 1969, and Great Banquet, which branched off of the Methodist Walk to Emmaus in 1992. They are mavericks in the sense that their founders self-consciously and unapologetically diverged from the mainline weekend Christian Cursillo weekends, but they nonetheless approximate the methods and intentions of the mainline movements and provide their candidates and graduates with strikingly similar experiences and outcomes.

Christ Renews His Parish

Bob Edwards, who cofounded Christ Renews His Parish (CRHP) in Cleveland in 1969, told me that several factors led him to branch off of Catholic Cursillos and start something new:

> We had sixty women in a course at one time and sixty men in their course at one time—there was a huge demand for Cursillos. A Cursillo was held every month, and people would drive from all over to get there. It was hard on the parishioners because they had to drive all over the place and then for the ultreyas it was even more running around to get there. We decided to go parish-based instead of diocesan-based because it was better for parishioners. Keeping it in-house was more convenient and less stressful for parishioners in the end.[2]

The waiting list for Cursillos in Edwards's own diocese could be years long. In addition to witnessing the unmet demand for Cursillos in the Cleveland area in the 1960s and 1970s, Edwards was deeply dissatisfied with his Cursillo weekend, "the most BORING experience of my life!" He thus joined with then-priest John Jacoby to form CRHP as a shortened version of Catholic Cursillos, thirty hours instead of seventy-two, and parish-based since he believed that parishes would benefit from renewed and refreshed members. Moreover, Edwards and Jacoby wanted to create a more ecumenical Christian experience than CdC. From CRHP's founding, any Christian, regardless of denomination, was eligible to make a CRHP experience so long as it was within her or his parish boundaries. While telling me CRHP's history, Edwards paused a moment to chuckle at his movement's acronym, whose pronunciation he admits not having thought through very carefully at the time: "We wanted something that was parish-based and Christ-centered, and the name just sort of happened. Unfortunately, I didn't think about the acronym enough because it was CRHP, and that's what people call it. I guess I should be grateful I didn't name it Christ Renews *a* Parish—then it would be called 'Crapper!'"[3]

As cofounder of the movement, Edwards knew CRHP's history by heart, saying that "1969 was the first official CRHP. It was held in Parma, Ohio, a suburb of Cleveland, at Holy Family parish, the largest parish in Cleveland." According to Edwards, today CRHP has been held in 1,100–1,200 U.S. parishes. He said that he and Frank Wardega, CRHP's key facilitator, assisted forty to forty-five parishes a year in beginning the process: "It is definitely spreading. I don't like to call it a movement because it is not a business." In fact, Edwards asked me not to write that CRHP is a "movement" because he liked to think of CRHP as spreading "according to God's plan, not man's plan." When I asked how he preferred me to refer to CRHP, he replied that it is "a parish process. A 'movement' implies something that this, Christ Renews His Parish, really doesn't do. In movements you have annual meetings and lots of regular meetings. When we initiated CRHP I said, 'Over my dead body will we have meetings and all of that.'" Edwards had a problem with the Fourth-Day movements that have websites, sell literature, and are, in his estimation, "a little slick." CRHP has no national website, does not sell literature, and spreads primarily through word-of-mouth. Edwards said this is the best kind of growth because it is "being directed by God" in parishes around the country and world. "People hear about CRHP from others and want to have it in their own parish. They don't hear about it from an organization or from a website, which I think makes CRHP more, shall we say, legit in many ways."[4]

The 1980 CRHP manual still serves as the group's written touchstone. Unlike the mainstream in-covenant Fourth-Day movements, which all have tracts and other writings to complement the manuals, CRHP has one book—its manual. The fifth edition of the handbook, published in 2011, is fully compatible with the third edition (1980) and the fourth edition (1997), CRHP handbooks currently in use. Christ Renews His Parish is a copyrighted parish renewal process (to use Edwards's term) that, unlike the other groups chronicled in the book, does not have a national office. CRHP does not advertise and has no full-time staff members. Since 1969, its weekend has been used as the primary instrument of personal and parish renewal in more than 1,179 parishes in thirty-five U.S. states and in five other countries.[5]

According to Edwards, CRHP was an "improvement" on Catholic Cursillos that was modeled on the SEARCH retreats that were popular in the 1960s and 1970s and founded by Jacoby. Moreover, Edwards took issue with Catholic Cursillos' method of teaching process. In CRHP, "there are no rollos or teachings. You can't critique someone else's life." In a two-day CRHP experience, small-group dynamics are emphasized. A social leveling takes place that does not privilege anyone's authority or knowledge.

Another big difference at the time between Cursillos and CRHP was that CRHP was more intentionally Scripture-heavy. "Unlike Cursillo," said Edwards, "we have always used the Bible, not the *Summa Theologica*."[6] Edwards was correct in his assessment of early U.S. Catholic Cursillos, which emphasized experiential theology over Scripture, yet the movement has become more Bible-focused in recent years. My own Cursillo weekend, which I described in chapter 4, was replete with biblical references. Each rollista provided numerous Scripture passages that supported her talk's focus, and she used them to reinforce the rollo's larger message. Catholic Cursillos and other Fourth-Day movements today incorporate Scripture, in particular New Testament readings on the life of Jesus, but to say that the weekends are Scripture-heavy or Bible classes would be inaccurate.

Although participants in CRHP weekends consult its handbook, the New Testament is considered to be CRHP's manual. In the two days of CRHP renewal, priests, sisters, and laity from a territorial parish—which can include non-Catholics and non-Christians who live in a geographically defined area—discuss given predetermined topics. Rollos are not given but specific areas to discuss are provided. CRHP volunteers and candidates alike are encouraged to "share their faith life" and to "witness their experience of the Lord" in the areas of "renewal," "new life in Christ," "spirituality," "Christian community," "reconciliation," "the Eucharist," "Scripture," "Father's loving care for us," and "Discipleship."[7]

Another point of distinction between CRHP and Fourth-Day movements is that in contrast to its parent movement, the diocese-based Catholic Cursillo movement, CRHP has always been parish-based. Only men and women from a given parish are allowed to participate in a CRHP experience. Edwards and Jacoby were both Catholics but were critical of Catholic renewal programs such as Cursillos, which they believed "sucked the energy out of" parishes, as Edwards put it. Bonnín himself encouraged cursillistas to reach the "faraway" in their own "environments," and Edwards and Jacoby interpreted this as providing an opportunity for men and women to infuse their parishes (their environments) with a newfound zeal and energy.[8] In doing so they addressed the centrality of parish life for U.S. Christians, in particular for Catholics. As

Edwards and Jacoby wrote in the first 1980 CRHP manual, "In spite of many experimental community models being tried and offered on many levels, the territorial parish is where people are. Most people simply would never leave their parish. Their parish would be their experience of church. In most parishes the need was the same—for small, workable groups of parishioners who would commit themselves to coming together on a regular basis to share their faith, pray, study, and eventually become involved in authentic and effective lay ministry."[9]

Edwards and Jacoby believed from the start that a parish-based encounter with Christ would ultimately be more effective and that the renewals would take root in people's parishes. Ideally, as they stated in the first CRHP handbook, "Meeting the Lord in your child's classroom or experiencing Christian community in the social hall transforms the parish buildings into sacred space. The parish begins to become home for its people."[10]

The goal was for CRHP to provide a constant stream of renewed parishioners to the parish and a steady pace of renewal. A diocese-based renewal like the Catholic Cursillo, they contended, would not be as effective as a parish-based one because its graduates were dispersed geographically and would not have a common place to funnel their renewed selves and faith. Edwards and Jacoby were onto something important here, as CRHP and other parish-based weekend and two-day renewals have proven popular in midwestern parishes in particular.[11] It does seem that the shortened duration and concentrated geographic scope has made a lasting impact on parishes that have sponsored and that continue to sponsor CRHP. The CRHP graduates I have spoken with all say that they like the shortened duration, which they say works better for today's busy families. CRHP graduates also emphasize that their personal faith has been renewed and that they have taken their newfound faith to their parishes. Some graduates say that their parishes have been "completely transformed" by the weekend experience.

The experience of Kate Hodel, who lives in the Kansas City metro area and calls herself a "practicing Catholic," supports the argument that CRHP creates healthier parishes because the parish is at the center of U.S. Catholics' lives.[12] In 2005 Kate traveled more than ten hours from her own Church of the Ascension parish in Overland Park, Kansas, to Elizabeth Ann Seton parish in Indianapolis to make her CRHP with a group of women from her parish. She returned "on a mission," she says, to bring CRHP to her own Kansas City parish. Not long after her "amazing" CRHP experience in Indianapolis, she says, "a contingent of Indiana folks came to our parish and helped us put on a CRHP. Ever since then, I can say that CRHP has been a wonderful thing for our parish because so many people's faith has been renewed. I am honored to be a part of this exciting time in my parish and to see the positive changes that are occurring."[13]

When I asked her about how CRHP has impacted her parish, Hodel replied: "We have had a huge response to CRHP since we brought it here. I can think of two huge benefits off the top of my head, the first is that people get connected to each other in ways they hadn't connected before. Parishioners of all ages are now connected and have formed small faith communities since their CRHP. Secondly, I can say that CRHP has revitalized our parish. We have more involved and active parishioners than we did before and I'd say that parish involvement has increased three times what it was before we had CRHP."[14]

Hodel remembered Edwards fondly as a "very special person because he founded this revitalization program for our parishes, and now CRHP has taken on a life of its own."[15] She likened Edwards's role in the movement to that of a "rock who created ripples." She agreed wholeheartedly with Edwards's insistence on a thirty-hour program restricted to residents of the parish. Hodel said she did not make a Cursillo because it was too much time away from her family; for her, CRHP's shortened, condensed experience acknowledged parents' busy lives and their multiple commitments.

Catholics like Hodel who have gone through a CRHP weekend say that it was a time for them to reflect on God and to deepen their faith. Melissa Knoblett-Aman, Catholicism editor for BellaOnline, writes that her February 2008 CRHP retreat was "a wonderful experience that truly renewed and deepened my relationship with Jesus. Being part of the formation team was an amazing spiritual journey with a group of women I now consider my sisters." Knoblett-Aman went on to serve on the CRHP formation team seven months later and is actively involved in CRHP. She encourages fellow Catholics to make the overnight retreat, writing, "If you have the opportunity to participate in a Christ Renews His Parish retreat, do! It is so worth it. And if you feel the call to continue, listen and respond with a 'Yes!' You won't be disappointed. The weekend is amazing; continuing with the formation process is even more so."[16]

Knoblett-Aman's enthusiasm for CRHP was seconded by Hodel, now executive director of the Ignatian Spirituality Center in Kansas City: "CRHP clarified who I am as a person and introduced a discernment process for me. I now focus on my spirituality so much more and identify with Ignatian. I am now cognizant of being a child of God and what I believe defines me more now than what I do for a living."[17] In addition to her work for Ignatian, from which she said she derives immense satisfaction, Hodel chairs the inner-parish mission committee, which has worked with other Kansas City area laity and priests who want to bring CRHP to their parish. She said that an important lesson she has taken from her work with CRHP is that "it is important to look for God moments and to acknowledge that while things don't always work out as we want them to, what we get, in the end, is a true blessing from God."[18]

Since making her CRHP in April 2004, Hodel has gone from working full-time to part-time and spends more time now with her spouse and teenaged son and daughter. "I am very, very blessed to have made my CRHP because it has helped me be a better role model for my kids. I was relentlessly busy before and rarely took the time to stop and reflect and meditate. That has all changed since making my CRHP, and I feel so much more centered now, more at peace." For Hodel, CRHP was more appealing than Cursillo because in CRHP, husbands are not required to make their weekend prior to their wives. This made things easier for Kate, whose husband is "on a different path right now.... maybe he will make a CRHP at some point but maybe he won't."[19] CRHP nonetheless welcomed her as a Catholic Christian who desired a spiritual experience independent of her spouse's experience. In other words, in CRHP, a married woman's spiritual growth is not contingent on her husband's faith or lack thereof, and it is not assumed that her spiritualty is in tandem with her husband's—or that it should be. CRHP does not assume or expect the same spiritual compass for husbands and wives, and because of this flexibility, it can welcome women whose husbands have not made their two-day experience as well as men whose wives may not desire the experience for themselves.

Hodel's case thus points to a significant issue for the U.S. Catholic Cursillos. I have spoken with several female cursillistas who were not happy with the U.S. Catholic rule that wives must wait for their husbands to make the weekend first. Kathy, a lifelong practicing Catholic in central Illinois, said she was "angry, hurt, and more than a little disillusioned" when her priest told her she would not be allowed to make her Cursillo weekend until her husband made his (something he was not at all interested in doing at the time, she said). Kathy said that although her husband went into his weekend "uninterested" and signed up for it only so she could make hers, he "ended up loving his Cursillo weekend and getting a lot out of it." Today, he is heavily involved in his local movement, while Kathy, "still angry," she said, refuses to make hers in protest of what she considers to be a sexist rule.[20] Cursillistas tend to cite the rule to legitimate both the patriarchal orientation of the weekends and an accepted understanding—an imagined patriarchy, if you will—that men need to feel they are the heads of their households. These legitimations of the engenderment of the weekend's patriarchy are curious and ahistorical, especially since Eduardo Bonnín did not devise such a rule. CRHP, which does not have the rule, can be said to be in covenant with Bonnín in this important way, and its growth—eclipsing that of the Catholic Cursillos in some dioceses—can be attributed in part to its progressive attitude toward marriage.[21]

CRHP is a non-Fourth-Day movement offshoot that, like other Christian Cursillo spinoffs, does not adhere to Fourth-Day movements' insistence on the seventy-two-hour retreat. Some, like Bob Edwards, do not want to be a part of the "exclusive Fourth-Dayers" because they "think they have a lock on experiencing Christ, but they don't." For Edwards, the Catholic Cursillo weekend was "way too long and . . . way too boring." Nonetheless, although modified (in its policy regarding women's participation) and shortened, CRHP remains a version of Catholic Cursillos, with the emphasis on transforming individuals' lives so they can transform their environments (in CRHP's case, the parish).

This promise of transformation is what links all of the Christian weekend retreat movements, Fourth Day and non-Fourth Day alike. Candidates enter the experience not knowing much about the details of the three days, but knowing that their friends and neighbors have experienced conversions, new outlooks on life, and renewed marriages as a result of their weekend experiences. Indeed, like the men and women who make a Fourth-Day weekend retreat, those who experience an offshoot weekend tend to become more involved in their churches and parishes. Ruth, whom I met during the Kairos Inside weekend, attends an active and large Catholic parish in Indianapolis. She made her CRHP weekend about ten years ago and was the lay director for several years. She said that the men and women who go on a CRHP weekend "absolutely" become the leaders of the parish and motivate others to become more involved in church life and in community organizations as well.[22] CRHP is "very active" at Ruth's parish church, St. Monica's, where—as in Hodel's Overland Park, Kansas, parish—there are waiting lists to make the thirty-hour course. Ruth had to wait over a year to make her CRHP and said it was "well worth the wait."

Yet not all parishes are experiencing the same level of success. St. Barnabus, another Indianapolis parish, has reduced its CRHP "weekends" to one a year, down from the two per year it has offered for some time. I met a couple at the Kairos Inside closing at Rockville Correctional Facility in southern Indiana who have been very involved in CRHP at St. Barnabus, and they bemoaned its current state there. Mark, who is in his late sixties, said that there are "just too many options" for Christians today and that CRHP "just becomes one of many things to do." He compared the current state of CRHP in his parish to what he had just witnessed at the Rockville Correctional Facility Kairos Inside closing: "Here they have a captive audience, and of course these women want to experience something new and different. They don't have many options." What Mark did not mention here—and what Hodel did allude to during our interview— is the crucial component of a weekend's success in a parish-based retreat such as CRHP: a priest's involvement and support. The CRHP manual emphasizes that the success of the parish renewal depends on parish priests and parishioners' collaboration. In the manual's "Who Does It" section, this in-house collaboration is underscored: "The secret of the 'who' is that you can't rent a priest or a team of experts. You have to do it yourself. Shared responsibility flows most effectively out of shared ministry."[23]

The four priests at St. Monica's are active in CRHP and work closely with their parishioners; as a result of the reciprocal relationship and a shared form of governance, the two-day experience is thriving in their parish. Likewise, Tres Dias is thriving at Westminster Presbyterian Church in Rockford, Illinois, in no small part because its copastors, as I noted in chapter 4, are deeply involved in the movement and have required their entire staff to make a Tres Dias weekend. CRHP appeals to Christians because of its ecumenical Christian outlook, its focus on the parish, and its more updated, twenty-first-century outlook on gender relations.

Great Banquet

A more recent Fourth-Day offshoot has also been successful in its ecumenical Christian focus and outreach. Great Banquet, a seventy-two-hour interdenominational Christian weekend retreat for adults, was founded by Rev. Jack Pitzer in 1990, and its youth version, Awakening, was founded in 1992. A direct spinoff of Walk to Emmaus, Great Banquet is part of Lampstand Ministries, the "covering corporation" that Pitzer founded in 1990 and continues to lead.[24] As senior pastor of Lampstand Presbyterian Church in his hometown of Decatur, Illinois, Pitzer oversees the thirty Great Banquet communities and nine Awakening movements. States where Great Banquet communities currently exist include Indiana, Illinois, Ohio, Texas, Tennessee, Kentucky, Virginia, and Florida.[25] Pitzer attended the "number five Walk to Emmaus weekend" in Nashville in the fall of 1979. Shortly thereafter moved with his wife, Roberta, and their four young children to Madisonville, Kentucky, where he was installed as the senior pastor of First Presbyterian Church and where he lived and preached for twenty-three years. After thirty years away, Pitzer believes that God "called me back to my hometown."

I first heard of Great Banquet during the 2010 Orlando gathering of Fourth-Day movement leaders. The gathering has been by invitation only for the past sixteen years and included Victor Lugo (Catholic Cursillo) Tracy Schmidlin and Steve Gielda (Via de Cristo), Greg Engroff (Walk to Emmaus), John McKinney and Paul Weis (Tres Dias), John Thompson (KPMI), and Thom Neal (NEC). Since 1994, leaders of the six in-covenant Fourth-Day movements have been meeting to discuss their movements and to "bounce ideas off of each other," according to Gielda, vice president of outreach of Via de Cristo. Jack Pitzer of Great Banquet has never been invited to this annual gathering, and Engroff, urged me to "check out Great Banquet's website" to understand why. At my prodding, Engroff offered some information about Pitzer, and minced few words, saying that he "basically stole from Walk to Emmaus. He stole our information and repackaged it as Great Banquet." Engroff was especially suspicious of Pitzer's financial motives, viewing him as a contemporary prodigal son, and suggested that he was profiting off a movement over which he has total control. In a telephone interview with me, Pitzer dismissed the charges and said he fervently believes that Great Banquet is a more authentic ecumenical Christian expression of renewal and that "all people, not just some" are included "at the table with Jesus Christ."[26]

After my trip to Orlando to meet with Fourth-Day movement leaders, I checked out the various Great Banquet–related websites and links. I was especially interested in Pitzer's claim that he had attended Upper Room Cursillo number 5 in Nashville in the fall of 1979, and that he helped found the Walk to Emmaus in Nashville. Pitzer claims to have begun the first Walk to Emmaus movement outside of Nashville in 1981. Great Banquet is advertised on Lampstand Ministries' website as a tool that God uses to "advance and establish His Kingdom in many places.... Jack has found that God can work miracles in people's lives if they give Him 3 days of their time. He says that the Great Banquet does his job for him, which is for people to 'know Jesus as Savior and Lord and to make Him known.'"[27]

Pitzer advertises Great Banquet as being in line with "its counterparts Cursillo, Emmaus, and Tres Dias" in that it is an "orderly, structured weekend designed to strengthen and renew the faith of Christians." And, as in other Fourth-Day movements, in Great Banquet laity and clergy work together for the "renewal of the church."[28] When Pitzer and I spoke on the phone, he emphasized his early involvement with the Upper Room Cursillos. Because Upper Room Cursillos were ecumenical, Pitzer, an ordained Presbyterian minister, was welcomed as both a participant and as a founding father, he says, of Walk to Emmaus. He had first heard about Upper Room Cursillos while he was attending seminary and living in eastern Tennessee. Pitzer chuckled recalling this time, saying that "it was hard enough finding toilets that flushed there, let alone an Upper Room Cursillo weekend!" Intrigued by the stories he heard from those who had gone through a weekend, he said he "wanted to find out what made it so damn special, you know?"[29] It was when he and his family moved to western Kentucky in 1975, he said, that he was able to become involved with what was then called Upper Room Cursillos. "They put me to work right away because I'm clergy, and every weekend needs a clergyman present." He recalled the moment when the movement formally became Walk to Emmaus as a time that was "not pretty, let me tell you."[30] In this, Pitzer's story aligns with other cursillistas' retelling of the U.S. National Secretariat's actions toward Protestant Cursillo groups. "What happened was that the Catholic Cursillo folks threatened to sue Upper Room over the use of the word *Cursillo* because they had intercommunion," Pitzer said. "The real catalyst for Walk to Emmaus was the threat of this action being taken." Pitzer went along with the newly constituted Walk to Emmaus and led men's weekends in Madisonville, Kentucky. Aware of his own denominational ties and the "Methodist direction that Walk to Emmaus was moving toward," Pitzer met with Walk to Emmaus founders Maxie Dunham and Rev. Bob Wood in 1981 and expressed his interest in "moving more toward a Presbyterian context." While the two men were receptive to his ideas, he said, once they left the movement, he had no supporters and Upper Room began to make Walk to Emmaus less ecumenical and more Methodist. The "dirt side" of the founding of

Great Banquet was how he felt pushed away by the movement he said he helped found:

> Let me put it this way, Upper Room has become more draconian, and they now require all kinds of credentials of its spiritual directors that they didn't used to have. Basically a spiritual director has to now be Methodist, but this was not always the case. The Bloomington-Normal director, who has been involved with the movement for a long time and has led a very active community there, would not qualify today because he is not a Methodist. So what Upper Room is doing is exactly what the Catholics did to them—moving from being ecumenical to nonecumenical, and I have a problem with that.[31]

According to Pitzer, because of the "draconian measures" of Walk to Emmaus, some Emmaus communities have "jumped ship" and are now Great Banquet communities. Pitzer emphasized the ecumenical origins that are a mainstay of his organization: "We are truly ecumenical. We may lean toward Presbyterian principles, but we have always been and for as long as I'm in charge will be ecumenical."[32] What he means by "Presbyterian principles" is a greater focus on confession, given the larger history of Presbyterianism. There is a strong confessional focus in Great Banquet, and individual sinfulness is emphasized more than it is in the mainline Fourth-Day movements. "We don't know who Jesus is," said Pitzer, "until we realize that Jesus died for our sins. We need to confess our sins to be able to know Jesus." In a recorded workshop for Great Banquet team leaders, Pitzer emphasizes "our sinful nature" and that "we are targets for Satan, who tries to bewitch us; and if he doesn't get us, our sinful nature can, or the distractions of the world will get us."[33]

According to Pitzer, it was the departure of Bob Wood and Maxie Dunham as Walk to Emmaus's leaders that prompted him to see himself as "called by God" to branch off and form his own movement. He spent a year studying Catholic Cursillo documents, he said, "going back to the original," and he "rewrote Upper Room Cursillo" during that year. Pitzer stressed that it was his involvement in many movements, including the National Episcopal Cursillo, Catholic Cursillo, Tres Dias, Walk to Emmaus, and a Walk to Emmaus offered to inmates, that gave him the ability to incorporate aspects from all of the movements into the one he was forming. He said that he wanted to retain the original "essence" of the Catholic Cursillo weekend as well as the "flexibility" he experienced during the prison Cursillo weekend: "What I learned from the prison experience was that you need to be willing to change the course of events depending on how people respond. What I had experienced was that Emmaus and other movements were becoming too rigid in their method and they didn't have this kind of openness."[34] Pitzer insisted that what became Great Banquet was informed by the essence of Cursillos, the flexibility of prison ministry, and Presbyterianism, "because it is the pool I live in."[35]

Great Banquet's three-day structure consists of fifteen talks, five given by clergy and ten by laity, as in Fourth-Day movements. It similarly features small-group discussions and group dynamics such as poster-making sessions. Great Banquet's three days hinge on the themes of "Knowing Yourself" (Friday), "Knowing Jesus" (Saturday), and "Knowing the World" (Sunday), paralleling the themes and order of Fourth-Day movement weekends. Moreover, the fifteen short talks—"Discovering Your Priorities," "God's Gift of Grace," "Ministry of All Believers," "Response to Gift of God's Grace," "Way of Relationship," "Truth through Study," "Sacramental Grace," "Life of Christian Action," "Obstacles to Grace," "Disciples," "Change Environments," "Life of Grace," "Christian Community in Action," "Staying Power," and "Establishing Priorities"—all drive home the same basic messages as do Fourth-Day rollos, namely, that a life of introspection and knowing oneself is necessary for a life of effective outreach to others. Living a productive Christian life means knowing oneself, developing a relationship with Jesus, and working with other Christians in community. Knowing Jesus and being an effective apostle necessitates studying the Bible, which is part of deepening one's personal piety. Fourth-Dayers, CRHP graduates, and those who are part of Great Banquet share this intentionality.

Pitzer insisted that it was ultimately the Holy Spirit that led him to found Great Banquet. When he ran Walk to Emmaus weekends in Madisonville, he'd always "throw a big feast Saturday night—I mean a *real nice* dinner." News of the fabulous meals reached members of the larger community, and each year people who were not part of the weekend "just showed up to be fed." Pitzer instructed the team leading the weekend to "go ahead and feed folks who show up." He recalled one instance when a father and two young children "showed up for a handout, and we fed them. I will never forget how huge the eyes of the children were—they were like saucers. I don't think they had ever seen so much food." As Pitzer put it,

"God sponsored these people. Every year that we held a Walk to Emmaus weekend we had folks show up to eat. Many of them stayed for the rest of the weekend, and some of them are still involved in the movement." While he was overseeing Emmaus weekends in Madisonville in the early to mid-1980s the parable of the Great Banquet (Luke 14:15–24) came to him, and he realized the focus of his weekend: "I've been running movements since 1981, and this Scripture, more than any other, spoke to what I do. There are lots of excuses for not going to the great feast, but most of them are cold feet, not good excuses for not attending the Lord's banquet."[36] Pitzer said that while he has never had the "yoke of oxen to tend to" (Luke 14) as an excuse, he has "gotten the excuse from a couple of farmers that they had to check on a bull!" According to Pitzer, Great Banquet appeals especially to people who have gone through "all kinds of 'amputations,'" like a divorce or a death in family. Great Banquet is for everyone but especially for "people who have had parts of them killed, people who have had a hard time getting to where they have wanted to go in life. In this way they are 'lame' like those talked about in Luke 14 as well as blind because they can't see where they want to go."[37] Pitzer derived inspiration from other chapters and verses, including Luke 10:25, "which says to love your neighbor with all your heart, soul, and strength, and to love your neighbor as yourself." This, he said, is the focus of Great Banquet.[38] In fact, all of the movements examined in this book include feasts of some kind, as well as a candlelight ceremony following the dinner (like the one I experienced during my own Cursillo weekend). That food and fellowship are emphasized by all Fourth-Day movements is something Pitzer does not acknowledge.

Pitzer formed Lampstand Ministries, the "tent ministry corporation" encompassing Great Banquet and its youth version, Awakening, in 1992. Since 1999 he has been the head pastor of Lampstand Presbyterian Church in Decatur, where he continues to supervise Great Banquet and Awakening. Pitzer said that the movement has also been successful among "independent Christian churches, those that are not denominationally affiliated."[39]

One denominationally affiliated church where Great Banquet has been successful is Trinity Lutheran Church on the south side of Indianapolis. When John Herfurth was called as pastor to Trinity in 1992, the congregation "had been through a lot of conflict, and many people, while they went to church each Sunday, hadn't experienced Christ."[40] Herfurth soon noticed that the leaders of the church had all been through a Great Banquet weekend. Inspired by "the many gifts they brought to the church," he made his own weekend two years after his arrival. The weekend experience was "powerful" for Herfurth, who described it to me as a time "when you don't just talk about Jesus, you get to feel and experience the love of Jesus firsthand." Deeply moved by his weekend encounter with Christ, Herfurth soon after became the spiritual director for the men's weekends. He said he encourages specific individuals to make the weekend encounter but emphasized that "you want to approach these folks in a certain way; you don't want them to think they're half a Christian before they make the weekend or if they decide to not make it." He said he has tried to steer members of the clergy toward the weekend but without success: "I think that clergy are threatened by more intimate encounters with Christ. Most are uncomfortable with the intimacy and emotion that is experienced on the weekend. We all have our walls that need to be broken down, and I think that it is hard for clergy to tear down those walls and expose their hearts."[41]

Entering the weekend "with an open heart" is crucial, said Herfurth, if one is to have a "full experience with Christ." Amanda Hoover, the spiritual director for Trinity Great Banquet's women's weekends, agreed, saying that Great Banquet has been a "real blessing" for her church and that "many hearts" have been opened. Hoover said that, like many members of her congregation, she went to church regularly before her Great Banquet weekend but only "because I thought that this is just what you are supposed to do." She said that the entire weekend was "so powerful" for her and the other "guests" because it all led up to "seeing and experiencing the power of forgiveness and grace and above everything, the love of Christ."[42] Herfurth said that it is difficult to separate out the weekend's many components because each builds on the previous one and leads to the next in a pattern of "progression and power." A real "turning point" for Great Banquet weekend guests, according to Hoover, is the "dying moments" and "grace" talks because at those points the guests experience a "tumbling down" of the walls they have built up over the years. The guests are asked to forgive others, "a major thing for everyone because it is when we forgive others that we truly let Christ into our hearts and know Him."[43]

The challenge for Trinity Great Banquet has been to "get people involved in Fourth-Day activities," such as group reunion meetings and the monthly worship gatherings. According to Herfurth, the fact that Trinity Great Banquet attracts team leaders and weekend guests from a wide array of Christians all over Indianapolis, which makes it so effective and dynamic, also makes holding group reunions a challenge, as "people are really spread out and not everyone goes to the same church." Hoover said that the "weakest point" of Trinity Great Banquet is the irregularity and inconsistency of regular group reunion meetings. Yet while people are not active in reunion groups, she noted, they do not hesitate to sign up to serve at a Great Banquet weekend because "it was such a wonderful experience for them, so they want to continue that experience by experiencing it again, this time from a different role." Herfurth said his biggest concern now is figuring out how to facilitate more regularly held reunion groups, because "you want people in relationships and you want people to be in relationships with fellow Christians who have shared experiences. While the weekend experience is wonderful, I think the focus should also be on how to continue that weekend experience and feeling once it is over." Here Herfurth echoed other pastors, laypeople, and leaders of Fourth-Day movements and their spinoffs. My sources for this book all emphasized that the weekend is "just the beginning" and that the "Fourth Day" is for the rest of one's life and is to be shared and lived with other Christians. Making the Great Banquet weekend is "powerful" and "a way to experience Christ's love for us," but the guests who go through the weekend must change their lives once the weekend is over, said Herfurth. "The Banquet is a very powerful weekend and then you go back to your regular life. It is the same reason why diets don't work—it is hard to change your lifestyle but if you want to continue to see and to experience positive results you must be disciplined and continue a new way of life." The essential motivator for Herfurth, to "show people the love of Christ because so many people do not know Him," is a key component of all of the Fourth-Day movements and their spinoffs. And in a world that is "broken," Great Banquet has "changed people's lives," according to Hoover, because they "realize that Jesus loves them and that their sins are forgiven. They experience grace firsthand."[44]

While the Christian Cursillo spinoff experiences CRHP and Great Banquet are not considered to be in covenant by leaders in the Fourth-Day movements, the historical reality is that CRHP and Great Banquet are, like the in-covenant movements, based directly on the Catholic Cursillo weekend. We can also consider CRHP and Great Banquet to be mavericks because of their critiques of mainstream in-covenant Fourth-Day movements and their decisions to branch off of the mainline Christian Cursillo weekends. Edwards, Jacoby, and Pitzer critique the mainline

Cursillo weekends for being too long in duration and too rigid, and for what they viewed as the sexism of mainline Cursillos, which require or strongly advise that wives make their Cursillo weekend after their spouses. Moreover, the founders of CRHP and Great Banquet critique mainline Cursillos as not ecumenical enough. CRHP and Great Banquet owe their existences to the CdC, and their founders interpret their respective weekends as more authentic than the in covenant weekends—closer to the original Mallorquín weekend. CRHP's identity as a parish-based, shortened version of the CdC that is open to any Christian within the parish boundaries has proven successful. CRHP is more popular than the Cursillos in some dioceses, where it has replaced the CdC as the premiere Christian weekend experience, akin to the way Great Banquet has proven more popular than Walk to Emmaus in places like southern Indiana.[45] Case studies of the maverick yet still mainstream CRHP and Great Banquet show that even movements that have branched off of the branches—Fourth-Day movements—remain informed by the purpose and methods of weekend Cursillos and continue to resonate with U.S. Christians.

EPILOGUE

Cursillo Weekends, Fourth-Day Spirituality, and the Future

You might say that the Cursillo is a serenity prayer actualized, or the beatitudes of Saint Francis. You *can* be an instrument of peace. I see the Cursillo as an actualization of the serenity prayer, "I'm not quite the person I want to be, but I'm not the person I used to be either." The Cursillo is a process, we strive to be better—we know we'll never be perfect, but we strive for it.
—Jesse Ramírez, San Diego, July 22, 2005

As we have seen, Catholic and Protestant Cursillos are lay-sponsored, parachurch, church-supported weekend retreats that address individual Christians as important, vital members of the larger Church body. Although some within the Cursillo movement shun the term *retreat*, in my own experience at a Cursillo and interviewing more than 200 cursillistas between 2005 and 2011, the word accurately captures the intensive spiritual experiences and exercises that happen on a Cursillo weekend, whether Catholic or Protestant. As we have seen, six tables of five to six candidates and one mentor per table eat, sleep, pray, and worship together for seventy-two-hours, from Thursday to Sunday evening. Whether it is a Catholic Cursillo, a Tres Dias weekend, a Kairos Inside Weekend, or any of the other Fourth-Day weekends or their offshoots, the course is carefully orchestrated according to a manual by a team of dedicated Cursillo lay leaders who dedicate months of planning to sponsoring a successful weekend. Candidates have been carefully screened by veteran cursillistas for their readiness to undertake the course. Once a candidate has been accepted, he or she goes through the pre-Cursillo, a period of sponsorship. During this time before the actual course is held, which can last for months or weeks, each candidate meets with a veteran cursillista who helps to prepare him or her for the experience. Ideally, the sponsor continues to be a spiritual mentor long after the course is over, in a period known as the post-Cursillo.[1]

My own Catholic Cursillo sponsor, Doris O'Keefe, met with me on several occasions and we also spoke on the phone as part of the preparation for my making my Cursillo, number 959 in the Diocese of Peoria. Doris asked me questions about my faith life and what I wanted to "get" out of the Cursillo. I had interviewed Doris four and a half years prior to this experience. We met at a dinner arranged and hosted by a mutual friend, another cursillista I had interviewed, and hit it off immediately. I was struck by Doris's gentle demeanor, her graciousness, and her steady Catholic faith. We talked about mothering and the stresses and joys of being mothers and wives. As I had many of the cursillistas I had interviewed, I felt a connection with Doris and it was more of a conversation and less of an interview.[2]

At Doris's recommendation, shortly after meeting her and her husband, Jerry, I met and interviewed Father Duane Jack of St. Patrick's Church in Orion, Illinois. Father Duane was instrumental in bringing Catholic Cursillos to the Quad Cities area in 1971 and has been active in the movement since then. He has been the spiritual director of the Northwest area region since the first Cursillos were held at the Villa de Chantal, the former convent and Catholic girls' school run by the Visitation Sisters in Rock Island, Illinois. Father Duane is both a historian of the movement in Illinois and an active participant. An avid supporter of this book project, he asked me if I wanted to make a Cursillo as part of my research.

Father Duane and I agreed that only the weekend's team leaders, Doris, and he would know about my book research so that the women on the weekend would not be influenced by my identity.[3] At the time I interviewed Father Duane, my son Declan, who will be a kindergartener when this book goes to press, was a toddler. Although I had wanted to make my Cursillo earlier than I eventually did in the spring of 2011, the demands and pleasures of another pregnancy meant that I would have to wait to make my own Cursillo weekend. The youngest of my three children, Josie, was a little over two years old when I made my Cursillo weekend. I felt ready to make my weekend and, since my daughter was still nursing, the team leaders graciously accommodated my needs and provided me with a private room for pumping. I had experienced such generosity a year earlier during the Kairos Inside weekend I participated in and observed. My hesitation to be away from my children for three days points to a very real challenge for Fourth-Day movements, and indicates a reason for the success of shortened weekend experiences such as

Christ Renews His Parish (CRHP) and the Christian Experience Weekend (CEW). It is difficult for parents to be away from their children for three days. Leaders in the various movements are aware of the challenges in attracting younger couples and all cited attracting younger couples as a priority. In some places, like Thom Neal's South Carolina National Episcopal Cursillo (NEC) community, Fourth-Day movement leaders are encouraging sponsors to help out with childcare to make it easier for mothers and fathers of young children to make their course.[4]

My experience with priests, pastors, and laity in charge of sponsoring Christian Cursillo weekends has been overwhelmingly positive. I came away from both weekend experiences—Kairos Prison Ministry International and Catholic Cursillo—with a renewed faith in men and women and with a new understanding of the importance of joining a group reunion in the post-Cursillo, Fourth-Day phase. While I do not necessarily share all of the views of those women who were part of my Cursillo weekend, I do respect them and their commitments. Even when I do not agree with them, I understand why they believe what they do and do what they do. There was a strong prolife theme on my Cursillo weekend, for instance, and while I consider myself personally prolife, I see much complexity—as well as problematics—in the contemporary prolife/prochoice discourse. I advocate for comprehensive sexual education and access to birth control, which the Roman Catholic Church explicitly condemns, as Pope Paul V detailed in his 1968 encyclical *Humanae Vitae*.[5] Thus, when rollistas and other cursillistas talked about picketing Planned Parenthood clinics and being "so happy when a girl walked out of the clinic without getting an abortion—Amen to that Lord!," I was uneasy in my chair, wondering to myself, "What happened next?" I couldn't help but think, "Where is this young woman today and how is her child faring?" and "Wouldn't access to birth control help empower women and reduce the numbers of abortions and unwanted children?"[6] The moments most moving for me were those when table members had chances to bond. I enjoyed making posters and talking with the other women at our table St. Catherine of Siena. While I enjoyed the rollos and the poster-making sessions that followed them, the really powerful moments for me, and for the majority of cursillistas I have interviewed, came during the smaller breakout sessions with table members. Sharing three meals a day for three days with the six other candidates at my table gave us time to talk about our families, our struggles, and our faith. We opened up to each other, exposing our deepest fears as well as hopes and dreams, during the candlelight prayer session. And most of the women on my weekend, myself included, were overcome with emotion when we walked from the center to the chapel at Christ the King parish church next door and were greeted with songs and hundreds of lit candles held by cursillistas. We were tired, even overwhelmed, from a long day, and the songs in the softly illuminated chapel moved all of us to tears. Later that night, talking about the experience over decaf coffee and cookies, my cohorts expressed the surprise, excitement, and "inner peace" they had felt when they first saw the lit candles and were greeted by smiling cursillistas. "It seemed like that is what Christianity is supposed to be all about," one woman said, while the woman sitting next to her squeezed her hand and exclaimed, "I felt so special and loved. It felt wonderful!" For weekend candidates such as this woman, experience trumped theology and the kind of politicized theology we find in contemporary prolife discourse.

A highlight of the weekend for me came after chapel and mass, walking into the dining room with the ladies from my table and finding tables arranged to resemble a cross and covered in deep-red tablecloths. Candles adorned the tables as well as loaves of freshly baked bread and a glass of wine for each candidate and weekend team member. I had just had a difficult experience in the chapel, and seeing this version of the Last Supper again moved me to tears. As a non-Catholic who teaches American Catholicism and who has written extensively on U.S. Catholicism, I know well the Church's official stance against intercommunion, and I dutifully crossed my arms to receive a blessing from Father Duane. As a Christian who is involved in my own church—Edwards Congregationalist United Church of Christ (UCC) in Davenport, Iowa—taking communion has many meanings to me and is something I look forward to every month as it is practiced in the UCC. Even though I am well aware of the Catholic Church's stance, being denied communion stung, and for the first time during my Cursillo weekend I felt like an outsider. So walking from the chapel feeling hurt and being offered communion with the women of my table hit an emotional chord in me. The cracked wheat bread, baked from scratch that morning as a form of palanca by cursillistas, was the best bread I think I ever tasted, and the wine, made by a cursillista who keeps a small home vineyard, was deliciously sweet.

Some of these meaningful moments were planned by the weekend's team leaders, some were not. The entire weekend is structured with the explicit intent of bringing cursillistas to a closer relationship with Christ. It communicates forcefully that cursillistas need others to continue to grow in their faith and that the "Fourth Day" is all about joining a group reunion and continuing an intentional journey with Christ. Father Duane and Doris were instrumental in my making my weekend, and I appreciate the way they encouraged my own spiritual growth and development and, at the same time, my scholarship. I never once felt as though I had to compromise my standards of scholarship and have been encouraged by both of them to ask questions. They both recognized not just my scholarly interests but my spiritual ones, too, and they believed that the Cursillo experience and a group reunion would be beneficial to me on an academic as well as a personal level. My Protestant faith was valued, and I was allowed to make my Cursillo even though my husband had not made his. The fact that my husband, a non-Catholic, had made his TEC while a junior at a Catholic high school helped, but in the end, exceptions were made to accommodate my research, and I am grateful. As a Catholic priest who is ecumenically inclined, Father Duane is part of the Diocese of Peoria's long history of outreach to Protestants.

During my Cursillo weekend I couldn't help but reflect on my place in the history of Cursillos and on the fact I was making my weekend in a diocese that has demonstrated ecumenicism at the same time that it has evidenced a resurgence of Catholic triumphalism, most particularly in the last twenty years. Aside from my disappointment at not receiving communion, given my own beliefs and what the ritual means to me on a personal level, I experienced fellowship and inclusion all weekend long. Father Duane and Doris were sincere in wanting me to have a deep spiritual experience—their encouragement was not to make me Catholic. In fact, only one woman during my weekend joked that "now all we need for you to do is join the Catholic Church!" I went along with my tablemate's joke and chuckled along with her, knowing that she probably really did want me to join her Church because it was such an important part of her life. A cradle Catholic, my tablemate couldn't imagine belonging to another faith tradition.

Although priests' and pastors' involvement is essential to a Catholic Cursillo, when we go back to Eduardo Bonnín's writings and directives, although he recognized clergy's pivotal role in supporting the movement and encouraging parishioners to make the course, he never intended for priests to dominate the weekend. Father Duane's involvement seemed to illustrate what Bonnín envisioned—supportive, available, but not overbearing. Father Duane's rollo on the sacraments was moving and informative. Judging from their responses, the candidates appreciated his theological insights. A slightly built yet dynamic man who appears decades younger than his age, Father Duane is also very funny. His biker impersonation during some of the weekend's downtime made everyone in the room laugh. In the course of my research I came to appreciate not only the dedication of the clergy who particulate in the weekend but also their sense of humor and zest for life. Here we are reminded of Tanya Muzzarelli's story, related in chapter 3, of dressing up Pastor Dave like a baby during the Rockford Tres Dias weekends.

While Eduardo Bonnín cautioned weekend leaders against what he called "oddities" in his *Spiritual Testament*, and while some Fourth-Day leaders worry about too much improvisation, as we have seen, I can't help but wonder that if some adaptations are in order to lighten the intensity of the long weekend. The various priests, pastor, and laity I have met in the course of the research for this book have shown an amazing zest for life and like to have fun. Weekend sessions like the motorcycle skit highlight the enduring *amistad* between clergy and laity and indicate the centrality of community for a Cursillo weekend. Bonnín, after all, is remembered by his Mallorquín friends as someone who encouraged friendships among and between laity and clergy. He is remembered by his friends as a deep thinker, a man of profound spiritual insights, but also someone who could always make you laugh.

The history of Cursillo and its transmission to the United States shows how religion moves with its adherents and how it morphs, depending on the context. Cursillo's history necessarily prompts scholars of U.S. religious history to look for the ways the movements we are studying overlap with international efforts. We can no longer afford to be isolationists in our work, because much of what came to dot the U.S. religious landscape of the mid-to-late twentieth century came from somewhere else. Religion in the United States has always had transatlantic, international, and global influences. What was happening in 1940s on the island of Mallorca ended up resonating in the cultural and theological manifestations of U.S. Catholicism and Protestantism in the 1960s, 1970s, 1980s, 1990s, and the present. The history of the Cursillos de Cristiandad is a global one in which the United States played an important role, as U.S. cursillistas in turn helped to establish communities outside of the United States as part of their "living the Fourth Day."

When we employ an ethnographically oriented history and talk with individuals who have been involved with Cursillos for a long time, we are able to understand the global impact of a Mallorquín Catholic layman and role he played in spreading the movement in the United States, with the help of Catholic laymen, laywomen, and clergy.

Religion moves—it ebbs and flows with the people who carry it with them, and as scholars of religion, the historian and ethnographer Thomas Tweed reminds us, we must pay close attention to the ways religion travels as well as *why* it travels.[7] The Cursillo weekend was originally brought here on airplanes in the hearts and minds of cursillistas from Mallorca, men who were committed to seeing the weekend bear fruit in the United States. They sponsored weekend courses and from there the movement spread across the United States as Catholics—and later Protestants—wanted to experience a Cursillo weekend in their parishes, dioceses, and churches. As part of his extensive travels throughout the United States, Bonnín also visited Protestant Cursillo communities and showed his support and enthusiasm for these versions of the CdC. This brings us back to Miguel Sureda's contemporary observation that Bonnín was for unity among Christians and devised a weekend meant to revitalize Christianity for Catholics and Protestants.

The Mallorquín Catholic Cursillo traveled from Mallorca to mainland Spain to Colombia to Italy, then the United States and Mexico within thirteen years of the 1944 Cala Figuera CdC. Bonnín was a religious ambassador who has been under the radar of U.S. religious historians, as have the laity and clergy who helped spread the movement. If we are to understand religion as it is lived and practiced in the United States and in other countries, we must examine what Christians in other places are doing and saying, because their actions and words can and do have a direct impact on how Christianity, in this case, the Cursillos de Cristiandad, is lived in the United States.

American cursillistas' narratives show that for most of them, the universal appeal of the Cursillo experience trumps rigid denominationalism. What has emerged is nothing less than a distinctive language of experience and emotion. Cursillistas of Fourth-Day movements as well as their offshoots, and regardless of their Christian denomination or ethnic identities, use a strikingly similar language of experience. Theirs is a religion of the heart, and an ethnographically oriented history of the Cursillo movement in the United States points to current as well as future trends in religion where universal experience is discussed and emphasized more than what divides cursillistas theologically. It is precisely this shared experience and language that has ensured Christian Cursillos' health, and as long as the various movements continue to nurture a language and experience that transcends church, ethnic, and class affiliation, it will still be around fifty years from now.

The research I conducted for this book suggests that the nonecumenically oriented U.S. Catholic and Episcopal Cursillos will face real challenges in maintaining and growing their movements in the next half century, as American Christians have demonstrated their proclivity to downplay denominationalism in favor of ecumenicism and interdenominationalism. Moreover, Catholic Cursillos' diocesan organizational structure seems to have hindered their U.S. growth, in contrast to the parish-based efforts of Christ Renews His Parish (CRHP). Those men and women who have been on a CRHP can more readily see the fruits of their efforts to revitalize their communities when they are parish-focused. Yet, Catholic cursillistas' efforts are not necessarily focused on revitalizing their churches, to return to Bonnín's Mallorquín vision, but rather intend to "affect their environments"—their homes, neighborhoods, workplaces, churches, schools. If the Catholic Cursillo movement can effectively market itself in this way—if it can provide a path to individual spiritual renewal that leads to profound changes in all aspects of life—this could allow it to place itself at the center of spiritual renewal in the twenty-first century.

Via de Cristo and Walk to Emmaus, while denominationally situated, exhibit a blend of openness and denominational specificity that will continue to appeal to Christians who desire to experience a Cursillo and a Fourth-Day community with Christians of different denominations. The nondenominational Christian Tres Dias should continue to appeal to Christians who attend nondenominational churches or, if they themselves are denominationally situated, who place a higher value on the universal label of "Christian" than they do on a specific denomination with specific creeds. Tres Dias's future might be linked with the spread of Protestant evangelicalism and Pentecostalism, both in the United States and globally, since an increasing number of its members are evangelically inclined. Thus, having begun as an interdenominational Christian movement not tied to one denomination, Tres Dias might just become the most "denominational" of all the Fourth-Day movements, if it becomes an evangelical Christian organization whose members are megachurch evangelicals who prefer to be called "Christian." For, although contemporary Protestant evangelicals think of themselves as postdenominational, their theologies are not necessarily ecumenically inclined. To them, "Christian" is a label for a particular kind of Christian, one who is born again and who exhibits certain signs of salvation. As with all movements, the past, present, and future of the interdenominational Tres Dias is tied to those who are currently in charge, and if future trends perpetuate what the movement has seen in the past twenty years, it has the potential to become the most widespread of the Fourth-Day movements, yet, should it become increasingly evangelical, it will sacrifice ecumenism for a new kind of denominationalism.

As with Tres Dias, Kairos Prison Ministry International (KPMI) has become more evangelical over the years, and its future successes rest with the global spread and appeal of evangelicalism. As more evangelically inclined Christians are drawn to reforming men and women in prison, KPMI would seem to be an appealing choice. Moreover, like Tres Dias, Kairos is not affiliated with one denomination and welcomes participation by all Christians.

Offshoots of the in-covenant Fourth-Day movements such as Great Banquet and Christ Renews His Parish seem to be well positioned for increased success, as their structures (fewer hours away from family) make it easier for men and women to participate. And it is significant that CRHP, as I noted in chapter 7, is parish-based rather than diocesan based. Parish-based renewal in the U.S. context seems especially auspicious for Catholic movements in particular, since U.S. Catholicism has a long history of being centered in the parish. This outlook lends itself to a sense of ownership on the part of parishioners, since they can see tangible results in their churches. As we saw in chapter 5, the diocese-based TEC movement has experienced a more stagnation than its parish-based offshoot Kairos (not to be confused with KPMI) weekend experience for young adult Catholics. Like its parent, the U.S. Catholic Cursillo weekend, TEC's more recent history has shown that a diocesan base might hinder its continued and future growth.

Cursillistas believe that they must live the rest of their lives as reborn men and women; they are revitalized Christians with a mission to make the world a better place. In our ethnographic and historical examination of the Mallorquín and U.S. Cursillo movements, I hope it has become clear that the emotion, praise, and worship that are part of the Fourth-Day and offshoot movements come not so much from nineteenth-century Protestant camp meetings and revivals as they do from more recent movements like the postwar Mallorquín Catholic weekend Cursillos. A dynamic, lay-focused strain of Iberian Catholic spirituality that originated on Mallorca has come to impact hundreds of thousands of

U.S. Christian lives since the late 1950s—and millions globally. Today, as in 1944 Mallorca and 1957 Waco, Texas, cursillistas, whether Catholic or Protestant, are renewed and reenergized Christians who try to live their faith in demonstrable ways. Living their faith is tantamount not only to following in Christ's footsteps but also to trying to be "the hands and feet of Christ," and they will continue to do this work in the foreseeable future.

APPENDIX ONE

Cursillo Chronology

August 1944: The first three-day Catholic Cursillo weekend is held in Cala Figuera, Santanyí, Mallorca, Spain. Founded by Eduardo Bonnín Aguiló, the weekend is called "Cursillo of Conquest."

May 1957: The first U.S. Cursillo de Cristiandad is held in Waco, Texas.

October 9–11, 1965: The first Teens Encounter Christ is held in Battle Creek, Michigan, at the Sisters of Mercy Lodge. The cofounders are Father Matt Fedewa and Sister Mary Concetta (aka Dorothy Gereke), who had made their Catholic Cursillo and used their experience as a model for the TEC weekend. Sister Concetta has also been active in the Better World Movement (an interfaith, communitarian movement founded by a priest in Rome) and numerous other retreats.

1965–70: Teens Encounter Christ ALIVE retreat weekends, early TEC weekends before the TEC handbook was written and the TEC conference was formed, are held in Lansing, Michigan.

1969: The first Christ Renews His Parish is held in Parma, Ohio, a Catholic, parish-based (not diocese-based like Catholic Cursillos), ecumenical encounter. There is no national webpage, and it is not a "movement," according to Bob Edwards, one of its founders.

1970: The first official Three-Day National Episcopal Cursillo Weekend in the Episcopal Church is conducted with help from Roman Catholic sponsors in the Diocese of Iowa.

1972: The first Lutheran Cursillo weekends are held in Iowa and Florida. The founders had attended Catholic Cursillo weekends in these two states in 1971 and formed the Lutheran Cursillo modeled after the Catholic Cursillo weekend experience.

November 2–5, 1972: The first Tres Dias is held in Newburgh, New York. Founder Dave McManigal had made his Catholic Cursillo a year earlier. Tres Dias is non-denominational and ecumenical.

1974: Rev. Robert Woods, one of the three main initiators of the Methodist Walk to Emmaus, attends a Catholic Cursillo in Peoria, Illinois.

1975: Danny Morris, one of the three main initiators of the Walk to Emmaus, attends a Lutheran Cursillo in Miami Springs, Florida.

1975: The first National Episcopal Cursillo Seminar is held in the Diocese of Dallas.

1975: Tom Johnson, an attorney and Catholic cursillista from Miami, attends an ecumenical Cursillo gathering in Atlanta.

September 1976: Kairos Prison Ministry International, is officially formed after Tom Johnson works with Miami-area pastors to organize the first prison Cursillo at Union Correctional Institution in Raiford, Florida.

1976: Maxie Dunham, one of the three main initiators of the Walk to Emmaus, attends a Catholic Cursillo in Peoria, Illinois.

1977: The first unofficial men's and women's Upper Room (Methodist) Cursillo weekends are held in Peoria, Illinois. The founders (Rev. Robert Woods, Danny Morris, and Maxie Dunham) use Catholic Cursillo handbooks and literature.

November 1978: The first official Upper Room Cursillos are held at Belmont United Methodist Church in Nashville, the headquarters of Upper Room Ministries, with help from Peoria, Nashville, and Atlanta Catholic Cursillo communities. The course is Methodist-based but ecumenical.

1979: The first Kairos Prison Ministry International weekend is held in Miami, Florida, with the support of the National Secretariat of Catholic Cursillos. Following this first Kairos weekend, the Cursillo Secretariat asks others who are holding Cursillo weekends in prison to stop using the Cursillo name and join Kairos.

1979: The National Episcopal Cursillo Committee is formed in Atlanta.

July 11, 1980: Tres Dias forms as a national organization. John McKinney is elected as first president. Tres Dias is incorporated as a not-for-profit corporation in New York State and is recognized by the Internal Revenue Service.

1981: The National Cursillo Center in Dallas informs Upper Room Cursillo that it must discontinue using the word *Cursillo* in its name because its course is ecumenical. The founders of Upper Room meet and officially change the name to Walk to Emmaus.

1981: The Teens Encounter Christ Conference is formed. Father Jim Brown, Father Matt Fedewa, and Dorothy Gereke (the former Sister Mary Concetta) travel to Rome to present Pope John Paul II with the first TEC manual.

1981: The first Lutheran Via de Cristo Cursillo is held at Cross and Crown Lutheran Church in Atlanta. The Catholic Cursillo *Leader's Manual* is used.

1982: The National Cursillo Center in Dallas informs Via de Cristo Cursillo that it must discontinue using the word *Cursillo* in its name because its course is ecumenical. Members meet and rename the movement Via de Cristo. A minority group maintains the name Lutheran Cursillo and becomes nonecumenical.

1984: Walk to Emmaus becomes international when communities are chartered in Australia.

1985: The first Upper Room Ministries Cursillo Chrysalis is held at Hermitage United Methodist Church in Peoria, Illinois. Bishop Gerry Hughes asks Upper Room to discontinue using Teens Encounter Christ materials and the TEC name because Chrysalis is ecumenical and TEC is not. Subsequently, Upper Room drops the word *Cursillo* from its name.

1985: Tres Dias becomes international when communities are chartered in Korea and Germany.

APPENDIX TWO

Glossary

Bonnín Aguiló, Eduardo: Born in Palma de Mallorca, Spain, in 1917, Bonnín was the founder and one of the main architects of the weekend Cursillo "short course in Christianity" movement. He died in Palma in 2008.

Cursillistas: People who have "made" their Cursillo weekend.

Cursillo de Cristiandad (CdC): The three-day "short course in Christianity" weekend retreat that was founded by Eduardo Bonnín Aguiló in 1944 in Cala Figuera, Santanyí, Mallorca, Spain.

De Colores (many colors): Expression used by cursillistas to refer to their changed postweekend status as renewed Christians. Also refers to a Mexican folk song that has been the trademark song of the CdC since 1949. Protestant cursillistas also use the expression as well as the song in their weekends.

Fourth Day: The post-Cursillo, "the rest of your life," after the three-day weekend is over.

Fourth-Day movement: Catholic and Protestant weekend Cursillos that consider the "Fourth Day," after the three-day Cursillo weekend, to be the rest of the cursillista's life.

Fundación Eduardo Bonnín Aguiló (FEBA): A nonprofit organization in Palma de Mallorca, Spain, dedicated to maintaining the memory of the founder of the Cursillo de Cristiandad movement, Eduardo Bonnín Aguiló, and archiving his vast collection of writings and photographs. http://www.feba.info.

Group reunions: Small groups of cursillistas that meet on a regular basis to encourage each other in the Fourth Day.

Leader's School: A working three-day weekend for Cursillo leaders that was developed by Eduardo Bonnín Aguiló. This weekend is a replica of the regular Cursillo three-day weekend, with an emphasis on the continued education of leaders within the movement. Also called Cursillo de Cursillos.

Organismo Mundial de Cursillos de Cristiandad (OMCC): The international office of the CdC established in 1980.

Post-Cursillo: See Fourth Day.

Pre-Cursillo: An undetermined period of time before the Cursillo candidate makes the weekend course. The candidate meets with his or her sponsor, who helps to prepare him or her for the three-day Cursillo experience.

Rollo **(short talk):** Ten rollos are given by laity during the Cursillo weekend, and five are given by clergy.

Ultreya **(onward or going forth):** A reunion of group reunions. In the United States, *ultreyas* are held once a month; in Palma, Mallorca, they are held every Monday in a South Palma seminary.

Notes

Preface

1. Examples of such devotions include Kenneth and Gloria Copeland, *He Did It All for You* (Fort Worth, Tex.: Kenneth Copeland Ministries, 2005); *Pursuit of His Presence: Daily Devotionals to Strengthen Your Walk with God* (Tulsa, Okla.: Harrison House, 2002); and *From Faith to Faith: A Daily Guide to Victory* (Tulsa, Okla.: Harrison House, 1999). In addition to their coauthored books, the Copelands have each penned their own books, including Gloria Copeland, *God's Will Is Prosperity* (Fort Worth, Tex.: Kenneth Copeland Ministries, 1978); Kenneth Copeland, *The Laws of Prosperity* (Kenneth Copeland Ministries, 2010), and *Prosperity: The Choice Is Yours* (Fort Worth, Tex.: Kenneth Copeland Ministries, 1985).

2. Heather Rankle, interview with author, Tres Dias International Secretariat, Rockford, Ill., March 14, 2010.

Introduction

1. Throughout the book, I will use the term *Cursillo de Cristiandad* and the abbreviation CdC to refer to the three-day weekend experience that originated in Mallorca in 1944. Other designations I will use include Cursillo (to refer to the Catholic version); short course in Christianity; Cursillo weekend; Cursillo retreat; and Cursillo encounter. I will refer to the Protestant versions of the weekend retreat by their specific names, such as Tres Dias, Via de Cristo, and Walk to Emmaus.

2. It was Bishop Juan Hervás who renamed Bonnín's "Cursillos of Conquest" weekend Cursillo de Cristiandad ("Cursillos in Christianity") when he arrived in Mallorca as auxiliary bishop in 1946. *First Conversations at Cala Figuera* (Dallas: National Cursillo Center, 2004), 80.

3. In her book *Righteous: Dispatches from the Youth Evangelical Movement* (New York: Viking, 2009), Lauren Sandler makes a strong case for calling the twenty-first-century movement of evangelical youth the "Disciple Generation." She relates calls the movement a newer version of previous Christian awakenings. Though this is a smart and savvy portrayal of evangelical youth today, it is telling that this author, a journalist, finds it necessary to contextualize this movement by relating it to eighteenth- and nineteenth-century antecedents.

4. The scholarship on Vatican II and post–Vatican II Catholicism, for example, has mostly examined how American Catholics responded to the Church Council, and to U.S. social movements (second-wave feminism, Vietnam, post–civil rights America), but the premier Catholic lay movement of the 1960s, the Cursillo movement, has received little or no mention in peer-reviewed academic literature.

5. This book offers an in-depth study of mainline Christian laypeople's moods and motivations, as well as a history of an important but unrecognized post-1950s

Christian movement. It addresses what Kevin M. Schultz and Paul Harvey call the missing history of Catholics and Protestants: "If history is the study of change over time, then to ignore one of the important factors (religion) that has motivated Americans throughout this nation's history is not only to write bad history, but to fail to understand many of the driving forces that animate those that live around us." Schultz and Harvey, "Everywhere and Nowhere: Recent Trends in American Religious History and Historiography," *JAAR* 78, no. 1 (2010): 152.

6. Throughout the 1970s and 1980s, the northern Illinois Catholic Cursillos were held at the Villa de Chantal until more spacious accommodations were required. Since 2002, Catholic Cursillos in this region have been held at the Believers Together Center at Christ the King parish church in Moline, Illinois.

7. Five years later, in 2010, a new magnet school opened its doors to K–12 students. I am connected to the Villa and to local Cursillo culture, having interviewed dozens of local cursillistas who attended their Cursillo at the Villa. Moreover, my sons, Cormac and Declan, are students at the school (Rock Island Center for Math and Science, RICMS) and my daughter, Josie, will attend once she is of school age. Katherine Burton's *Bells on Two Rivers: The History of the Sisters of the Visitation of Rock Island, IL* (Milwaukee: Bruce Publishing, 1965) documents the history of the Villa de Chantal.

8. Only recently has Bonnín been credited in print as the primary initiator and founder of the CdC. The Fundación Eduardo Bonnín Aguiló (FEBA) has corrected the historiographical error that Juan Hervás founded the movement.

9. Cursillistas are trained at leaders' schools, which usually take place over a weekend. During this time, cursillistas practice their rollos and prepare for the weekend they will be working.

10. I am grateful to Augustana College for providing me with a Freistat Research Grant to travel to Mallorca in June 2011 to conduct archival research and ethnographic research to complete this book. The information gained during this trip has been invaluable for this book and for our understanding of the larger Cursillo de Cristiandad movement and the impact it has had on Catholic and Protestant cultures in the United States and around the world.

11. Elaine Peña has recently noted the dissonance between these institutionally driven standard accounts of religious phenomena and popular, lay accounts, noting how ethnography is a way of addressing inconsistencies of accounts and making sense of storytelling. Peña, *Performing Piety: Making Space Sacred with the Virgin of Guadalupe* (Berkeley: University of California Press, 2011).

12. Since the publication of David Hall's *Lived Religion in America* (Cambridge: Harvard University Press, 1997), the term "lived religion" has been invoked so much that it is in danger of losing its usefulness as a category for understanding religion.

13. Kristy Nabhan-Warren, *The Virgin of El Barrio: Marian Apparitions, Catholic Evangelizing, and Mexican American Activism* (New York: New York University Press, 2005).

14. I made my Catholic Cursillo at the Believers Together Center at Christ the King parish church in Moline, Illinois, March 17–20, 2011. My experiences and observations will be included in chapter 6. Christ the King and the Believers

Together Center are part of the Diocese of Peoria, which welcomes non-Catholic participants in its Cursillos. I thank Father Duane Jack and my sponsor, Doris O'Keefe, for encouraging me in the writing of this book and for welcoming my participation in the weekend.

15. Robert Wuthnow, *"I Come Away Stronger": How Small Groups Are Shaping American Religion* (Grand Rapids, Mich.: William B. Eerdmans, 1994), *Sharing the Journey: Support Groups and America's New Quest for Community* (New York: Free Press, 1994), and *The Restructuring of American Religion: Society and Faith since World War II* (Princeton, N.J.: Princeton University Press, 1988).

16. Robert Putnam, *Bowling Alone: The Collapse and Revival of American Community* (New York: Simon and Shuster, 2000); Robert Putnam and Lewis Feldman, *Better Together: Restoring the American Community* (New York: Simon and Schuster, 2003); Robert Putnam and David E. Campbell, *American Grace: How Religion Divides and Unites Us* (New York: Simon and Schuster, 2012).

17. There is a vast literature in the sociology of religion on post-1950s immigration and religion, as well as on religion and suburbanization. See R. Stephen Warner and Judith Wittner, eds., *Gatherings in Diaspora: Religious Communities and the New Immigration* (Philadelphia: Temple University Press, 1998); Helen Rose Ebaugh and Janet Saltzman Chafetz, *Religion and the New Immigrants: Continuities and Adaptations in Immigrant Congregations* (Walnut Creek, Calif.: AltaMira, 2000); and Lois Ann Lorentzen et al., eds., *Religion at the Corner of Bliss and Nirvana: Politics, Identity, and Faith in New Migrant Communities* (Durham, N.C.: Duke University Press, 2009) for insights into religion and immigration. For books that explore religious and identities and contestations among American suburbanites and exburbanites, see James Hudnut-Beumler, *Looking for God in the Suburbs: Religion and the American Dream* (New Brunswick, N.J.: Rutgers University Press, 1994); and Nancy L. Eisland, *A Particular Place: Urban Restructuring and Religious Ecology in a Southern Exburb* (New Brunswick, N.J.: Rutgers University Press, 1999).

18. Putnam, *Bowling Alone*, 69.

19. See Wuthnow, *"I Come Away Stronger,"* and *Sharing the Journey*.

20. Eduardo Bonnín Aguiló, *Colaboración en la revista "Testimonio"* (Palma de Mallorca: FEBA, 2007), 17.

21. While revisionist works like Thomas A. Tweed's *Retelling U.S. Religious History* (Berkeley: University of California Press, 1997) and Philip Goff's more recent *The Blackwell Companion to Religion in America* (Boston: Blackwell, 2010) challenge scholars of U.S. religion to shift our geographic, engendered, racialized, and denominational biases, the vast majority of U.S. religious histories still adhere to deeply engrained geographic, denominational, and engendered ways of telling religious histories.

Chapter One

1. See Francisco J. Romero Salvadó, *The Spanish Civil War: Origins, Course, and Outcomes* (New York: Palgrave MacMillan, 2005), for an excellent treatment of the history of the war.

2. The first Catholic Cursillos de Cristiandad for *muchachas* (young women were the focus of the first CdC for women) were held in Bogotá, Colombia, in June 1953.

3. Cristina González Duqué, e-mail correspondence.

4. Ibid.

5. Ibid.

6. Travel guides have long noted Mallorca as an ideal hiking destination, and serious bikers train on the challenging Mallorquín roads year-round. For a recently published book on hiking and walking the island, see June Parker and Paddy Dillon, *Walking in Mallorca: Classic Mountain Walks in Mallorca* (Milnthorpe, United Kingdom: Cicerone, 2010).

7. Catalina ("Cati") Granados, FEBA office, Palma de Mallorca, interview with author, 23 June 2011.

8. Eduardo Bonnín Aguiló, *My Spiritual Testament* (Palma de Mallorca: FEBA, 2009), 27.

9. The cathedral has been the subject of several academic books and is featured in travel guides and tourist-oriented books today. See Baltasar Coll, *Mallorca Cathedral*, trans. Nuria Llanso Jornet (Palma de Mallorca, 1977); Ralph Adams Cram, *Cathedral of Palma de Mallorca*, Medieval Academy of America Publications, vol. 14 (Cambridge, Mass.: Periodicals Service, 1932); and Robert A. Scott, *The Gothic Enterprise, A Guide to Understanding the Medieval Cathedral*, 2d ed., rev. (Berkeley: University of California Press, 2011).

10. Bonnín Aguiló, *My Spiritual Testament*, 26.

11. Ibid., 27.

12. Ibid., 25.

13. Ibid., 27.

14. Ibid., 29.

15. Ivan Rohloff, *The Origins and Development of Cursillo* (Dallas: National Ultreya, 1976), 20.

16. Gerald E. Poyo, *Cuban Catholics in the United States, 1960–1980* (South Bend, Ind.: University of Notre Dame Press, 2007), 16.

17. Stanley G. Payne, foreword to José M. Sánchez, *The Spanish Civil War as a Religious Tragedy* (South Bend, Ind.: University of Notre Dame Press, 1987), ix.

18. Sánchez, *Spanish Civil War*, 94.

19. Ibid.

20. Michael Mann, *Fascists* (Cambridge: Cambridge University Press, 2004), 324. Mann asserts that CEDA was not fascist, because it "supported traditional state institutions and specifically rejected paramilitarism," and that "it was actually as varied as the Socialist Party, but with a difference—this church-centered party was more disciplined." Mann notes that "'fascist' became the standard word used by the European left and center-left for authoritarians who wished to imprison them" (331).

21. Mann, *Fascists*, i.

22. Salvadó, *Spanish Civil War*, xv.

23. Mann, *Fascists*, 3.

24. Salvadó, *Spanish Civil War*, xiv.

25. Ibid., 122. As Salvadó writes, on September 30, 1936, the bishop of Salamanca, Enrique Pla y Deniel, "graciously offered Franco his palace in which to establish the Nationalist headquarters," effectively "lending the civil war a confessional character" (122).

26. Ibid., 131.

27. Sánchez, *Spanish Civil War*, 102.

28. Ibid., 19.

29. Ibid.

30. Stanley G. Payne, *Fascism in Spain, 1923–1977* (Madison: University of Wisconsin Press, 1999), 369.

31. Ibid.

32. Julio A. Gonzalo González, *Cursillos in Christianity: Origins and First Expansion* (Madrid: Asociación Española Ciencia y Cultura, 2008).

33. Saint James's tomb is housed in the Cathedral of Santiago de Compostela in Galicia, northwest Spain. Pilgrimage to Saint James's tomb peaked in the Middle Ages, when this was one of the most important pilgrimage sites in Europe. In the early to mid-twentieth century, Spanish Catholic Action aimed to resurrect this tradition as rite of passage for Christians. Saint James, who was killed for supporting his brother, the apostle John, was credited by Spanish Catholics with aiding them in defeating the Moors. Pilgrimages to honor him have continued since the eighth century. Mallorquín scholar Guillermo Biblioni explains the sixteen-year gap between the youth congress and the pilgrimage it inspired as being primarily for reasons of "seguridad, luego por la Guerra Civil y, finalmente, por otros motivos desconocidos." He goes on to assert that "Pese a todo, la juventud jamás perdía la esperanza de que su proyecto sería un día realidad" (for reasons of "security, and because of the Civil War and finally for other unknown reasons." "Most of all, the youth never lost the hope that they believed could one day be realized."). Biblioni, *Historia de los Cursillos de Cristiandad* (Madrid: Libroslibres, 2002), 25.

34. Rohloff, *Origins and Development of Cursillo*, 31.

35. Pilgrimages to the Lluc monastery in northwest Mallorca remain popular today, as legend has that the black Madonna who resides here originally appeared in the thirteenth century to a young Moorish shepherd. She is said to have chosen this location for her residence, and today the Santuari de Lluc and the monastery together form Mallorca's most popular pilgrimage site.

36. Payne, *Fascism in Spain*, 324.

37. Ibid., 323.

38. Quoted in ibid., 324.

39. Biblioni, *Historia de los CdC*, 28.

40. "Ni un solo joven de España sin amor de Cristo en el alma, y con la ayuda de Santiago a reconquistar el mundo para Cristo" ("Not a single young man in Spain without the love of Christ in his soul, and with the aid of Saint James to reconquer the world for Christ").

41. See the following *Proa* issues: May–December 1938; January–August 1939; January, April, May, June, August–December 1940; January, February, April, June, August–December 1941; January–June and September–December

1942; January–December 1943; January–February and April–December 1944; all issues January–December 1945; all issues January–December 1946; all issues January–December 1946, 1947, 1948, 1949, 1950, 1951, 1952, 1953, 1954, 1955; January–September 1956; March 1957–December 1957; all issues January–December 1958, 1959, 1960.

42. Jonathan Ebel, "The Great War, Religious Authority, and the American Fighting Man," *Church History* 78, no. 1 (March 2009): 109. In his article Ebel shows that in the late nineteenth and early twentieth century U.S. Protestant and Catholic clergy "worked tirelessly to convince men that Christianity was for them, implicitly linking their own cultural capital to the religious lives of men" (101). See also Clifford Putney, *Muscular Christianity: Manhood and Sports in Protestant America, 1880–1920* (Cambridge: Harvard University Press, 2001); and Gail Bederman, "'Women Have Had Charge of the Church Work Long Enough': The Men and Religion Forward Movement of 1911–1912 and the Masculinization of Middle-Class Protestantism," *American Quarterly* 41, no. 3 (September 9, 1989), 432–65, for other insightful studies of how U.S. Protestantism was masculinized in the early to mid-twentieth century.

43. Rohloff, *Origins and Development of Cursillo*, 30.

44. González, *Cursillos in Christianity*, 72.

45. Rohloff, *Origins and Development of Cursillo*, 35.

46. Since the 1945 Catholic Action Cursillo and the 1949 San Honoratio CdC, Cursillo course graduates all receive a specially made cross. The Catholic Cursillos de Cristiandad, the Lutheran Via de Cristo, the Methodist Walk to Emmaus, the National Episcopal Cursillo (NEC), Kairos Prison Ministry International, Tres Dias, TEC, and numerous other Catholic and Protestant offshoots of Catholic Cursillos all have their signature crosses and will be examined in more detail in later chapters.

47. Eduardo Bonnín, *The How and the Why* (Madrid: Libroslibres, 1971), 21.

48. "Puros angelos apostólicos," and as communicating "su fuego a la tierra y hacer que arda, cumpliendo la sentencia evangélica." *Juventud de Acción Católica*, January 1941.

49. Payne, *Fascism in Spain*, 31.

50. Rohloff, *Origins and Development of Cursillo*, 25.

51. González, *Cursillos in Christianity*, 35. The figure given for the number of pilgrims ranges from 70,000 to 100,000. González says there were 100,000, but most other sources say 70,000.

52. *Proa*, no. 122 (January 1949): 2, http://www.ictisp.com/~rrodrigu/cursillos/eng/chapter1-4.htm.

53. Bernardo Vadell, *Los orígenes mallorquines de los Cursillos de Cristiandad en EE.UU. (Texas, 1957–1959)* (Dallas: National Cursillo Center, 2008), 21.

54. http://www.ictisp.com/~rrodrigu/cursillos/eng/default.htm (chap. 3).

55. Guillermo Estarellas de Nadal, interview with author, FEBA office, Palma de Mallorca, June 23, 2011.

56. Michael Mann, *Fascists* (Cambridge: Cambridge University Press, 2004), 257.

57. Bonnín Aguiló, *My Spiritual Testament*, 30.
58. Ibid., 28.
59. National Cursillo Center, *Leader's Manual* (Dallas, Tex.: Office of the National Secretariat, 1981), 4.
60. Biblioni, *Historia de los CdC*, 33.
61. Guillermo Estarellas de Nadal, interview with author, June 23, 2011.
62. Bonnín Aguiló, *My Spiritual Testament*, 34.
63. Ibid.
64. The Blessed Virgin Mary remains central to weekend Cursillo in Mallorca and around the world. Antonio Pérez Ramos, spiritual director of the Palma de Mallorca Cursillos, emphasized the centrality of Mary for the weekend Cursillo during his talk at the Saturday, June 25, 2011, leaders' school held at the seminary Collegi Sant Pere in Palma de Mallorca. Mary, Pérez Ramos asserted, was and is an inspiration for all cursillistas: "Era una mujer extraordinaria, la madre de Jesús y la más importante madre para todos nosotros. Ella es la madre Maria, Madre de Jesús, Madre de la Iglesia" ("She was an extraordinary woman, the mother of Jesus and the most important mother to us all. She is the mother María, Mother of Jesus, Mother of the Church.").
65. Personal witness given by Salvador Escribiano Hernández, participant of the First Cursillo at Cala Figuera de Santanyí, Mallorca, Spain (August 20–23, 1994).
66. Ibid.
67. Ibid.
68. Ibid.
69. Bonnín Aguiló, *My Spiritual Testament*, 35.
70. Francisco Forteza, "Person," in *First Conversations at Cala Figuera* (Dallas: National Cursillo Center, 2004), 28.
71. Eduardo Bonnín Aguiló, "Friendship," in *First Conversations at Cala Figuera* (Dallas: National Cursillo Center, 2004), 76.
72. Bonnín, *The How and the Why*, 1966.
73. Ibid., 34–35.
74. Ibid., 37.
75. Thanks to the first outside reader of the manuscript, who encouraged me to emphasize the broader context for pre–Vatican II discussions of the laity in which Bonnín and his Cursillo weekends were ensconced.
76. Yves Congar, *True and False Reform in the Church*, rev. ed. (Collegeville, Minn.: Liturgical Press, 2011). See also *At the Heart of Christian Worship: Liturgical Essays of Yves Congar* (Collegeville, Minn.: Liturgical Press, 2010).
77. Pope John XXIII, *Princeps Pastorum*, Catholic Action, no. 43 (November 28, 1959).
78. Bonnín Aguiló, *My Spiritual Testament*, 53.
79. Bonnín, *The How and the Why*, 33–34.
80. Ibid., 25–26.
81. As I noted above, while his close friends all say he was a leader in Catholic Action, Bonnín has gone on record to disassociate himself from the movement,

saying he was merely a bystander and not a member. Bonnín writes in *My Spiritual Testament*: "I did not belong to Catholic Action, but I used to attend their meetings, which I never liked, and which led me to be very critical of the people who constituted those meetings" (30).

82. To make an even broader historical claim, if we examine the history of American Christian revivalism starting in the eighteenth century, the prevailing message has been to embrace Christ, his love, and to go out and be apostles. Christians in the wake of the Great Awakenings of the eighteenth and nineteenth centuries went out and lived their faith. Christians heeding Jonathan Edwards's messages worked hard to share their renewed piety with the world; evangelical Christians after the Second Great Awakening formed numerous societies to aid the poor, and men adopted the language of "business of the heart." John Corrigan, *Business of the Heart: Religion and Emotion in the Nineteenth Century* (Berkeley: University of California Press, 2002).

83. Guillermo Estarellas de Nadal, interview with author, June 23, 2011.

84. Ibid.

85. González, *Cursillos in Christianity*, 63.

86. Bonnín Aguiló, *My Spiritual Testament*, 35.

87. Ibid., 33.

88. While recent religious studies scholarship has complicated the usage of the term *religious experience*, I will use the concept in this book as it is the chosen language of my interlocutors. Catholic and Protestant cursillistas in Mallorca and the United States use the terms *religious experience*, *spiritual experience*, and *experience* interchangeably when they talk about their Cursillo weekend, and I will adhere as closely to their language as possible in this book, analyzing it where it is appropriate and where it helps us to more deeply understand what happens on a Cursillo weekend. I agree with Ann Taves when she argues that it is important to disaggregate "religious experience" in order to understand more fully the various elements of that experience, including the "psychobiological, the social, and cultural-linguistic processes." The Cursillo weekend is a complex religious, social, psychological, and anthropological event with many factors working to influence the cursillistas and what they take away from it. None of the cursillistas I have interviewed would say that what they experience on the weekend is somehow predetermined by outside forces. They do acknowledge that the Holy Spirit is "working" and is "at work" during the weekend, but they do not indicate that the Holy Spirit determines what happens ahead of time. Cursillistas do, however, believe that the weekend experience is one of a kind and cannot be replicated. The weekend is different for each person and is a once-in-a lifetime experience, they say. Cursillistas understand what they see, feel, taste, touch, and smell on their Cursillo weekend to be a combination of the Holy Spirit working in their lives; the power of the rollos and experienced laypersons giving the talks; the friendship and camaraderie they feel with their tablemates; and the delicious food that is homemade for them each day by volunteer cursillistas who give palanca. Taves, *Religious Experience Reconsidered: A Building Block to the Study of Religion and Other Special Things* (Princeton, N.J.: Princeton University Press, 2009), 8.

89. Miguel Sureda, interview with author, FEBA office, Palma de Mallorca, June 14, 2011. Second quote from comments of first outside reviewer, University of North Carolina Press, February 2012.

90. For an intriguing sociohistorical examination of how men, women, and children have imagined Jesus Christ and have adapted his story to fit their own, see Stephen Prothero, *American Jesus: How the Son of Man Became a National Icon* (New York: Farrar, Straus, and Giroux, 2004).

91. Eduardo Bonnín, Francisco Forteza, and Bernardo Vadell, *The Structure of Ideas (Vertebration)* (Dallas: National Cursillo Center, 1995), 4.

92. It is the radical experience of and with Christ, the self, and community during the Cursillo weekend that transcended denominational boundaries, and attracted Protestants in the 1960s. Protestants observed Catholic cursillistas who were living their faith and who had a new outlook on the purpose and meaning of life. Their friends' and neighbors' renewed commitment to their faith was deeply inspiring and moving to them. These Catholic cursillistas were on fire for Christ and spoke of their love of the Holy Spirit. In the mid-1960s Protestants, intrigued, wanted to experience this weekend for themselves and, with the support of Catholics, made a Catholic Cursillo. Protestant cursillistas went on to form their own movements that were—and are today—based directly on the Catholic Cursillo.

93. Bartolomé Arrom, interview with author, FEBA office, Palma de Mallorca, June 14, 2011. Marcene Marcoux is the only noninsider to question whether 1949 is the correct date of the first Cursillo. She writes, "If the meeting at San Honorato is declared the first Cursillo, then more credence can be given to the leadership of Juan Hervás and men like Juan Capó, the rector at the time. Hervás was the highest authority in the diocese and the one ultimately involved with overseeing this religious work. Credit can then be given to his position that the Cursillo was the development of his pastoral plan and one of the first steps in his idea for spiritual renewal. But if, as others admit, this was not the first Cursillo but an extension of the courses begun before Hervás was ever in Mallorca, then there is more credence to Bonnin's role as the founder." Marcoux, *Cursillo: Anatomy of a Movement* (New York: Lambeth, 1982), 18–19. While she does not cite the 1944 Cala Figuera Cursillo as the first, she raises important questions that highlight the struggle over power and authority in the 1940s and 1950s as well as how the history of the CdC has been interpreted.

94. Bonnín, Forteza, and Vadell, *Structure of Ideas*, 34.

95. Ibid., 35.

96. Ibid., 51.

97. Bonnín Aguiló, *My Spiritual Testament*, 29.

98. Ramón Rosselló Nadal, interview with author, FEBA office, Palma de Mallorca, June 15, 2011.

99. Alphonsus Duran, *The Essence and Purpose* (Madrid: Ultreya, 1966), 10.

100. Ibid., 11.

101. Bonnín Aguiló, *My Spiritual Testament*, 59.

102. Rohloff, *Origins and Development of Cursillo*, 30.

103. Ibid., 31.

104. Bonnín, *The How and the Why*, 23.

105. In the Cursillos de Cristiandad, clergy have always been an important part of the weekend and present five of the fifteen rollos over the course of the three days.

106. Guillermo Estarellas de Nadal, interview with author, 23 June 2011.

107. Bonnín Aguiló, *My Spiritual Testament*, 53.

108. Rohloff, *Origins and Development of Cursillo*, 74.

109. Guillermo Estarellas de Nadal, interview with author, June 23, 2011.

110. Rohloff, *Origins and Development of Cursillo*, 72.

111. Ibid., 86.

112. Juan Ruiz, president's letter, *OMCC Newsletter*, February 1, 2009, 2–3.

113. Ibid., 3.

114. Bonnín Aguiló, *My Spiritual Testament*, 54.

115. Juan Hervás, *Leader's Manual for Cursillos in Christianity* (Madrid: Ultreya, 1964), 47.

116. Rohloff, *Origins and Development of Cursillo*, 88.

117. Hervás, *Leader's Manual*, 32.

118. Ibid., 57.

119. "Carta pastoral sobre los Cursillos de Cristiandad," *Boletín oficial del Obispado de Mallorca*, 385–86.

120. Ibid., 391. Enciso makes clear that the only acceptable extra-Church instruction and teachings that are to be found in Catholic Action.

121. Jesús Enciso Viana, "Carta pastoral sobre los Cursillos de Cristiandad," 397–98.

122. Miguel Sureda, interview with author, June 14, 2011.

123. Ramón Rosselló Nadal, interview with author, June 14, 2011.

124. M. Carlos Calatayud Maldonado, "I Went to a Cursillo: Testimony of a Layman," *Christ to the World* (1964): 485.

125. Ibid., 496.

126. Ibid., 493.

127. Ibid., 488.

128. Ibid., 494.

129. Damien Rico, interview with author, Mimi's Café, East Chicago, Ill., June 16, 2010. All of the 250 Catholic and Protestant cursillistas interviewed for this book emphasized the centrality of group reunion meetings, ultreyas, and other gatherings to help individual cursillistas maintain a healthy and centered spiritual life.

Chapter Two

1. In this chapter, as in the others, the terms *CdC*, *Cursillo*, and *Cursillo de Cristiandad* will be used interchangeably to refer to the seventy-two-hour weekend first developed and offered by Eduardo Bonnín Aguiló in 1944 in Cala Figuera, Mallorca.

2. Most published accounts say that the 1949 San Honorario Cursillo was the first Cursillo and rarely mention the 1944 Cala Figuera Cursillo, the latter of which is

cited as the first-ever Cursillo by national secretariats around the world today. Most written accounts of Cursillo attribute its spread and success to Bishop Juan Hervás, giving little credit to Bonnín. Julio A. Gonzalo González, *Cursillos in Christianity: Origins and First Expansion* (Madrid: Asociación Española Ciencia y Cultura, 2008), gives most of the credit to Hervás and misspells Bonnín's name throughout his book ("Bonin," "Bounin"). González's account of the Cursillos' history champions the cardinals, bishops, and priests who supported the weekends and barely mentions Bonnín and his colleagues. Ivan Rohloff's *The Origins and Development of Cursillo: 1939–1973* (Dallas: National Ultreya, 1976) is a much more thorough historical and theological investigation than González's and is the only published history of the movement to date. Rohloff credits Bonnín with being the founder of Cursillos and spends considerable time explaining the drama that surrounded their origins and early years.

3. In Catholic Cursillos, women lead women's weekends and men lead men's weekends. On women's weekends, the candidates are exclusively female, and on men's weekends, the candidates are exclusively male. The weekends are not strictly segregated among volunteers, however, as women volunteer to work during men's weekends and men at women's weekends. Cursillistas cook, clean, and pray for the weekend candidates and see themselves as part of one large community of renewed Christians. In the U.S. Cursillo movement, husbands make their weekend first and their wives make theirs shortly after. In Mallorca, there is no uniform rule, and wives can make their weekend before their spouse. According to Miguel Sureda, a longtime leader in the Mallorquín Cursillo movement and a close friend of Bonnín, "Whoever is more spiritually ready to make Cursillo goes first, whether it is the woman or the man." Miguel Sureda, interview with author, FEBA office, Palma de Mallorca, June 14, 2011.

4. All of my Mallorquín cursillista interlocutors emphasize that it was these men, "los iniciadores," who came together to lead the first Cursillo. My ethnographic interviews are substantiated by Guillermo Biblioni, *Historia de los Cursillos de Cristiandad: Mallorca, 1944–2001* (Madrid: Libroslibres, 2002), 32.

5. See Juan Capó Bosch, *The Group Reunion* (Dallas: National Cursillo Center, 1969) and *Lower Your Nets* (Dallas: National Cursillo Center, 1975); Bernardo Vadell, *Los orígenes mallorquines de los Cursillos de Cristiandad en EE.UU. (Texas, 1957–1959)* (Dallas: National Cursillo Center, 2008); Eduardo Bonnín, Bernardo Vadell, and Francisco Forteza, *Structure of Ideas (Vertebration)* (Dallas: National Cursillo Center, 1995); Juan Hervás, *Cursillos in Christianity: Instruments of Christian Renewal* (Dallas: Ultreya, 1950), *Leader's Manual* (Madrid: Ultreya, 1964), and *Questions and Problems Concerning Cursillos in Christianity* (Dallas: National Cursillo, 1965).

6. Bartolomé Arrom, Ventura Rubí, and Miguel Oliver have also been mentioned as important cursillistas who helped craft the movement. Bonnín, Forteza, and Vadell, *Structure of Ideas*, 2. I had the honor of interviewing "Tomeu" Arrom in June 2011, and he provided an important historical perspective as well as personal information that has greatly benefitted this book.

7. Bishop Enrique Enciso died in 1964 and his successor, Obispo Alvarez Lara, was named one year later. For ten years, then, Bonnín's movement was forced to go underground.

8. Guillermo Biblioni writes that in his published work, Hervás credits Capó with initiating the movement, and nowhere does he mention Bonnín. Biblioni, *Historia de los CdC*, 192.

9. Ibid., 33.

10. According to Ivan Rohloff, three individuals most influenced Cursillos in the years during which they spread rapidly throughout the world (1962–73): Juan Hervás, Eduardo Bonnín, and Juan Capó. These men wrote books, traveled around the globe, and each in his way helped spread the movement. Rohloff, *Origins and Development of Cursillo*, 105. As clergymen, Hervás and Capo had a more pro-clerical influence in the movement, and their writings were published by Spain's National Secretariat—giving them a seal of approval. By contrast, Bonnín published outside of Spain or was not published at all. FEBA has published many of his writings, and today volunteers are cataloguing his many works.

11. FEBA is largely responsible for publishing Bonnín's articles and books and for offering an important corrective to the perception that Hervás was the founder of the movement.

12. When we examine the histories of other Fourth-Day movements and spinoffs of Cursillo, we see that men and women in the armed services spread their respective movements where they were (and are) stationed. In addition to Catholic Cursillos, we find this phenomenon most especially with Tres Dias and TEC.

13. Father Gabriel Fernández, "The First Cursillo Weekends," in *Fiftieth Anniversary of the Cursillo Movement in the United States of America* (Dallas: National Cursillo Center, 2007), 1.

14. In contrast to U.S. Catholic Cursillos' lay focus, Catholic Cursillos in Mexico were much more clerical, a legacy that continues today. During my Mallorquín fieldwork I did meet a priest, Father Urbano, who was sent by his bishop to study the "authentic" Cursillo for one year. Father Urbano returned to Mexico to implement Bonnín's version of the CdC a year after we met. Our e-mail correspondence since our initial conversation in June 2011 confirms that the Cursillo movement in Mexico assumed a trajectory different from that of the movement in the United States.

15. Biblioni, *Historia de los CdC*, 203.

16. While Bernardo Vadell can be considered one of the lay Catholic leaders in the early U.S. Cursillo movement, he later joined a Spanish political organization that critiqued the Church and left his faith. González, *Cursillos in Christianity*, 119. My Mallorquín interlocutors mentioned Vadell's leaving his faith and expressed sadness that one of the most successful apostles of Cursillos became what they called an anarchist.

17. Vadell, *Orígenes mallorquines*, 29–30.

18. According to González, *Cursillos in Christianity*, Father Fernández arrived in the United States from Spain in 1955; "He had been involved in one of the very

first Cursillos in Majorca together with Don Juan Capó and Eduardo Bonning [sic]" (119). Guillermo Biblioni also writes that Father Fernández knew Juan Capó and Eduardo Bonnín in Palma de Mallorca (*Historia de los CdC*, 203).

19. Fernández, *Fiftieth Anniversary of the Cursillo Movement*, 1.

20. Vadell, *Orígenes mallorquines*, 19.

21. For definitive sources on Eisenhower, see Stephen E. Ambrose, *The Supreme Commander: The War Years of Dwight D. Eisenhower* (New York: Anchor, 2012), and *Eisenhower: Soldier and President* (New York: Simon and Schuster, 1991); Jean Edward Smith, *Eisenhower in War and Peace* (New York: Random House, 2012); and Jim Newton, *Eisenhower: The White House Years* (New York: Doubleday, 2011).

22. See Paul Preston, *The Spanish Civil War: Reaction, Revolution, and Revenge*, rev. ed. (New York: W. W. Norton, 2007).

23. Fernández, "First Cursillo Weekends," 1.

24. Bonnín, Forteza, and Vadell, *Structure of Ideas*, 179.

25. Ibid., 36.

26. Ibid.

27. Ibid.

28. Oscar J. Martínez, *Border People: Life and Society in the U.S.-Mexico Borderlands* (Tucson: University of Arizona Press, 1994), 251.

29. Ibid.

30. Mexican-descent men and women in the early to mid-twentieth-century Waco, as in most southwestern cities then and since, experienced discrimination by white non-Hispanics. Mexican-descent Waco residents lived in an area known as Calle Dos, or Second Street, in downtown Waco. Calle Dos had originally been established by city planners in the late nineteenth century as a red-light district known as "The Reservation." The district was closed, under pressure from federal officials, when the U.S. Army base Camp MacArthur was proposed. The first waves of Mexican immigrants during and after the Mexican War moved into houses, the only ones affordable and available to them, that had been abandoned by displaced prostitutes. See "Waco History Project," http://wacohistoryproject.org, for more details on the history of Waco and its Mexican-descent, non-Hispanic white, and African American residents.

31. Vadell, *Orígenes mallorquines*, 88.

32. González, *Cursillos in Christianity*, 118–19.

33. Fernandez, "First Cursillo Weekends," 1.

34. Vadell, *Orígenes mallorquines*, 39.

35. Ibid., 46–47.

36. Hervás, *Leader's Manual*, 8.

37. Fernández, *Fiftieth Anniversary of the Cursillo Movement*, 71.

38. National Cursillo Center, *Leader's Manual* (Dallas, Tex.: Office of the National Secretariat, 1981), 8.

39. Vadell, *Orígenes mallorquines*, 31.

40. In Waco, the city where the first U.S. Cursillo was held, the Waco Army Airfield Basic army training school was established in 1949. It was renamed

James Connally Air Force Base in 1951 to honor a Waco-born pilot killed in Japan in 1945.

41. González, *Cursillos in Christianity*, 120. *Ultreya* ("forward" or "onward") is a greeting that was used by Santiago de Compostela pilgrims to encourage each other on their path.

42. Timothy Matovina, *Latino Catholicism: Transformation in America's Largest Church* (Princeton, N.J.: Princeton University Press, 2011), 50.

43. The base is named for the World War I aviator First Lieutenant John J. Goodfellow Jr., a San Angelo native killed in France in September 1918 while conducting visual reconnaissance over German lines. Marcene Marcoux writes that the date—November 9, 1961—is "critical as it marks the first English version of cursillo in the States. . . . now, at last, the cursillo could become a serious force affecting American Catholicism." Marcoux, *Cursillo: Anatomy of a Movement* (New York: Lambeth, 1982), 26.

44. Ibid.

45. Hervás, *Leader's Manual*, 8.

46. Ibid., 9.

47. Hervás, *Leader's Manual*, 9.

48. The U.S. National Cursillo Center's website is http://www.cursillo.org. In the October 2011 online Cursillo national mailing, Father Peter M. Jaramillo, S.S.A., the national spiritual advisor for U.S. Cursillos, writes that CdC weekends are held in six languages in "some 150 plus dioceses, and almost 1,000,000 Cursillistas . . . presently numbered in the USA" (2).

49. The U.S. Cursillo movement today includes four main ethnic and language groups: Spanish-speaking, English-speaking, Vietnamese, and Korean.

50. University of Notre Dame Archives, PMRH 129/05, Joseph Green, *Marriage, Sexuality . . . A Brief Report on the Cursillo Movement in the USA*.

51. Ibid.

52. University of Notre Dame Archives, PMRH 116/02, YCS 1962 Cursillo, "Dear Father" letter sent to Father LaMarre of Saginaw, Mich., February 14, 1962.

53. The history of anti-Catholicism in America is well documented. For especially good academic sources, see Jenny Franchot, *Roads to Rome: The Antebellum Protestant Encounter with Catholicism* (Berkeley: University of California Press, 1994); and Mark S. Massa, SJ, *Anti-Catholicism in America: The Last Acceptable Prejudice* (New York: Crossroads, 2005).

54. Green, *Marriage, Sexuality*.

55. Bonnín, Forteza, and Vadell, *Structure of Ideas*, 105.

56. Ibid., 104.

57. Ibid.

58. Green, *Marriage, Sexuality*.

59. Ibid.

60. Green, *Marriage, Sexuality*; University of Notre Dame Archives, Ed Salmon letter to priest, May 14, 1973.

61. University of Notre Dame Archives, NC News Service, Domestic, August 5, 1971.

62. University of Notre Dame Archives, "To: Catherine, From: The Archbishop," Chancery Building, San Antonio Inter-office Correspondence, July 18, 1967.

63. Green, *Marriage, Sexuality*; University of Notre Dame Archives, Ed Salmon, "Chicago Cursillo Movement... For Your Information."

64. Ron Caronti, telephone interview with author, January 26, 2011.

65. Green, *Marriage, Sexuality*; Salmon, "Chicago Cursillo Movement."

66. Green, *Marriage, Sexuality*; Ed Salmon letter, May 14, 1973.

67. Bishop Gilbert Chavez, interview with author, Diocese of San Diego, July 26, 2005.

68. Ibid.

69. Notably, in the October 2011 U.S. National Secretariat newsletter, Father Peter M. Jaramillo, S.S.A., the national spiritual advisor of the CdC, emphasizes that the Cursillo movement is at its core a lay movement and that laity and clergy are to work together: "Eduardo Bonnín clearly and specifically emphasized, that Cursillos in Christianity is a movement of lay initiative, in which priests contribute in their primary role. And that Cursillo can only persevere and grow 'with a perfect fit between priests and laity.' The Cursillo, more now than ever, must be anchored in a faith that lives in close union, in friendship with everyone, lay and clergy, without... the 'dictatorial' attitude from either side."

70. Miguel Sureda, interview with author, FEBA office, Palma de Mallorca, June 16, 2011.

71. Miguel and María Sureda, interview with author, FEBA office, Palma de Mallorca, June 16, 2011.

72. University of Notre Dame Archives, NC News Service, Domestic, August 5, 1971.

73. Bonnín, Forteza, and Vadell, *Structure of Ideas*, 103.

74. University of Notre Dame Archives, CPIC/MPIC Parish and Institutional Records, Reel 13, Letter on St. Anthony Retreat Center letterhead, Rev. Bill Alcuin.

75. Ibid.

76. University of Notre Dame Archives, "roundup on cursillos," "De Colores" Cursillo Conference, 1971.

77. Ibid.

78. Ibid.

79. For recent scholarly discussions of the Vatican II Council and what it meant for U.S. Catholics and Catholicism in the United States in particular, see Chester Gillis, *Roman Catholicism in America* (New York: Columbia University Press, 2000), esp. chaps. 3 and 4. See also Mark S. Massa, SJ, *The American Catholic Revolution: How the '60s Changed the Church Forever* (Oxford: Oxford University Press, 2010); and Melissa J. Wilde, *Vatican II: A Sociological Analysis of Religious Change* (Princeton, N.J.: Princeton University Press, 2007).

80. University of Notre Dame Archives, CDAD 5/40, Anthony Padovano Papers, Fr. Timothy Joyce, letter to "Tony," April 8, 1964.

81. "Atlantans Attend National Cursillo Encounter," *Georgia Bulletin: The Official Newspaper of the Roman Catholic Archdiocese of Atlanta*, July 18, 1974.

82. Hervás, *Leader's Manual*, 39.

83. Ibid.

84. Miguel Sureda, interview with author, FEBA office, Palma de Mallorca, June 14, 2011.

85. Eduardo Bonnín Aguiló, *My Spiritual Testament* (Palma de Mallorca: FEBA, 2009), 40.

86. Interlocutors have informed me that some parishes in upstate New York, Nashville, and Atlanta unofficially welcomed Protestants to make a Catholic Cursillo. Moreover, intercommunion was offered at these weekends, a practice denounced by the U.S. National Secretariat.

87. I was welcomed as one of two non-Catholics at the Women's Cursillo no. 959 at the Believers Together Center, Moline, Illinois, in March 2011. The center, completed in 2001 and part of the Diocese of Peoria, is the site of all of the Northwest region's Cursillos.

88. Father Tom has had a long and eventful career as a priest. He recently retired as pastor of two western Illinois churches: St. Thomas Catholic Church in Camp Point and Holy Family in Mt. Sterling. He was the pastor at Holy Family for nineteen years and was also the pastor in Camp Point in 2007. A native of Canton, Illinois, Father Tom was considered to be "on loan" from the Peoria diocese. He served in many roles in the Peoria and Springfield diocese in his forty-nine years as a Roman Catholic priest. After his ordination in 1963, Father Tom began as assistant pastor of St. Patrick in Peoria for seven years, then as Navy chaplain for a year, and then served the Visitation parish of Kewanee. He then was pastor of St. Thomas in Peoria Heights for nineteen years before moving to St. Edward in Chillicothe for two years and then on to Holy Family in Mt. Sterling. In Mt. Sterling, part of the Springfield diocese, Father Tom helped renew the Brown County Ministerium, an ecumenical group of churches.

89. Victor Lugo, telephone interview with author, November 14, 2009.

90. Peoria Cursillo Center, "Peoria Cursillo History, Part 1," http://www.peoria-cursillo.org/index.cfm?load=page&page=182.

91. Moreover, we can further speculate on the National Secretariat's missed opportunities when we compare its actions with those of another late 1960s Catholic renewal movement that has seen greater global success, the Catholic Charismatic Renewal Movement (CCR). Like the Cursillo movement, the CCR emphasizes lived experience and action over intellectualism and Church theology. CCR has had greater global successes than Cursillo. It is, according to the historian Edward Cleary, the "fastest growing movement in the Catholic Church in Latin America given its combination of rootedness in Roman Catholic doctrine and symbols but also its enthusiastic Pentecostal-style praise and worship." Cleary, *The Rise of Charismatic Catholicism in Latin America* (Gainesville: University of Florida Press, 2011), 1.

92. Knowing that I was interested in Bonnín's travels to the United States, González read through his diaries looking for relevant data. She orally translated his jottings from Mallorquín Catalan to Spanish, and I transcribed in my field-note journal what she read aloud to me.

93. Like Bonnín, Dorothy Gereke, formerly known as Sister Mary Concetta and one of the cofounders of Teens Encounter Christ (TEC), has traveled across the United States and abroad as an ambassador for the weekend-experience-turned-movement that she helped to found. Like Bonnín, Gereke, now also known as "Mama TEC," was (and still is today in her mid-eighties) committed to seeing the "fruits" of an intentional weekend of spirituality continue to grow. I will document the history of TEC and Gereke's role in it in chapter 5.

94. Cristina González and numerous FEBA volunteers have gone through Bonnín's global travel schedule and have recorded his travels to the following countries and dates (listed in alphabetical order): Alemania (Germany) (June 1976, April 1997, October 2001); Angola (July 1973); Argentina (October 1981, November 1991, August 1992, May 1993, November 1994); Australia (September 1991, September 1998); Austria (December 1971, September 1974, October 1992); Bolivia (April 1998); Brasil (Brazil) (July–August 1966); Canadá (Canada) (January 1992, July 1992, July 1993, April 1994, April 1995, September 1995, May 1996); Chile (August 1988, April 1998); China (July 1998); Colombia (August 1968); Corea del Sur (South Korea) (April–May 1972, September 1992, October 1997); Costa Rica (July 1978); Ecuador (July 1995); El Salvador (July–August 1966, January 1992, August 1993, July 1996); Escocia (Scotland) (July 1995); Estados Unidos (United States) (August–September 1961, May 1962, July–August 1996, July 1971, May 1983, May 1988, January 1991, April 1991, May 1992, July 1992, April 1993, April, September 1994, August 1995, September 1995, October 1995, February 1996, March 1996, June 1996, March 1997, April 1997, May 1997, June 1997, December 1997, July–August 1998); Filipinas (Philippines) (April–May 1972, October–November 1995); Guam (October 1996); Guatemala (May 1985, July 1996, June 1998); Honduras (July 1993, July 1996); Hungría (Hungary) (November 1997); Inglaterra (England) (June 1990, July 1995); Italia (Italy) (October 1955, May 1966, April 1985, September 1986, October 1991, September 1992, April 1993, November 1993, December 1993, June 1994, May 1995, December 1995, September 1996, November 1996, February 1997, September 1997, October 1997, May 1998, September 1998, November 1999); Irlanda (Ireland) (June 1978, September 1994, July 1997); Japón (Japan) (April–May 1972); Macao (Macau) (April–May 1972); Méjico (Mexico) (May 1962, August 1963, 1970, September 1980, January 1992, November 1992, March 1994, September 1994, January 1995, November 1996, August 1998); Nicaragua (February 1972, July 1996); Panamá (Panama) (August 1993); Perú (Peru) (July–August 1996); Portugal (February 1981, April 1982, April 1983, January 1997, February 1998); Puerto Rico (August 1990); Santo Domingo (Dominican Republic) (July 1980); Tailandia (Thailand) (September 1993, October 1994); Taiwán (Taiwan) (April–May 1972, November–December 1982); Venezuela (June 1976, July 1988).

95. Marcoux, *Cursillo*, 30.

96. By contrast to these packed summer travels, Bonnín's August 1966 schedule was much more modest: he visited only New York and Philadelphia.

97. During this time, according to González, Bonnín suffered from chronic shingles that caused him intense pain. Cristina González, interview with author, FEBA office, Palma de Mallorca, June 23, 2011.

98. He continued his travels from Toronto, and flew to Buenos Aires, Barcelona, Milan, South Korea, Frankfort, and Vienna. From Vienna, Bonnín flew to Dallas for the National Secretariat Meetings. From Dallas he flew to Guadalajara, and then went on to visit cursillistas in Little Arkansas and Hot Springs, Ark.; and Jacksonville, Fla.

99. In September 1995, Bonnín went to Miami, Cancun, Campeche, "muchos lugares en México [many places in Mexico]," Toronto, Edmonton, Calgary, Vancouver, Victoria, Calgary, and New York. In October 1995, his travels took him to Guatemala, Denver, Dallas, Laredo, San Antonio, Tucson, and Los Angeles, and in 1996 he visited Atlanta, Jacksonville, Boston, Toronto, Montreal, Miami, Guatemala, Nicaragua, El Salvador, Los Angeles, and Miami. In 1997, he traveled to Philadelphia, Fresno, and Sacramento, and in July and August 1998, he went to Miami, New York, St. Louis, and Peoria.

Chapter Three

1. Cursillistas have explained to me that leaders in the movement screen candidates to make sure they "can handle" the intense emotional highs and lows that individuals who make the course tend to experience. Yet this screening seems rather arbitrary, ineffective even, when we consider the testimonies of many of the cursillistas I interviewed. At least half of these men and women were experiencing what they described as emotional, financial, and familial "lows" at the time they made their course. Women like Carmen Uriostegui and Rosita Aldrete and men like Damien Rico and Chris Sandovál spoke at length about their emotional fragility. It was precisely because of this vulnerability, to use their language, their "openness to the Spirit," that they embraced the weekend experience and were psychologically and emotionally healed and ready to live a fruitful, meaningful Fourth Day as participants in their community and church.

2. We will examine the fifth in-covenant Fourth-Day movement, Kairos Prison Ministry International (KPMI), in chapter 6. Founded by Catholics, KPMI is interdenominational and has a distinctive and focused mission—to bring Christ to incarcerated men and women and their families.

3. Ivan Rohloff, *The Origins and Development of Cursillo* (Dallas: National Ultreya, 1976), 37.

4. Bob Franks, "A Visit with Eduardo Bonnin," April 2, 1998, unpublished manuscript.

5. Ibid.

6. Via de Cristo members Ellie Henning and Randy Mullin were, according to Henning, "privileged to have an interview with Eduardo Bonnin [*sic*], the founder of the Cursillo Movement, from Mallorca, Spain," while taking part in a Jacksonville, Florida, Fourth-Day movement gathering.

7. Victor Lugo, telephone interview with author, November 14, 2009.

8. My heartfelt thanks go out to the leaders of the in-covenant movements who invited me out to Orlando in late January 2010 to have dinner with them and interview them for this book.

9. Via de Cristo Ultreya, February 1, 2010, Prince of Peace, Orlando, Fla.

10. Paul and Tracy Schmidlin, Orlando, Fla., February 1, 2010.

11. Greg Engroff, telephone interview with author, December 1, 2009.

12. "Aqui se celebró el 1° cursillo de cristiandad del mundo a 20 y al 23 agosto 1944. Cursillos de Portugal, Decolores."

13. María Sureda and Cristina González both said that the current owner of what in 1944 was called the "Mar i Pins" chalet was confused and perplexed by the tour buses and throngs of Italian and Portuguese Catholics who traveled to his home to take photos. Cristina said with a chuckle, "Ahora que sabe sobre Eduardo y los cursillos y comprende porque tantas personas han tomado fotografías de su casa durante los años" ("Now he knows about Eduardo and the Cursillo movement and understands why so many people have taken photographs of his home over the years").

14. None of the randomly chosen Mallorquines I asked on the street, in restaurants or in hotels had any idea who Eduardo Bonnín was, and only one knew anything about the CdC movement. The one person who had heard "something about" the CdC was the caretaker of our rented villa in Cala Figuera. Catalina ("Cati") Granados had lived in Mallorca her whole life and had a vague idea of what the CdC was, even though Mar i Pins was a mere two blocks from our villa and her office.

15. "Genesis of Tres Dias," www.tresdias.org.

16. Ibid.

17. Ibid.

18. Ibid.

19. Ibid.

20. Ibid.

21. Ibid.

22. The cross-giving tradition began in Mallorca with the first CdC in 1944, and each of the Fourth-Day movements has its own signature cross.

23. "Genesis of Tres Dias."

24. "History," www.tresdias.org.

25. Tres Dias, *Essentials*, ratified 1980, Poughkeepsie, N.Y. See http://www.tresdias.org/f/w.htm.

26. Ibid.

27. We also find this global outreach with the Catholic Cursillo spinoff Teens Encounter Christ (TEC), which we will examine in chapter 5.

28. John McKinney, e-mail correspondence, June 20, 2012.

29. Ibid.

30. John McKinney, telephone interview with author, January 18, 2010.

31. Ibid.

32. Ibid.

33. John McKinney, telephone interview with author, January 10, 2010.

34. Chad Smits, interview with author, Tres Dias Secretariat, Rockford, Ill., March 13, 2010.

35. The first Methodist Cursillos (1977–80) were called Upper Room Cursillos. In 1981, the Upper Room Cursillos' name was changed to Upper Room Walk to

Emmaus. "Cursillo" was dropped from the name at the request of the U.S. National Catholic Secretariat.

36. Rev. Robert ("Bob") Wood, January 2, 2010, telephone interview with author.
37. Ibid.
38. Ibid.
39. Rev. Robert Wood, *The Early History of Walk to Emmaus* (Nashville, Tenn.: Upper Room Ministries), 9.
40. Rev. Robert Wood, telephone interview with author, January 2, 2010.
41. Ibid.
42. Ibid.
43. Ibid.
44. Ibid.
45. Wood, *Early History*, 22.
46. Ibid.
47. Ibid., 23.
48. Ibid., 22.
49. Ibid., 23.
50. Ibid., 25.
51. Danny Morris, telephone interview with author, January 5, 2010.
52. Ibid.
53. According the Engroff, in addition to the 302 communities active in the United States (as of September 1, 2011), there is an ever-increasing number of active international communities in five countries with plans to establish Emmaus. These countries include Australia (25 communities plus National Board); Bahamas (1); Barbados (2); Brazil (7 plus national board); Costa Rica (1); Czech Republic (1); England, UK (4 plus national board); Estonia (1); Fiji (1: start-up); Germany (1); Ghana (1); Guatemala (1: start-up); Honduras (1: start-up); Hong Kong (2); Ireland (1); Jamaica (1); South Korea (2 plus national board); Malaysia (1); Mexico (2); Mozambique (2); St. Maarten (the Netherlands) (1); New Zealand (1); Nicaragua (1: start-up); Norway (2); Puerto Rico (2); Romania (1); Russia (1); Saint Lucia (1); Saint Vincent (1); Singapore (1); South Africa (16 plus national board); Swaziland (1); Sweden (1); Switzerland (1); Taiwan (1); Trinidad and Tobago (1); Ukraine (1); and Zimbabwe (2 plus coordinating board). Greg Engroff, e-mail correspondence with author, August 26, 2011.
54. Greg Engroff, telephone interview with author, November 10, 2009.
55. Greg Engroff, e-mail correspondence with author, August 26, 2011.
56. Colleen McDannell, *Material Christianity: Religion and Popular Culture in America* (New Haven, Conn.: Yale University Press, 1998), 269.
57. Rev. Robert Wood, telephone interview with author, January 2, 2010.
58. Malcolm Gladwell, *The Tipping Point* (New York: Back Bay Books, 2002).
59. Victor Pérez, telephone interview with author, December 16, 2009.
60. Ibid.
61. Ibid.
62. Ibid.

63. Wood's work with Via de Cristo is chronicled in the National Lutheran Secretariat for Via de Cristo's website under the "Archives" tab, http://www.viadecristo.org/.

64. Wood, *Early History*, 27.

65. "Archives," "1981 to 1985," http://www.viadecristo.org/.

66. Ibid.

67. Ibid.

68. Ibid.

69. Ibid., "Archives," "1986–1990."

70. Ibid.

71. Ibid., "Archives," "1991 to 1995."

72. Ibid.

73. A 2010 ELCA News Release reported that more than half of the forty-one new ELCA congregations started in 2010 were immigrant congregations, with an emphasis on Indonesian and Hispanic communities (http://www.elca.org/Who-We-Are/Our-Three-Expressions/Churchwide-Organization/Communication-Services/News/Releases.aspx?a=4570).

The ELCA prides itself on evangelical outreach and features its success stories in "Stories of Faith and Action," http://www.elca.org/Our-Faith-In-Action/Stories-of-Faith-in-Action/Outreach.aspx.

74. I should note that the fifth in-covenant Fourth-Day weekend, Kairos Prison Ministry, which is the focus of chapter 6, is currently experimenting with a seventy-two-hour weekend with two to three fewer talks. Kairos is distinctive from the other Fourth-Day movements because all of its weekends take place inside medium- to maximum-security prisons ("inside weekends") or with inmates' family members ("outside weekends"). We will examine one of these pilot weekends in chapter 6.

75. Although the founder of the movement is acknowledged to be Eduardo Bonnín Aguiló, Juan Hervás, the priest who helped popularize the movement, is still officially credited by the National Lutheran Secretariat on its website with developing the Cursillo method on which Via de Cristo has been modeled.

76. Tracy Schmidlin, interview with author, Winter Park, Fla., January 30, 2010. Schmidlin is mindful of Eduardo Bonnín's critiques of Cursillos that he specifies in *My Spiritual Testament* (Palma de Mallorca: FEBA, 2009), chap. 6, "About the Weaknesses of the Cursillos," 43–45. Yet while Schmidlin agrees with Bonnín that "oddities" of the weekend need to monitored, she does not have a problem with coed weekends, something Bonnín himself did not advocate.

77. Tracy Schmidlin, interview with author, , January 30, 2010.

78. Thom Neal, telephone interview with author, April 26, 2010.

79. Steve Gielda, e-mail correspondence with author, August 21, 2011.

80. According to Schmidlin, 137 weekends are on record for 2010: 45 men's, 51 women's, and 41 coed or mixed weekends. Schmidlin added that there are 44 "local secretariats" in the United States with interest in 3 more. The five international communities include Bolivia, Finland, Latvia, Papua New Guinea, and Sweden. In

our August 26, 2011, e-mail correspondence, Schmidlin wrote that "at the moment Bolivia is on hold because the country is not stable at the moment but the interest is there. We have had interest in two countries in Africa, but again the political unrest is making things a bit difficult. . . . We will continue to pursue it though."

81. Sue Davis, telephone interview with author, April 27, 2010.

82. Ibid.

83. Thom Neal, telephone interview with author, April 26, 2010.

84. National Episcopal Cursillo, "A Statement in Response to Discussions on 'Interdenominational Cursillo,'" order no. 219, Booklet no. 20 (2010): 4.

85. Ibid., 7.

86. http://www.acswebnetworks.com/episcopalcursillo/article106392.htm.

87. Ginny Schoneberg, "National Episcopal Cursillo, 1970–1990," unpublished manuscript.

88. Ibid.

89. Ibid.

90. Thom Neal, telephone interview with author, April 26, 2010.

91. Ibid.

92. Ibid.

93. Ibid.

94. Ibid.

95. NEC Newsnotes, NECC Meeting, February 2011, Diocese of North Carolina, http://www.nationalepiscopalcursillo.org/newsnotes.211.pdf.

96. Thom Neal, telephone interview with author, April 26, 2010.

97. Ibid. Neal's expression "frozen chosen" is meant to be a tongue-in-cheek critique of those Christians who believe they were predestined by God to be saved but who do not live their faith in demonstrable ways (they are "frozen"). I have heard other cursillistas I interviewed use this expression, as well as Christians not interviewed for this book.

98. Ibid.

99. Ibid.

100. Ibid.

101. See http://religions.pewforum.org/affiliations.

102. Schoneberg, "National Episcopal Cursillo."

103. *NEC Library* (Conway, S.C.: National Episcopal Cursillo, 2008), chap. 18, "Health and Well-Being of the Movement," 10.

104. Thom Neal, telephone interview with author, April 26, 2010.

105. According to the Mallorquín cursillistas I interviewed in June 2010, Eduardo Bonnín did not approve of mixed-gender weekends.

106. *NEC Library*.

107. Like American lay and clerical Catholics, who responded to the reforms of Vatican II and the shifting U.S. social landscape, American Protestants felt called by their churches and the larger societal changes to revitalize their personal faith and their churches. See Robert Wuthnow, *The Restructuring of American Religion* (Princeton, N.J.: Princeton University Press, 1990), *After Heaven: Spirituality in America since the 1950s* (Berkeley: University of California Press, 1998); and

Wuthnow and Robert Edison, eds., *The Quiet Hand of God: Faith-Based Activism and the Role of Mainline Protestantism* (Berkeley: University of California Press, 2002).

108. The sociologist of U.S. religions Wade Clark Roof writes that the 1950s and 1960s were a time of eroding denominational boundaries and rising "voluntarism" among American Protestants, Catholics, and Jews. Old hierarchies were eroding and laity were taking greater roles in their churches as well as in larger society." See Roof and William McKinney, *American Mainline Religion: Its Changing Shape and Future* (New Brunswick, N.J.: Rutgers University Press, 1987). For a fuller understanding of "baby boomers" and the shift from religious to spiritual language in the 1950s and 1960s, see Roof, *A Generation of Seekers: The Spiritual Journeys of the Baby Boom Generation* (San Francisco: Harper, 1994) and *Spiritual Marketplace: Baby Boomers and the Remaking of American Religion* (Princeton, N.J.: Princeton University Press, 2001).

U.S. religious historian Robert S. Fuller examines 1950s and 1960s U.S. Christianity and the changing political and social climate, which had a deep impact on the way Catholics and Protestants saw themselves in the modern world. Catholics and Protestants experienced the upheavals of the 1960s and began thinking about religious community in new ways. Pastors remained important to the life of churches and in the individual lives of churchgoers, but as Christian laypersons experienced the various reforms to their churches, many saw their clergy less as hierarchical figures and more as mentors and friends in their religious and spiritual journeys. See Fuller, *The Fifties Spiritual Marketplace: American Religion in a Decade of Conflict* (New Brunswick, N.J.: Rutgers University Press, 1997) and *The Sixties Spiritual Awakening* (New Brunswick, N.J.: Rutgers University Press, 1994).

109. Tanya Muzzarelli, interview with author, Tres Dias International Secretariat, Rockford, Ill., March 13, 2010.

110. Dave Smazik, interview with author, Tres Dias International Secretariat, Rockford, Ill., March 13, 2010.

111. Derek Schurman, interview with author, Tres Dias International Secretariat, Rockford, Ill., March 13, 2010.

112. Jeff Johnson, interview with author, Tres Dias International Secretariat, Rockford, Ill., March 13, 2010.

113. John Connor, interview with author, Tres Dias International Secretariat, Rockford, Ill., March 13, 2010.

114. Tanya Muzzarelli, interview with author, March 13, 2010.

115. John Connor, interview with author, March 13, 2010.

116. West Point graduates established the first Tres Dias community in South Korea in 1985, and since this time Tres Dias, like Christianity more generally, has flourished there. The Tres Dias Korean Region (TDKR) Committee was founded in 2008 by a subcommittee of the Tres Dias International Secretariat, and in 2012 will hold an assembly. Representatives from Korean-speaking communities in New York and California are helping to coordinate planning, an experience, writes Don Bohl, that is injecting new vitality into their own programs. Bohl, Tres Dias Summer/Fall newsletter, 2011, p. 3, http://www.tresdias.org).

117. Thomas A. Tweed, *Crossing and Dwelling: A Theory of Religion* (Cambridge: Harvard University Press, 2010).

118. Kurt Horberg, interview with author, law office of Telleen, Horberg, Smith & Carmen, PC, Cambridge, Ill., March 12, 2011.

Chapter Four

1. While a number of scholars have noted the influence of Mexican-descent Catholics and other Hispanic Catholics (primarily Puerto Rican and Cuban) in popularizing the movement in the United States, none have analyzed in depth how these men and women experience Cursillo in their everyday lives. For sources that touch on the role of Mexican-descent Catholics and other U.S. Hispanic Catholics in popularizing the movement in the United States and the meanings of Cursillo for Hispanic Americans, see Rodolfo Acuña, *Occupied America: The Chicano's Struggle towards Liberation* (San Francisco: Harper and Row, 1972); Ana-María Díaz-Stevens, *Oxcart Catholicism on Fifth Avenue* (South Bend, Ind.: University of Notre Dame Press, 1993); and Ana María Díaz-Stevens and Anthony Stevens-Arroyo, *Recognizing the Latino Resurgence in U.S. Religion* (Boulder, Colo.: Westview, 1998). Anthony Stevens-Arroyo notes the significance of Cursillos for Hispanic Catholics in "Latino/a Catholic Theology," in *Handbook of Latina/o Theologies*, ed. Edwin David Aponte and Miguel A. de la Torre (St. Louis: Chalice, 2006), 175–77. David Badillo mentions that Cursillos have been important for Puerto Rican, Mexican American, Cuban American, and Dominican Catholics and their efforts to maintain distinctively Latino and Catholic identities; Badillo, *Latinos and the New Immigrant Church* (Baltimore: Johns Hopkins University Press, 2006).

2. While it was not difficult for me to forgo a laptop for three days, going without my cell phone was a challenge, as I wanted to text my husband to see how the kids were faring. In particular, I worried how my daughter was doing without "mommy." Doris O'Keefe, my ever-considerate sponsor, dropped off a note for me on Saturday telling me that she had talked with Steve and that everyone was "doing great!" Her brief note helped make the rest of my absence from home easier.

3. Sue Davis, telephone interview with author, April 27, 2010.

4. Although there is no such rule in Mallorca, the birthplace of the CdC, the U.S. Cursillo Center and National Secretariat are firm in their stance that husbands must make their CdC weekend before their wives. While some Cursillo communities have bent the rules to allow women to make the course first, this is rare and strongly discouraged by the National Secretariat and most U.S. priests involved in Cursillos.

5. I observed and participated in a Kairos Prison Ministry Inside Weekend (KI) in spring 2010 and made a Catholic Cursillo at the Believers Together Center in Moline, Illinois, in March 2011. The Believers Together Center is one of few places in the country where Catholic Cursillos are open to non-Catholic Christians.

6. The Cursillo movement itself is considered by many Catholics to be cofounded by Eduardo Bonnín Aguiló, a Spanish lay Catholic, and Bishop Juan Hervás, both of whom have written handbooks on the history and "essence" of the

Cursillo weekend, as well as guidelines for priests and laity involved in the weekend courses. Although the National Cursillo Center has in the past promoted Hervás as the official founder of the movement, first-generation veteran cursillistas think otherwise. The San Diegans I interviewed all asserted that Bonnín was the "true" founder and that Hervás has been given most of the credit. Since the beginnings of the movement, laity and priests have worked together, giving rollos and planning the weekend, yet the movement is fundamentally a lay one—supported by priests and the Church hierarchy but run by laymen and women. Laymen and women give ten of the fifteen weekend talks and a layperson, called the rector, organizes and sponsors the weekend course. *The Structure of Ideas (Vertebration)* (Dallas: National Cursillo Center, 1995), which Bonnín coauthored with Francisco Forteza and Bernardo Vadell, focuses on the importance of lay involvement for the success of the course and the future of the Church itself. Interestingly, Bonnín devotes only half a page to the priest's role and there makes it very clear that priests are important components to the weekend course but that they should not "interfere with or interrupt the progress of the Cursillo at any moment" (Bonnín, Forteza, and Vadell, *Structure of Ideas*, 61). Priests have historically given five of the ten rollos during the Cursillo weekend, and they also serve as spiritual directors of the weekend. The Notre Dame University archives house the Gerhardt Niemeyer papers, which include numerous Cursillo talks given by Pastor Niemeyer in the 1980s. The National Cursillo Center's *Leader's Manual* (Dallas: Office of the National Secretariat, 1981) lays out the official guidelines for the course.

7. If a candidate is selected and cannot pay the application fee, it will be waived.

8. Teens Encounter Christ (TEC), a Catholic Cursillo spinoff we will examine in chapter 5, has its own word for palanca: "wheat." Wheat is biblically significant for the TEC movement, which finds inspiration in John 12:24, "Unless a grain of wheat falls into the ground and dies, it remains only a single grain; but if it does die, it produces a rich harvest." Volunteers are encouraged to make and give wheat throughout the weekend, during which they repeatedly invoke the words, "Wheat, wheat, and more wheat."

9. Father Duane and O'Keefe suggested—like almost all my interlocutors—suggested that I make my Cursillo weekend in order to gain a deeper understanding of its inner workings. Moreover, they all hoped that I would be spiritually moved by my experience. Father Duane and O'Keefe both urged me to keep my identity as a researcher private, so as not to influence the other candidates' experiences. I agreed that it would not be a good idea to let my fellow candidates know I was writing about them and our weekend. I am convinced that this was the right decision, and I sincerely hope that the women who were on the weekend—the team leaders, volunteers, and candidates alike—will not be offended if they happen to read this book. Except for the individuals who knew about my identity as a researcher, I have changed all of the names of the women on my weekend.

10. I decided to wait until my youngest was two years old to make my weekend. Making my Cursillo after I had conducted most of the qualitative research kept the latter from being overly determined by my own experience. I asked my interlocutors questions and listened carefully when they talked about their three days and

about their Fourth Day. Probably the biggest negative of waiting until the end of my research to make my weekend was that I might have asked additional questions of my interlocutors had I made my weekend earlier.

11. In the Catholic Cursillo weekend these meditations are called "Know Thyself" and "The Merciful Father."

12. *The Fundamental Ideas of the Cursillo Movement* (Dallas: National Cursillo Center, 1972), 141.

13. Rollo no. 1, "Ideal," March 18, 2011.

14. Ibid., 144.

15. The Serenity Prayer, written by the famous American Protestant theologian Reinhold Niebuhr, has become iconic among U.S. Christians, cursillistas included: "God grant me the serenity to accept the things I cannot change, the courage to change the things I can, and the wisdom to know the difference."

16. Rollo no. 6, "Study," March 19, 2011, 150.

17. Ibid.

18. Ibid., 151.

19. Rollo no. 7, "Sacraments," March 19, 2011.

20. Rollo no. 9, "Obstacles to the Life of Grace." This deacon, like all the other rollistas, gave us a list of Scripture readings that addressed obstacles to a life of grace, as well as how to remedy our sins. These included Romans 6:1-23, Ephesians 6:11, I John 3:8, Matthew 26:41, Wisdom 3:9, John 1:14-17, Romans 12:6-13, and Ephesians 2:8-10.

21. Rollo no. 7, "Sacraments," 156-57.

22. Ibid., 158.

23. Ibid., 160.

24. Rollo no. 14, "Total Security." The rollista cited the following Scripture to support her points about the importance of Christian community in action: Matthew 6:33, 10:20, 18:20, 10:16, and Luke 14:26-30.

25. Rollo no. 15, "Fourth Day," March 20, 2011, 164.

26. Ibid.

27. On the Kairos Inside weekend I observed, the agape bags were given to the candidates on Saturday afternoon, while on the women's weekend I attended we were given our palanca bags on Sunday afternoon. The majority of cursillistas I interviewed said that they received their palanca or agape bags on Saturday.

28. According to the *Leader's Manual*, "Palanca means prayer and sacrifice which is offered to God to obtain something. Palanca should accompany all apostolic action. The Spanish word 'palanca' means 'lever.' It came to be used to describe 'intendencia' (prayer and sacrifice), because a lever allows a person to move things which are beyond his strength, just as prayer and sacrifice allow an apostle to accomplish more than he would be capable of otherwise." National Cursillo Center, *Leader's Manual*, 316.

29. Palanca letter, Women's Cursillo no. 959, Northwest region, Diocese of Peoria, spring 2011.

30. Ibid., 169.

31. Jesse Ramírez, interview with author, San Diego, Calif., July 23, 2005.

32. Elva Hernández, interview with author, East Chicago, Ind., June 29, 2006.

33. In contrast to what Sigmund Dragastin has called the "religious fanaticism" of the Cursillo and "the long term hazards" of the Cursillo process, cursillistas say that they find deep meaning in the structured weekend course, and they point to the authenticity of their experiences. Dragastin, "All That Glistens Isn't: A Look at the Cursillo Exercise," *Una Sancta* 23, no. 1, 44–51.

34. *The Purpose of the Movement* (Dallas: National Cursillo Center, 1974), 81–82.

35. Louie González, interview with author, East Chicago, Ind., June 28, 2006.

36. Jesse Ramírez, interview with author, July 22, 2005.

37. Louie González, interview with author, June 28, 2006.

38. Damien Rico, interview with author, Mimi's Café, East Chicago, Ind., June 27, 2008.

39. Adelina Torres, interview with author, Office of Hispanic Ministries, East Chicago, Ind., June 26, 2008.

40. Ramona ("Mona,") Sandovál, interview with author, East Chicago, Ind., June 29, 2006.

41. Catalina González, interview with author, East Chicago, Ind., June 28, 2006.

42. Rosita Aldrete, interview with author, Quinta de Guadalupe, San Diego, Calif., July 21, 2005.

43. Mary Farrell Bednarowski, "'Our Work Is Change for the Sake of Justice': Hope Community, Minneapolis, Minnesota," in *Religion and Healing in America*, ed. Linda L. Barnes and Susan S. Sered (New York: Oxford University Press, 2005).

44. Rebecca Lester, *Jesus in Our Wombs* (Berkeley: University of California Press, 2005), 42.

45. Louie González, interview with author, June 28, 2006.

46. Catalina González, interview with author, June 28, 2006.

47. John Corrigan, *Business of the Heart: Religion and Emotion in the Nineteenth Century* (Berkeley: University of California Press, 2002), 3.

48. Carmen Uriostegui, interview with author, Oceanside, Calif., July 26, 2005.

49. Corrigan, *Business of the Heart*, 3.

50. M. Carlos Calatayud Maldonado, "I Went to a Cursillo: Testimony of a Layman," *Christ to the World* (1964): 496.

51. The first women's weekend was held in 1953 in Bogotá, Colombia, and the second in 1958 in Tarragona, Spain. The first women's weekend in the United States was held in 1961 in San Antonio, Texas. Guillermo Biblioni, *Historia de los Cursillos de Cristiandad: Mallorca, 1944–2001* (Madrid: Libroslibres, 2002), 231, 232, 205.

52. Biblioni writes that Capó and other Church leaders invoked machismo and argued that the CdC should remain for men only because women's souls could not be edified as could men's. Bonnín insisted that the Cursillos were for both men and women and that everyone's soul could be edified and awakened during the weekend. Biblioni, *Historia de los CdC*, 121. Bonnín believed that men's and women's weekends should be separate, not because he was a chauvinist, Mallorquín cursillistas say, but because he believed that men open up more around men and women more around women and that separate courses provide the best environment for women to grow spiritually without distractions (i.e., from men) and for

men to grow spiritually without distractions (from women). Every Catholic cursillista with whom I have spoken—whether Mallorquín, Mexican American, or U.S. white non-Hispanic—agrees with the separate men's and women's courses. Where there is disagreement is over whether or not husbands should make their weekend before their wives. Mallorquín cursillistas like Miguel Sureda, one of Eduardo Bonnín's closest friends, say that the spiritual head of the home should make her or his Cursillo first and that this is not always the husband. U.S. cursillistas are more conservative on this issue and almost every U.S. cursillista I have interviewed, men and women of Mexican descent and white non-Hispanic alike, say that husbands should make their weekend first.

53. "Frente a quienes abogaban por la apertura de talles cursillos, don Juan Capó y su grupo los rechazaban esgrimiendo endebles argumentos, teñidos de solapado machismo." Biblioni, *Historia de los CdC*, 121.

54. All ten Mallorquín women I interviewed in Palma in June 2011 spoke about Bonnín's lack of machismo. The female cursillistas I met at a Palma ultreya gathering as well as at the leaders' school also spoke about his progressive attitude toward women.

55. Carmen Uriostegui, interview with author, July 26, 2005.

56. Doris O'Keefe, telephone interview with author, May 2009.

57. Bishop Gilbert Chavez, interview with author, San Diego, Calif., July 26, 2005.

58. Field notes, San Diego, July 2005. Bishop Chavez did grant me permission to make my Cursillo in San Diego. Echoing my female cursillista's sentiments, he thought that making my Cursillo in the Spanish-speaking movement would give me a better sense of the origins of the movement and would be a more authentic experience. Because I had a young son and another child on the way, I was unfortunately not able to make my Cursillo in San Diego, but did make my Cursillo (in English) in spring 2011 in the Diocese of Peoria.

59. During our interview (July 26, 2005), Bishop Chavez did say that there is never a shortage of female candidates for Cursillo weekends, but that they have had to cancel men's weekends for lack of male candidates.

60. Elizabeth Brusco, *The Reformation of Machismo: Evangelical Conversion and Gender in Colombia* (Austin: University of Texas Press, 2010).

61. W. Bradford Wilcox, *Soft Patriarchs, New Men: How Christianity Shapes Fathers and Husbands* (Chicago: University of Chicago Press, 2004).

62. John Blackwell, "The Walk to Emmaus: Culture, Feeling, and Emotion," *Ethos* 19, no. 4 (December 1991): 450.

63. Louie González, interview with author, East Chicago, Ind., June 29, 2006.

64. Ibid.

65. Chris Sandovál, interview with author, East Chicago, Ind., June 29, 2006.

66. Ibid.

67. Louie González, interview with author, June 29, 2006.

68. Miguel Arredondo, interview with author, East Chicago, Ind., June 29, 2006.

69. Deacon Rob Litavich, interview with author, Barnes and Noble, Merrillville, Ind., June 30, 2008.

70. Jesse Ramírez, interview with author, July 23, 2005.

71. This sentiment was echoed by the Mexican-descent men interviewed for this book, including Louie González and his father, Ray González, Chris Sandovál, Miguel Arredondo, Jesse Guadiana, and Damien Rico of East Chicago; and Enrique Aldrete, Jesse Ramírez, Frank Barrios, José Herréra, and Enrique Mendez of San Diego, all quoted or referred to in this chapter.

72. Jesse and Maria Ramírez, interview with author, San Diego, Calif., July 23, 2005.

73. Father Duane Jack, interview with author, St. Patrick Church, Orion, Ill., June 23, 2008.

74. Ron Caronti, telephone interview with author, January 26, 2011.

75. John Connor, interview with author, Westminster Presbyterian Church, Rockford, Ill., March 13, 2010.

76. Ibid.

77. Tom Miller, interview with author, Westminster Presbyterian Church, Rockford, Ill., March 13, 2010.

78. Wayne, interview with author, Westminster Presbyterian Church, Rockford, Ill., March 13, 2010.

79. Michael, interview with author, Westminster Presbyterian Church, Rockford, Ill., May 12, 2010.

80. JoEllen Rowe, interview with author, Rockville Correctional Facility, Rockville, Ind., May 13, 2010.

81. John Bruckman, interview with author, Rock Island, Ill., January 6, 2008.

82. Robert Wuthnow, *After Heaven: Spirituality in America since the 1950s* (Berkeley: University of California Press, 1998), 50.

83. Trysh Travis, *The Language of the Heart: A Cultural History of the Recovery Movement from Alcoholics Anonymous to Oprah Winfrey* (Chapel Hill: University of North Carolina Press, 2009), 5.

84. Ibid., 11.

85. Ibid.

86. See Wuthnow, *"I Come Away Stronger": How Small Groups Are Shaping American Religion,* and *Sharing the Journey: Support Groups and America's New Quest for Community.*

87. Bob and Rhoda Franks, interview with author, Cool Beanz coffeehouse, Rock Island, Ill., January 26, 2011.

88. Pixies, "Monkey Gone to Heaven," *Doolittle* (Elektra Records, 1989).

89. Tanya Muzzarelli, interview with author, Westminster Presbyterian Church, Rockford, Ill., March 13, 2010.

90. Ibid.

91. Steve Gielda, Fourth-Day talk, Via de Cristo Ultreya, Prince of Peace Lutheran Church, Orlando, Fla., January 31, 2010.

92. Rita Gustafson, interview with author, Java, Rock Island, Ill., October 9, 2008.

93. Ibid.

94. Linda, interview with author. It proved to be much easier as a researcher to locate cursillistas who enjoyed their weekend and who became involved in a Fourth-Day movement than to find men and women who did not enjoy the

weekend. A study of cursillistas who do not go on to be involved in their Fourth Day would be a welcome addition to the scholarship on the movement.

Chapter Five

1. Father Matt Fedewa, interview with author, Festus, Mo., June 18, 2010. During our interview, Father Matt talked about how the early 1960s SEARCH and Better World movements influenced him and Sister Mary Concetta when they developed TEC. Both movements encouraged breakout discussions after talks were given and encouraged collaboration.

2. There is a vast literature on the Vatican II Council and the events that preceded it. See Mark S. Massa, SJ, *The American Catholic Revolution: How the '60s Changed the Church Forever* (Oxford: Oxford University Press, 2010); John W. O'Malley, SJ, *What Happened at Vatican II* (Cambridge: Belknap Press of Harvard University Press, 2010); O'Malley, Ed., *Did Anything Happen at Vatican II?* (New York: Continuum, 2007); and Melissa J. Wilde, *Vatican II: A Sociological Analysis of Religious Change* (Princeton, N.J.: Princeton University Press, 2007) for some of the best and current academic sources on what led up to Vatican II, the Vatican II Council, and the council's legacy.

3. For a fascinating sociological examination of conservative Catholic dissent after Vatican II, see Michael W. Cuneo, *The Smoke of Satan: Conservative and Traditionalist Dissent in Contemporary American Catholicism* (Baltimore: Johns Hopkins University Press, 1999). Cuneo shines light on the reasons conservative and traditionalist Catholics were and are deeply disappointed in Vatican II and why and how they want to go back to a pre–Vatican II Catholicism. Colleen Carroll's *The New Faithful: Why Young Adults Are Embracing Christian Orthodoxy* (Chicago: Loyola University Press, 2004) examines the recent trend among college-aged American Christians toward more conservative, what Carroll calls "orthodox," forms of their denominations and faith traditions. The young adults' lament in her book dovetails that of the Catholic conservatives and traditionalists in Cuneo's book in that they all long for a return to a glorified and sanitized past and are reacting to what they believe is a morally relativistic mainline Christianity.

4. Sister Concetta was especially involved in retreats inspired by Vatican II. In 1964 she made her Cursillo, and in April 1965 she made an Exercise in Christian Living weekend that was an adaptation from the Better World Movement (in which she had been involved).

5. Ronald Reiter, telephone interview with author, December 1, 2009. Father Jim Brown, OAR, according to Ron, "met with Father Matt in the mid-1970s to get the history of TEC. Father Jim recognized that TEC had grown out of control and developed the National TEC Conference in 1981 to help guide and organize the TEC movement. Most of the youth movements don't have a national office but ours does. We also have two bishops: An Episcopal moderator affiliated with the NCCB [National Council of Catholic Bishops] who help support the movement."

6. Father Matt Fedewa, interview with author, June 18, 2010.

7. Ibid.

8. Ibid.
9. Ibid.
10. Ibid.
11. Ibid.
12. Dorothy Gereke, interview with author, Festus, Mo., June 18, 2010.
13. The SEARCH retreat originated in San Mateo, California, in 1963 as a weekend experience for high school seniors. SEARCH weekends, offered in Catholic high schools around the country in the 1960s and 1970s, were precursors to TEC weekends. Today, Catholic high schools in mostly Western states continue to offer the retreat.
14. Dorothy Gereke, telephone interview with author, January 27, 2010.
15. Other weekends held at the Battle Creek, Michigan, Lila Post Hospital Lodge between 1965 and 1968 include Catholic Cursillo, Marriage Encounter, the Michigan State University Apostolic Formation Weekend for Vatican II, the Christian Community Movement for a Better World (also known as the Better World Movement), and Renewal through Vatican II workshops for Sisters and Clergy.
16. Father Matt Fedewa, interview with author, June 18, 2010.
17. Dorothy Gereke, interview with author, June 18, 2010.
18. Father Matt Fedewa, interview with author, June 18, 2010.
19. The Lila Post Montgomery Hospital was run and staffed by the Detroit Sisters of Mercy Order and was named after Lila Post, the second wife of C. W. Post, of Post cereal fame. According to Dorothy, Lila Post had the hospital built and chose the sisters to run the hospital, even though she herself was not Catholic. Dorothy says that Lila had had a good experience with sisters at other hospitals where she and her husband had been treated and was committed to Catholic-run hospitals. The hospital is now part of the Battle Creek Health System, and the Detroit Sisters of Mercy are no longer involved. The nursing school closed in 1956, and what became known as the Lodge was the first TEC Center in the United States. There were twenty-eight private rooms, a big living room (which became the liturgical chapel), and a parlor (which became the weekend's Eucharistic chapel). The suites were occupied by the sisters and priest working the weekend. According to Dorothy, the groups would have to crowd in for chapel. There were beds and mattresses in each room. The Lodge, which was adjacent to the hospital and was where the early TECs were held, is now a parking lot.
20. Ronald Reiter, telephone interview with author, December 1, 2009.
21. Reverend William J. Fitzgerald, introduction to original TEC manual, unpublished document (Battle Creek, Mich.: TEC Lodge, Feast of the Assumption, [August 15,] 1966), 1.
22. Sisters of Mercy, introduction to original TEC manual, 1.
23. Original TEC manual, 8.
24. Ibid., 4.
25. Ibid.
26. Ibid.
27. For an insightful collection of primary sources on U.S. Catholics' views on womanhood, and the engendering of girls and boys, see Paula Kane, James

Kenneally, and Karen Kennelly, *Gender Identities in American Catholicism* (New York: Orbis, 2001). For a historical examination of how American Catholic women, both lay and religious (nuns) have been gendered within U.S. Catholic culture, see Kathleen Sprows Cummings, *New Women of the Old Faith: Gender and American Catholicism in the Progressive Era* (Chapel Hill: University of North Carolina Press, 2010).

28. For an excellent historical look at the changing roles of women religious in the United States, see Amy Koehlinger, *The New Nuns: Racial Justice and Religious Reform in the 1960s* (Cambridge: Harvard University Press, 2007).

29. The Apostolic Formation Weekend, also called the "Vatican II Weekend," at TEC Lodge for Michigan State University students was held at the Lodge at Lila Post Hospital, Battle Creek, Mich., October 20-22, 1967.

30. TEC Rally, sponsored by the TEC Student Representatives Committee, 1967-68, Sunday, May 5, 1968, Central Fieldhouse, Battle Creek, Michigan, program, 4.

31. "Teen Encounters Christ Rally Draws 1,000 Here," *Battle Creek Enquirer*, May 6, 1968, 6. "Youths Learn Christian Love during Three-Day Exercise," *Flint Journal*, December 23, 1967, 7; "MBW Attends TEC Rally," *Atmosphere* 5, no. 5 (June-July 1968): 1, 3; "Pictorial Report on a Battle Creek Rally: Teen Encounters Christ," *Lansing Catholic Weekly*, May 10, 1968, 6; "Teen Encounters Christ: A New Spiritual Exercise Captures the Teenage Mind," *Catholic Weekly*, May 13, 1966, 15; "Youth Reflects at TEC: A Place to Seek Ideals, Spiritual Uplift," undetermined newspaper source, February 24, 1968.

32. The rally's imagining of Jesus and identifying him as a long-haired spiritual guru fits within the long history of Americans identifying with Jesus and making him into what they believe a spiritual leader would look like and say. For a fascinating historical look at how Americans have identified with Jesus over the centuries, see Stephen Prothero, *American Jesus: How the Son of Man Became a National Icon* (New York: Farrar, Strauss, and Giroux, 2004).

33. Dorothy Gereke, telephone interview with author, February 3, 2010.

34. Dorothy Gereke, telephone interview with author, January 27, 2010.

35. Ibid. Dorothy added more details important to understanding the intensity of TEC's formative years: "We ended the first weekend in May [1965] with a big rally at the Battle Creek auditorium, and there were 1,331 people there! Some of the students had helped set this rally up, and there was a priest in Grand Rapids who helped as well." She and Father Matt helped start eight centers in the first year (1965-66), and "in the first three and a half, four years I worked at 105 TEC weekends."

36. Dorothy Gereke, interview with author, June 18, 2010.

37. Father Matt Fedewa, Christmas letter to Sister Mary Concetta, n.d. (c. 1967).

38. In her *New Women of the Old Faith: Gender and American Catholicism in the Progressive Era* (Chapel Hill: University of North Carolina Press, 2009), Kathleen Sprows Cummings shows how women religious and clergy cooperated with one another to support higher education for U.S. Catholic women. Historical tensions between men and women religious notwithstanding, Cummings chronicles a history of cooperation and reciprocity among nuns and priests in the Progressive Era.

The more contemporary cooperation between the Detroit Sisters of Mercy and the clergy who were part of the Diocese of Lansing is another illustration of men and women religious working together for a common cause.

39. Ronald Reiter, telephone interview with author, December 1, 2009.
40. Father Matt Fedewa, interview with author, June 18, 2010.
41. Ibid.
42. Ibid.
43. Ibid.
44. Archbishop Roger Schwietz, telephone interview with author, January 26, 2009.
45. Father Matt Fedewa, interview with author, June 18, 2010.
46. Fitzgerald, introduction to original TEC manual, 1.
47. Sisters of Mercy, introduction to original TEC manual, 2.
48. Dorothy Gereke, telephone interview with author, January 27, 2010.
49. The Catholic Cursillo movement in the United States inspired and spawned a variety of Catholic and Protestant movements, including the Better World Movement and SEARCH. During the religious renewal and experimentation of the 1960s and early 1970s, these three movements were part of a larger Christian renewal in the United States.
50. Father Matt Fedewa, interview with author, June 18, 2010. Father Matt Fedewa made his Cursillo in August 1963 at the age of thirty. Sister Concetta made her Cursillo in January 1964 at the age of forty-one.
51. Archbishop Schwietz, telephone interview with author, January 26, 2009.
52. One other key player in TEC's early years is Father James ("Jim")Brown, OAR, who in June 2010 was not physically up to journeying to Festus. According to Archbishop Roger Schwietz, Father Jim was instrumental in TEC's early years. Archbishop Schwietz first met Father Jim when he was transferred to Omaha, Nebraska, in the early 1970s. There he was part of Creighton University's seminary. While he was in Omaha, TEC was begun at the request of the archbishop of Omaha. Father Jim Brown "really got TEC going in Omaha," says Archbishop Schwietz, and for his part, Schwietz worked closely with him. "From Father Jim," Schwietz said, "I learned how TEC was intended to operate and that he was working on a TEC manual. You see, there were several different manuals at the time in the Midwest, and Father Jim Brown and the Omaha group really worked to consolidate TEC and provide one manual in 1978 for all to follow." Archbishop Schwietz, telephone interview with author, January 26, 2009. TEC executive director Ronald Reiter seconded Schwietz's assessment during our first conversation on December 1, 2009: "Another person who is important to the history of the movement is Father Jim. Father Jim is now eighty-nine years old and at the time he was at Boy's Town in Omaha, Nebraska. He had heard about TEC and called Father Matt and had him meet him. It was Father Jim who wrote the first TEC manual."
53. Father Matt Fedewa, Christmas letter to Sister Concetta, c. 1967.
54. Dorothy Gereke, telephone interview with author, January 27, 2010.
55. Dorothy Gereke, interview with author, Festus, Mo., June 17, 2010.
56. Ibid.

57. Father Matt Fedewa, "Evolution of an Experiment: TEC (Teens Encounter Christ)," *Catholic High School Quarterly* (1967): 22.

58. Ibid., 22.

59. Ibid., 23.

60. Dorothy Gereke, telephone interview with author, January 27, 2010.

61. Dorothy Gereke, telephone interview with author, February 3, 2010.

62. Sisters of Mercy, introduction to original TEC manual, 1.

63. Fedewa, "Evolution of an Experiment," 24.

64. Ibid., 23.

65. Father Matt Fedewa, "T.E.C.," unpublished manuscript, submitted to the Diocese of Lansing, Mich., June 1969, 2.

66. Ibid., 1.

67. Ibid., 5.

68. Josh, interview with author, Augustana College, Tredway Library, Rock Island, Ill., May 19, 2008.

69. Archbishop Schwietz, telephone interview with author, January 26, 2009.

70. For this chapter I interviewed six young men and five young women who made their TEC. In addition, I interviewed one young female and one young male who made the TEC-spinoff Kairos weekend. I also interviewed one college-aged Methodist female who made her Chrysalis weekend (the young adult version of the Walk to Emmaus) in high school.

71. Josh, interview with author, May 19, 2008.

72. Kate, interview with author, October 5, 2008.

73. Ibid.

74. Tim, interview with author, Augustana College, Rock Island, Ill., November 10, 2010.

75. Chris, interview with author, Augustana College, Rock Island, Ill., October 15, 2010.

76. Chad, interview with author, Rock Island, Ill., September 13, 2009.

77. At the time of our interview on February 11, 2010, Amanda's religious history included her recent membership in Grace Church, a nondenominational Christian church in Glendale, Arizona, where she lived until attending college in the Midwest. She attended Grace Bible camp in Arizona and Oregon and was preparing to be a camp counselor at Grace Bible Camp in San Diego in summer 2011. Amanda attends a Lutheran church when she visits her family in Illinois.

78. Amanda, interview with author, Augustana College, Tredway Library, Rock Island, Ill., February 11, 2010.

79. Ibid.

80. Ibid.

81. Ibid.

82. Dorothy Gereke, telephone interview with author, February 3, 2010.

83. Ibid.

84. Father Matt Fedewa, interview with author, June 18, 2010.

85. Dorothy Gereke, telephone interview with author, February 3, 2010. Today Dorothy is an associate member of the Sisters of Mercy. She says she has come "full

circle"—she was a sister, then left her order in 1969, and is back with her order as an associate today. In April 2010 she traveled to Detroit for a retreat with other associates like herself. "Associates" are called "oblates" by some orders like the Benedictines. "I wanted to travel to Detroit to make my formal commitment because this is where I started. I will be with my former community once again, taking on a new commitment. As a lay associate it is our commitment to live out the spirit of Mother McCauley, the founder of the Sisters of Mercy." Dorothy says that the first TEC weekend was held in Battle Creek at the Lodge, October 9–11, 1965. "I have really come full circle now as an associate of the Sisters of Mercy. Mother McCauley . . . never intended to found an order—but so many women wanted to work with her, and she ended up going to Ireland to work with cloistered sisters there. She knew that the cloistered life would not work in America, and when she came to Detroit she founded the Sisters of Mercy in 1831."

86. Mary O'Brien, interview with author, Cool Beanz coffeehouse, Rock Island, Ill., November 2, 2010.

87. Father Matt Fedewa and Dorothy Gereke learned in October 2010 that they had won the award. They received it at NFCYM's annual conference in New Orleans, December 8–12, 2010.

88. Wes Six, interview with author, Augustana College, Rock Island, Ill., January 18, 2007.

89. Justine Nguyen, interview with author, Augustana College, Rock Island, Ill., January 18, 2007.

90. Father Matt Fedewa, interview with author, Festus, Mo., June 18, 2010.

91. Ronald Reiter, executive director, TEC, e-mail correspondence with author, August 17, 2011.

92. The twenty-four U.S. states in which TEC is currently active are Massachusetts, Pennsylvania, Maryland, West Virginia, Kentucky, Louisiana, Michigan, Ohio, Illinois, Indiana, Wisconsin, Minnesota, North Dakota, South Dakota, Iowa, Kansas, Nebraska, Missouri, Oklahoma, Alaska, Montana, Colorado, Florida, and Georgia.

93. The new TEC centers that Ron Reiter hopes will emerge by summer 2012 are planned for Austin and Corpus Christi, Texas; and Louisville, Kentucky. The national office is communicating with the following former TEC Centers about reopening Joliet, Illinois; La Crosse, Wisconsin; and Spokane and Seattle, Washington. Reiter, e-mail exchange with author, August 17, 2011.

94. According to Ronald Reiter, NET has been "hugely successful" in St. Paul, where it is linked with TEC. More than 30,000 young Catholic adults have been through a TEC-NET in St. Paul, says Ron. NET is part of TEC's "go forth," and TEC alumni involved in NET give a year to evangelizing across the United States. Youth involved in NET stay with a family and focus on a parish that they are assigned. NET, based in the Twin Cities, Minnesota, has two full-time paid employees and a six-figure budget. For more details, see http://netusa.org/home/.

95. Ronald Reiter, telephone interview with author, December 1, 2009.

96. Ibid. According to Ron, most TECs are held at a TEC center, and there are fifty TEC centers nationally and internationally. He emphasizes that "being diocesan-based gives TEC more legitimacy, as anyone can go, and youth from all over

the diocese come to take the course." Ron also notes that the Midwest is a stronghold for the TEC movement. The Diocese of Peoria is an important diocese for TEC as there are six TEC centers in this diocese alone: Believers Together Center in Moline; three TEC centers in Peoria itself; one TEC center in Bloomington-Normal; and one TEC Center in Peterstown. Ron adds that in 2009 there were more than 400 weekends in the Northwest region (which includes Illinois).

97. Father Matt Fedewa, interview with author, June 18, 2010.

98. In addition to the TEC-inspired, parish-based Kairos, another parish-based weekend for Catholic young adults that is currently popular in the Chicagoland area is Logos.

99. During our interviews, Father Matt, Dorothy, and Ron Reiter all emphasized that it is important for new people to become involved in TEC's leadership in order to avoid power struggles and the sense of ownership that people tend to get when they have been in leadership positions for too long. The "new blood" they refer to is about cycling new people into leadership positions and inviting others to retire who have been involved for many years and need to, according to Father Matt, "step aside to let new folks come in and lead."

100. The sociologist Christian Smith is widely regarded as the premier sociologist of teens and emerging adult spirituality. He coined the term *moralistic therapeutic deism* (MTD) to describe what he views, based on his quantitative and qualitative data, as the weak theology of most U.S. Christian youth. See Smith and Melinda Lundquist Denton, *Soul Searching: The Religious and Spiritual Lives of American Teenagers* (Oxford: Oxford University Press, 2009), for Smith's definition of MTD and his entrée into understanding U.S. teenagers' spirituality. See also Smith and Patricia Snell, *Souls in Transition: The Religious and Spiritual Lives of Emerging Adults* (New York: Oxford University Press, 2009); and Smith, Kari Christoffersen, Hilary Davidson, and Patricia Snell Hertzog, *Lost in Transition: The Dark Side of Emerging Adulthood* (New York: Oxford University Press, 2011).

101. In addition to the primary source documents I have obtained from TEC archives, personal archives, and interviews, academic sources for this chapter include Smith and Denton, *Soul Searching*; Kenda Creasy Dean, *Almost Christian: What the Faith of Our Teenagers Is Telling the American Church* (New York: Oxford University Press, 2010); Lauren Sandler, *Righteous: Dispatches from the Evangelical Youth Movement* (New York: Viking, 2006); and the National Study of Youth and Religion (NSYR) http://youthandreligion.org, for quantitative data on contemporary American teens and religious persuasions.

102. While most of the other Fourth-Day movements have their own prison ministry, Kairos Prison Ministry International is the only one whose sole focus is on inmates and their families.

Chapter Six

1. At the invitation of Kairos International director John Thompson, I observed and participated in a Kairos Inside weekend at Rockville Correctional Facility for women in southern Indiana on May 13–16, 2010. My research was facilitated by

JoEllen Rowe, the warm and enthusiastic director of women's weekends in Indiana, as well as all of the Kairos volunteers, who were gracious with their time and who supported my work. Rita Steed, the facility's volunteer services director, was immensely helpful and forthcoming with information, and like many of the Kairos female volunteers, remained accessible well after the weekend experience was over. Thanks to Rita, I received permission to bring my electric breastpump for the weekend. I am grateful for and humbled by the degree to which Rita and the Kairos women accommodated my needs.

2. While the names of Kairos volunteers will be used, for privacy reasons, the names of the weekend's guests will be changed.

3. The one exception was me: though also a "Hoosier," I hail from the northwest part of the state, which many consider to be more culturally connected to Chicago than to southern Indiana.

4. John Thompson, executive director, Kairos Prison Ministry International, e-mail correspondence with author, August 16, 2011.

5. See http://kpmifoundation.org/about-us/kairos-history/ for more details.

6. For an excellent ethnography on the women's section of Aglow International in the United States, see R. Marie Griffith, *God's Daughters: Evangelical Women and the Power of Submission* (Berkeley: University of California Press, 1997).

7. For a well-researched and thoughtful academic source on college fraternities and sororities, see Alan D. DeSantis, *Inside Greek U: Fraternities, Sororities, and the Pursuit of Pleasure, Power, and Prestige* (Lexington: University Press of Kentucky, 2007).

8. Unlike other Christian-based prison reform movements, Kairos Prison Ministry International (KPMI) is a nonprofit organization run by volunteers that works with inmates who have voluntarily signed up for the weekend-long course. In *AU v. PFM* (2006), the U.S. District Court in Des Moines, Iowa, ruled a faith-based in-prison rehabilitation program known as InnerChange Freedom Initiative (IFI) to be unconstitutional. According to Winnifred Fallers Sullivan, *Prison Religion: Faith-Based Reform and the Constitution* (Princeton, N.J.: Princeton University Press, 2009), "*AU v. PFM* is acknowledged to be one of the most significant recent court cases considering the application of the establishment clause of the First Amendment to the U.S. Constitution to the new 'faith-based' social services" (1). Both KPMI and IFI are faith-based initiatives and hope to impact prisoners' lives by introducing Jesus Christ. While there are similarities between the objectives of the two programs, as both aim to show that a relationship with Christ is the key to a better, reformed life, there are important differences as well. IFI was a state-supported Christian rehabilitation program, one of former President George W. Bush's faith-based initiatives, while Kairos is not state supported and is run by volunteers. Kairos predated the faith-based initiatives of the 2000s by more than twenty years and is offered in medium- to maximum-security prisons to a small group of inmates who voluntarily sign up to take the course. Kairos is one of several religiously based programs at the facility where I attended the Kairos Inside weekend I describe in this chapter. Other offerings at this facility included interfaith prayer meetings, Aglow, and Sunday morning worship services.

9. For example, in 2008, Aglow women held a two-day retreat in Central California's Women's Facility. Their focus, like that of Kairos Prison Ministry International, was "to teach the women how to receive the healing that God promises by releasing their pain, grief, un-forgiveness or other emotional barriers" (http://www.aglow.org/aglownewscontent.aspx?id=2096).

10. Important sources for the analysis in this chapter include Sullivan, *Prison Religion*; Megan Sweeney, *Reading Is My Window: Books and the Art of Reading on Women's Prison's* (Chapel Hill: University of North Carolina Press, 2010); Courtney Bender, *God's Love We Deliver* (Chicago: University of Chicago Press, 2004); R. Marie Griffith, *God's Daughters: Evangelical Women and the Power of Submission* (Berkeley: University of California Press, 1995); and Griffith, *Born Again Bodies* (Berkeley: University of California Press, 2004).

11. KPMI, *Kairos Newsletter*, May–June 1995.

12. Ibid.

13. Significantly, the date of the first Cursillo is erroneously given as 1949, instead of the correct 1944.

14. John Thompson sent me "The Prison Story" as a pdf.

15. See L. Shannon Jung, *Sharing Food: Christian Practices for Enjoyment* (Minneapolis: Fortress, 2006), for a good overview of the centrality of food and hospitality for Christians. Kairos Prison Ministry International emphasizes food and Christian fellowship in its weekend. See also Brendan Byrne, *The Hospitality of God: A Reading of Luke's Gospel* (Collegeville, Minn.: Liturgical Press, 2000), for a New Testament exegesis of the importance of hospitality for Christians.

16. Cindy, interview with author, Rockville, Ind., May 15, 2010.

17. Megan Sweeney, *Reading Is My Window: Books and the Art of Reading in Women's Prisons* (Chapel Hill: University of North Carolina Press, 2010), 7.

18. JoEllen Rowe, interview with author, Rockville Correctional Facility, March 14, 2010.

19. Courtney Bender, *Heaven's Kitchen: Living Religion at God's Love We Deliver* (Chicago: University of Chicago Press, 2003).

20. Byrne, *Hospitality of God*.

21. Kairos Prison Ministry International Inc., *Program Manual: Medium/Maximum Security Prisons, Men and Women* (Winter Park, Fla.: KPMI, 2005), sec. 4, p. 5.

22. Ibid., sec. 4, p. 4.

23. Ibid., sec. 4, p. 5.

24. There were some critical voices, however. Tom in Tres Dias told me that there is too much food served and that the weekend was "gluttonous." Some women told me that they had a hard time not being able to exercise—"so much sitting!"—and that it was difficult to pass up so much food. But more women, notably, said that the weekend was a welcome "break" from the demands of parenting and careers. They welcomed being "pampered." Doris O'Keefe, who made her Catholic Cursillo in Rock Island, Illinois, in 1977 remembers how "wonderful" it was to "relax, talk with other women about my faith, to be fed and to not have to wash a single dish!" Women in particular talked at length about how they were usually the ones taking care of others and said their weekend Cursillo offered them a rare occasion when

they were the focal point of care and concern. In contrast to women who welcomed such a respite, men seem to have a more difficult time being taken care of—especially by other men who run the weekend encounters.

25. R. Marie Griffith, *Born Again Bodies: Flesh and Spirit in American Christianity* (Berkeley: University of California Press, 2004).

26. Ibid., 143.

27. Ibid., 143.

28. Kairos Prison Ministry International Inc., *2010 Pilot Program Manual*, (Winter Park, Fla.: KPMI, 2010), 14.

29. Great Banquet and Christ Renews His Parish (CRHP) will be examined in chapter 7.

30. KPMI solicited feedback from select communities in the spring and summer of 2010 and a Program Review Ad Hoc Committee met that summer to discuss what changes to make to KPMI's manual.

31. JoEllen Rowe, interview with author, Rockville, Ind., March 14, 2010.

32. KPMI, *Program Manual* (2005), sec. 3, p. 31. See http://kairosofindiana.org/cookie for detailed instructions on how to make the cookies.

33. Bender, *Heaven's Kitchen*.

34. KPMI, *Program Manual* (2005), sec. 3, p. 9.

35. In the introduction to the collection of essays *American Sanctuary: Understanding Sacred Spaces* (Bloomington: Indiana University Press, 2006), Louis P. Nelson writes that "Those seeking to construct and contain sacred space use both word and form to do so. Often the sacred emerges from within the common or everyday landscape and the sanctity of the place is simply declared with little or no immediate material change to the site" (6).

36. Because I was not a full-fledged volunteer and was considered by the weekend leaders to be an outside observer, I was given access to all of the weekend events and was invited to take part in the rituals.

37. Randy Rothwell, "Sanctuary," *Be Magnified* (Integrity Media, 2010).

38. Kairos Prison Ministry International Inc., "Freedom Guide,"(Winter Park, Fla.: KPMI, 2005), 2.

39. Malcolm X, *The Autobiography of Malcolm X,* as told to Alex Haley (New York: Ballantine, 1987). See esp. chap. 11, "Saved," for Malcolm's powerful rendering of his conversion experience while imprisoned.

40. The 2010 KI weekend I describe here was a "pilot program," one of several experimental KI weekends being held across the United States. One of the changes in the pilot program is combining four of the talks into two so that there are thirteen instead of fifteen talks. Everyone I spoke with about the changes thought they improved the weekend experience, saying that fifteen talks was "a little too much" and that the combined talks "worked out great" because they held the attention of the offenders and left more time for chapel and silent reflection.

41. Eduardo Bonnín Aguiló, *My Spiritual Testament* (Palma de Mallorca: FEBA, 2009), 44.

42. Ibid., 44–45.

43. KPMI, *Program Manual* (2005), sec. 6, p. 5.

Chapter Seven

1. In addition to Christ Renews His Parish (CRHP) and Great Banquet, other Fourth-Day movement spinoffs include Credo, which is modeled after Tres Dias but focuses on a specific population: abused and battered women. According to Tanya, who lives in Rockford, Illinois, and is involved in both Tres Dias and Credo, in order to qualify for the course the women have to be off drugs, "clean" for at least ninety days. Credo's weekend course is held at Bishop Lane in Rockford, a retreat center. Tanya works with Credo as part of her Fourth Day and says that seeing these women "just come alive and for once have hope" is deeply moving and "keeps me doing what I am doing." The participants, a majority of whom are African American, change on the last day into white clothes, symbolizing their "starting a new life, one of hope and love." Way of Christ is a spinoff of Via de Cristo, a mainline in-covenant Fourth-Day movement that itself branched off of Catholic Cursillos (unlike Way of Christ, Via de Cristo is acknowledged as being in covenant with Eduardo Bonnín's vision and thus with the original Catholic Cursillos de Cristiandad).

2. Of all of the interviews conducted for this book, my telephone interview with Bob Edwards (December 10, 2009) is one of the most memorable. Edwards was a no-holds-barred kind of guy and did anything but romanticize his Cursillo experience. He was pragmatic, even a bit irreverent, and I appreciated that about him. He was a supporter of this book and spoke without reservation. Bob Edwards passed away on November 14, 2010, and will be missed by many.

3. Bob Edwards, telephone interview, December 10, 2009.

4. Ibid.

5. Information sent to me by e-mail from Frank Wardega, July 20, 2011.

6. Bob Edwards, telephone interview, December 10, 2009.

7. Bob Edwards and Edward Jacoby, *Synopsis: A Parochial Spiritual Renewal Process* (Cleveland: Christ Renews His Parish, 1980), 9.

8. It can also be said that Bonnín did not intend for the CdC to be a church renewal weekend and that CRHP is focused on church renewal.

9. Edwards and Jacoby, *Synopsis*.

10. Ibid.

11. These shorter Cursillo spinoffs, which are not in covenant, tend to be parish- rather than diocese-based. They include the young adult, parish-based renewal weekends Kairos (not KPMI) and Logos; as well as the adult Catholic Christian Experience Weekend (CEW), currently popular in central and western Iowa; and Adoration, Community, Theology, Service (ACTS), which is offered in the Archdiocese of Cincinnati. The CEW was founded in 1974 by priests and women religious in Dubuque and aimed to reach more laypeople by not requiring them to miss a Friday workday and by offering a more ecumenical Christian weekend. In addition, wives were not required to wait until their husbands had made their weekend. Other Catholic Cursillo spinoffs include Koinonia. Both Koinonia and the CEW are Christian spirituality movements modeled after the Cursillo weekend but parish- rather than diocese-based and shortened from three days to two. Koinonia is ecumenical Christian and grew directly out of the Catholic Cursillo movement,

although it is not in covenant. Koinonia's first weekend was held in Findley, Ohio, in 1972. Like the in-covenant Catholic and Protestant Cursillo weekends, Koinonia spread across the United States with the help of Catholic cursillistas. Men and women from Koinonia have helped out on Cursillo weekends and Kairos Prison Ministry weekends, offering yet more evidence of U.S. Christians taking part in Cursillo-inspired movements, whether they are officially Fourth Day or not, and working together to bring their faith to others.

12. Leading scholars of U.S. Catholicism have long noted that for American Catholics, the parish is at the center of their Catholic identity. See John McGreevy, *Parish Boundaries: The Catholic Encounter with Race in the Twentieth-Century Urban North* (Chicago: University of Chicago Press, 1998), for a wonderful study of how urban ethnic Catholic identities shaped the worldview of U.S. Catholic men and women; Eileen McMahon, *What Parish Are You From? A Chicago Irish Community and Race Relations* (Lexington: University Press of Kentucky, 1996), for a detailed study of the centrality of ethnic and religious identities for Chicago Catholics; Chester Gillis, *Roman Catholicism in America* (New York: Columbia University Press, 2000), for a solid historical overview of U.S. Catholicism and the centrality of the parish to U.S. Catholics' identities; Colleen McDannell, *The Spirit of Vatican II: A History of Reform in America* (New York: Basic Books, 2011), for a vivid examination at the place of the parish for U.S. Catholics; and Mark S. Massa, SJ, *The American Catholic Revolution: How the '60s Changed the Church Forever* (Oxford: Oxford University Press, 2010), for a close look at 1960s U.S. Catholicism and parish identities. See also John Seitz, *No Closure: Catholic Practice and Boston's Parish Shutdowns* (Cambridge: Harvard University Press, 2011), an excellent ethnohistorical study of parish shutdowns and parishioners' responses.

13. Kate Hodel, telephone interview with author, February 11, 2011.
14. Ibid.
15. Ibid.
16. http://www.bellaonline.com/articles/art58494.asp.
17. Kate Hodel, telephone interview with author, February 11, 2011.
18. Ibid.
19. Ibid.
20. Kathy, interview with author, Rock Island, Ill., April 10, 2011.
21. CRHP's success in midwestern dioceses in particular (Indiana, Illinois, Ohio) parallels the success of the parish-based Kairos young adult weekend, an offshoot of the diocese-based TEC. Just as CRHP has eclipsed Cursillo in some dioceses, Kairos has eclipsed TEC, including across the state of Michigan.
22. Ruth, interview with author, KPMI weekend, Rockville, Ind., May 13–16, 2010.
23. Edwards and Jacoby, *Synopsis*, 5.
24. http://www.lampstand.net/.
25. "Great Banquet Community Locations," http://lampstand.net/.
26. Jack Pitzer, telephone interview with author, June 3, 2010.
27. See http://lampstand.net/.
28. Ibid.
29. Jack Pitzer, telephone interview with author, May 11, 2010.

30. Ibid.
31. Ibid.
32. Ibid.
33. *Great Banquet Orientation* (Lampstand Ministries, 1995), CD.
34. Jack Pitzer, telephone interview with author, May 11, 2010.
35. Ibid.
36. Ibid.
37. Ibid.
38. *Great Banquet Orientation*.
39. Jack Pitzer, telephone interview with author, May 11, 2010.
40. Pastor John Herfurth, telephone interview with author, June 3, 2010.
41. Ibid.
42. Amanda Hoover, telephone interview with author, June 3, 2010.
43. Ibid.
44. Ibid.
45. As of 2001, the CRHP Parish Census reported statistics were as follows: 741 parishes/congregations; 2 countries (United States and Italy); 67 dioceses/areas; and 28 state parishes/congregations. CRHP is most active in the Midwest, with 301 weekends in Ohio, 138 in Illinois, and 114 in Indiana (http://www.stjudefw.org/crhpparishcensus.html#Diocese).

Epilogue

1. See *The Purpose of the Movement* (Dallas: National Cursillo Center, 1974); *The Fundamental Ideas of the Cursillo Movement* (Dallas: National Cursillo Center, 1972); and Juan Capó Bosch, *Lower Your Nets* (Dallas: National Cursillo Center, 1975) more detailed information on the pre-Cursillo and discerning process.
2. Indeed, the majority of the interviews conducted for this book were highly pleasurable. Cursillistas were eager to share their stories of faith with me and were always open to my questions, at times even wanting my analysis of what they were telling me. On average, the interviews lasted one and a half to two hours.
3. As I have already noted, I have thought a lot about my undercover identity and do think it was the right thing to do. There were times during the course where I thought about sharing with my St. Catherine of Siena tablemates that I was writing about Cursillos, but I firmly believe that if I had divulged my identity this would have reduced their willingness and ability to share. Like most of the women at my table, I am a middle-class non-Hispanic white woman; a daughter, wife, mother, Christian, and a seeker. Focusing on what connected us was more important in the end than singling myself out as a scholar. I made my Cursillo weekend out of a scholarly interest as well as a personal one. I was looking for spiritual nourishment as much as I was seeking to understand more deeply the weekend dynamics. I came away from the course with a deep respect for those who organize and run the weekend as well as admiration for the women who make the weekend and expose themselves emotionally. I also came away from the course with some questions and critiques. I was uncomfortable with the prolife message as well as images of

fetuses during the opening chapel time as well as in some of the rollos. When I shared this with my Mallorquín cursillista interlocutors, they were shocked and said that this would never happen in Mallorca and that "politics" should not intervene in the Cursillo weekend.

4. As we saw in chapter 5, leaders such as Neal have encouraged sponsors to help out with childcare. One of the reasons why CRHP has been so successful is because it is shorter—forty-eight hours instead of seventy-two—and individuals go home for the evening so parents can be with their children. While CRHP is not considered to be an in-covenant Fourth-Day movement, it has been successful in attracting younger men and women of childbearing years to its retreats because it is more flexible with its time commitments. See chapter 7 for a more in-depth discussion of CRHP and its outreach.

5. See http://www.vatican.va/holy_father/paul_vi/encyclicals/documents.

6. Thus, while I enjoyed my weekend experience and came away from my Cursillo with an even greater appreciation for my husband and children, and for God's many graces in my life and in my family's, there were parts of the weekend like, the prolife rhetorical moments, that were difficult for me to experience and clouded my enjoyment of the weekend. What the contemporary U.S. prolife movement must address is the lack of education and access to birth control for many women. Similarly, contemporary U.S. abstinence-only movements may have good intentions, but they fail young women and men in their refusal to educate them and to prepare them fully. As Mark Regnerus and others have shown, "red states" have higher rates of out-of-wedlock pregnancy, divorce, and domestic violence. Regnerus, *Forbidden Fruit: Sex and the Lives of American Teenagers* (Oxford: Oxford University Press, 2001). The Roman Catholic Church, which has steadfastly refused to legitimate the use of birth control other than "natural family planning," must also reassess its stance. Theologies and policies that prohibit or make difficult the knowledge and purchase of birth control medicine (pills, patch, etc.) can be viewed as irresponsible and complicit in the number of unwanted pregnancies. Moreover, it is women who are blamed in the event of an unwanted pregnancy and are privately and increasingly publicly vilified if and when they consider an abortion. Moreover, sexual violence in the form of incest, abuse, and rape are legitimated by the theological discourse that the pregnancy is part of "God's plan"—that there is some divine reason why the fetus is in existence.

7. Thomas A. Tweed, *Crossing and Dwelling: A Theory of Religion* (Cambridge: Harvard University Press, 2010).

Index

Action: and CdC, 3, 87; and U.S. Cursillo movement, 71; and Protestant Cursillos, 90, 100; and Via de Cristo, 111, 112; and Fourth-Day movements, 128; and Cursillo weekends, 134, 139, 140, 142; and Kairos Prison Ministry International, 198; and Teens Encounter Christ, 198; and Kairos Prison Ministry Inside Weekend, 202, 224
Adoration, Community, Theology, Service (ACTS), 298 (n. 11)
African Missionary Order, 201
Agape, 102, 132–33, 143–44, 187, 203, 205, 208–9, 214, 220–23, 284 (n. 27)
Agape letters, 199, 220–21
Aglow International, 202, 203, 295 (n. 8), 296 (n. 9)
Aguiló Forteza, Mercedes, 22, 23
Albrecht, Fidelis, 57
Alcoholics Anonymous (AA), 161–62, 164
Alcuin, William ("Bill"), 73
Aldrete, Enrique, 151, 287 (n. 71)
Aldrete, Rosita, 12, 150–51, 276 (n. 1)
Álvarez Lara, Rafael, 58, 270 (n. 7)
American Catholicism: and U.S. Cursillo movement, 1, 2, 7, 18; and social movements, 3, 259 (n. 4); historiography of, 10–11, 14; Mexican-descent Catholics, 12, 14, 15–16, 18; ecumenicism of, 17–18, 75, 76, 86; renewals of, 18; and laity, 86–87; and Teens Encounter Christ, 168; as parish-based, 253
American religious history: assumptions of, 11–12, 15, 17, 18, 259–60 (n. 5), 261 (n. 21); and ethnography, 13–15; and regionalism, 18; and Midwest, 79; and narratives of Cursillo weekends, 152; and food theology and praxis, 206, 209, 210; and pluralism, 226–27; international influences on, 250, 251
Amistad (friendship): and Eduardo Bonnín, 8, 17, 21, 41, 44, 59, 77, 78, 273 (n. 69); and ecumenicism, 77, 78; and Fourth Day, 86
Androver, Francisco, 37
Archdiocesan Cursillo Center, Chicago, Illinois, 71
Armed services: and spread of CdC, 61, 62, 64–65, 67, 96, 106, 270 (n. 12), 270–71 (n. 40); and Tres Dias, 96, 270 (n. 12), 281 (n. 116)
Arredondo, Miguel, 157, 287 (n. 71)
Arrom, Bartolomé ("Tomeu"), 46, 269 (n. 6)
Australia, 104, 106, 107, 201
Austria, 59
Awakening, 195, 235, 236, 240
Azpiazu, José Joaquín, 28

Badillo, David, 282 (n. 1)
Barrios, Frank, 287 (n. 71)
Bednarowski, Mary Farrell, 151
Believers Together Center, Christ the King parish church, Moline, Illinois, 12–13, 260 (n. 6), 260–61 (n. 14), 282 (n. 5)
Bender, Courtney, 214
Better World Movement (BWM), 170, 181, 288 (nn. 1, 4)
Biblioni, Guillermo, 59, 154, 263 (n. 33), 270 (n. 8), 271 (n. 18), 285 (n. 52)
Birth control, 247, 301 (n. 6)
Blackwell, John, 156

303

"Blooming where we are planted," 2, 3, 17, 45, 124, 126, 142, 153
Bloy, Leon, 37
Bohl, Don, 281 (n. 116)
Bohonek, Chad, 190
Bonnín Aguiló, Amalia, 22
Bonnín Aguiló, Eduardo: founding of CdC, 1–2, 4, 8, 20–21, 24, 26, 33, 36–40, 47–48, 54–55, 58, 59, 68, 84–85, 91, 110, 260 (n. 8), 267 (n. 93), 268 (n. 1), 269 (n. 2), 270 (nn. 8, 10), 279 (n. 75), 282–83 (n. 6); and Catholic Action, 1–2, 26–27, 35, 36, 42, 44, 45, 47, 59, 265–66 (n. 81); Catholicism of, 2, 8, 20, 21, 22, 23, 24–25, 36, 41–42, 81; and lay focus of CdC, 2, 8, 36, 37, 38, 40, 41, 42, 43, 44–45, 48, 49, 54–55, 57, 59, 69–70, 72–74, 76, 80, 81, 273 (n. 69); "reaching the faraway" concept, 2, 37, 44, 48, 107, 128, 131, 205, 214, 230; and tricolored origami birds, 4, 21; Mallorquín cursillistas' memories of, 6, 20–21; marginalization of, 7–8; and ecumenicism, 8, 76–77, 78, 79, 98; legacy of, 8, 98; methods established by, 9, 44–45, 46, 70, 83, 87, 107, 111, 112, 114, 116, 128, 134, 148, 154, 198, 221, 234, 249, 250, 252, 279 (n. 75), 280 (n. 105), 285–86 (n. 52), 298 (n. 1); and search for meaning and connectedness, 16–17, 24; personality of, 20, 21, 39, 47, 81–82, 88, 250; family background of, 22–23; education of, 23–25; military service of, 25–26, 36–37, 46; and pilgrimage, 35, 40; as spiritual leader, 43, 46–47, 91–92, 169, 277 (n. 14); ostracization of, 48–49, 51–53, 56, 59; and Hervás, 50, 51; and "Cursillos clandestinos," 52–53, 56; and structure of CdC, 59; and U.S. Cursillo movement, 60, 68, 80–83, 271 (n. 18); writings on CdC, 62, 77, 270 (nn. 10, 11), 282–83 (n. 6); travel of, 80, 81, 82–83, 91, 251, 274 (n. 92), 275 (nn. 94, 96), 276 (nn. 98, 99); health problems of, 82, 275 (n. 97); and standardization, 85, 86; and Protestant Cursillos, 88–91, 97–98, 276 (n. 6); and Fourth-Day movements, 90, 112, 204–5
Bonnín Aguiló, Elvira, 22
Bonnín Aguiló, Fernando, 22
Bonnín Aguiló, Jordi, 22
Bonnín Aguiló, Josefa, 22
Bonnín Aguiló, Luisa, 22
Bonnín Aguiló, María, 22
Bonnín Aguiló, Mercedes, 22
Bonnín Aguiló, Pilar, 22
Bonnín Piña, Fernando, 22, 23
Bourdieu, Pierre, 151
Brazil, 106
Brown, Jim, 169, 193, 194, 288 (n. 5), 291 (n. 52)
Bruckman, John, 161
Brusco, Elizabeth, 156
Burke, Carol, 95
Burke, George, 95
Bush, George W., 295 (n. 8)

Camp, Jeremy, 191
Canada, 201
Capó Bosch, Juan: and spread of CdC, 49, 60–61, 267 (n. 93), 270 (n. 10), 271 (n. 18); writings on CdC, 58, 59, 270 (n. 10); and gender, 154, 285 (n. 52); and Hervás, 270 (n. 8)
Caronti, Marie, 68, 71
Caronti, Ron, 68, 71, 72, 159
Carroll, Colleen, 288 (n. 3)
Casting Crowns, 191
Cathedral of Santa Maria ("la Seu"), Palma de Mallorca, 24, 53, 262 (n. 9)
Cathedral of Santiago de Compostela, Galicia, 29, 263 (n. 33)
Catholic Action (CA): and Eduardo Bonnín, 1–2, 26–27, 35, 36, 42, 44, 45, 47, 59, 265–66 (n. 81); and pilgrimages, 2, 26, 29–30, 32, 33, 34–35,

36, 41, 45, 263 (n. 33); establishment of, 26–27; and Spanish Falangism, 28, 29, 44; Cursillos sponsored by, 30, 32–33, 34, 35, 36–37, 39, 42, 44, 47, 48, 49, 51, 59, 167, 264 (n. 46); Pilgrim Scouts, 30, 33; and Hervás, 50; and Enciso, 52, 58, 268 (n. 120)

Catholic Action for Youths, 26, 33, 50

Catholic Charismatic Renewal Movement (CCR), 274 (n. 91)

Catholic clergy: involvement in CdC, 9, 14, 36, 48, 49, 50, 51, 52, 55, 57, 58–59, 65, 268 (n. 105), 270 (n. 10); giving rollos, 9, 36, 43, 46, 48, 130, 268 (n. 105), 283 (n. 6); and Spanish Catholicism, 35; and Eduardo Bonnín, 36, 72; and Catholic Action Cursillos, 48; suspicions of CdC, 49, 52, 58, 74; and U.S. Cursillo movement, 69, 70–74, 122; and Tres Dias, 97; and Protestant Cursillos, 108; women religious cooperating with, 177, 290–91 (n. 38)

Catholic Cursillos: as Fourth-Day movement, 9; emphasis on Catholic identity, 9–10, 282 (n. 1); history of, 13, 19, 58; churches as setting of, 16; cross-giving in, 33, 93, 264 (n. 46); in U.S., 57, 59–67, 68, 69, 70–77, 84, 90, 252, 253, 272 (nn. 43, 48); and gender, 57, 234, 243, 269 (n. 3); and armed services, 59–60, 270 (n. 12); Protestants making, 77, 78–79, 84, 86, 88–89, 90, 93–94, 95, 99, 249, 274 (nn. 86, 87), 282 (n. 5); nonecumenical stance of, 90, 93, 94, 97, 104, 108–9, 128, 252; demographics of, 120; and laity, 132, 245; and Teens Encounter Christ, 188; and Kairos Prison Ministry Inside Weekend, 224; and transcendence of denominational boundaries, 267 (n. 92)

Catholicism: and Catholic identity, 3, 29, 299 (n. 12); Fourth-Day movements' effect on, 5; as feminized, 31, 32; Protestantism's relationship with, 69, 99–100, 104; and ecumenicism, 86, 87; and parish life, 230–31, 253, 299 (n. 12); missing history of, 260 (n. 5); masculinization of, 264 (n. 42). *See also* American Catholicism; Spanish Catholicism

Catholic triumphalism, 8, 10, 24, 27, 29, 76, 77, 80, 249

Chavez, Gilbert E., 71–72, 155, 286 (nn. 58, 59)

China, 106

Christian Experience Weekend (CEW), 247, 298 (n. 11)

Christian megachurches, 125, 252

Christian Weigh-Down diet, 209

Christ Renews His Parish (CRHP): and Kairos Prison Ministry Inside Weekend, 212, 224; as spinoff of Fourth-Day movements, 225, 227–28, 234, 242, 298 (n. 1); and ecumenicism, 228, 235, 243; as parish-based, 228–35, 243, 252, 253; manual for, 229, 230, 231, 235; and gender, 233–34, 235, 243; popularity of, 243, 300 (n. 45); spread of, 247, 299 (n. 21), 301 (n. 4)

Chrysalis, 195

Church hierarchy: and popular and official piety, 7; control over laity, 40, 121, 281 (n. 108); and Catholic Action, 41; and Eduardo Bonnín, 48, 53, 76; and Hervás, 49, 50; and U.S. Cursillo movement, 68, 72, 94

Cleary, Edward, 274 (n. 91)

Clergy/laity cooperation: and Fourth-Day movements, 87, 122–24, 235; and Christ Renews His Parish, 235; and Great Banquet, 237; and Cursillo weekends, 249, 250, 283 (n. 6)

Clergy/laity power struggles: and popular and official piety, 7–8;

and Eduardo Bonnín, 8, 41–42; and Torres, 49; and Hervás, 51; and U.S. Cursillo movement, 72, 73, 74–75; and Leader's School, 72–73; and Vatican II Council, 74–75
Cold War, 63
Colombia, 59, 251
Communism, 62, 63
Concetta, Sister Mary. *See* Gereke, Dorothy Neibauer
Confederación Española de Derechas Autónomas (Spanish Confederation of the Autonomous Right, CEDA), 27, 262 (n. 20)
Confraternity of Christian Doctrine (CCD), 185
Congar, Yves, 40–41
Conger, George, 95
Congreso de la Juventud Masculina de Acción Católica (National Congress of Young Men's Catholic Action), 30
Connor, John, 123, 159, 160
Conversion, 35, 135
Corrigan, John, 152
Costa Rica, 201
Credo, 298 (n. 1)
Crowder B., David, 191
Cummings, Kathleen Sprows, 290–91 (n. 38)
Cuneo, Michael W., 288 (n. 3)
Cursillistas: connection to faith community, 1, 2, 9, 10–11, 19, 86, 128, 133, 142, 145, 148, 151, 153, 162–63, 284 (n. 24); as active members of church, 1, 9, 17, 73, 74, 100, 101, 117, 123; renewal experienced by, 2, 10–11, 15, 18–19, 83, 127, 128, 147–48; and deepening of spiritual life, 2–3, 4, 5, 9, 10, 86, 100, 128; Mallorquín cursillistas, 4, 13, 16; as ambassadors of spirituality, 5; cultural and historical significance of stories, 6–7; and candidates for weekend retreats, 7, 9, 51, 85, 117, 132, 133–34, 245, 269 (n. 3), 276 (n. 1); and sponsorship period, 7, 85, 117, 118, 133–34, 245; as spiritual mentors, 7, 245, 246; rollos given by, 9, 43, 46, 47, 130, 260 (n. 9), 266 (n. 88), 283 (n. 6); Leader's Schools for, 9, 51, 61, 70, 72–73, 76, 93, 260 (n. 9); and palanca letters, 9, 133, 143–44, 157, 192; ethnographic interviews with, 12, 246, 251, 300 (n. 2); sense of purpose and meaning, 15, 85–86, 117, 276 (n. 1); religious involvement of, 16; and experiential theology, 88, 125, 128, 230; and Protestant Cursillos, 94; and Cursillo weekends, 127, 132, 146–53, 247, 285 (n. 33); religious experience of, 266 (n. 88). *See also* Reunions of cursillistas

Cursillo de Cristiandad (CdC): founding in Mallorca, 1–2, 3, 8, 9, 21–22, 24, 26, 58, 269 (nn. 4, 6); Eduardo Bonnín's founding of, 1–2, 4, 8, 20–21, 24, 26, 33, 36–40, 47–48, 54–55, 58, 59, 68, 84–85, 91, 110, 260 (n. 8), 267 (n. 93), 268 (n. 1), 269 (n. 2), 270 (nn. 8, 10), 279 (n. 75), 282–83 (n. 6); popularity of, 2, 48, 50; and transforming environment, 3, 17, 26, 27, 36, 37, 39, 40, 41, 43, 45, 46, 50, 51, 76, 114, 116, 252; cultural importance of, 5, 8; spread of, 5, 58–67, 270 (n. 12); history of, 6, 8, 11, 13, 15, 53, 58, 83, 91, 250, 269 (n. 2); and weekend retreats, 7; and renewal of Christian spirituality, 8, 17, 19, 21, 39, 40, 42–43, 44, 51, 54; naming of, 8, 44, 50, 56, 259 (n. 2); Hervás as founder, 8, 56, 58, 68, 73, 110, 260 (n. 8), 267 (n. 93), 269 (n. 2), 270 (nn. 8, 11), 279 (n. 75), 282–83 (n. 6); recent, less authentic branches of, 9; Cala Figuera weekend, 10, 36, 37–39, 44, 45, 49, 50, 51, 60, 85, 91, 251, 267 (n. 93), 268 (n. 1), 268–69 (n. 2), 277 (n. 13); and language of violence, 21, 27, 28, 39, 46, 63; psychological discovery in, 37; group dynamics of, 39; goal of, 40; role of clergy in, 41–42, 49, 51, 57, 58–59, 60; nine major thrusts of, 42; San Honorato weekend, 43, 45, 48, 257 (n. 93), 268 (n. 2); impact of fascism on, 44–45, 46, 54, 63, 69; vertebration as purpose of, 45, 51, 133; cross-giving in, 48; Enciso's criticisms of, 52; and "Cursillos clandestinos," 52–53, 56, 58; worldwide expansion of, 56; lack of cohesiveness of, 58, 59; as nonecumenical, 92; and religious experience, 266 (n. 88). *See also* Lay focus of CdC

Cursillo Movement USA, 68

Cursillos de Adelantados de Peregrinos (Cursillos for Advanced Pilgrims), 33–34

Cursillos de Jefes de Peregrinos (Cursillos for Pilgrim Leaders), 2, 20, 21–22, 33, 35, 36, 39, 45, 47, 56

Cursillos of Conquest, 8, 45, 49, 51, 52

Cursillo weekends: candidates for, 7, 9, 51, 85, 117, 132, 133–34, 245, 269 (n. 3), 276 (n. 1); dynamics of, 126; and universal Christian spirituality, 127, 128; cursillistas' experience of, 127, 132, 146–53, 247, 285 (n. 33); core principles of, 128; and emotionality, 129, 131–32, 137, 139, 141, 147, 149–50, 152, 154, 156–61, 248; and sponsorship, 129, 133–34, 141; and rollos, 130, 131, 135, 136–43, 247, 249, 283 (n. 6), 284 (nn. 20, 24); and prayer, 130, 136, 142, 149–50, 248; structure of, 130, 248; and enjoyment, 130–31, 145; and meditations, 131, 135, 136, 139, 141–42; and personal reflection, 131, 141; and laity, 132, 133, 283 (n. 6); and women, 132, 134, 153, 154, 155, 156, 158, 285 (n. 51), 286 (n. 54), 296–97 (n. 24); and men, 132, 134, 153–62, 286 (n. 59), 297 (n. 24); and team leaders, 132, 136, 142–43, 248; preparations for, 132–34, 283 (n. 6); schedule of events, 134–44; Friday events, 136–39; Saturday events, 139–41; and evangelization, 141–42; Sunday events, 141–43; and reunions of cursillistas, 143, 145, 148, 160, 162–65, 287–88 (n. 94); and palanca, 143–44, 157, 248, 284 (n. 28); and Fourth Day, 144–53, 247; writings on, 282–83 (n. 6). *See also* Cursillistas

Davis, Jeff, 129–30
Davis, Sue, 113, 119, 127, 129–31
"De Colores," 2, 4, 48, 115, 119, 148
Demetrius, Sister, 201
Denominationalism: and cursillistas' Christian universalism, 3, 10, 88, 98, 267 (n. 92); interdenominationalism, 87, 92, 99, 201, 276 (n. 2)
Detroit Sisters of Mercy, 166, 170, 172–73, 177, 180, 186, 194, 291 (n. 38), 292–93 (n. 85)
Diocesan Secretariat of Cursillos, 49, 51
Diocese of Peoria, Illinois: ecumenicism of, 17–18, 77, 78, 79, 84, 99, 100–101, 103, 108, 249; and Cursillo weekends, 67, 78, 79, 93, 129, 246, 274 (n. 87); and Teens Encounter Christ, 196
Disciple Generation, 259 (n. 3)
Dragastin, Sigmund, 285 (n. 33)
Dunham, Jerry, 99
Dunham, Maxie, 99, 102, 237, 238
Duran, Alphonsus, 47

Ebel, Jonathan, 264 (n. 42)
Ecumenicism: and language of emotion and healing, 3; and Eduardo Bonnín, 8, 76–77, 78, 79, 98; and denominational tensions, 10; of

American Catholicism, 17–18, 75, 76, 86; and Protestant Cursillos, 17–18, 75–80, 86, 87, 89–91, 97, 100, 237; and lay focus of CdC, 60, 79; and U.S. Cursillo movement, 67, 75–80, 252, 274 (nn. 86, 87); nonecumenicism of U.S. National Secretariat, 75–80; and intercommunion, 76, 77, 87, 88, 90, 97, 100, 124, 188, 237, 248, 249, 274 (n. 86); and Fourth-Day movements, 86–88, 124, 126; and Walk to Emmaus, 90, 99, 104, 108, 113, 237, 252; and Tres Dias, 97–98, 108, 113, 117, 126, 252, 253; and Via de Cristo, 108, 109, 110, 113, 252, 279 (n. 63); and Great Banquet, 235, 236, 238, 243
Edward, Jonathan, 266 (n. 82)
Edwards, Bob, 226, 228–32, 234, 242–43, 298 (n. 2)
Eisenhower, Dwight, 62
Emotionality: and men experiencing CdC, 1, 21, 39; ecumenical language of, 3; and focus on heart, 3–4; and U.S. Cursillo movement, 61, 68; and Protestant Cursillos, 90, 123; and Cursillo weekends, 129, 131–32, 137, 139, 141, 147, 149–50, 152, 154, 156–61, 248; and Kairos Prison Ministry Inside Weekend, 160–61, 221, 225; and Teens Encounter Christ, 189, 190; and screening of candidates, 276 (n. 1)
Enciso Viana, Jesús, 52–53, 56, 58, 59, 268 (n. 120), 270 (n. 7)
Engroff, Greg, 84, 90–91, 104–5, 236, 278 (n. 53)
Episcopal Church USA, 117–18
Episcopal Cursillo Leaders Workshop (ECLW), 115
Essert, Bob, 95
Essert, Mary, 95
Estarellas de Nadal, Guillermo, 21, 36, 37, 41–42, 46, 48, 49, 58

Estonia, 106, 107
Ethnography: methodology of, 10–14, 260 (n. 11); and American religious history, 13–15
Evangelical Lutheran Church of America, 111, 279 (n. 73)
Evangelical youth: National Evangelization Teams, 196, 293 (n. 94); as Disciple Generation, 259 (n. 3)
Evangelization: Eduardo Bonnín's concept of "reaching the faraway," 2, 37, 44, 48, 107, 128, 131, 205, 214, 230; and Catholic Action, 35; and Pius XI, 40; and John XXIII, 41; and CdC, 42, 43, 44, 46–47, 50, 59, 63; and U.S. Cursillo movement, 62, 69, 74; and Tres Dias, 87, 117; and Protestantism, 88, 98–99, 252–53; and Protestant Cursillos, 92; and National Episcopal Cursillo, 113, 119, 121; and Via de Cristo, 117; and Walk to Emmaus, 117; and Cursillo weekends, 141–42; and Teens Encounter Christ, 188; and Kairos Prison Ministry Inside Weekend, 202
Exercise in Christian Living, 181, 288 (n. 4)

Facebook, 105
Falange Española Tradicionalista (Traditionalist Spanish Falange, FET), 28–29, 31, 40, 44
Fedewa, Matt: and Teens Encounter Christ, 165, 166, 167, 168–72, 174–88, 193–97, 288 (nn. 1, 5), 290 (n. 35), 294 (n. 99); Catholicism of, 168, 170, 171, 177–78, 184–85; and inner-city ministry, 194
Fernández, Gabriel, 60–62, 64, 270–71 (n. 18)
Ferragut, José, 26, 37, 41, 58
Finland, 113
Fitzgerald, William J., 172, 179–80
Fonseca, Juan, 66

Ford, Wayne, 110
Forteza, Francisco, 39, 58, 62–63, 69–70, 73, 283 (n. 6)
Fourth Day: cursillistas as spiritual mentors, 7, 245, 246; and cursillistas' sense of purpose and meaning, 15, 85–86, 117, 276 (n. 1); settings of, 16; history of, 19, 41; living the Fourth Day, 45, 126, 128, 187, 250; and sponsorship, 85; and Walk to Emmaus, 104; and National Episcopal Cursillo, 118–19; and Cursillo weekends, 144–53, 247
Fourth-Day movements: and experience of religion, 4, 251; and Spanish terminology, 9; history of, 13–14, 86–88, 92; spread of, 83; and Eduardo Bonnín, 90, 112, 204–5; and Protestant clergy, 122; and laity, 132; and Cursillo weekends, 134, 243; and food, 210, 240, 296–97 (n. 24); spinoffs of, 225, 226–28, 229, 234, 242, 243, 251, 298 (n. 1); annual leader gatherings, 236. *See also* Catholic Cursillos; Kairos Prison Ministry International; National Episcopal Cursillo; Protestant Cursillos; Tres Dias; Walk to Emmaus
France, 59
Franco, Francisco, 28, 29, 34, 49, 263 (n. 25)
Franks, Bob, 84, 88, 89, 98, 163
Franks, Rhoda, 84, 88, 89, 98, 163
Fromm, Erich, 37
"Frozen chosen," 116, 117, 280 (n. 97)
Fuller, Robert S., 281 (n. 108)
Fundación Eduardo Bonnín Aguiló (FEBA), 21, 80–81, 260 (n. 8), 270 (nn. 10, 11)

Gender: and Catholic Action, 1, 2, 33; masculinist language, 8, 16, 34, 44, 53, 61, 62–63, 69, 153–54; and husbands making their weekend before wives, 8, 72, 130, 133, 154–55, 233–34, 249, 269 (n. 3), 282 (n. 4), 286 (n. 52); masculine Christianity, 29, 32, 34, 264 (n. 42); masculinist overtones of pilgrimage, 31, 32; and Catholic Cursillos, 57, 234, 243, 269 (n. 3); and U.S. Cursillo movement, 58, 61, 269 (n. 3), 282 (n. 4); and Protestant Cursillos, 86, 243; and coed weekends, 114, 120–21, 279 (nn. 76, 80); Cursillo weekends transcending, 127, 160–61; Cursillo weekends invoking, 138; and separate weekends, 158, 285–86 (n. 52); and Teens Encounter Christ, 173; and Kairos Prison Ministry Inside Weekend, 210–11, 215, 218–19; and Christ Renews His Parish, 233–34, 235, 243. *See also* Men; Women
Gereke, Dorothy Neibauer: and Teens Encounter Christ, 165, 166–68, 170–88, 193–95, 197, 275 (n. 93), 288 (n. 1), 289 (n. 19), 290 (n. 35), 294 (n. 99); Catholicism of, 167, 168, 170, 184–85, 288 (n. 4), 292–93 (n. 85); as administrator of Lila Post Montgomery Hospital, 170, 171, 175, 176, 180, 289 (n. 19); and Cursillo weekends, 181
Gereke, Paul, 193–94
Germany, 59, 96, 124
Ghana, 104
Giacosta, Charles, 103, 108
Gielda, Steve, 112–13, 164, 236
Gladwell, Malcolm, 106
God's Love We Deliver, 214
González, Catalina, 150, 151
González, Julio A. Gonzalo, 43, 269 (n. 2)
González, Louie, 148, 151, 157, 287 (n. 71)
Góngalcz, Martha, 148
González, Ray, 287 (n. 71)

González Duqué, Cristina, 21, 22, 23, 80-82, 274 (n. 92), 275 (nn. 94, 97), 277 (n. 13)
Goodfellow, John J., Jr., 272 (n. 43)
Goodfellow Air Force Field, San Angelo, Texas, 67, 272 (n. 43)
Grace: sanctifying grace, 52; and U.S. Cursillo movement, 60; and Protestants making Catholic Cursillos, 89; and Walk to Emmaus, 102-3; and Cursillo weekends, 135, 137-38, 141, 142, 162
Granados, Catalina ("Cati"), 23, 277 (n. 14)
Great Awakenings, 3, 259 (n. 3), 266 (n. 82)
Great Banquet: and food, 206, 239; and volunteers for Kairos Prison Ministry Inside Weekend, 212; as spinoff of Fourth-Day movements, 225, 227-28, 242, 298 (n. 1); and ecumenicism, 235, 236, 238, 243; and clergy/laity cooperation, 237; structure of, 239, 253; and reunion meetings, 241-42
Green, Joseph, 68, 69, 70-71
Griffith, Marie, 209
Guadiana, Jesse, 287 (n. 71)
Gustafson, Rita, 164-65

Hall, David, 260 (n. 12)
Happening, 119
Harvey, Paul, 260 (n. 5)
Henning, Ellie, 276 (n. 6)
Henseler, Tom, 17, 77, 79, 100-101, 106, 274 (n. 88)
Herfurth, John, 226, 240-42
Hernandez, Antonio, 66
Hernández, Elva, 146-47, 149
Hernández, Salvador Escribiano, 38-39
Herrera, José, 127, 147, 287 (n. 71)
Hervás, Juan: naming of CdC, 8, 44, 50, 56, 259 (n. 2); credit for founding of CdC, 8, 56, 58, 68, 73, 110, 260 (n. 8), 267 (n. 93), 269 (n. 2), 270 (nn. 8, 11), 279 (n. 75), 282-83 (n. 6); and lay focus of CdC, 49, 50, 51; and Catholic Action, 50; and legitimacy of CdC, 50-51; changes to CdC, 51-52, 53, 55, 56, 58, 59, 69, 270 (n. 10); and ultreyas, 73; writings of, 84-85, 282-83 (n. 6); and "Authentic Cursillo Method," 109
Hodel, Kate, 231-33, 235
Holy Spirit: cursillistas connecting with, 3, 266 (n. 88); and CdC, 36, 37, 43, 45, 49; cursillistas motivated by, 41, 49, 125; and U.S. Cursillo movement, 64; and Walk to Emmaus, 104, 105-6; and Via de Cristo, 110, 113
Hong Kong, 101, 106, 107
Hoover, Amanda, 241, 242
Horberg, Kurt, 125
Hughes, Gerald, 75-76, 78, 79, 97, 101, 103-4, 108-9

InnerChange Freedom Initiative (IFI), 295 (n. 8)
International Catholic Organizations of the Pontifical Council for the Laity, 67
Internet: and Walk to Emmaus, 105, 107
Islam: and Catholic triumphalism, 24, 29
Italy, 251

Jack, Duane: and Cursillo weekends, 7, 131, 133-34, 136, 140, 158-59, 246, 248-50, 261 (n. 14), 283 (n. 9)
Jacoby, John, 228, 229, 230-31, 242-43
James the Greater, Saint, 29, 32, 263 (nn. 33, 40)
Jaramillo, Peter M., 272 (n. 48), 273 (n. 69)
Jars of Clay, 191
Jesus Christ: cursillistas as hands and feet of, 2, 91, 99, 104-5, 116, 254;

mystical Christ, 3, 45, 46, 47; and pilgrimage to Santiago de Compostela, 31, 32, 34, 35; and CdC, 37, 38, 39, 40, 42–43, 45, 46, 52; and friendship, 39–40; laity as part of body of, 41; historical versus living Christ, 47, 54, 76, 77; renewing relationship with, 71, 89, 90, 91, 92, 119, 123, 130, 131, 136, 139, 146, 147, 149, 151, 153, 232, 240–41, 242, 248; Paschal Mystery of, 168, 171, 178, 179, 187, 194, 196; and Teens Encounter Christ, 174, 290 (n. 32)

John Paul II (pope), 10

Johnson, Jeff, 122–23

Johnson, Tom, 201

John XXIII (pope), 41, 74

Joyce, Timothy, 75

Judaism, 129–30

Julió, Juan, 43

Juntas de Ofensiva Nacional-Sindicalista (Boards of the National-Syndicalist Offensive, JONS), 29

Juventud Española de Acción Católica (Spanish Youth Catholic Action, JEAC), 30

Kairos (renewal weekend), 195–96, 197, 253, 294 (n. 98), 298 (n. 11), 299 (n. 21)

Kairos Prison Ministry Inside Weekend (KI): inmates' experiences of, 7, 202, 209–10, 215, 222–24; ethnography of, 13–14, 198, 246; and emotionality, 160–61, 221, 225; and cookies, 199, 200, 210, 213–15; and food, 199, 200–201, 202, 205–11, 212, 296 (n. 15); and agape letters, 199, 220–21; clothing guidelines for volunteers, 200; volunteers for, 200–201, 202, 203, 204, 205–9, 211, 212, 213–16, 217, 219, 220–22, 224, 225, 295 (n. 8); and CdC method, 201–2; and agape, 203, 205, 208, 209, 214, 220–23, 284 (n. 27); and reading, 206, 207; "Freedom Guide," 206–7, 218, 219; and rollos, 207, 216, 218, 219–20, 297 (n. 40); and family language, 208, 217, 220; Kairos Angels, 212–13, 221; manual of, 215, 216, 219, 225; structure of, 215–20, 279 (n. 74); cross ceremony, 216, 217; rice paper ritual, 217–18; and reunion meetings, 223, 224–25

Kairos Prison Ministry International (KPMI): as Fourth-Day movement, 9, 198; and Catholic Cursillo ecumenicism, 89; and Cursillo weekends, 128; and laity, 132; as interdenominational, 201, 276 (n. 2); "The Prison Story," 204–5; and evangelical Protestantism, 253; cross-giving in, 264 (n. 46)

Kairos Prison Ministry Outside Weekend (KO), 201, 279 (n. 74)

Knoblett-Aman, Melissa, 232

Koinonia, 298–99 (n. 11)

Lackland Air Force Base, San Antonio, Texas, 62, 64

Laity: being church, 2, 10, 41, 42, 60, 66, 127, 138, 147, 148, 223; and popular and official piety, 7; Eduardo Bonnín's help in spiritual development, 20; and Catholic Action's Cursillos, 33, 48; Vatican II theology of, 40, 41, 74–75, 100, 121, 173, 181, 188, 280 (n. 107); pre–Vatican II discussions about, 40, 265 (n. 75); and Paul VI, 41; and American Catholicism, 86–87; and Protestantism, 86–87, 121, 280 (n. 107); and American Christian retailing, 105; and Cursillo weekends, 132, 133, 283 (n. 6); and food theology and praxis, 206, 209. *See also* Clergy/laity cooperation; Clergy/laity power struggles

Lampstand Ministries, 236–37, 240

Latvia, 113

Lay focus of CdC: and Eduardo Bonnín, 2, 8, 36, 37, 38, 40, 41, 42, 43, 44–45, 48, 49, 54–55, 57, 59, 69–70, 72–74, 76, 80, 81, 273 (n. 69); and Cursillo weekends, 4, 132; scholarship on, 5, 259 (n. 4); and popular and official piety, 7; and clergy's role, 9, 48, 50, 59, 65, 73, 74, 268 (n. 105); and U.S. Cursillo movement, 10, 14, 60, 65, 69–72, 73, 80, 273 (n. 69); and impact on environment, 43, 45, 46, 50, 51, 76; and Hervás, 49, 50, 51; and Enciso, 52; and empowerment, 53, 66, 74, 80, 86; and ecumenicism, 60, 79; and Protestant Cursillos, 60, 86, 87, 96, 245

Leclerc, Jacques, 37
Legionnaires of Mary, 65
Lemcke, Jerry, 145
Leo XIII (pope), 27
Lila Post Hospital Lodge, 171, 175, 176, 177, 180–81, 186, 289 (nn. 15, 19)
Lila Post Montgomery Hospital, 170, 171, 180, 289 (n. 19)
Litavich, Rob, 157–58
Lived religion, 11–12, 260 (n. 12)
Lluc monastery, Mallorca, 24, 26, 30, 38, 263 (n. 35)
Logos (renewal weekend), 294 (n. 98), 298 (n. 11)
Lucado, Max, 140
Lugo, Victor, 77–78, 88–89, 236
Lutheran Cursillo. *See* Via de Cristo
Lutheran Kogudus movement, 110
Lyphout, Josh, 188, 189, 190

Maier, Helmut, 94
Malaysia, 106, 107
Maldonado, Carlos Calatayud, 53–54, 56, 153
Mallorca: and founding of CdC, 1, 3, 5, 8, 9, 21–22, 24, 26, 58, 269 (nn. 4, 6); and Spanish Civil War, 21, 27, 28; terrain of, 22–23, 24, 262 (n. 6); Lluc monastery, 24, 26, 30, 38, 263 (n. 35); and pilgrimages, 30; awareness of Eduardo Bonnín, 91–92, 277 (n. 14)

Mann, Michael, 28, 262 (n. 20)
Marcoux, Marcene, 267 (n. 93), 272 (n. 43)
Maritain, Jacques, 37
Maritain, Raïsa, 37
Marriage: husbands making weekend before wives, 8, 72, 130, 133, 154–55, 233–34, 249, 269 (n. 3), 282 (n. 4); and Walk to Emmaus, 99, 101; and National Episcopal Cursillo, 119; and Christ Renews His Parish, 233, 234
Martínez, Oscar J., 63
Mary Concetta, Sister. *See* Gereke, Dorothy Neibauer
Masculine Christianity, 29
Maslow, Abraham, 37
Matovina, Timothy, 66
McDannell, Colleen, 105
McKinney, John, 6, 96–98, 106, 108, 124, 125, 236
McManigal, David, 93–95
Men: CdC geared toward, 1, 2, 16, 21, 37, 42–43, 46–47, 51, 53–54, 85, 154; and pilgrimage, 29, 31–35, 263 (n. 40); Cursillos of Catholic Action for, 33; and U.S. Cursillo movement, 57–58, 61, 63–64, 71–72; and Protestant Cursillos, 86; and Cursillo weekends, 132, 134, 153–62, 286 (n. 59), 297 (n. 24); and Teens Encounter Christ, 169, 173, 179, 185; and Kairos Prison Ministry Inside Weekend, 203, 204, 211; and Great Banquet, 241. *See also* Gender
Mendez, Enrique, 287 (n. 71)
MercyMe, 191
Mexico, 59, 251
Miller, Pat, 118

Miller, Tom, 160
Mir, Juan, 37, 41, 58
Miralles, José, 50
Morris, Danny, 99, 102, 103, 104, 108
Morris, Rosalie, 99
Mozambique, 104
Mullen, Nicole C., 191
Mullin, Randy, 276 (n. 6)
Murga, Tim, 190
Muzzarelli, Tanya, 121–22, 123, 164, 250, 298 (n. 1)
Mysticism, language of, 8

National Conference of Catholic Bishops, 67
National Cursillo Center, 67, 77, 85, 103–4, 108, 147–48, 272 (n. 48), 283 (n. 6)
National Cursillo Encounter, 205
National Episcopal Cursillo (NEC): as Fourth-Day movement, 9; as non-ecumenical, 87, 92, 113, 117, 119, 120, 128, 252; and Catholic Cursillo ecumenicism, 89, 92, 113, 114; history of, 92, 113–21; and coed weekends, 114, 120–21; cross-giving in, 114, 264 (n. 46); symbols of, 114–15; and English language, 115; and Spanish language, 115; organizational structure of, 118; demographics of, 120; and laity, 132; and childcare, 247, 301 (n. 4)
National Evangelization Teams (NET), 196, 293 (n. 94)
National Federation of Catholic Youth Ministry (NFCYM), 167
National Lutheran Secretariat (NLS), 108, 110, 111, 112, 279 (n. 75)
Nation of Islam (NOI), 218
Neal, Betsy, 117, 120
Neal, Thom, 112, 113–17, 118, 119–21, 236, 247, 280 (n. 97), 301 (n. 4)
Nebreda, Alfonse, 179, 185, 186
Neimeyer, Gerhardt, 283 (n. 6)

Nelson, Louis P., 297 (n. 35)
Nguyen, Justine, 195
Niebuhr, Reinhold, 284 (n. 15)
Northern Illinois Tres Dias community (NITD), 96, 122–23

O'Brien, Mary, 194
O'Keefe, Doris, 7, 133–34, 141, 155, 246, 249, 261 (n. 14), 282 (n. 2), 283 (n. 9), 296 (n. 24)
O'Keefe, Jerry, 141, 246
Oliver, Miguel, 269 (n. 6)
O'Regan, Billy, 196
Organismo Mundial de Cursillos de Cristiandad (World Organization of Cursillos in Christianity, OMCC), 49–50, 67
O'Rourke, Edward W., 17, 78–80, 100

Palanca, 102, 132–33, 143–44, 157, 248, 284 (n. 28)
Palanca letters, 9, 133, 143–44, 157, 192
Palomino, Augustín, 54–55, 57, 60, 62–65
Papua New Guinea, 113
Paul V (pope), 247
Paul VI (pope), 10, 41
Payne, Stanley G., 27, 29
Peña, Elaine, 260 (n. 11)
Pentecostalism, 252
Pérez, Victor, 106–8
Pérez Ramos, Antonio, 265 (n. 64)
Pew Forum, 99
Piety: and CdC, 3, 36, 38, 40, 44, 87; popular and official piety, 7–8; and Eduardo Bonnín's family, 23, 24; masculine Catholic piety, 31, 32, 44, 61; and cursillistas' environment, 41; and U.S. Cursillo movement, 71; and Protestant Cursillos, 90; and Via de Cristo, 111, 112; and Fourth-Day movements, 128; and Cursillo weekends, 134, 138–39, 142; and Teens Encounter Christ, 187, 198;

and Kairos Prison Ministry Inside Weekend, 202, 224; and Great Banquet, 239

Pilgrimages: and Catholic Action, 2, 26, 29–30, 32, 33, 34–35, 36, 41, 45, 263 (n. 33); as embodied Catholicism, 29, 30; and Santiago de Compostela, 29–30, 32, 33, 263 (n. 33), 264 (n. 51); Great Pilgrimage, 30, 32, 33, 34, 35, 41, 45, 47; and Lluc monastery, 30, 263 (n. 35); children's pilgrimages, 30–31; and Marian sites, 30–31; masculinist overtones of, 31–32, 263 (n. 40); and Eduardo Bonnín, 40

Pilgrim Scouts, 30, 33, 47
Pitzer, Jack, 226, 235–40, 242–43
Pitzer, Roberta, 236
Pius X (pope), 40
Pius XI (pope), 27, 40, 48
Pius XII (pope), 26, 34, 40, 41, 46, 49
Pla y Deniel, Enrique, 263 (n. 25)
Plesch, Amanda, 190–93, 292 (n. 77)
Plus (friar), 37
Portugal, 59, 91
Post, Lila, 289 (n. 19)
Post-Cursillo. *See* Fourth Day
Poyo, Gerald E., 28
Pre-Cursillo, 7, 85, 117, 118, 133–34
Primo de Rivera, José Antonio, 28
Proa (magazine), 29–32, 34–35, 65
Prolife movement, 138, 140, 247, 248, 300–301 (n. 3), 301 (n. 6)
Promoter's Crucifix, 33
Promoter's School, 33
Protestant clergy, 9, 14, 97, 122
Protestant Cursillos: and universal Christian spirituality, 3, 10, 88, 98, 102, 267 (n. 92); context of Mallorquín origins, 10, 83, 90, 251, 253–54; history of, 13, 19, 57, 89; churches as setting of, 16; and ecumenicism, 17–18, 75–80, 86, 87, 89–91, 97, 100, 237; cross-giving in, 33, 264 (n. 46); and lay focus of CdC, 60, 86, 87, 96, 245; and U.S. Cursillo movement, 69, 76–79; and Eduardo Bonnín, 88–90, 97–98, 251; popularity of, 101; spread of, 124–26. *See also* National Episcopal Cursillo; Tres Dias; Via de Cristo; Walk to Emmaus

Protestantism: and CdC, 1, 2, 3–4; and Great Awakenings, 3; Fourth-Day movements' effect on, 5; historiography of, 10–11; and ecumenicism, 17, 78; renewals of, 18; masculinization of, 32, 264 (n. 42); and grace, 52; Catholicism's relationship with, 69, 99–100, 104; and laity, 86–87, 121, 280 (n. 107); denominational reforms, 88; rise of evangelicals, 88, 98–99, 252–53; and revivals, 152, 253; missing history of, 260 (n. 5)

Puerto Rico, 106
Putnam, Robert, 15, 16

Race relations, 63
Rahner, Hugo, 37
Rahner, Karl, 37
Rainbow: as symbol of Fourth-Day movements, 4, 114–15
Ramírez, Jesse, 146, 158, 245, 287 (n. 71)
Ramírez, María, 158
"Reaching the faraway": Eduardo Bonnín's concept of, 2, 37, 44, 48, 107, 128, 131, 205, 214, 230
Regnerus, Mark, 301 (n. 6)
Reiter, Ronald ("Ron"): and Teens Encounter Christ, 167–68, 169, 172, 177, 182, 196–97, 291 (n. 52), 293 (n. 93), 293–94 (n. 96), 294 (n. 99)
Religious experience, 88, 266 (n. 88), 274 (n. 91)
Resseter, Daniel, 64
Reunions of cursillistas: and renewed Christian life, 4, 131; and ultreyas, 12, 15, 54, 72, 268 (n. 129); settings of, 16; and Eduardo Bonnín's origami birds, 21; impact of, 54, 85–86,

268 (n. 129); and sponsorship, 85; and Tres Dias, 99; online groups, 107; and Walk to Emmaus, 107; and National Episcopal Cursillo, 114, 119; and Cursillo weekends, 143, 145, 148, 160, 162–65, 287–88 (n. 94)
Rico, Damien, 54, 148, 276 (n. 1), 287 (n. 71)
Riutort, Bartolomé, 37, 41, 58
Riutort, Jaime, 37, 41, 58
Rivera, Severo, 66
Rock Island Center for Math and Science (RICMS), 260 (n. 7)
Rockville Correctional Facility, Indiana, 199, 294–95 (n. 1)
Roggers, Karl, 37
Rohloff, Ivan, 34, 49, 269 (n. 2), 270 (n. 10)
Rollos (short talks): Catholic clergy giving, 9, 36, 43, 46, 48, 130, 268 (n. 105), 283 (n. 6); cursillistas giving, 9, 43, 46, 47, 130, 260 (n. 9), 266 (n. 88), 283 (n. 6); discussion groups following, 9, 130, 141; and Eduardo Bonnín, 36–37; and CdC, 38, 39, 43, 47; anecdotes in, 39, 137, 207; development of, 43; purpose of, 46; power of, 53–54, 266 (n. 88); and Protestant Cursillos, 90, 122; and Walk to Emmaus, 102; and Via de Cristo, 112; and National Episcopal Cursillo, 119; and Cursillo weekends, 130, 131, 135, 136–43, 247, 249, 283 (n. 6), 284 (nn. 20, 24); and Kairos Prison Ministry Inside Weekend, 207, 216, 218, 219–20, 297 (n. 40); and Great Banquet, 239
Romero Salvadó, Francisco J., 28
Roof, Wade Clark, 281 (n. 108)
Rooster: as symbol of Fourth-Day movements, 4, 114–15
Rosselló Nadal, Ramón, 46–47, 53
Rothwell, Randy, 217
Rowe, JoEllen, 161, 207, 214, 219, 220, 224, 295 (n. 1)

Rubí, Ventura, 269 (n. 6)
Ruiz, Juan, 50
Rullán, Andrés, 37, 41, 58
Rupert, Ron, 93
Russia, 107, 124

Sáiz, José Ángel, 35
Sala, Pedro, 49
Salgado, Arias, 29
Salmon, Ed, 71
Sánchez, José M., 28
Sandler, Lauren, 259 (n. 3)
Sandovál, Chris, 157, 276 (n. 1), 287 (n. 71)
Sandovál, Mona, 149–50
San Gaya, Sebastian de, 39
San Salvador Cursillo, 34
San Salvador shrine, Mallorca, 30
Santiago de Compostela: as pilgrimage site, 29–30, 31, 33, 34, 263 (n. 33), 264 (n. 51); Great Pilgrimage of 1948, 30, 32, 33, 34, 35, 41, 45, 47; *ultreya* as greeting, 272 (n. 41)
Scharfenberg, Peter, 96
Schmidlin, Paul, 90, 91
Schmidlin, Tracy, 84, 90, 91, 112, 236, 279 (n. 76), 279–80 (n. 80)
Schoneberg, Ginny, 118–19
Schultz, Kevin M., 260 (n. 5)
Schurman, Derek, 122
Schwietz, Roger, 178–79, 181–82, 188–89, 291 (n. 52)
Schwob, Rene, 37
Scott, Chris, 190
Sears, Eugene, 186
Seeking Each Other and Receiving Christ's Hand (SEARCH), 170, 181, 183, 229, 288 (n. 1), 289 (n. 13)
Sepulvada, Julio, 66
Serenity Prayer, 138, 284 (n. 15)
Seventh Diocesan Gathering (1947), 35
Shamblin, Gwen, 209
Sheen, Fulton, 64
Singapore, 107
Six, Wes, 195

Small-group movement: and sense of community, 15, 16; and Kairos Prison Ministry Inside Weekend, 204; and Christ Renews His Parish, 230
Smazik, Dave, 121–22, 250
Smith, Christian, 197, 294 (n. 100)
Smits, Chad, 98–99
Smits, Deb, 98–99
Social status, 54, 127
South Africa, 104, 201
South Korea, 96, 124, 281 (n. 116)
Spain: fascism in, 8, 16, 21, 22, 27–29, 31, 32, 33, 34–35, 36, 44, 54, 62, 63, 154, 262 (n. 20); nationalism in, 24, 27, 28, 29, 33, 44, 63; National Secretariat of Cursillos, 270 (n. 10)
Spanish Catholicism: CdC remaking, 2, 16–17, 21, 22, 43; CdC's challenging of, 8, 22; effect on American Christian culture, 11; authoritarianism of, 21, 22, 24, 27, 28, 29, 31, 35, 36, 37, 63; and Spanish Civil War, 27, 28–29; and Catholic identity, 29, 31; "Catholic Integrism," 29, 35, 36, 44; masculinization of, 32, 33; and fascism, 34, 35, 37; and institutionalized Christ, 45
Spanish Civil War, 21, 27–29, 31, 263 (n. 25)
Spanish Falangism, 28–29, 31, 40, 44
Spanish Guinea, 59
Steed, Rita, 200, 202, 223, 224, 295 (n. 1)
Stern, Robert, 66
Study: and CdC, 3, 87; and U.S. Cursillo movement, 71; and Protestant Cursillos, 90; and Via de Cristo, 111, 112; and Fourth-Day movements, 128; and Cursillo weekends, 134, 139, 140, 142; and Teens Encounter Christ, 198; and Kairos Prison Ministry Inside Weekend, 202, 224
Sullivan, Winnifred Fallers, 295 (n. 8)

Sureda, María, 20, 72
Sureda, Miguel, 21, 44, 52–53, 72, 76–77, 251, 269 (n. 3), 277 (n. 13), 286 (n. 52)
Sweden, 113
Sweeney, Megan, 207

Taizé, 94–95
Taves, Ann, 266 (n. 88)
Technology: and websites, 105, 107, 229, 236; and Cursillo weekends, 128, 282 (n. 2)
Teens Encounter Christ (TEC): emphasis of, 9–10; and laity, 132; and Fedewa, 165, 166, 167, 168–72, 174–88, 193–97, 288 (nn. 1, 5), 290 (n. 35), 294 (n. 99); and Gereke, 165, 166–68, 170–88, 193–95, 275 (n. 93), 288 (n. 1), 289 (n. 19), 290 (n. 35), 294 (n. 99); and Paschal Mystery of Christ, 168, 171, 178, 179, 187, 194, 196; and Vatican II Council, 168, 173–74, 178, 183–85, 197–98; founding of, 168–77; and Notre Dame weekend, 169, 170–71; manual for, 171, 172–73, 180, 186, 187, 291 (n. 52); and rally of 1968, 173–74; and group dynamics, 181–82; development of, 182–87; and round tables, 183; typical weekend structure, 187–89; and Catholic Cursillos, 188; alumni of, 188, 189–93, 194; and wheat, 191, 192–93, 283 (n. 8); relevance of, 195–98, 253, 293 (n. 92); organizational structure of, 197, 293–94 (n. 96); cross-giving in, 264 (n. 46); and armed services, 270 (n. 12)
Thibon, Gustavo, 37
Thompson, John, 201, 205, 236, 294 (n. 1)
Todd, Ivan, 94, 95
Torres, Adelina, 149
Torres, Bartolomé, 49
Torres, Hector, 66
Travis, Trysh, 162

Tres Días: as nondenominational Fourth-Day movement, 6, 9, 87, 92, 95, 96, 97, 98, 99, 252, 253; and Catholic Cursillo ecumenicism, 79, 89, 92, 93–94, 95; history of, 92, 93–99; cross-giving in, 95, 264 (n. 46); spread of, 95–96, 98, 99, 107, 124, 125, 126, 253, 281 (n. 116); organizational structure of, 96, 123; and armed services, 96, 270 (n. 12), 281 (n. 116); and ecumenicism, 97–98, 108, 113, 117, 126, 252, 253; and Walk to Emmaus, 102; and Spanish language, 116; demographics of, 120; and laity, 121–23, 132; and Cursillo weekends, 128, 159–60; and food, 206, 296 (n. 24); spinoffs of, 298 (n. 1)

Truth, 45, 46, 63

Tweed, Thomas, 125, 251

Twelve-step programs, 161–62, 164

Ultreya (magazine), 65

Ultreyas: group reunion meetings, 12, 15, 54, 72, 268 (n. 129); and "Cursillos clandestinos," 53, 56; and U.S. Cursillo movement, 61, 72; and ecumenicism, 76; importance of, 85; and Protestant Cursillos, 90; and Vía de Cristo, 112; and National Episcopal Cursillo, 119; and Cursillo weekends, 131, 143; coed ultreyas, 153

United Kingdom, 104, 106

United Methodist Church (UMC), 99, 105, 106

Upper Room Cursillos. *See* Walk to Emmaus

Upper Room Ministries, 90–91, 99, 102, 103–4, 105, 106, 238

Uriostegui, Carmen, 6, 152–53, 155, 276 (n. 1)

U.S. Cursillo movement: in Waco, Texas, 1, 60–64, 65, 271 (n. 30), 271–72 (n. 40); history of, 3, 6, 8, 10–11, 13, 15, 19, 55, 56, 59–60, 91; spread of movement, 5, 64, 65–67, 69, 71, 72, 128; and lay focus of CdC, 10, 14, 60, 65, 69–72, 73, 80, 273 (n. 69); context of Mallorquín origins, 10, 56–57, 68, 76, 250–51, 253–54; ethnography of, 15; and reunions of cursillistas, 16; and church involvement, 17; and Midwest, 17–18, 79; renewal of, 18–19; impact of, 44, 54; institutionalization of, 55, 84–85; and Spanish language, 57, 58, 63, 66, 67, 68–69, 71, 81, 91, 94, 95, 116, 181, 272 (n. 49), 286 (n. 58); and Palomino, 57, 60, 62–65; and Vadell, 57, 60–65, 69–70, 270 (n. 16); and English language, 57, 64, 66, 67, 68–69, 71, 79, 81, 94, 116, 181, 272 (nn. 43, 49); and gender, 58, 61, 269 (n. 3), 282 (n. 4); and armed services, 59–60; and Eduardo Bonnín, 60, 68, 80–83, 271 (n. 18); National Secretariat of, 65, 67, 69–70, 72, 75–80, 94, 97, 98, 102, 103, 104, 108, 110, 113–14, 237, 274 (nn. 86, 91), 278 (n. 35), 282 (n. 4); and ecumenicism, 67, 75–80, 252, 274 (nn. 86, 87); and popular and official Catholicism, 68–75; and anti-Catholicism, 69; and Leader's School, 72–73; and Korean language, 272 (n. 49); and Vietnamese language, 272 (n. 49)

U.S. Hispanics: and religious studies, 14, 18; transnational existence of, 15–16; and U.S. Cursillo movement, 54, 57, 61, 63–66, 68, 71–72, 91, 127, 128, 282 (n. 1); racism experienced by, 63–64, 271 (n. 30); and ethnic identity, 66, 282 (n. 1); and National Episcopal Cursillo, 115; and Cursillo weekends, 146–53, 156, 157, 158, 287 (n. 71)

U.S.-Mexico War, 63

U.S. National Catholic Secretariat, 8

U.S. social movements, 3, 15, 259 (n. 4)

Vacari, 119
Vadell, Bernardo, 35, 54–58, 60–65, 69–70, 73, 270 (n. 16), 283 (n. 6)
Van Caster, Marcel, 188
Van de Meer of Malcheren, 37
Vatican II Council: Catholic Action predating, 1; renewals of, 18, 88, 95; theology of laity, 40, 41, 74–75, 100, 121, 173, 181, 188, 280 (n. 107); and U.S. Cursillo movement, 71, 72, 74–75, 76, 79–80, 86; and Teens Encounter Christ, 168, 173–74, 178, 183–85, 197–98; and Fedewa, 170, 171, 178, 184–85; and Gereke, 170, 178, 184–85, 288 (n. 4); and dress codes for women religious, 173; parishes built in the round, 183; scholarship on, 259 (n. 4); and conservative Catholic dissent, 288 (n. 3)
Vertebration, 45, 51, 133
Via de Cristo: and Lutheran Church, 6, 9, 75; and Catholic Cursillo ecumenicism, 79, 89, 92, 108–9; and interdenominationalism, 87, 92; and Eduardo Bonnín, 88, 90, 110, 111, 276 (n. 6); history of, 92, 108–13; spread of, 107, 110, 113, 279–80 (n. 80); and ecumenicism, 108, 109, 110, 113, 252, 279 (n. 63); organizational structure of, 111; and authenticity, 111, 112–13; and immigrants, 111, 279 (n. 73); coed weekends, 114, 279 (nn. 76, 80); and Spanish language, 116; demographics of, 120; and Cursillo weekends, 128; and laity, 132; and Fourth Day, 145; reunions of cursillistas, 163, 164–65; and food, 206; and Kairos Prison Ministry Inside Weekend, 224; cross-giving in, 264 (n. 46); spinoffs of, 298 (n. 1)

Villa de Chantal convent, Moline, Illinois, 5–6, 246, 260 (nn. 6, 7)
Virgin Mary: devotion to, 9–10, 12; and Lluc monastery, Mallorca, 24, 30, 38, 263 (n. 35); Eduardo Bonnín's devotion to, 24, 38, 51; and San Salvador shrine, 30–31; and CdC, 38, 51–52, 265 (n. 64); Legionnaires of Mary, 65

Walk to Emmaus: as Methodist and ecumenical Fourth-Day movement, 9; and Catholic Cursillo ecumenicism, 79, 89, 92; and interdenominationalism, 87, 92, 99; and Eduardo Bonnín, 88, 90–91; and ecumenicism, 90, 99, 104, 108, 113, 237, 252; history of, 92, 99–108, 277–78 (n. 35); international communities, 104, 106, 278 (n. 53); cross-giving in, 105, 264 (n. 46); spread of, 105–7, 243; and Spanish language, 116; demographics of, 120; and Cursillo weekends, 128; and laity, 132; and men, 156; and food, 206; and Kairos Prison Ministry Inside Weekend, 224; spinoffs of, 227; and Great Banquet, 235–36; and Pitzer, 236, 237–40
Ward, William ("Bill"), 122
Wardega, Fred, 229
Warren, Rick, 42, 43
Way of Christ, 298 (n. 1)
Websites: and Walk to Emmaus, 105, 107; and Fourth-Day movements, 229; and Great Banquet, 236
Weis, Paul, 236
Wesley, John, 102
West, Matthew, 191
Wilcox, W. Bradford, 156
Women: role in fascist-controlled Spain, 31; and CdC, 51, 85, 262 (n. 2), 276 (n. 1); and U.S. Cursillo movement, 57–58, 71, 72; and

Protestant Cursillos, 86, 87; and Cursillo weekends, 132, 134, 153, 154, 155, 156, 158, 285 (n. 51), 286 (n. 54), 296–97 (n. 24); and Teens Encounter Christ, 172–73, 179, 180; and Kairos Prison Ministry Inside Weekend, 199, 203, 204, 211; and Great Banquet, 241. *See also* Gender

Wood, Jan, 101
Wood, Robert ("Bob"), 99–106, 108, 237, 238, 279 (n. 63)
World War I, 32
Wuthnow, Robert, 15, 16, 161, 163

Youth. *See* Teens Encounter Christ

Zimbabwe, 104